Jameis1of1 has written a game-
media may hate but NFL fans

– Jacquez Green
University of Florida Athletic Hall of Famer
Former NFL WR with the Buccaneers, Redskins and Lions

Jameis Winston is one of the most misunderstood and polarizing athletes in the history of Tampa Bay sports. Winston's life is an incredible study in how negative, misinformed and inaccurate media coverage, race and collegiate allegiances have poisoned the local fan base. Jameis1of1 takes a hard look at comparative and even era adjusted stats that prove Jameis compares favorably to Super Bowl era Hall of Fame quarterbacks. When looked at objectively it's really quite obvious Winston's on a Hall of Fame pace.

- JP Peterson
Award Winning Tampa Bay Sports Journalist
Fox Sports Sun Host

To me, as a football player, the best thing anyone can say about you is that you were a great teammate and Jameis was one of the best teammates I've ever had. There are few players that can match his competitiveness and desire to win.

– Joe Hawley
Former Buccaneers Starting Center
www.ManVanDogBlog.com

Jameis1of1's book will be the litmus test to judge whether one is infected with *Winston Derangement Syndrome* or not, as the only people who will dislike his book are biased Jameis-haters who prefer false narratives to truth!

– Chris Smith
Director of Content: *The Unfiltered Sports Network*
www.UnfilteredSportsNetwork.com

This book does an excellent job of telling stories and sharing the Gospel in a way that is refreshing and encouraging.

– Jason Romano
Author - *Live to Forgive* / Host - *Sports Spectrum* Podcast

Anyone who considers themselves a fan of Jameis Winston and doesn't read this book isn't a real fan of Jameis Winston. Read this book!

- Samer Ali
Host: *Loose Cannons* Podcast

Author Jameis1of1 has written the definitive book on Jameis Winston! He also compares the statistics of every single modern era Hall of Fame quarterback to Winston as well as to each other, all while adjusting for era to eliminate even the appearance of bias. *Jameis Winston Derangement Syndrome* is an NFL stat-geek's dream, a biased media member's nightmare and belongs in every Buccaneers fan's library!

– Ashlie Abrahams
Host: *Talk The Plank* Podcast

Jameis1of1 exposes the biased media and refutes fake news with a mountain of evidence in a fun book every NFL fan should own!

– James Hill
Youtuber aka *MrBucsNation*

When an NFL player is as polarizing as Buccaneers QB Jameis Winston, it's easy for many to shovel dirt on his career without any push-back. Author Jameis1of1 takes a deeper statistical look into his on field performance to see what the data actually says about Winston's play and where he stacks up when compared to the greatest quarterbacks of all time. The results are fascinating!

– Ren Daxt
Co-Host: *ThePewterCast* Podcast

Jameis Winston personally inspires me to work hard and to know that I can do anything I put my mind to, so I'm thrilled Jameis1of1 wrote a book that details Jameis' life from grade-school to the present day and also refutes the media's lies with facts! *Jameis Winston Derangement Syndrome* is a book that deserves to be read, shared and promoted by every Buccaneers fan!

– Cory Hays
Host: *All Things Bucs* Podcast

Jameis Winston may be the most polarizing player in football today, but he's also unquestionably on a Hall of Fame statistical pace and this book proves it with a mountain of hard data and original era adjusted statistics that will blow your mind!

– Dean Jensen
Businessman and father of Bucs Starting Center Ryan Jensen

Author Jameis1of1 takes no prisoners in *Jameis Winston Derangement Syndrome* as he destroys the lazy and false narratives spun by the main stream sports media regarding Jameis Winston with irrefutable truth. If you want to improve your understanding of NFL QB history, see how every Hall of Fame quarterback stacks up against each other and become a higher-football-IQ fan. Buy this book!

– Brodie Perry
College Football Scout in the 813

There are some great reporters that cover the Buccaneers and some great statisticians that produce wonderful research, but no one covers Jameis Winston or produces the voluminous amount of statistical research regarding Jameis Winston, as Jameis1of1 does. *Jameis Winston Derangement Syndrome* is one book every Bucs fan should own!

– Susan Gilbert
Board certified member of the Association of Medical Illustrators
www.medartist.com

Author Jameis1of1 left no stone unturned in unbiasedly comparing Jameis Winston to every Hall of Fame quarterback statistically, even adjusting for era whether or not doing so would make Winston look better or worse. He also proves with facts backed by a monstrous amount of citations that the false narratives surrounding Winston are a product of a biased main stream media. If you want the truth, read *Jameis Winston Derangement Syndrome*!

– Rasheed Farid
Businessman who expects Jameis Winston to be in the HOF one day

Baker Mayfield, Kevin Durant and others who've felt wronged by the media have nothing on Jameis Winston and this book proves it!

– Donny Downs
Buccaneers Superfan and Gulf War Veteran

The media is infected with *Winston Derangement Syndrome*, so much so that I can't even enjoy watching ESPN's *First Take* anymore! However, Jameis1of1 is basically what Max Kellerman would be if Kellerman were infinitely more logical, rational and unbiased. Read this book and increase your football IQ!

- Vince Cassiddy
Lifelong NFL Fan and Detroit Lions Season Ticket Holder

Words will never be able to describe the impact Jameis has had on my life. He is a daily reminder to be the best version of myself I can be. Jameis1of1 has written a book that doesn't just set the record straight with facts and truth; he's written a book that inspires its readers as well!

– Jeff Sullivan
Biggest Bucs fan in Orlando

Jameis Winston doesn't know me from Adam but he's been a major inspiration in my own life, as watching him overcome adversity and deal with the biased media has given me the strength to overcome many of my own obstacles. *Jameis Winston Derangement Syndrome* is filled with enough statistics to make your head spin and exposes the biased media marvellously, but it also details Jameis the person and is a fun read. Author Jameis1of1 has written a masterpiece!

– JJ Patel
Biggest Buccaneers Fan in Philadelphia

NOTE TO THE MEDIA

I, Jameis1of1, would not only be willing to participate via voice, camera, or in-person on any and all segments discussing Jameis Winston. In fact, I challenge each and every member of both the main stream and independent media to invite me to participate in such segments.

As a Biblical Christian theologian, you can most definitely expect me to carry myself with the utmost class and professionalism. In fact, even if you search through my entire Twitter history you will not find one single tweet I do not stand behind, as I have never even lost my cool dealing with the crazies – many of them main stream media members – that lurk on Twitter.

Nevertheless, be aware that if you allow me to partipate in a segment where any other guest is ill-prepared or doing little more than spinning false narratives, I will gladly expose said guest's errors – professionally and without malice of course – and likely make him or her look foolish to your audience. However, such would certainly make for good theatre, provoke a great deal of audience feedback and therefore be great for your ratings.

Finally, please also understand that fame does not appeal to me whatsoever. I wrote my book under a pseudonym as I have no desire to be personally recognized and because I believe all that matters is the content of this book, rather than the character who wrote it. That said, if I am to appear on any segment via camera or in-person, I will be *disguised* in a way. However, again, such would likely make for good theatre and be great for ratings.

Sincerely,

Jameis1of1

Jameis Winston Derangement Syndrome:

How Media Bias Causes Us to Overlook the

Start of a Hall of Fame NFL Career

_____

Jameis1of1

Jameis Winston Derangement Syndrome: How Media Bias Causes Us to Overlook the Start of a Hall of Fame NFL Career

For more information about this author, visit:

https://www.twitter.com/jameis1of1

Dedicated to the One True God of the Bible and His *created** son Jameis Winston

For whether we live, we live unto the Lord; and whether we die, we die unto the Lord: whether we live therefore, or die, we are the Lord's. For to this end Christ both died, and rose, and revived, that he might be Lord both of the dead and living. – Romans 14: 8-9

* In no way am I implying that Jameis Winston is different than any other created human being, or that the nickname *Jameis Christ* that some bestowed upon him when he was at Florida State University is appropriate, let alone that he is in any way comparable to the uncreated Son of God (i.e. Jesus Christ) with the above phraseology, as all of us mere mortals are *created* children of God. As the passage above makes clear, *we* – as in every single one of us – belong to the Lord.

Also, please note that while I am fully aware that the above dedication may offend some readers, I trust that such offended individuals can simply understand that I do not believe I should have to hide my Biblical Christian faith – especially in writing a book about an athlete like Jameis Winston who also professes faith in Jesus Christ – any more than one should have to hide their race, creed or color in this day and age.

NOTE ON THE TYPE USED IN THIS BOOK

I have used the popular serif typeface *Times New Roman* which was created by Stanley Morrison and Victor Lardent and commissioned by the London, England newspaper *The Times* in 1931.

However, I feel I should point out that no font is perfect and with *Times New Roman*, especially in 11 point size which is generally used in this book, when an *r* and *n* appear next to each other in a word, such can appear as an *m* to some readers. For example, the word *discern* could appear to some as *discem* while the name *Warner* could appear to some as *Wamer*. Please keep such in mind as you read this work.

NOTE ON THE CITATIONS FOLLOWING THE STATISITCAL TABLES IN THIS BOOK

This book is jam packed with nearly 900 citations as I believe in hard data and offering corroborating evidence in copious amounts. I even tend to favor citing a specific source multiple times if I mention a specific factoid multiple times. However, I also realize such can make for a less enjoyable reading experience for some; therefore at times I have forgone re-citing sources in an effort to make the book more enjoyable for you the reader.

However, I feel it necessary for me to explain how the citations following each statistical table work as I realize they could be confusing for many.

The longest string of citations following one of the statistical tables in this book reads as follows:

[141][744] [369] [705] [706] [230] [745] [746] [747] [748] [231] [749] [750] [751] [713] [232] [752] [753] [754] [755] [233] [756] [757] [758] [759] [234] [760] [761] [762] [763] [235] [764] [765] [766] [767] [236] [768] [769] [770] [771] [237] [772] [773] [774] [775] [238] [776] [777] [778] [779] [239] [780] [781] [782] [714] [240] [783] [784] [785] [786] [241] [787] [788] [789] [790] [242] [791] [792] [793] [794] [243] [795] [796] [797] [798] [244] [799] [800] [801] [802] [245] [803] [804] [805] [697] [211] [806] [807] [808] [809] [246] [810] [811] [812] [813] [247] [814] [815] [816] [817] [248] [818] [819] [820] [821] [249] [822] [295] [823] [824]

The above may look like a daunting list of citations to many readers and they may not understand what such means. However, it is actually quite simple. The very first citation corresponds to the first player mentioned at the top of the respective table – generally Jameis Winston – while each succeeding citation would also point to a statistic for said quarterback, until you come upon a citation for the next quarterback listed below Jameis Winston, and so on and so forth, until you reach the final citation for the final quarterback detailed in the table.

ACKNOWLEDGMENTS

I would like to thank various individuals and organizations that played a part in bringing this book to fruition in one way or another.

Firstly, I'd like to thank the Winston family and especially Jameis' father Antonor and his lovely mother Loretta. The two of you raised a young man that has been able to consistently take the proverbial weight of the world upon his shoulders and still perform at a high level. You even raised that young man in such a way that he has been able to endure the hatred of the masses infected with *schadenfreude* and the false narratives of the biased media infected with *Winston Derangement Syndrome* while keeping a smile on his face and handling his business. May the One true God of the Bible's perfect will always be done in your lives!

Secondly, I'd like to thank youth football coach Fred Green who coached Jameis Winston in *Pop Warner*, Mark Freeman who trained Jameis in his younger years, Otis Leverette who continues to train and mentor Jameis (and who contributed a magnificent foreword to this very book), Matt Scott who coached Jameis at Hueytown High School, as well as Florida State University (especially: Head Coach Jimbo Fisher, Recruiting Coordinator Dameyune Craig and Quarterbacks Coach Randy Sanders) and the entire Tampa Bay Buccaneers organization (especially: The Glazer family and GM Jason Licht) for believing in, coaching, training, recruiting, drafting and handing the keys of your respective kingdoms to Jameis Winston. Every burgeoning legend in the making needs people to believe in him or her and all of you had the foresight to do just that with the golden-armed young man from Bessemer known as *Jaboo*.

Thirdly, I'd like to thank all of the biased main stream sports media members as well as all of the silly Jameis-haters on social media for being as transparently biased and laughingly illogical as you are. Your insanity, which I long ago labelled *Winston Derangement Syndrome*, helped me realize just how needed this book is.

Fourthly, I'd like to thank all the individuals who have sent me messages of inspiration and encouraged me to defend the most maligned young QB in NFL history. You know who you are and please know that I appreciate each and every one of you very much.

Fifthly, I would like to thank my wife and children for their undying love, support, understanding and prayers. I love each of you with all my heart and soul and thank God for blessing me with the best family any man could ever hope to have. As each of you know, I literally wouldn't trade my life for the life of anyone else on earth; so from the bottom of my heart, I say a million times, thank you!

Finally, my greatest thanks goes to God: Father, Word and Holy Spirit. I couldn't take a single breath, let alone author this book, without You. You are my Creator, my Savior, my love, my life, my everything, and my greatest goal is to do Your will and to see Your will done.

PERSONAL NOTE FROM THE AUTHOR

Various main stream sports media members, a former CEO of an NFL team and even one Hollywood actor have personally insulted, cursed, muted and/or blocked on Twitter and even threatened and attempted to dox me. They did so simply because I wrote an article or tweeted 100 percent accurate statistics that refute the false narratives surrounding Jameis Winston, or used logical, rationale and common sense arguments to refute the seemingly all-pervasive *Winston Derangement Syndrome* that infects said individuals.

The above said, if I have been subjected to that sort of absurdity for merely writing short articles or debating football topics in tweets of 140 characters or less, I can only imagine how much hatred and slander may be headed my way once this book hits the market. However, perhaps the media has learned its lesson and realized it's better not to poke the bear that is Jameis1of1 so to speak, as no one who has ever engaged me in an online debate centered around Jameis Winston with the intention to make Winston look like anything other than a talented young quarterback on a Hall of Fame statistical pace, has come out looking good when all was said and done.

Regardless, I do feel that it is appropriate for me to include a personal note at this time, as a sort of pre-emptive explanation for what I imagine I will be falsely accused of by Jameis-bashers or even those who simply don't like me for whatever reason.

All of the above said, allow me to state that I believe any decent human being should denounce sexual harassment, assault and the like. In fact, such a statement should be a given in a civilized society. Likewise, any man or woman who has been convicted or been proven to have sexually assaulted another man or woman, deserves to not only be denounced by the public but to be punished for his or her crimes by the justice system.

I have personally witnessed the pain and suffering that envelops a woman who has reported a sexual assault and never received the justice she sought, as I took my own sister when she was in high school to the police when she filed her rape complaint, and to this day she has never received the justice she sought. I even know what it feels like to be the victim of – at the very least – an *attempted* sexual assault when I was still in grade school. However, I was able to escape the grasp of an adult male and run into and lock myself in my house when he tried to molest me.

The above said, please do not misinterpret anything written in this book as unsympathetic to any man, woman or child who has been sexually assaulted. Also, please do not misinterpret anything written in this book as a defense of assault of any kind.

Finally, please do not misinterpret anything written in this book as some sort of attack on the Democratic or Republican parties. I do not live in America, was not born in America and certainly do not vote in American elections. Also, as a Biblical Christian theologian that believes I owe 100% of my allegiance to my Lord and Savior Jesus Christ of Nazareth, no matter who the secular leader is at any given time I love and pray for that person whether I agree with their policies or not. In short, I'm probably unlike anyone you've ever met before, unless you know another theologian that has also studied NFL quarterbacks for decades, invests in high-end collectibles, quotes Tupac Shakur, Thomas Sowell and Gandhi, and gets mistaken for an Eastern Orthodox priest at times.

All of the above said, I do however strongly believe in the innocent until *proven* guilty concept. Likewise, I strongly believe that judging an innocent person to be guilty is just as reprehensible as judging a guilty person to be innocent. Furthermore, I do not believe in playing God, pretending to be omniscient, or judging individuals based on unknowable actions or events. I believe in hard data, proof, statistics and the like and in following the evidence wherever it leads. I hope you can respect these viewpoints of mine even if you don't agree with everything you read in the following pages of this book.

FOREWORD

I've been to church more times than I can remember, but one Sunday school class I attended at *Friendship Missionary Baptist Church* in Americus, Georgia, circa 1994, and the message I heard, still speaks to my heart as much today as it did when I heard it for the first time.

The particular message that Sunday was about the great Biblical prophet known as John the Baptist and his unwavering zeal to spread God's word no matter the cost. I heard about John baptizing sincere seekers of the One true God in the Jordan River, and how as his ministry grew amongst the people, his fame spread throughout the land as well, to the point that many even asked him if he were the *Christ* (see John 1:19-28), that is to say, the promised Messiah of holy Scripture.

And when I heard the minister recount the words that John the Baptist spoke when he was asked whether he was the Christ, it was those very words that would change my life forever.

To be specific, when John the Baptist was asked whether he was the Christ or not, he stated:

I am the voice of one crying in the wilderness, Make straight the way of the Lord, as said the prophet Esaias. ... there standeth one among you, whom ye know not; He it is, who coming after me is preferred before me, whose shoe's latchet I am not worthy to unloose. – John 1:23b, 26b, 27

It was at that moment, upon hearing John the Baptist's words, that I realized my Creator had created me for a purpose greater than merely serving myself or simply doing all I could to make sure that I personally succeeded. It was at that moment that I realized God had created me to not only be a blessing to others, but to serve someone in the future who was greater than I was in that present.

Fast forward approximately 13 years to a *Rivals Camp* in Vestavia Hills, Alabama, when my previous calling turned into a present reality, as that is when I first met a tall, skinny kid with a poor 40 yard dash technique named Jameis Lanaed Winston.

I watched the lanky youngster from afar and observed a kid with undoubted athletic potential, yet little understanding of basic running mechanics. Without any invitation or even forethought I walked through the crowd of coaches and trainers, looked the young man in the eye, and began coaching and teaching him. To my surprise he not only listened but learned and then instantly performed with true prodigy like precision. It's difficult to explain, but I had no doubt that I had found someone greater than myself in this young man.

After a mere 20 minutes or so of working with young Jameis, his father, Antonor Winston, approached me and introduced himself. Shortly after that first meeting I would become Jameis Winston's personal trainer and mentor, while also being blessed to be mentored by Antonor himself, as make no mistake about it, Antonor Winston was the architect of the man we now know as Famous Jameis Winston, and was both a compass and anchor for his son and myself from that day forward.

Since that day I have never ceased being a trainer and mentor for Jameis and this is a credit to him, to his work ethic, character and loyalty. You see, while I knew that Jameis, as well as his father, were both uncommon individuals in a world of very common individuals, and while I had no doubt that young Jameis had greatness in him, I had met other individuals in the past who also had at least the potential to be great, but who for one reason or another, never fulfilled that potential.

Many athletically gifted young men can throw, run and even read defenses, but only a very select few seem to have the innate ability to remain loyal to the people God has strategically placed in their lives. Jameis Winston was such a person as a young man and remains such a person to this day.

Many athletes are comfortable simply being the best of the worst, never realizing that they were writing a post-dated check to merely being average. Later on in their lives they realize that they never fulfilled their true athletic potential, let alone the high calling God had on their lives. However, I don't worry about that happening to Jameis Winston, as while he has all the talent necessary to be among the best to ever play the game of football, it's his intangibles that have made him a person greater than myself and someone who will use his rise to greatness as a vehicle to truly serve the masses.

John the Baptist was a radical and a man who would leave an indelible footprint on mankind. Such was the common yet uncommon trait that he and the Lord and Savior Jesus Christ shared! And, while I certainly am not claiming to be a man as great as John the Baptist whom Jesus Himself said was the greatest prophet ever born (Luke 7:28) and while I am also not likening Jameis to the sinless Creator and Savior of the world, Jesus Christ, I am drawing a parallel between the mere human relationship John and Jesus shared and the relationship I share with Jameis.

I was drafted by the Miami Dolphins and played for the Washington Redskins, San Diego Chargers and San Francisco 49ers during my NFL career. Not bad for a kid that attended Middle Georgia Junior College. I also founded *Modernday Fitness* and have trained over 150 athletes that have signed DI or DII scholarships. I've even been recognized by the Alabama House of Representatives for my NFL career and off-field service. Not bad for a kid from Americus, Georgia, a city with a population of around 17,000.

However, while I thank God for my life and while it has certainly been anything but common, in my own mind I never truly attained the athletic success I felt my talent allowed me to attain. Nevertheless, what I did gain from my time in the NFL was a very uncommon wisdom thanks in large part to my own short-comings. I thank God for such, as it was those short-comings and the wisdom that came from them that has aided me in helping to develop a world-class man and athlete, Jameis Winston. You see, *Jaboo* is bigger than a mere game; *Famous Jameis* is a movement!

It may take some time for the masses to catch up, to ignore the false narratives and to recognize the greatness in Jameis. However, don't expect Jameis to just sit idly by and wait for people's opinions to change regarding him, because he's about his Father's business and he's dedicated to being the best quarterback and man he can be. And I for one am happy I was placed in his life by God and given the responsibility of helping him reach his potential, potential I have no doubt he will ultimately reach!

Otis Leverette
Former NFL Defensive End
Founder of *Modern Day Fitness*
Jameis Winston's Mentor & Trainer

PREFACE

The profession of book writing makes horse racing seem like a solid, stable business.

– John Steinbeck [I]

Writing an article on spec is a gamble; writing an entire 400 plus page book that is filled with nearly 900 citations on spec could be called insane. However, that's exactly what I did.

Why did I do it? Simply put, I literally felt *called* by God to not only write this book but to finish this book in time for it to be published before the start of the 2019 season. Please don't misunderstand me; I am not in any way claiming this book is inerrant or some sort of holy writ. I'm simply telling you why I wrote this book and why I worked so hard to finish it so quickly.

I've written countless articles and authored more than ten books in various genres with each one being published by conventional publishers and two even being sports books. However, when I proposed this book to various publishers and even showed a large portion of the manuscript to a couple choice publishers I'd worked with in the past, their reply was almost always the exact same, "It's a great concept / manuscript and certainly salable but it's about a quarterback we're not interested in publishing a book about".

It was clear that *Winston Derangement Syndrome* existed amongst publishers just as it did amongst the media, if not in the publishers themselves at least in their general audience which said publishers felt the need to pacify.

When one considers that books have been published by conventional publishers about convicted criminal athletes O.J. Simpson, Lawrence Taylor, Mike Tyson, Lenny Dykstra and the like, it is absolutely incredulous that Jameis Winston – a young man who has never even been arrested, let alone convicted of a crime at any time in his entire life – could be considered *persona non grata* by mammon seeking publishers, simply because they know just how real *Winston Derangement Syndrome* is and just how many people have been infected with such a disease from listening to the biased main stream media. In fact, I have no real doubt that I absolutely could have received a publishing contract and even a hefty advance on future royalties if I would have proposed a book demonizing Jameis Winston as a person and belittling his accomplishments as a player instead of writing the book I wrote.

However, as author David Lagercrantz stated:

> *There is no money in the world that would compensate me for writing a lousy book.* [II]

The way I see it, a truly lousy book is not merely one that is poorly written or boring, but one that contains inaccurate statistics, provably false narratives and the like. That is the sort of book I have no intention of ever writing regardless of the amount of compensation available to me.

Regardless, when I realized I wouldn't receive a contract let alone an advance, I didn't shelve the manuscript for this book. I decided I would continue researching, writing and crafting the book you are now reading, no matter the cost. And you better believe I knew the cost could be great.

I'm a theologian, businessman, freelance writer, author, investor, and home-schooling father of eight with three children currently enrolled in seminary and five children still needing me to educate them on a daily basis. Free time isn't exactly something I have a great deal of. However, I couldn't shake the feeling that this book needed to be written, that I needed to write it, and that I needed to do so quickly!

Author Terry Tempest Williams once said:

> *The only book worth writing is the book that threatens to kill you.*
> [III]

While I certainly was never at death's door whilst writing this book, sometimes it felt that way, as after a long day attending to my usual work I'd spend a few hours with my family, tuck my children into bed around 11pm and then grab my trusty laptop and write till around 7 AM each day, get a few hours of sleep and start over again the next day. This routine allowed me to finish the book quickly, but there were consequences.

Both I and my angel of a wife experienced separate health scares and even a serious financial test, as an extended family member defrauded us out of nearly $200,000 while I was writing this book. Said struggles caused me to set this book aside and concentrate on more obviously pressing matters each time. However, even when I was personally laid up in bed, I felt the need to finish the book and to do so as quickly as possible.

Nevertheless, one thing that aided me greatly was my precious wife's counsel that money is merely green paper, isn't important, and that I certainly shouldn't worry about whether this book would sell or not, but merely concern myself with finishing the book and then simply let God take care of the rest.

It seems my angel of a wife would get along well with author Ann Patchett, who stated:

I think people become consumed with selling a book when they need to be consumed with writing it. [IV]

While I'm not a rich man – though I admit the word *rich* is entirely relative and I certainly consider myself the richest man on earth thanks to the relationships I have with my Creator and family – and would certainly be thrilled to see this book become a commercial success, I know my wife was right. I wrote this book simply because I felt *called* to do so, and what God does with it from here on out is entirely up to Him.

It seems fitting to quote two of my favorite Scripture passages here, as they fit with the above and corroborate my wife's wise advice perfectly:

And whatsoever ye do in word or deed, do all in the name of the Lord Jesus, giving thanks to God and the Father by him.

– Colossians 3:17

Better is a little with righteousness than great revenues without right. A man's heart deviseth his way: but the LORD directeth his steps.

– Proverbs 16: 8-9

All of the above said, if this book gets trashed by the media, or even if it is simply ignored, so be it.

If it turns into a cherished work by Buccaneers fans, so be it.

If it gets thrown into a pile and lit on fire while biased media members infected with *Winston Derangement Syndrome* dance around chanting curses directed at me, so be it.

God's will be done.

Table of Contents

Note to the Media	VI
Dedication	IX
Note on the Type Used in this Book	X
Note on the Citations Following the Statistical Tables in this Book	XI
Acknowledgements	XII
Personal Note from the Author	XIV
Foreword by Otis Leverette	XVI
Preface	XX
Escaping the Sports Media Matrix	25
Full Disclosure	27
The Phenom	34
Troubles in Tallahassee	43
Triumph in Tallahassee	64
The Greatest QB in NCAA History?	77
The Franchise	87
Rookie Revelation	95
Jameis Winston vs. the Greats, Part I	108
QBWINZ is Not a Stat … However	120
Sophomore Sensation	127
Jameis Winston vs. the Greats, Part II	141
Junior Juxtaposition	151
Jameis Winston vs. the Greats, Part III	170
MeToo & Jaboo	180
Guilty Until Proven Innocent	197
Talking Heads Playing God	206
Senior Survivorship	221
Jameis Winston vs. the Greats, Part IV	245
Exposing Media False Narratives	255
What about Those #QBWinz Again?	297
What about Turnovers?	305
Where Does Jameis Winston Rank?	314
The Final Word	328
Postface	340
Note to Readers	342
References	343
Bibliography	370
Index	399
About the Author	403

Escaping the Sports Media Matrix
17 Stand-alone Haikus forming One Poem

Bias infected
the main stream sports media
to the hurt of fans.

Stories replaced truth
and sports fans bought the stories
without fact-checking.

Lowered sports IQ's
were the effect of fake news
which MSM* wants.

Low-sports-IQ trolls
seemed to replicate themselves
and madness ensued.

Today sports fans are
both smarter and dumber than
they ever have been.

Wisdom depends on
whether you do your research
or stare at TV.

The sports talking heads
are just paid story tellers
not real truth-tellers.

It's the media
that needs truth spoken to it
as they're the power.

Talking heads reign now
and pick heroes and villains
to praise and slander.

Jameis Winston is
the most slandered and slighted
quarterback ever.

Jameis Winston news
must have a negative slant;
So much for freedom.

Freedom *of* the press
isn't freedom *in* the press;
Thought police abound.

A nail that sticks out
is one that gets hammered down;
That may never change.

The sickness known as
Winston Derangement Syndrome
is easily cured.

Stats, logic and truth
easily refute the lies
the media spins.

Convenient lies are
easier to accept than
inconvenient truths.

Will anything change?
This book's irrefutable,
so of course it will!

– Jameis1of1

* MSM = Main Stream Media

If people in the media cannot decide whether they are in the business of reporting news or manufacturing propaganda, it is all the more important that the public understand that difference, and choose their news sources accordingly

– Thomas Sowell [1]

The media's the most powerful entity on earth. They have the power to make the innocent guilty and to make the guilty innocent, and that's power. Because they control the minds of the masses.

– Malcolm X [2]

Truth will ultimately prevail where there is pains to bring it to light.

– George Washington [3]

FULL DISCLOSURE

Whoever is careless with the truth in small matters cannot be trusted with important matters.

– Albert Einstein [4]

I desire to see the statistical truths and factual statements I present in this book accepted by you the reader. Therefore, I believe that by covering the *small matters* in this chapter truthfully, such will serve to allow you the reader to trust me when I cover the *important matters* in the forthcoming chapters of this book.

Also, please know that I am a perfectionist with OCD who despises statistical errors and have therefore made sure that every statistic and fact quoted in this book is accurate. However, I encourage all readers to be good *Bereans* (see Acts 17:11) and to fact-check me whenever they feel the need to do so, as this book certainly isn't the inerrant word of God and if there is even one error in it, I welcome being alerted to such a fact so that I can correct such in future editions of this work.

In the interest of full disclosure I will say that I did not decide to expose the biased media for their *Winston Derangement Syndrome* simply because I thought doing so would be a fun mental exercise. I also did not research Jameis Winston's statistics and compare him with other past and present quarterbacks because I was bored and had nothing better to do with my time. I am a busy man and while I greatly enjoy researching a vast number of subjects, love statistics and have considered myself a connoisseur of quarterbacks for many years, I also value my private and family time greatly.

The fact is that I have been an investor in high-end sports cards and memorabilia for decades. In the mid to late 90s, I invested close to 50% of my net worth in Kobe Bryant rookie cards and when I sold them I was able to purchase a home with cash. Later I invested a solid amount in LeBron James memorabilia and sports cards and when I sold, netted a 600% ROI. I have also sunk sizeable sums and received solid returns investing in and selling the sports cards and memorabilia of various NFL quarterbacks.

At present, I own a share of the most valuable and impressive collection of Jameis Winston true 1/1 (i.e. one of one, or the only one in existence, akin to an original painting rather than a mere lithograph) autographed rookie sports cards on earth, known as the *Lucky 13 Collection*. And, you better believe that when I make a major investment in high-end sports cards of an athlete, I spend a great deal of time researching that athlete to make sure I am investing wisely.

When I began considering investing in Jameis Winston, a player as notorious as he is notable, I knew I had to research him more than I ever researched any other player I invested in in the past. In short, I knew I couldn't let emotionalism or fandom get in the way of logic and rationale.

That I was not a fan of Florida State University or even the Tampa Bay Buccaneers when Jameis Winston was drafted was a major plus, as such made it easy for me to base my decision to either invest in or refuse to invest in Winston, on serious statistical research, an unbiased eye-test, true expert opinions of Winston's football acumen and other relevant data, rather than a mere feeling, let alone a feeling based on biased fandom. And, after conducting said extensive research, I felt confident enough in Jameis Winston's future prospects as an NFL quarterback to invest a sizeable sum into a collection of his high-end sports cards and memorabilia.

Since becoming an investor in the aforementioned Winston collection and since creating the *@Jameis1of1* Twitter profile, I have had many interesting debates with main stream media journalists, statisticians and even a former NFL team CEO, as well as the standard batch of fans, trolls, haters and the like. However, one extremely common reply I receive whenever I enlighten someone with statistical facts, accurate historical comparisons, etc., that they did not previously know, is that I must be biased towards Jameis Winston to even tweet such factual statistics in the first place.

However, as economist and social theorist Thomas Sowell stated:

> *It is hard to imagine a more stupid or more dangerous way of making decisions than by putting those decisions in the hands of people who pay no price for being wrong.* [1]

While many folks who are actually biased against Jameis Winston like to reject the truths detailed in this book, on the mere basis that I must be biased towards Winston, the fact is that there is nothing on the line for them if their opinions about Winston are erroneous. However, I have *put my money where my mouth is* so to speak and therefore will absolutely pay a price if I am wrong about Winston. This said, as I am the one with money on the line, logically, I am the one who actually spent more time truly researching Winston, crunching the numbers, doing the historical comparisons and the like, and therefore I am the one who is more likely to hold accurate beliefs based on actual hard data rather than mere biased opinion.

Regardless, as the great author, E.B. White stated:

> *I have yet to see a piece of writing, political or non-political, that doesn't have a slant. All writing slants the way a writer leans, and no man is born perpendicular, although many men are born upright.* [5]

While I may not be able to claim to have been born *perpendicular* or completely without bias, I certainly strive to be *upright*, meaning righteous in my judgment and accurate in my assessments. I also reject mere opinion, even my own mere opinion, in favor of statistical truth and hard data, as while opinions are often provably false, accurate statistics are irrefutable facts, as mathematician and biostatistician Karl Pearson stated:

Statistics is the grammar of science. [6]

The above said – and as I explained in a Twitter debate with one main stream sports media journalist who ranted about bias when he couldn't refute the statistics I was tweeting and then had a public melt-down and ultimately blocked me, apparently to prevent me from curing him of his *Winston Derangement Syndrome* – I rely so heavily on statistics rather than mere human opinions because I am an investor and know full well that personal bias, emotionalism and even mere fandom of a particular team can destroy an investment and corrupt the mind of an investor in short order. Therefore, that I am an investor in a high-end Jameis Winston sports card and memorabilia collection does not make me any more biased toward Jameis Winston over other quarterbacks than owning Pepsi stock makes me biased toward Pepsi over my preferred brands: Virgil's, Reed's and Blue Sky.

For example, my favorite basketball player of all-time is Kobe Bryant, and as mentioned above, Bryant is responsible for making me a great deal of money as an investor in the past. However, I willingly acknowledge that Michael Jordan, LeBron James and Kareem Abdul-Jabbar all had greater careers than Bryant had and all therefore deserve to be ranked higher on a GOAT (i.e. Greatest of All Time) list than Bryant does.

Of course when I explain such to various main stream sports media members, as well as the usual illogical social media types, I am generally hit with personal insults, childish rants, a string of curse words and the like, as such folks simply do not like the facts I tweet. Yet such folks also cannot refute any of the factual statistics I present either, so they simply rant and rave about *bias* and pretend such facts don't exist.

I have been blocked on Twitter by various main stream sports media figures for no other reason than that I presented facts that didn't fit with the narratives they were trying to spin. In fact, I even had one extremely unethical main stream sorts media journalist have a major melt-down while debating me on Twitter before unethically attempting to dox me and then blocking me when he realized he couldn't get me to lose my cool and realized any future replies from me would expose his own bias even further.

However, as the prodigious Irish playwright and polemicist George Bernard Shaw stated:

> *It is the mark of a truly intelligent person to be moved by statistics.* [7]

That the seemingly vast majority of sports fans are not just unmoved by statistics if those statistics contradict their mere biased opinions, but actually detest such statistics, literally makes me feel sorry for such individuals in the same way I feel sorry for a cancer patient who continues to smoke through the stoma in his or her throat. I simply do not understand how anyone can be presented with the truth about anything and then reject said truth and even fight against it; such illogic strikes me as a form of insanity, or should I say, *derangement*, as in *Winston Derangement Syndrome*.

And, while I enjoy debating with biased journalists and even dialoguing with absolute trolls and haters, there are certainly times when conversing with such leads me to remember a couple of Bible verses, one from Proverbs 23:9 and the other from Matthew 7:6b, which state:

> *Speak not in the ears of a fool: for he will despise the wisdom of thy words ... neither cast ye your pearls before swine, lest they trample them under their feet, and turn again and rend you.*

Regardless, I still try to set aside time each week to go on Twitter, expose biased journalists and analysts, interact with my readers, and as one of my readers put it, *do God's work.*

The above said, no, I did not start researching Jameis Winston simply because I was bored or because I wanted to expose the media's obvious bias against one random athlete. I did so because I was considering investing in high-end Winston sports cards and memorabilia and because after I made such an investment, I continued to follow his career and re-evaluate his performance each season to determine whether I should hold or sell said investment. To this day neither I nor any of the other investors in our group has ever advertised a single card in the *Lucky 13 Collection* for sale, as each and every one of us remains confident in Jameis Winston's future as a Hall of Fame quarterback, thanks in large part to the various statistical truths and other relevant data presented in this book.

All of the above said, I have little doubt that many will reject the irrefutable truths in this book, simply because they'd rather believe entertaining lies (i.e. false media narratives) when it comes to Jameis Winston than accept inconvenient truths. However, as businessman, author and philanthropist W. Clement Stone said:

> *Truth will always be truth, regardless of lack of understanding, disbelief or ignorance.* [8]

I also have little doubt that many will reject the truths in this book simply because I, a man using the pseudonym *Jameis1of1*, am the one disseminating such truths. However, as human rights activist Malcolm X said:

> *I'm for truth, no matter who tells it.* [2]

I also have little doubt that many will reject the truths in this book simply because they may not know anyone else who believes such truths and do not hear any popular talking head in the main stream sports media broadcasting such truths. However, as Gandhi said:

> *Even if you are a minority of one, the truth is the truth.* [9]

Nevertheless, just as I was ridiculed by many for sinking nearly 50% of my net worth into Kobe Bryant rookie cards, called insane for refusing to dump said investment even when Kobe was still riding the bench during his 2nd season, trolled by those who pretended to be omniscient and liked to play God because I refused to do the same and would only rebuke Bryant for committing adultery after he was arrested and charged with a crime in 2003 and the charges were later dropped with him admitting to committing adultery, I am now experiencing déjà vu with my investment in Jameis Winston. Of course, just because I was proven to be prescient with the statistical projections I made based on the age-related first and second year stats of Kobe Bryant and with my major financial investment in his high-end sports cards, such does not mean I will end up being proven prescient when it comes to my views and investment in Jameis Winston.

However, I am 100% sure of two things. Firstly that the great author Miguel de Cervantes was right when he said:

Truth will rise above falsehood as oil above water. [10]

And, secondly that my greatest prayer in life is for God's will to be done, whatever that may be and whatever that may bring, because as Jameis Winston himself once said:

I'm so thankful that everything God does is perfect. [11]

THE PHENOM

Phenom: a phenomenon, especially a young prodigy. [12]

Jameis Lanaed Winston's picture could be displayed under the word *phenom* in any dictionary. In fact, former NFL defensive end, founder of Modernday Fitness and Winston's long-time personal trainer Otis Leverette once wrote:

> *When people describe you with words like phenom and prodigy, you transcend from being a man into a movement. That's what the last six years have been like for Jameis.* [13]

Not only did little Jameis start playing football at just four years of age [14], his parents, Antonor and Loretta:

> *signed their boy up for football mostly for the photo opportunities. They knew how ridiculous 4-year-old Jameis would look, his body swallowed up by a baggy uniform, tottering around a field occupied by 7- and 8-year-old behemoths. But Jameis felt at home.* [15]

Little Jameis' coach was the renowned Fred Green, who was:

> *instantly enamored with the tiny kid wearing the helmet two sizes too big. He was amazed by the way the kid attacked much older competition without a hint of fear.* [15]

Winston is said to have called his first audible as a *Pop Warner* quarterback when he was just 7 years old [16] and by age 10 young Jameis had a personal trainer – Mark Freeman – who over the next few years would spend three plus hours a day, 3-4 days per week training Jameis. This training included not just on-field work but *chalk talk* where Winston would have to draw up plays on a blackboard and answer every question Freeman threw at him, which he always did. [15] According to Freeman:

I knew Jaboo was going to be special. [15]

Winston would end up playing quarterback for 7 years in *Pop Warner* and lead his teams to a combined record of 50 wins and zero losses, that's right, 50-0! [17]

Journalist Connor Muldowney stated the following after viewing game-tape of a dominant 11 year old Winston:

It's crazy to see Winston's accuracy on the long ball and his ability to throw on the run even as a young player. It's almost as if he was born to play football and everything he did was extremely impressive. Watching him run even a youth offense is intriguing as you probably couldn't take your eyes off the video for the duration. [17]

Some of you reading the above may scoff at young Jameis compiling an absurd 50-0 perfect record as a *Pop Warner quarterback* thinking such doesn't mean anything. However, according to longtime NFL Executive and three time Super Bowl champion Michael Lombardi:

Bill Parcels' golden rule was to draft prospects with at least 23 wins in college. It told him that a player knew what it took to be successful and was committed to doing the little things that got the job done. You can't bluff your way to 23 wins, not even in Pop Warner. [18]

Lombardi actually mentions Winston in his very next sentence, but as this chapter deals with young Jameis rather than college age Jameis, Lombardi's quote about *Pop Warner* will suffice.

By the time Jameis Winston reached high school he was already a legend known by the moniker *Jaboo*. Current Tampa Bay Buccaneers head coach and then Arizona Cardinals head coach Bruce Arians stated:

> *Jaboo's been a legend since he was in the ninth grade ... Just a tremendous athlete. A very bright guy, but had a cannon for an arm* [19]

The High School Years

As a 14 year old freshman in 2008, Winston enrolled at Hueytown High School and won the starting QB job on the varsity team immediately, starting all 11 games that season and leading the team to a winning record. After the season, his coach Jeff Smith stated:

> *It's still hard to believe he was a freshman quarterback starting on the varsity. He's just so talented with so much potential* [20]

However, the Hueytown High School Golden Gophers football team had not won a regional title since 1974 and had an abysmal 43-81 win/loss record over the 12 seasons before Jameis *Jaboo* Winston arrived. Winston would have his work cut out for him if he wanted to turn such a moribund program into an powerhouse in the great football state of Alabama [21]. Yet that is exactly what the legend known as *Jaboo* would do!

As a sophomore, even when the Golden Gophers young team struggled and finished with a mere .500 record, Winston's legend continued to grow and the plaudits surrounding him continued to flow. In fact, after he competed in a football camp in Tuscaloosa, Alabama, Winston's trainer Otis Leverette stated:

> *I knew it ever since he got out there at a camp in Tuscaloosa as a sophomore competing with 5-star seniors, and anybody with two working eyes could clearly see that Jameis was the best quarterback there. I've seen some kids go to these camps and, for*

lack of a better term, pee down their legs when they get out there
with that level of competition. It was like no moment was ever too
big for him. [13]

During Winston's junior season he led the Golden Gophers to the best
season in their 90 year school history. And, while the team lost its final
game of the season in the 3rd round of the Alabama state playoffs, it took
the eventual state champion Spanish Fort Toros – a powerhouse that
shutout their opponent in the state title game – to end Hueytown's historic
season [22].

Then, as a senior in 2011, Winston and his Golden Gophers bested what
they had done the year before, thereby once again having the greatest
season in school history. Hueytown finished the season with a school
record 13 wins and captured their first regional title in 38 years [23]. As for
Winston himself, he finished the season with 2,424 passing yards, a 69%
completion rate and 28 touchdown passes against just 2 interceptions. He
also rushed for 1,065 yards and recorded 15 more touchdowns on the
ground.

Winston's high school coach – Matt Scott – once said about his star QB:

He's wired completely different than anybody I've ever been
around ... His football IQ is through the roof. [15]

It wasn't just Winston's high football IQ that Coach Scott loved but
Winston's competitive fire as well, which Scott explained by stating:

Every Friday night, he was the meanest son of a gun out there.
I've never been around anyone as competitive as he is ... People
say quarterbacks shouldn't get too high or too low, but I mean to
tell you, when he's in a rage, he's pretty good. [15]

Otis Leverette echoed Coach Scott's statement when he described
Winston as follows:

> *When it comes to football, Jameis is like that dog over the fence who is wagging his tail, and you think it's the nicest dog you've ever seen, and then you jump over there and he will bite the hell out of you. He's always had this Will Smith from the Fresh Prince type of personality, but with some Navy SEAL in him, too. If we're having a water break, he'd act like he was four years old with the other kids. But when he got back on the field, he instantly snapped into a trained assassin. He could do it in a matter of minutes. When I saw that, I knew I had something special.* [13]

Following his senior season, Winston was named to the Under 19 USA Football National Team, as well as named a:

- Alabama Sports Writers Association's Class 5A Back of the Year [21]
- Alabama Gatorade State Player of the Year [21]

- ESPNHS first team All-American [21]

- Parade All-American [24]

- Under Armor All-American [24]

- USA Today first team QB on the All-USA Team [24]!

In Jameis Winston's four year high school career, he accounted for an astounding 9,853 total yards and 103 total touchdowns [25] while his teams compiled a 35-13 win/loss record, won 5 state playoff games and even won their first regional title in 38 years. However in the 12 years before Winston arrived the team went just 43-81 and won just two playoff games total, and in the 4 years after Winston left the team went just 16-25 and didn't win a single playoff game [21]. In short, Jameis Winston was to the Hueytown Golden Gophers what LeBron James was to the Cleveland Cavaliers … everything!

The Elite 11 MVP

After graduating from high school with a 4.0 GPA [26] Jameis Winston participated in the 2011 Elite 11 quarterback competition run by Student Sports LLC and coached by former NFL Super Bowl winning QB Trent Dilfer. At the culmination of the camp Winston was named Co-MVP [27].

Below is a complete list of all 22 quarterbacks to win an Elite 11 MVP award between the first year of the competition in 1999 and 2017, the most recent year with an MVP that has played at least one season of college football [27]:

- 2017: Justin Fields
- 2016: Tua Tagovailoa
- 2015: Shea Patterson
- 2014: Blake Barnett
- 2013: Sean White
- 2012: Asiantii Woulard
- 2011: **Jameis Winston**, Tanner Magnum and Neal Burcham
- 2010: Jeff Driskel
- 2009: Jake Heaps
- 2008: Aaron Murray
- 2007: Blaine Gabbert
- 2006: John Brantley
- 2005: Matthew Stafford
- 2004: Mark Sanchez
- 2003: Rhett Bomar and Matt Tuiasosopo
- 2002: Kyle Wright
- 2001: Ben Olson
- 2000: Brodie Croyle
- 1999: Brock Berlin

Two things instantly become clear when reading the previous list. Firstly, that the vast majority of Elite 11 MVPs never live up to their potential even on the collegiate level, let alone on the NFL level. Secondly, that

Jameis Winston's name jumps off this list as one phenom that lived up to the hype in spades.

In fact, of the 22 quarterbacks awarded an Elite 11 MVP trophy over the aforementioned 19 year period, the only quarterback other than Jameis Winston to have ever won a National Title is Alabama's Tua Tagovailoa and the only quarterback other than Jameis to be a #1 overall NFL draft pick was Matthew Stafford, while Jameis is the one and only quarterback to have ever won a Heisman trophy. Winston is therefore the one and only Elite 11 MVP who has ever gone on to win a Heisman trophy, National Championship and become a #1 pick in the NFL Draft, a sort of QB phenom *Triple Crown* if you will.

In short, Jameis Winston is, by far, the greatest collegiate quarterback to have ever won the MVP trophy in the history of the Elite 11, the most prestigious high school quarterback competition in existence!

The Five Star Prospect's Five Star Prospect

CBS' 247Sports – the king of national high school prospect ranking websites – has a database known as the 247Sports Composite which is described as "the industry's most comprehensive and unbiased prospect ranking". [28] The 247Sports Composite of star-rated high school football players dates back to the year 2000 with the highest rating a prospect can receive being the coveted *Five Star* rating. And, in 2012 Jameis Winston not only received the coveted Five Star rating but was also named the #1 quarterback in the nation as well. [29]

Beginning in that first year of 2000 and ending in the year 2016 – the most recent year for a quarterback prospect (i.e. Dwayne Haskins of Ohio State University) who entered the recent 2019 NFL Draft – the 247Sports Composite has awarded a Five Star rating to just 56 quarterbacks, an average of just under 3.3 such incoming freshman NCAA QBs each year. [28]

Below is a complete list of all 56 quarterbacks to receive a Five Star rating from said composite, listed in order from the highest to the lowest graded in each season [28]:

- 2016: Shea Patterson and Jacob Eason
- 2015: Josh Rosen, Blake Barnett and Kyler Murray
- 2014: Kyle Allen
- 2013: Max Browne and Christian Hackenberg
- 2012: **Jameis Winston** and Gunner Kiel
- 2011: Jeff Driskel and Braxton Miller
- 2010: Phillip Sims
- 2009: Matt Barkley, Russell Shepard, Garrett Gilbert, Aaron
    - Murray and Tajh Boyd
- 2008: Terrelle Pryor, Dayne Crist and EJ Manuel
- 2007: Jimmy Clausen, Ryan Mallett, Tyrod Taylor, Aaron Corp,
    - Cam Newton and John Brantley
- 2006: Matthew Stafford, Mitch Mustain and Tim Tebow
- 2005: Mark Sanchez and Ryan Perrilloux
- 2004: Rhett Bomar, Xavier Lee, Anthony Morelli, Chad Henne,
    - Mat Tuiasosopo and Bobby Reid
- 2003: Kyle Wright, Chris Leak and Robert Lane
- 2002: Vince Young, Ben Olson, Marcus Vick, Trent Edwards,
    - James Banks and Justin Zwick
- 2001: Brodie Croyle, Joe Mauer, D.J. Shockley and Cecil
    - Howard
- 2000: Brock Berlin, Jeff Smoker, Chance Mock, Casey Clausen
    - and Jason Campbell

Just as when one reads the list of Elite 11 MVP award winners, two things instantly become clear when reading the above list. Firstly, that the vast majority of Five Star rated quarterbacks never live up to their immense potential even on the collegiate level, let alone on the NFL level. Secondly, that once again Jameis Winston's name jumps off this list as one phenom that lived up to the hype in spades.

In fact, of the 56 quarterbacks awarded a Five Star rating over the aforementioned 17 year period, the only quarterbacks other than Jameis Winston to have ever been named to an NFL Pro Bowl were Cam Newton, Vince Young and Matthew Stafford, and Winston was the youngest of the four to earn a Pro Bowl nod. Likewise, of the 56 quarterbacks, the only two that have thrown more career NFL TD passes than Jameis Winston to date are Matthew Stafford who has played 6 more NFL seasons than Winston and Cam Newton who has played 4 more NFL seasons than Winston.

In short, Jameis Winston is the five star prospect's five star prospect and the epitome of what a *phenom* truly is!

TROUBLES IN TALLAHASSEE

Suppose one reads a story of filthy atrocities in the paper. Then suppose that something turns up suggesting that the story might not be quite true, or not quite so bad as it was made out. Is one's first feeling, 'Thank God, even they aren't quite so bad as that,' or is it a feeling of disappointment, and even a determination to cling to the first story for the sheer pleasure of thinking your enemies are as bad as possible? If it is the second then it is, I am afraid, the first step in a process which, if followed to the end, will make us into devils.

– C.S. Lewis [30]

As a man who considers himself an unworthy servant of the One true God of the Bible above all else, I do not want to think of any human being as being a *devil*, as I recognize that the devil (i.e. Satan) is real (see Matthew 4:1-11) and that devils (i.e. fallen angels) actually exist (see Revelation 12:7-11). However, all it takes is for one to spend about 15 minutes on a social media site to realize that many modern day human beings have become the exact sort of individuals C.S. Lewis described in the above quote, and that such people do indeed act like devils, or even the devil himself, as the Scriptures describe the devil as a *liar* (John 8:44) and as *the accuser* (Revelation 12:10). And, if there is one thing individuals on social media seem to like to do more than anything else, it is to accuse others of violating various laws, rules, customs and the like, even if they need to lie in order to levy such accusations against the object of their wrath.

Jameis Winston learned the above lesson at a very young age, as according to journalist David Hale:

> *He was perhaps the most polarizing person in his hometown at
> age 15* [26]

And, at 17 years of age, when Winston elected to attend Florida State
University rather than Nick Saban's national powerhouse Alabama
Crimson Tide, he knew he was making a lot of enemies in his home state,
and confessed:

> *Well you know it's been tough, tough the whole time. I feel
> confident in my decision. I am just comfortable and that's where I
> wanted to be ... God has blessed me the whole way ... Alabama
> fans are going to hate me. But I am not worried about pleasing
> fans or people.* [31]

Winston was also once quoted as saying:

People don't like when you have success [26]

Success – especially on the football field – is one thing that has always
come easy for Jameis Winston. However, it's one thing for a young man
to be booed, jeered and taunted by mere rabid football fans that wish he
would have elected to attend Alabama instead of Florida State or wish he
would have thrown an interception instead of a game-winning touchdown
pass against their favorite team. It's an entirely different thing for a young
man to be accused of being a bad human being and to be called a criminal,
especially when such a young man has never even been arrested, let alone
convicted of a crime, at any time in his entire life. Yet that is exactly the
sort of treatment Jameis Winston received from both the media and large
numbers of the general public as well during his redshirt freshman season
in Tallahassee.

Soda Pop Piracy or Unsubstantiated Silliness?

In July 2012 police were called to a Burger King after an employee
accused Winston of taking free drinks of soda. [32] However, the Police

declined to interview Winston about the alleged incident and no further action was taken. [33]

What? The Police refused to even interview the alleged, infamous *Soda Pop Pirate*? Obviously the Police should have tasered Winston upon arrival and the public should have stoned him in the town square for even being accused of such a heinous act. Of course, for all anyone knows, the Burger King employee that reported Winston to the Police was actually just upset that Winston refused to grant an autograph or selfie request.

Squirrelduggery or Sensationalized Story?

In November 2012 Jameis Winston and an FSU teammate were briefly detained by police for hunting squirrels, an activity that was fully legal as it was done both off-campus and during Florida's squirrel hunting season. [34] Winston was not arrested and the officer that briefly detained him and took the pellet gun and pellets returned them to Winston. [35]

However, even though Winston was participating in a legal activity, not arrested and not charged with a crime, that didn't stop *USA Today* from running an article with the provocative title *Jameis Winston stopped by police at gunpoint in 2012* and insinuating that Winston could face code of conduct violations for hunting *on campus*. [35]

USA Today was forced to correct their story, as it was revealed that the trail Winston was hunting squirrels on was not *on campus* whatsoever. The reporter who wrote the story was also exposed as someone from Gainesville, Florida, where Winston's Seminoles rival the Florida Gators were located, and someone who had been attempting to dig up dirt on Winston for the previous 12 weeks. [34]

The reporter's actions bring a passage of Scripture to mind:

> *Thou shalt not raise a false report: put not thine hand with the wicked to be an unrighteous witness.*

> – Exodus 23:1-2

Of course the paper could have painted an accurate picture by running the article with a title such as:

> *Police briefly detained Jameis Winston for legally hunting squirrels*

The paper could have even ran the article using a pro-Jameis and anti-Police title such as:

> *White Police Officer holds Innocent African American QB at gunpoint*

Such a title is common place today and also would have been entirely true as the officer that brandished his firearm was Anthony Gioannetti, who is in fact a white male.

However various entities in the main stream media decided long ago that Jameis Winston as *villain* was the angle that worked best for them. They have been spinning narratives and running articles to that effect ever since. Fairness and justice be damned.

The BB Battle Champ?

Later in the same week of November 2012 Winston and the same teammate were investigated by the Police for causing property damage during BB gun *battles* to an apartment complex they were living in. The apartment manager had considered trying to evict four players including

Winston but ultimately the players paid for all damage caused and no actual action of any kind was taken. [35]

Certainly it may have been better for Winston to have been involved in rap battles rather than BB gun battles, but when one is a bona fide Alabama squirrel hunter, one would probably rather be the BB battle champ than the second coming of *B-Rabbit* from *8 Mile*.

The Crab Crook or the Humble Hook-up?

In April 2014 Winston received a citation for leaving a Publix grocery store with $32 worth of unpaid for crab legs and crawfish. [32] Initially Winston stated that he made a mistake and accepted full responsibility. However, when he was interviewed by Jim Harbaugh on the Draft Academy television show, Winston stated:

> *How I'm supposed to handle, like, if I just got them for free? I just say, 'I just messed up?' ... a week before, it was my buddy's birthday and we had got a cake. And we met a dude that worked inside Publix and he said, 'Hey, anytime you come in here, I got you.' So that day we just walked out and he hooked us up with that' ... And when I came in to get crab legs, I did the same thing and he just gave them to me and I walked out.* [36]

The masses – most of whom were not Florida State fans of course and had a reason to believe the worst about Winston – condemned Winston as some sort of low-life thug. Various memes mocking Winston flooded the internet and many people simply decided he must be guilty and even be a bad human being. Then the security video dropped. [37]

When the security video was released it became quite clear that Jameis Winston not only may have indeed had a *hook up* from a store employee, but that he merely apologized and accepted responsibility at the time of the incident to save said employee from losing his job.

47

In the security video one can easily see Winston slowly walking up to a seafood counter and picking up a plate of seafood that had been placed there by a Publix employee. Then, one can watch as Winston slowly meanders through the store with the plate of food in full view, even circling back to apparently look at another item on the shelf, before finally continuing on right out the front doors with the plate of food still in clear view. Winston never attempted to conceal the allegedly *stolen* food, never attempted to sneak out a back door or avoid cameras; in fact, he never made a suspicious movement of any kind.

Now, as a Christian who takes the Scriptures extremely seriously, I never want to pretend to be omniscient, play God, or judge unrighteously, be that by judging an innocent person to be guilty or by judging a guilty person to be innocent. Therefore, while I am not stating that I know for certain that Jameis Winston had a *hook up* from an employee of Publix, I most certainly believe the evidence in the form of the video tape – at the very least – *appears* to confirm what Winston told Jim Harbaugh when he was interviewed and therefore that no actual *theft* occurred whatsoever.

And, if Jameis Winston's behavior behind an NFL podium during post-game press conferences is any indication, it does seem to come naturally to him to take responsibility for other's faults and to refuse to throw anyone other than himself under the bus, even when it was indeed someone else who messed up on the field. Could it be that Winston merely took responsibility when it was really a Publix employee that gave him a *hook up* and should have fessed up to such? Could it be that Winston was simply protecting a friendly acquaintance from being fired from his job, in the same way he routinely protects teammates from being criticized by the media when he accepts responsibility for their poor play?

If that is what happened, that would mean the masses who castigated Winston as a thug and bad human being were themselves actually acting like bullies and bad human beings, and no one would ever want to believe such about themselves. That said, it's much more convenient for such people to simply continue to advance the idea that Winston must have been guilty of theft, as the alternative would be admitting that they themselves were guilty of bearing false witness against an innocent young man. Therefore, it is no surprise that to this day, many individuals on social media and even members of the main stream sports media continue to believe and state that Winston *stole* crab legs. Why? Simply because, as Protestant Christian minister Charles Spurgeon stated:

> *A lie can travel half way around the world while the truth is putting on its shoes.*

> – Charles Spurgeon [38]

A Chip off the ol' Favre?

On September 19, 2014, Florida State University suspended Winston for the first half against Clemson [39] after he shouted a popular yet vulgar internet meme in the Student Union. [40]

According to journalist Marc Tracy:

> *Winston's comments Tuesday ... played off a meme — a running gag, essentially — in which passers-by shout the phrase in videos ostensibly taken from live news broadcasts. ... The comments come at a time when there is public outcry over some football players' treatment of women, stemming primarily from the recently released video of the former Baltimore Ravens running back Ray Rice punching his then-fiancée in an elevator.* [40]

So, a 20 year old college student shouted a popular yet vulgar internet meme; okay, why was that national, front-page sports news? Because that 20 year old college student was Jameis Winston, and as the aforementioned journalist Marc Tracy pointed out, it happened shortly after the horrendous Ray Rice video dropped and therefore when social justice warriors were in a frenzy and chomping at the bit to exact social justice on any athlete that even *appeared* to be disrespecting women. Apparently shouting a popular internet meme that happened to be vulgar qualified, as social media did come down hard on Winston indeed. Yet, in reality, this was a non-story that became a story due to the social climate at the time it happened and because it featured Jameis Winston.

However, this Winston story reminds me of another story about a young mercurial quarterback. That quarterback's name was Brett Favre and he wasn't a redshirt college sophomore like Wiinston was, but a 23 year old father and NFL QB on his second team.

As the story goes, in late 1992 Favre participated as a judge in a *Hot Buns* contest, and during the contest an intoxicated Favre led a chant of a popular *2 Live Crew* song featuring vulgar lyrics. [41] Of course, the social media climate in 1992 was entirely different than it was in 2014, and even though Favre was an NFL QB at that time, he was nowhere near as popular or well-known at that time as Winston was as a mere redshirt sophomore college QB in 2014.

All things considered, it's quite obvious that the reason Winston was suspended for one game in his second collegiate season had more to do with the timing and the celebrity involved than the actual action itself. It certainly was not a reason for anyone to have considered Winston a thug, convict, or bad human being, even if it was a reason to consider Winston a typical 20 year old college student in need of maturation, like, well, any other 20 year college student.

Nevertheless, even if one were to give Winston the benefit of the doubt in each of the aforementioned situations – which isn't hard to do in all honesty, seeing as none of those situations resulted in any criminal charges or even a single arrest and most are things no one would bat an eye at if the person doing them was not named Jameis Winston – the next accusation covered in this book and how one interprets such, would likely define how one views Winston to this day.

In fact, even if all of the aforementioned allegations levied against Winston were unquestionably true, such would mean little more than he was a typical immature college kid. However, the next accusation covered in this book is the one accusation that has defined how the public and even the mainstream sports media views Jameis Winston to this day, be it as a criminal who got away with a heinous crime, or as an innocent person who was wrongly accused.

The Persecutor or the Persecuted?

In January of 2013 FSU student Erica Kinsman identified Winston to the Tallahasse police as the unknown assailant in her December 7, 2012 sexual battery incident report. However, Winston was never interviewed by the police and by February 2013 the case was closed. [41] Such was possibly due to the fact that Kinsman failed to identify her supposed attacker until a month after her initial report, despite the alleged assailant being the #1 ranked QB recruit in the country [29] and an individual that was a BMOC (i.e. Big Man on Campus) as evidenced by the media circus present on the day he signed his letter of intent to enroll at FSU and the fact that the popular website – www.TomahawkNation.com – published an article titled, *The Jameis Winston Experience: Seminoles Sign Top Quarterback* [42] on February 3, 2012, over 9 months before Kinsman filed her initial report, and approximately 10 months before she claimed Winston was the assailant.

However, it's even more likely that the reason the police did not seriously investigate Winston was that on top of the fact that Kinsman could not identify her assailant for approximately one month, she did state in her initial incident report that her assailant was a black male, between 5'9" and 5'11" tall, weighed 240 pounds and had *straight* black hair. [41] Winston however was listed as 6'4" tall and just 190 pounds by CBS' 247Sports [25] and did not have *straight* hair whatsoever. That said, Kinsman was 5-7" and 50 pounds off! By comparison, monstrous NFL QB Cam Newton [43] is just 6" taller and 30 pounds heavier than diminutive NFL QB Russell Wilson [44] and Tampa Bay Buccaneers fans will be shocked to know that gargantuan receiver Mike Evans [45] is 7" but just 46 pounds heavier than miniature cornerback Brent Grimes [46]! Can anyone who has seen Evans and Grimes play football possibly imagine mistaking the mammoth Evans (whose nickname is Godzilla) for

Brent Grimes with an extra 50 pounds of weight on his elfin body – who would also be sporting Katt Williams style *straight* hair – let alone after supposedly getting physically assaulted by Evans?

Regardless, Tallahassee interim Police Chief Tom Coe later revealed that Kinsman's attorney Patricia Carroll had lied previously, and that the fact of the matter was that the reason the investigation stalled was because Kinsman cut off contact with the Police and Carroll herself indicated to the Police that Kinsman did not wish to proceed with the case.

On November 13, 2013, after receiving various media inquiries about Kinsman's claims, Florida State Attorney Willie Meggs begins investigating the previously closed case by assigning it to the Special Victims Unit. The very next day Winston voluntarily provided a DNA-swab to the police. [41]

On November 17, 2013 Winston's lawyer calls on the State Attorney to refrain from making extrajudicial statements about Winston, yet the State Attorney states that the rights of the victim and not merely Winston need to be protected. [41] Such a fact doesn't quite fit with the media narrative that the State Attorney was running some big coverup, that's for sure.

Finally, on December 5, 2013, State Attorney Meggs announced during a press conference at the Leon County Courthouse that there would be no charges levied against Winston, while stating:

> *Her (Erica Kinsman, added) recall of the events of that night have been moving around quite a bit … We have a duty as prosecutors to determine if each case has a reasonable likelihood of conviction … After reviewing the facts in this case, we do not feel that we can reach those burdens.* [47]

Meggs also revealed the following facts:

- He did not believe that Kinsman could be counted on *to prove elements of a crime.* [47]

- Despite Kinsman claiming to have broken memory due to *heavy drinking* on the night in question, her toxicology report showed she had just a .04 blood alcohol level (which is the equivalent of a 120 pound female having just one can of beer [48]). [47]

- Kinsman's toxicology report showed no evidence of drugs in her system whatsoever. [47]

- The DNA of two men different men, including Winston, was found in the sexual assault kit. [47]

- Kinsman had no outward signs of trauma whatsoever. [47]

After the State Attorney announced his decision, Winston's lawyer Tim Jansen stated in regards to Winston:

> *He's absolutely innocent, and I'm glad and pleased that Willie did a full investigation and found the same thing we did. There's no evidence. He could not go forward with any charges.* [47]

Jameis Winston himself stated:

> *It's been difficult to stay silent through this process, but I never lost faith in the truth and in who I am.* [47]

After both the Tallahassee Police Department and later the Florida State Attorney's Office could find no reason to levy any sort of charge against Winston whatsoever, Florida State University itself convened a *Student Conduct Code* hearing in December of 2014. [49] The hearing was ruled over by retired Florida Supreme Court Chief Justice, Major Best Harding, who – for those who wonder if he was an FSU grad – earned his collegiate degrees from Wake Forest University and the University of Virginia and served on the Florida Supreme Court from 1991-2002. [50]

On December 19, 2014, Major Best Harding released his written decision. In it he stated the following:

> *The investigative hearing materials consisted of over 1,000 pages of documents as well as electronically stored data. ... supplemental materials submitted by the parties; witness testimony received at the hearing; and exhibits* [51]

> *Kinsman's statements concerning the night's events have changed over time* [51]

> *The medical exam and testimony of the SANE nurse, Ms. Walker, who performed Kinsman's exam are inconclusive.* [51]

> *lab reports show that there were no known drugs in Kinsman's system and that her blood alcohol level was within reason.* [51]

Major Best Harding concluded:

> *In sum, the preponderance of the evidence has not shown that you (Jameis Winston, added) are responsible for any of the charged violations of the Code. Namely, I find that the evidence before me is insufficient to satisfy the burden of proof.* [51]

Despite Jameis Winston being cleared of any wrong-doing by the Tallahassee Police Department and Florida State Attorney's Office, and then found guiltless in the Florida State University *Student Conduct Code* hearing conducted by an independent retired Supreme Court Justice, his accuser Erica Kinsman decided to sue him civilly in April of 2015 [52] in hopes of receiving a large sum of money from Winston. Such was right around the time Winston became the #1 overall pick in the 2015 NFL

Draft and received a $16,697,292 signing bonus as part of a four year $25,351,277 contract. [53]

In fact, according to a court filing from Winston's lawyer:

> *Ms. Kinsman's counsel demanded $7,000,000 from Mr. Winston and requested that he obtain an insurance policy "to protect her client's interests in the event he gets injured this year."*

> *Ms. Kinsman's counsel later sought a response or a counter-offer to her $7,000,000 demand and ended this phone call by stating, "by the way, if we settle you will never hear from my client or me again, in the press or anywhere."* [54]

However, Jameis Winston not give in to Kinsman's attempted money grab or pay her to go away as many past star athletes have done when faced with such a lawsuit. Instead, Winston actually countersued Kinsman for defamation and had his countersuit upheld by U.S. District Court Judge Anne C. Conway. [52]

Ultimately Winston and Kinsman settled their competing lawsuits amicably. [55] Winston haters promoted the idea that he paid Kinsman handsomely to avoid a trial, while Winston supporters promoted the idea that Kinsman paid him to avoid losing a great deal of money if and when the judge ruled against her on the defamation claim.

Personally, I do not know who paid who, or if any funds exchanged hands whatsoever. However, I do remember after the settlement news dropped, Winston's father stated that he was happy with the result and that his son didn't have to pay Kinsman a penny. I believe that since there was obviously a non-disclosure-agreement, had Winston's father's claims been untrue, Kinsman could have sued him. In short, if I had to guess what sort of settlement was reached, my guess would be that Kinsman did not receive a penny from Jameis Winston as I do believe she would have certainly lost the defamation claim filed against her, as many of her clearly defamatory and untrue statements were made publicly.

Now, please understand that as a Biblical Christian I personally denounce pre-marital sex of any kind, be it a casual hook-up or a loving encounter between fiancés, as the word of God is crystal clear that sex was created by God to be shared by husbands and wives only. That said, this section was not meant as a defence of Winston's actions, as I certainly do not approve of him fornicating with Erica Kinsman. The media, and in fact the majority of the world as a whole may have no problem with fornication these days, while at the same time being ready to publicly crucify someone over saying politically incorrect *words* or holding politically incorrect *beliefs*. I am not one of those people.

Regardless, all of the above said, the simple fact is that in this matter with Kinsman, Winston was cleared of any wrong-doing by the Tallahassee Police Department, and cleared of any wrong doing by the Florida State Attorney's Office, and found guiltless in the Florida State University *Student Conduct Code* hearing conducted by an independent retired Supreme Court Justice. Winston also countersued Kinsman after she allegedly attempted to extort $7,000,000 from him and sued him civilly, which resulted in the U.S. District Court Judge accepting and upholding Winston's countersuit and ultimately resulted in Kinsman dropping even her civil suit against him.

The Hunting Ground or The Propaganda Gang?

The Hunting Ground was a documentary film that premiered at the *Sundance Film Festival* about three months before the 2015 NFL Draft. The film was distributed by *CNN* [56] and *The Weinstein Company* [57], that's right, the same company founded by Hollywood outcast Harvey Weinstein.

Journalist Anne Hendershott stated:

> *For all of its flaws and fabrications, "The Hunting Ground," Harvey Weinstein's activist documentary film about sexual assault on college campuses, finally succeeded in helping to actually identify a real predator — the filmmaker himself. [57]*

In regards to the involvement of *CNN*, journalist Wendy McElroy stated:

> *The Hunting Ground does not provide the most basic safeguards of accuracy. .... The film is rife with misrepresentations or outright lies. ... Jameis Winston seems to be a particular target of "The Hunting Ground" and its supporters.... Unhappily, CNN has been heavily promoting a showing of the documentary. It is irresponsible to the point of unethical for a "news" channel to do so.* [56]

Consider also what journalist Stuart Taylor Jr. stated about the film and especially its treatment of Jameis Winston:

> *In making its case against Winston, the film conceals from viewers how Kinsman's story conflicts with the physical evidence, other witnesses, and her own past statements. It also distorts why the three investigations all found that the evidence does not prove that Winston raped Kinsman. In these respects, the film is strikingly similar to the gross, systematic distortions of the evidence by the New York Times to portray Kinsman as a truth-teller and Winston as a clearly guilty rapist.* [58]

Can you imagine what it would be like to have just turned 21 years old a few weeks ago and to find perhaps the most powerful newspaper in North America, and even the most powerful news network on earth, either involved in the creation of, and/or actively promoting, a propaganda film aimed at destroying your reputation, and which resorts to "outright lies" and "systematic distortions" to do so? Jameis Winston sure can!

However, while the film was popular and continues to be touted as a truthful expose by many social justice warriors who haven't bothered looking into the facts, journalist Robby Soave stated that the film is in fact:

> *a work of activist propaganda disguised as a documentary* [59]

One may wonder why so many people would believe a mere propaganda film, let alone act like it conveys Gospel truth and is worthy of being accepted by anyone with a moral compass. However, consider the following quote by former Mayor, as well as President of both Lafayette College and George Washington University, William Mather Lewis:

> *Today the world is the victim of propaganda because people are not intellectually competent.* [3.1]

The intellectual competence of various modern social justice warriors aside, the piece of propaganda known as *The Hunting Ground* was described by a group of 19 Harvard professors as a "purported documentary" that "provides a seriously false picture". [60]

This purported documentary was also described by *Variety* film critic Ella Taylor as follows:

> *a loaded piece of agitprop that plays fast and loose with statistics and our sympathy with victims of campus sexual assault. With death-defying leaps of logic on the basis of skimpy and distorted evidence, Kirby Dick and Amy Ziering's film does violence to both the legitimate fight for women's rights and the honorable cause of advocacy filmmaking.* [61]

In fact, the propaganda film has been widely condemned by various journalists, as the following comments attest to:

> *The only problem was that the film was based on a lie — none of the cases described in the film happened the way the filmmakers claimed they did.* [56]

CNN will air The Hunting Ground—a work of activist propaganda disguised as a documentary [59]

"The Hunting Ground" is not about fairness. It is about politics and ideology. For those consumed by either, the editing of truth and the destruction of innocents may seem a small price to pay. [57]

A film that factually and fairly examines what is happening on campuses regarding sexual assault, that looks at all the forces at work, that understands when there is an accuser there is also an accused, and that we need to hear both of their sides would be a useful contribution to this issue. The Hunting Ground is not that film. [62]

The film itself is inaccurate ...The film distorts the evidence and uses false statistics [63]

The film is slick, skillful propaganda. [64]

In regards to how the film and its creators – including *CNN* – were specifically determined to destroy Jameis Winston's reputation, consider the following statements from journalists:

> *A crew member from "The Hunting Ground," a one-sided film about campus sexual assault, has been editing Wikipedia articles to make facts conform with the inaccurate representations in the film. Edward Patrick Alva .... Alva is the assistant editor and technical supervisor for Chain Camera Pictures, the production company associated with "The Hunting Ground" director Kirby Dick. ... Alva took particular interest in editing the Wikipedia page of Jameis Winston ... Winston was cleared by three separate investigations, yet activists — and the film — claim this was due to a biased process and investigators seeking to protect a star football player. The film doesn't mention the holes in Erica Kinsman's accusation against Winston and in fact allows her to tell a story that contradicts physical evidence.* [63]

A so-called documentary about campus rape, The Hunting Ground, is set to air Thursday on CNN, which co-produced it. But a newly available e-mail from an investigative producer of the film spectacularly belies its pretensions to be honest, balanced journalism. Instead, the e-mail adds to the large body of evidence that that the film is highly misleading if not dishonest. ... The Herdy e-mail, sent to Kinsman's then-lawyer, included this assurance: "We don't operate the same way as journalists — this is a film project very much in the corner of advocacy for victims, so there would be no insensitive questions or the need to get the perpetrator's side" ... This e-mail appears directly contrary to claims by both Dick and CNN — which calls itself "the most trusted name in news" — that this is an accurate, balanced documentary, fair to both sides of every story. ... A second e-mail from Amy Herdy, dated February 12, 2014, asked accuser Kinsman's lawyer whether she was "ok with us sending [to Jameis Winston] the official request this week" for an interview. Herdy added: "I'm sure he will say no . . . and then I want him to have a gap of a couple of weeks to get complacent because then we will ambush him." [64]

After reading all of the above, it's abundantly clear that the only way one could believe that *The Hunting Ground* is a truthful documentary film that proves Jameis Winston is a criminal, is if one also believes that the film *Black Panther* is actually a biopic about Chadwick Boseman. And, if you happen to meet a person who believes either to be the case, as a wise man once told me, "you can't argue with insanity".

A Spotless Record?

While it may seem strange to hear, the fact is that Jameis Winston, to this very day, has a spotless criminal record. He has never been arrested in his entire life. He has never been convicted of, or even charged with, a crime at any time in his entire life. In short, you the reader have never met someone that has a more spotless criminal record than Jameis Winston.

Of course, Winston has indeed been accused of various things. However, anyone can be accused of anything, by anyone, at any time, for any reason. The *Duke Lacrosse Case* whereby three college athletes were falsely accused of rape [65], as well as the sad tale of former football star Brian Banks who spent over 5 years in prison for a rape that his accuser later admitted was entirely made up [66], proves such to be the case.

Many Seminole, Buccaneer, Winston and even just football fans in general, wonder why many individuals on social media and various main stream sports media members still spin the narrative that Jameis Winston is some sort of criminal. However, such folks are simply taking a page out of the infamous, communist Russian revolutionary Vladimir Lenin's playbook, when he stated:

> *A lie told often enough becomes the truth.* [67]

Regardless, as prevalent as repeating the false narratives surrounding Jameis Winston have been and continue to be, Winston's long-time personal trainer Otis Leverette believes the trials and tribulations have benefitted Winston, as he stated:

> *The hardships that he (Jameis Winston, added) has endured over the last couple of years, whether media-inflicted or self-inflicted, were almost essential to his growth.* [13]

However, many people will scoff at Leverette's statement, as the ancient yet absurd belief that when something bad happens to a person, such must be proof that said person deserved it, is still pervasive amongst social media trolls, social justice warriors and even casual sports fans alike. One wouldn't have to spend more than a few minutes on a site like Twitter to see multiple people saying that Tom Brady wouldn't have been suspended by the NFL if he wasn't guilty in *Deflategate*, or that the reason Greg Hardy lost an MMA fight was because he was charged with domestic violence in 2015 and arrested for cocaine possession in 2016.

Of course, such a belief is nonsensical on its face. In fact, such a belief is blatantly refuted by the Creator and Savior of the world, Jesus Christ, in John 9:1-3:

> *And as Jesus passed by, he saw a man which was blind from his birth. And his disciples asked him, saying, Master, who did sin, this man, or his parents, that he was born blind? Jesus answered, Neither hath this man sinned, nor his parents: but that the works of God should be made manifest in him.* – John 9:1-3

Likewise, the word of God actually corroborates the point Otis Leverette was making, namely that the trials and tribulations Winston has gone through, have benefitted him, when it states:

> *And we know that all things work together for good to them that love God, to them who are the called according to his purpose.* – 1 Corinthians 10:13b

That Jameis Winston professes to love God can easily be seen from even a cursory review of his social media posts, as well as from listening to an interview he gave during 2019 Super Bowl week – a week in which he was also a presenter at the *BET Gospel Awards* – when he stated:

> *I'm a man of God, you know, and to chase Him every single day, I have to do my, my work, my Christ work, and live a great life.* [68]

That Winston also believes trials and tribulations have benefitted him just as Leverette stated can be easily seen from the following quote from one of his *Instagram* posts.

> *God you get all the glory!!! ... You've taught me patience, perseverance humility and so much more through this game! Thank you!* [69]

And, that Jameis Winston takes the aforementioned Bible verse from 1 Corinthians seriously, and literally believes that God works all things to his good, is easily seen from his below *Twitter* post where he stated:

> *I'm so thankful that everything God does is perfect.* [11]

TRIUMPH IN TALLAHASSEE

Man's greatness consists in his ability to do and the proper application of his powers to things needed to be done.

– Frederick Douglass [70]

Coming into the 2014 NCAA Football season, not many people outside of Florida and Winston's hometown of Bessemer, Alabama, thought the Florida State Seminoles or their redshirt freshman quarterback would exhibit *greatness* consistently. Winston hadn't yet thrown a pass in a real collegiate game and the Seminoles were only ranked 10th in the nation. In fact, the Seminoles weren't even the highest ranked team in their own ACC Conference. That honor belonged to the Clemson Tigers who were quarterbacked by Heisman hopeful, senior quarterback Tajh Boyd, who was coming off a junior season in which he totaled 4,410 yards and 46 touchdowns in which he led the team to an 11-2 record and an Orange Bowl victory over Ohio State.

However, thanks to various mythical-type exploits by Winston during his redshirt season, such as when he heaved a football over *the roof* from the far end of the courtyard – a throw that only one person in Florida State University history was said to have ever been able to accomplish, and one which first round NFL Draft pick Christian Ponder never came close to accomplishing – which takes a 75 yard throw that must clear a 35' peak, there were some that new the kid named *Jaboo* was indeed destined for greatness. [15]

In fact, before Winston ever played his first collegiate game, FSU All-American defensive back Lamarcus Joyner stated:

You know great players when you see it ... Some guys, you question. Some guys, you try to beat around the bush. He's (Jameis Winston, added) just a talented kid and everybody knows it. [15]

However by the time Jameis Winston's very first collegiate game ended, the entire country had been put on notice that not only did Winston have remarkable, NFL first round draft pick type *ability*, but that he was also clearly capable of applying that ability to put forth a Heisman worthy performance in a game that mattered.

Winston's First Game

In Winston's first game – against conference rival Pittsburg – he looked like a mix between former Pitt QB and NFL Hall of Famer Dan Marino (as he completed an otherworldly 25 of 27 pass attempts for an absurd 356 yards and 4 TDs) and former FSU QB and Heisman winner Charlie Ward (as he ran for 25 yards and another TD). Winston totaled 381 total yards and accounted for all 5 of FSU's touchdowns as the Seminoles blew out the Panthers 41-13. [71]

USA Today's Corey Clark wrote about Winston's legendary first collegiate game:

> *With all the hype surrounding Florida State quarterback Jameis Winston heading into Monday night's season-opener, it seemed like an impossibility that he could live up to it. Instead, the redshirt freshman went out and had one of the greatest games in the history of Florida State football in a 41-13 win over Pitt ... a Pitt team that returned eight starters off a defense that finished in the Top 20 nationally.* [72]

Nevada, Bethune-Cookman & Boston College

Winston and the Seminoles then won their next three games – over Nevada, Bethune-Cookman and conference rival Boston College – routing their opponents by a combined score of 164-47. [73] Winston himself completed over 65% of his passes (42-64) for 692 yards, eight touchdowns and just two interceptions, while adding another 86 yards and one rushing touchdown. [74][75][76]

Winston's First Top 25 Test & Heisman Hype

Winston would get to face off against his first Top-25 team – Maryland – in the Seminoles' next game. The step up in competition didn't rattle the young gunslinger at all. Winston completed nearly 72% of his passes (23-32) for a career high 393 yards and 5 touchdown passes, while adding another 24 yards on the ground in leading the Seminoles to a preposterously dominant 63-0 victory. [77]

It was that dominant performance that truly started Winston's Heisman campaign. After the game *USA Today* ran an article titled, *Jameis Winston is chasing the Heisman Trophy* [78] while *Sporting News* ran an article titled, *Jameis Winston: Take notice, FSU quarterback is the real deal,* which stated:

> *As the final seconds ticked off the clock of FSU's 63-0 annihilation of Maryland, Jameis Winston signed garnet and gold hats by the brick wall behind the Seminoles bench.*

> *As if you didn't already know, he's a big deal in Tallahassee. And around the nation, too.*

> *It's time to quit straddling the fence on whether or not Jameis Winston is a real Heisman candidate.*

> *He is, people. Indeed, he is.* [79]

Death Valley Dominance & Heisman Frontrunner

Winston's next game would be the most important of his career, and not just because it was against the #3 ranked team in the country – the Conference rival Clemson Tigers – on the road in a hostile environment and would likely decide which team was going to win the Atlantic Division and therefore get to play in the ACC Championship Game. It was also because a dominant performance in a signature win for Winston would establish him not just as a Heisman candidate, but quite possibly as the favorite to win college football's most prestigious trophy.

The game was over by halftime.

Winston led the Seminoles to a 27-7 lead at half and the team cruised to a dominating 51-14 victory. It was the most points any team had ever scored in Death Valley and was the largest margin of victory ever against Clemson in Death Valley as well. [80]

Winston finished the game completing nearly 65% of his passes (22-34) for a new career high 444 yards and three touchdown passes while adding another touchdown on the ground in a truly remarkable performance. His Heisman candidate counterpart – Clemson quarterback Tajh Boyd – on the other hand had a terrible game, completing just 17-37 passes for an abysmal 156 yards and 1 touchdown while also getting picked off twice. [81]

There was a new Heisman frontrunner and his name was Jameis Winston. He also had a new nickname. No longer was he merely *Jaboo*; he was now *Famous Jameis*.

After the Death Valley beat down concluded, the *NY Times* published an article titled, *Winston Solidifies Stardom by Overwhelming Clemson*, in which journalist Tim Rohan stated:

> *This was Jameis Winston's introduction to stardom ... Florida State fans call him Famous Jameis. Remember the name ...*

Winston is already the face of the Seminoles, and now, having throttled Clemson, he could be the best hope for the A.C.C. [82]

An Undefeated Regular Season

The following six games were more of the same for Winston and the Seminoles, as in, an exhibition of pure dominance. Over those 6 games the Seminoles outscored their opponents by a combined score of 325-58 (54.2 – 9.7 on average), including drubbing their two in-state rivals, the #7 ranked Miami Hurricanes 41-14, and the Florida Gators in Gainesville 37-7, en route to an undefeated 12-0 season and an Atlantic Division title.

In those six games Winston completed over 66% of his passes (106-160) for 1,605 yards, 15 touchdowns and 5 interceptions. Even more impressive was that he put up such numbers despite exiting four of the six games before they were over as they were blow-outs. [83] [84] [85] [86] [87] [88]

ACC Championship Game

After finishing the regular season 12-0 and winning the Atlantic Division, the Seminoles' next game would be the ACC Championship Game against the Coastal Division champion Duke Blue Devils who finished their regular season 10-2 and on an eight game winning streak.

The game would be a complete blowout.

Winston and the Seminoles rolled to a 45-0 lead before giving up a garbage time touchdown and winning the game by a score of 45-7.

Winston himself would win ACC Championship Game MVP [89] after completing 19-32 passes for 330 yards and 3 touchdowns and adding another 59 yards and a touchdown on the ground. [89] Not bad for a 19 year old kid who only two days prior had been cleared by prosecutors investigating Erica Kinsman's unsubstantiated allegation against him. [90]

After the game Winston stated:

> *The football field is our sanctuary ... Every time I stepped on the field, every time we stepped on that field, everything that happened outside of our family, it was just zoned out.* [89]

I remember watching this game with my son and being amazed at Winston's performance. I even remember thinking Winston must have the same ability to compartmentalize his life and thrive on the field even when his off-the-field life was filled with stress, as the *Black Mamba*, Kobe Bryant had back in 2003.

Interestingly enough, Bryant gave himself the *Black Mamba* nickname after he had been arrested and charged by the police with sexual assault. [91] And, while Winston was never arrested, let alone charged with anything, he faced the same allegation Kobe Bryant had, and just like Bryant, had performed at an elite level despite the media circus and outside distractions surrounding him.

Winston's ACC Championship Game performance – and the MVP trophy he earned from it – was the first of many individual awards Winston earned before the Seminoles squared off with the 12-1 SEC Champion Auburn Tigers in the BCS National Championship Game.

Individual Award and Accolades

Winston would earn the following individual awards and accolades to add to his ACC Championship Game MVP trophy:

- ACC Offensive Player of the Year [92]
- ACC Player of the Year [93]
- Named Consensus All-American [94]
- AP Player of the Year Award [95]
- Davey O'Brien Award [96]
- Manning Award [97]

- Walter Camp Player of the Year Award [98]
- Heisman Trophy [99] [100]

Winston actually became the youngest Heisman trophy winner in collegiate history [100] and delivered the following, touching acceptance speech that brought his coach – Jimbo Fisher – to tears:

> *First and foremost I just want to thank God and the Heisman trustees and the Heisman -- past Heisman winners for allowing this dream to come true.*

> *So many people instilled in me trust and the process. From there, know the truth. I trusted in the process when I was playing for the Bessemer Tigers, won my first championship when I was 14 years old.*

> *My dad also told me, "J-Boo, good ain't never going to be good enough." And my beautiful mother was sitting there constantly rooting me on, motivating me even when our relationship wasn't as strong as it is right now. And my dad's friend, Chad Babin was telling me, "Leave him alone -- he['s] going to win the Heisman anyway."*

> *And I trusted in the process when coach Scott, back in Hueytown, Alabama, had came in and took over the program and told me he was going to make me the best quarterback in the nation as I was running a "Wing-T" offense my whole life.*

> *I trusted in the process when I went against the grain of making a -- a decision with coach [Jimbo] Fisher and "11" [FSU baseball coach Mike Martin] and "Meat" [Martin's son, the hitting coach], deciding whether I was going to play baseball, or go to the pros, or come to Florida State and play both sports.*

I trusted in the process with my main man, coach [Dameyune] Craig -- still -- I -- I still love that man to the day -- he left for Auburn for the -- for the job of his dreams. And coach Fisher sat me down and said, "Hey, I coached coach Craig, so I know I'm going to be able to prepare you real." And now that man['s] like a father figure to me.

I trusted in the process that evaluating facts and its truth is delivered with positive outcomes, because after all the things I've been through this past month -- I remember when my daddy trusted in the process, when he risked his job and was jobless three years ago, when I was out there, doing whatever I did to provide for my family, because I know he couldn't do it. Me and my momma having to pay bills; me and my momma making everything happen. And that man, he kept fighting me. But the truth prevailed because eventually, I got me a scholarship. I kept my education up. I kept bringing everything home. We ate every single night.

This Heisman isn't just for Jameis Winston. It's for Florida State. And I -- I love everybody in here. I can't be that much -- I mean I'm so blessed right now, man.... It means so much to me, but I got one thing to say: At Florida State, if we['re] going to do it then, we do it big then.

Thank ya'll. [101] [102]

BCS National Championship Game

The 2014 Vizio BCS National Championship Game was played on Jameis Winston's 20th birthday.

On the Seminoles opening drive of the game Winston led the team to a field goal and a 3-0 lead. However the Auburn Tigers would respond by scoring the next 21 points in the game and would hold a 21-3 lead when the Seminoles began their last possession of the first half. [103]

Winston then led the Seminoles on a 12 play, 66 yard touchdown drive. On 3rd & 7 from the Auburn 24 yard line, Winston scrambled for 21 yards down to the Auburn 3 yard line and junior running back Devonta Freeman than capped the drive off with a 3 yard touchdown run with just 1:28 left in the half. [104]

Winston entered halftime just 6-15 passing for 62 yards, a dismal NCAA passer rating of 74.7, a fumble lost and his Seminoles down 21-10. [104] It seemed his birthday would end in disaster and his chance at NCAA immortality would vanish, much as it had for another magnificent redshirt freshman QB who led his undefeated squad into the BCS Title game as well – Michael Vick – before Vick's squad would get demolished 46-29 and Vick would finish just 15-29 passing for 225 yards with no touchdowns and an NCAA passer rating of just 116.9. [105]

The third quarter wouldn't be much better for Winston's Seminoles as their four possessions went: punt, field goal, punt, punt. They entered the fourth quarter down 21-13.

Through the first three quarters the Heisman trophy winning Winston was just 11-24 passing for 120 yards, no touchdowns and a poor 87.8 NCAA passer rating.

Then crunch time came and the legend previously known as *Jaboo* and now known as *Famous Jameis* would put on a clutch performance for the ages.

After sophomore defensive back P.J. Williams intercepted Auburn's Nick Marshall and senior defensive back Lamarcus Joyner scooped up Williams' subsequent fumble, Winston and the Seminoles offense would get the ball at their own 44 yard line with 12:30 remaining in the game, down 21-13. [104]

Winston would lead a 5 play, 56 yard drive in which he completed all 3 of his passes for 40 yards and capped the drive with an 11 yard touchdown pass to bring the Seminoles within one point of the Tigers. [104]

After the Tigers went on a long 13 play drive that ended with a field goal, the Seminoles freshman receiver/returner Levonte Whitfield returned a kickoff for a touchdown, before the Tigers went on another long 8 play drive that ended with a touchdown of their own. The Seminoles were down 31-27 and there was just 1:11 left on the clock. [103] The game seemed over.

Jameis Winston had been sitting on the sidelines, watching the last 22 plays and nearly 10 full minutes of game time go by without his offense taking the field. [103] One can only imagine how nervous the 20 year old birthday boy was as he took the field, knowing that if he didn't deliver a touchdown drive in under 71 seconds of game-time, his mythical freshman season would lose its luster and even be regarded as a failure by his detractors.

However, for those old enough to remember Joe Montana's fabled 11 play, 92 yard game-winning drive in Super Bowl XXIII [106] and just how cool *Joe Cool* was, seeing Winston operate under far more difficult circumstances (as Winston had almost 2 full minutes less to work with, and unlike Montana could not rely on a field goal to tie the game as the Seminoles were down 4 points) with every bit as much of the proverbial ice water in his veins, was a joy to behold.

Winston started the drive off with a quick 8 yard pass to junior receiver Rashad Greene. He followed that up with a bullet slant pass to Greene who rumbled down the right sideline for a 49 yard gain. He then hit Devonta Freeman in the right flat for a short 6 yard gain. After the Seminoles called a timeout to stop the clock with 46 seconds remaining in the game, Winston came out of the timeout and feathered a touch 5 yard pass to senior receiver Kenny Shaw for a first down at the Tigers 12 yard line. [104]

Winston's next throw would be dropped by Greene, setting up a 2nd & 10. However, on the next play Winston would throw a beautiful pass into the left flat, to a tightly covered Freeman, who was tackled out of bounds at the 5 yard line. [104]

On 3rd & 3 from the 5 yard line and Winston slapping his hands and screaming for his center to hike the ball, the center apparently wasn't able to hear him and the Seminoles were whistled for a delay of game penalty. [104]

There was now just 21 seconds left in the game and Winston and his Seminoles faced a 3rd & 8 at the Tigers' 10 yard line. Winston dropped back and tried to hit Rashaad Greene on a slant pass to the left, however the ball fell incomplete and Auburn Tiger Chris Davis was flagged for pass interference. [104]

There was now just 17 seconds remaining in the game and the Seminoles had a 1st and goal at the Tigers' 2 yard line. The next play would cement Winston as irrefutably the most accomplished freshman quarterback in the history of NCAA Division 1 football. On the play Winston would drop back to pass but face heavy pressure, and just before a lunging defensive lineman could bat his pass down, Winston would throw a perfectly placed *jump pass* to sophomore receiver Kelvin Benjamin who landed in the end zone with Tigers' defensive back Chris Davis on top of him, giving the Seminoles the victory and the BCS National Title!

Winston, who through the first three quarters of this game had been just 11-24 passing for 120 yards, no touchdowns and a dismal 87.8 NCAA passer rating, would finish the last two touchdown drives 9-10 passing for 117 yards, two touchdowns and an otherworldly 254.3 NCAA passer rating.

To put Winston's clutch performance in perspective, consider the fact that in the 73 years since the NCAA began keeping passer rating data, no QB has ever had a higher season passer rating than 199.4. [107] [108] On the final 2 drives of Winston's freshman season, on his 20th birthday, with the

National Title on the line, and facing a deficit each time no less, he played flawless football (as again, his one incompletion was on a well thrown ball that his receiver merely dropped) and recorded a passer rating of 254.3, which is 27.5% higher than the highest season passer rating in NCAA history.

To further put Winston's clutch performance into perspective, the highest single season passer rating in NFL history was Aaaron Rodgers 122.5 rating, recorded in the 2011 season. [109] Eclipsing that rating by 27.5% would equal an absurd 156.2 passer rating. No quarterback in NFL history has ever had a 156.2 passer rating in Super Bowl history, and of course the Super Bowl is the only NFL equivalent to the BCS Title Game in college football.

Winston would finish the BCS Title game completing 20-35 passes for 237 yards, two touchdowns and no interceptions. He would also add another 48 yards on seven scrambles (though as college stats ridiculously incorporate yards lost when sacked into a quarterback's rushing totals, Winston was credited with 26 rushing yards on 11 carries, seeing as he was sacked 4 times for minus 22 yards) and was named MVP. [110]

After the game ended Florida State Head Coach Jimbo Fisher stated regarding Winston:

> *It was the best football game he's played all year ... and I'll tell you why, because for three quarters he was up and down and he fought. ... And to pull it out in the atmosphere and environment and with what was on the line tonight, to me if that's not a great player, I don't know who is.* [111]

After the game Winston was asked about being in such a pressure-packed situation and stated:

> *I was ready ... I wanted to be in that situation. That's what great quarterbacks do.* [112]

Winston also gave an emotional interview while leaving the field in which he stated:

> *We champions ... through everything that we went through, through all the haters, through every single thing, we came out victorious. And God did this. I'm so blessed.* [113]

Blessed? No doubt about it!

THE GREATEST QB IN NCAA HISTORY?

Some are born great, some achieve greatness, and some have greatness thrust upon them.

– William Shakespeare [114]

Jameis Winston – as a legitimate quarterback phenom – could certainly be said to have been born great. And, after completing the greatest freshman season in NCAA football history he could certainly be said to have achieved greatness. And, after having to orchestrate one of the greatest and most clutch game-winning drives in Championship Game history (which of course he did, splendidly) he could also be said to have had greatness thrust upon him.

However, it's one thing to be great and an entirely different thing to be considered one of the greatest of all-time, let alone *the* GOAT (Greatest of All Time).

Joe Theismann was a great NFL quarterback. Theismann won a regular season MVP and even a Super Bowl ring. However he has not been elected into the Pro Football Hall of Fame and there are no serious debates raging about Theismann being one of the greatest NFL quarterbacks of all-time.

No sensible person would argue with the fact that Jameis Winston was a great NCAA quarterback. However, those infected with the brain deteriorating *Winston Derangement Syndrome* will claim that Winston can't possibly be considered one of the greatest NCAA quarterbacks who ever played, let alone the GOAT. Those people would be wrong.

Now, it should be said that most GOAT debates are silly due to the fact that (a) most people debating base their arguments on personal opinions rather than hard data, and that (b) there is no scientific way to truly win such a debate.

As one of the greatest basketball players who ever lived – and very possibly the NBA GOAT – Kareem Abdul-Jabbar stated:

> *Finally, the GOAT question, which runs through the media like a nasty STD: "Who is the Greatest of All Time?" A month ago, LeBron claimed the title for himself during an ESPN interview ... It's a little disappointing hearing him play this imaginary game, which is akin to asking, Which superpower is better, flying or invisibility? I get asked this question a couple times a week, and my answer is always the same: The game has changed so much over the years that there is no leveling rubric to take into account the variables. So, sorry, LeBron, you're not the GOAT because it's a mythological beast. It's like asking, How big is the horn on a unicorn?* [115]

The above said, while it's not possible to concretely prove which quarterback was the greatest quarterback in NCAA history, it is at least a fun mental exercise to try to do so. It is also certainly much easier to create a logical and ordered list of the greatest NCAA quarterbacks ever if some parameters for how greatness is defined are set.

The Difference between *Best* and *Greatest*

When most football fans debate which players are the *best* at their respective positions, they generally mean which players have accomplished the most on an individual basis, meaning which players have won the most individual awards, or accumulated the best individual stats, independent of team success.

For example, many people – myself included – believe that Barry Sanders was the *best* NCAA running back of all time as well as the *best* pure runner in NFL history as well. However, Sanders was a full-time starter for just one collegiate season and only won one single playoff game in his 10 year NFL career and therefore is not generally considered the *greatest* NCAA or NFL running back of all time, as those titles are reserved for Archie Griffin and Jim Brown respectively.

On the flip side, when most football fans debate which players are the *greatest* at their respective positions, they generally mean which players have accomplished the most on both an individual *and* team basis.

For example, many people – myself included – believe that Terry Bradshaw deserves to be ranked higher on an NFL quarterback GOAT list than Dan Fouts, thanks in large part to the massive amount of team success he experienced, especially when compared to Fouts' utter lack of team success. However, many of those same people – myself included again – do not believe Bradshaw was a better individual quarterback than Fouts was, which the statistics and individual accolades Fouts amassed attest to.

The Parameters

All of the above said, when debating who were the *greatest* – not the *best* – NCAA quarterbacks of all time, I believe it's fair to eliminate any and all quarterbacks that did not win both a Heisman trophy as well as a National Championship (and no, a Co-National Championship, such as the one Gino Torretta won in 1991 does not count). For the sake of brevity I also believe it's fair to consider only modern-era quarterbacks rather than someone like Johnny Lujak – the obvious NCAA QB GOAT thanks to his three National Titles to go along with his one Heisman trophy and a 3rd place Heisman finish as well – who threw just 10 passes per game and finished with more interceptions than touchdown passes over his three collegiate seasons.

Also, before I list the seven modern era NCAA quarterbacks that have won both a Heisman trophy and a National Championship, I feel it is necessary to declare two honorable mention quarterbacks, one of which I actually believe is the *greatest* (not *best*) dual-threat quarterback in NCAA history.

The Honorable Mention Quarterbacks

The first honorable mention – the quarterback I feel is the *greatest* dual-threat quarterback in NCAA history – is Nebraska's Tommie Frazier. Frazier is one of only two modern quarterbacks to win two National Titles as a starting QB, and the only modern quarterback to ever win three National Title Game MVP trophies. [116] Frazier never won a Heisman, which eliminates him from our current debate, but in all honesty I do believe he was robbed of the Heisman trophy in 1995 when he finished in 2nd place behind Ohio State running back Eddie George. [117]

The second honorable mention is Alabama's A.J. McCarron. McCarron was blessed to play on the first iteration of Nick Saban's dynastic Alabama teams, and actually won his first National Championship during his redshirt year. [118] However, McCarron would win back to back National Titles in 2011 and 2012 and finish 2nd to Jameis Winston himself in the 2013 Heisman voting as well, which Winston won in a landslide by garnering nearly 8.5 times as many first place votes as runner-up McCarron did. [99] McCarron may not have won a Heisman, which eliminates him from our current debate, and he may have earned one of his three National Championship rings during his redshirt year, but any modern QB with three rings deserves an honorable mention in my book.

The Seven Quarterbacks in the GOAT Conversation

With the two honorable mention quarterbacks given their due respect, it's time to look at the seven modern quarterbacks that both won a Heisman trophy and a National Championship. In alphabetical order they are: Matt

Leinart, Cam Newton, Tim Tebow, Charlie Ward, Chris Weinke, Jameis Winston and Danny Wuerffel.

Also, I should mention here that while I am certainly aware some of Matt Leinart's accomplishments could have an asterisk next to them, I believe such is not only unfair to Leinart but absurd in the extreme. This said, I invite you to do as I have done, which is to trust your memory and to cherish what your eyes beheld when you watched Leinart, Reggie Bush, LenDale White and those dominant Trojan teams play football. Simply forget the NCAA rulings that came later, as they had nothing to do with what happened on the field.

Even with the field narrowed down to just seven quarterbacks, establishing concrete parameters that will allow one to logically rank said quarterbacks is of paramount importance.

If we were attempting to determine how to rank said quarterbacks on a list of the *best* – rather than the *greatest* – NCAA quarterbacks of all time, we may look at mere individual statistics, compare how much help each player had from his teammates, or even talk about the always subjective *eye-test*.

However, as we are attempting to rank the greatest NCAA quarterbacks of all time, we will simply compare their most important accomplishments, namely their career win/loss records, the amount of times they finished in the top 6 in Heisman voting (this was not an arbitrary number assigned by myself, as three of the seven players had a 6th place finish and none had a 7th – 10th place finish), National Titles won and National Title Game MVP trophies won.

When one compares the resumes of the seven quarterbacks using those parameters, two things become instantly clear.

The first thing that becomes clear is that Cam Newton and Chris Weinke fall behind the other five quarterbacks, as they are the only two quarterbacks that did not have more than one top 6 Heisman finish.

Likewise, they are the only two quarterbacks that did not win a National Title Game MVP trophy.

However when one simply compares the accomplishments of Weinke and Newton alone, one also quickly sees that Newton doesn't stack up to Weinke either.

Both players stayed in college four years. However while Newton spent two years riding the bench at the University of Florida before transferring to Blinn College while he was facing possible expulsion at Florida for three separate incidents of academic cheating [119] and therefore ended up starting just 14 games in Division 1, Weinke was QB1 on a team that went to three straight National Title games.

The above said, it's quite clear that Cam Newton ranks as the 7th greatest quarterback in NCAA history using the established parameters. Weinke ranks one spot ahead of him in 6th place.

The second thing that becomes clear is that Matt Leinart and Tim Tebow undoubtedly deserve to rank higher than the other remaining three quarterbacks. This is due to the fact that Leinart and Tebow are the only quarterbacks to have finished in the top 6 in Heisman voting three times [120] [121] [122] [123] [124] [125], as well as the only quarterbacks to have won two National Championships. [126] [127]

However when one compares the accomplishments of Leinart and Tebow alone, one can easily ascertain that Leinart – much more so than Tebow – deserves to be called the greatest NCAA quarterback of all time.

Both players played three full seasons as a starting quarterback and won two National Titles. However, while Tebow won his first National Title as a backup quarterback that recorded just 122 total passes and rushes over 14 games, compared to 442 such plays for starting QB Chris Leak [128], Leinart won both of his National Championships as a starting quarterback.

Likewise, in the one and only season that Leinart did not win the National Title, he still played in the National Title Game, and led the USC Trojans to a 12-1 record and a #2 final ranking. [129] Tebow on the other hand, in his greatest individual season, led the Florida Gators to a mere 9-4 record and a #13 final ranking. [130]

The above said, it is clear that Matt Leinart – at least under the parameters we have set in this chapter – ranks as the greatest quarterback in NCAA history, bar none. Tim Tebow ranks one spot below him in 2nd place.

Three quarterbacks needing to be ranked remain: Charlie Ward, Jameis Winston and Danny Wuerffel.

All three quarterbacks won one National Title and were named MVP of the game. [131] [132] [133]

Likewise, all three quarterbacks finished in the top 6 in Heisman voting two times. [134] [135] [117] [136] [99] [137]

However while Ward and Wuerffel played all four years and Winston played just two seasons [138], all three quarterbacks were only full-time starters for two seasons, and Winston actually won more games in his two seasons than Ward did in his four seasons combined. [139] [140] [141]

When comparing Wuerffel's four seasons at the University of Florida to Ward's four seasons at Florida State University one instantly sees that Wuerffel saw a great deal more game-time over his four seasons than Ward did. In fact Wuerfell threw for more than 5,000 extra yards than Ward and accounted for more than double the amount of touchdowns as Ward did over their respective careers. [139] [140]

The above, it seems quite clear that Danny Wuerffel deserves to be ranked higher on the list of the greatest NCAA quarterbacks of all time than Charlie Ward does.

It's also quite clear that Jameis Winston also deserves to be ranked higher than Charlie Ward, thanks in large part to him having more career wins in two years than Ward had in four years, a better career win percentage, and a massive statistical advantage as well. [139] [141]

However, deciding whether Winston should be ranked above or below Wuerfell is a tougher task. While Wuerfell played the aforementioned two extra seasons and therefore accumulated higher career stat totals, it was Winston that won his Heisman trophy in a landslide of 1,501 points over runner-up A.J. McCarron [99] while Wuerffel won a nail-biter by just 189 points over Iowa State running back Troy Davis. [137] It was also Winston that led his team to an undefeated season the year they won the National Championship while Wuerffel never experienced a perfect season.

Winning a unanimous MVP trophy in the NFL – which only Tom Brady has ever done [142] – is far more impressive than merely winning an MVP trophy, which a kicker – Mark Moseley – won in 1982. [143]

Likewise, completing a perfect season – which only quarterback Bob Griese and his 72' Dolphins have ever accomplished – is far more impressive than simply winning a Super Bowl.

The above said, Jameis Winston's landslide Heisman victory is far more impressive than Danny Wuerffel's narrow Heisman victory, and Winston's perfect season is far more impressive than Wuerffel's one-loss title winning season.

Just as people remember Tom Brady's 2010 NFL MVP season far more than they remember Mark Moseley's 1982 NFL MVP season, and just as people remember the 1972 Miami Dolphins perfect season far more than they remember the Super Bowl XL victory by the Pittsburgh Steelers in which Ben Roethlisberger was completely outplayed by opposing quarterback Matt Hasselbeck [144], they will remember Jameis Winston's undefeated, legendary freshman season, far more than they will remember Danny Wuerffel's one-loss senior season.

For all of the above reasons, I do believe it can be logically argued that Winston should rank one spot higher than Wuerffel on the list of greatest NCAA quarterbacks of all time.

The Final NCAA QB GOAT Rankings

All of the above said the final rankings for the greatest modern-era NCAA quarterbacks of all time looks as follows:

- GOAT: Matt Leinart
- Runner-up: Tim Tebow
- 3rd: Jameis Winston
- 4th: Danny Wuerffel

Note: The above four quarterbacks would make up the proverbial *Mount Rushmore* of the greatest modern-era quarterbacks in NCAA history.

- 5th: Charlie Ward
- 6th: Chris Weinke
- 7th: Cam Newton

While Winston may only be the third greatest modern-era NCAA quarterback of all time, he had irrefutably the greatest freshman quarterback season in NCAA history, and is also – again irrefutably – the greatest two year quarterback in NCAA history.

In fact, Winston is one of only two NCAA quarterbacks (along with Matt Leinart) in the history of college football to have an undefeated National Championship season in which he also won the National Championship Game MVP trophy and the Heisman trophy. And, Winston is the only freshman quarterback to ever accomplish such a feat.

That is the NFL equivalent of a rookie quarterback winning the regular season MVP award, going a perfect 19-0 and winning the Super Bowl as well as the Super Bowl MVP trophy as well. No NFL quarterback has ever pulled off such a feat, let alone a rookie quarterback, and no NCAA quarterback has ever accomplished what Winston accomplished in the 2013-14 NCAA season either.

Now some of you – especially those of you currently infected with the deadly *Winston Derangement Syndrome* – are probably gleeful that I did not bestow the title of GOAT NCAA QB on Winston, and even take pleasure in the fact that Winston only ranks 3rd on my list. All I will say to that is, 3rd is fantastic, and I doubt President Theodore Roosevelt would be upset today or covetous of Presidents Jefferson and Washington, because he was situated third in the line of sculptures on Mount Rushmore.

THE FRANCHISE

I'm not trying to compare myself to college competition, to another guy I'm against in the draft. ... I'm trying to be a Hall of Famer one day. This isn't about some competition on draft day. It's about being the face of a franchise.

– Jameis Winston [145]

When the 2015 NFL Draft rolled around the Tampa Bay Buccaneers had the #1 overall pick and were looking for a true franchise quarterback, someone that a coach could hand the ball to and expect to be a true *offense-carrier.*

There were two quarterbacks in the draft that many thought could be true franchise players, Winston, the *Most Scrutinized Draft Pick of All Time* [145], and Oregon's Marcus Mariota.

However, within short order it seemed the entire football world knew the Buccaneers had decided on Winston. That 2015 NFL Draft was the polar opposite of the 2018 NFL Draft, when almost no one seemed to know who the Cleveland Browns were going to take with the #1 overall pick until the Browns were on the clock on draft day itself.

On February 23, 2015, nearly two full months before the 2015 NFL Draft would take place, Sports Illustrated's Peter King stated:

> *They've left the starting gate, and Winston's got a couple of lengths on Mariota.* [145]

Buccaneers General Manager Jason Licht confirmed there was never any doubt that Winston was the QB they wanted when at his post-draft press conference he answered a reporter's question about how tempted he was to trade the #1 overall pick when teams called him with offers, by stating:

We were never tempted, we wanted to take him (Jameis Winston, added) the whole time. [146]

There simply was no question in Jason Licht's mind that Jameis Winston was a franchise QB, and many of the most respected names in NFL circles agreed with him.

Draft Experts Weigh In

Consider the following pre-2015-draft statements made about Winston:

From Draft Expert Todd McShay:

From purely on the field, the grade for Jameis Winston is just behind Andrew Luck's in the last ten years and there is nobody else in between [147]

From Draft Expert Mike Mayock:

I take (Jameis Winston, added) No. 1 from a talent perspective. I'm all over it from a talent perspective [148]

From Super Bowl winning NFL Head Coach Jon Gruden:

Not many people do what Jameis Winston did: first year as a starter winning a national championship, only one loss in his two years as a starter. He's got great charisma. He's polarizing for some people, but he's a rare talent. [149]

From Draft Expert Mel Kiper:

(Jameis Winston is, added) the most advanced QB in this class [150]

From NFL Network's Peter Schrager quoting a *trusted NFL source*:

He was put on this Earth to throw ... a football, a baseball ... whatever. He was meant to throw. [151]

Journalist Robert Klemko quoting a *high-ranking evaluator* from an NFL team:

> *The only guy who compares well to him (Andrew Luck, added) in the last five years is Jameis. A quarterbacks coach will tell you that Winston has fewer issues than Cam (Newton, added) ... Most guys are looking for a strong-armed pocket passer with the ability to read coverage. There's no projecting that with Jameis; he's already able to do it.* [152]

Draft Expert Matt Miller:

> *Best Prospect: Jameis Winston*
>
> *Most NFL-Ready: Jameis Winston*
>
> *Lowest Risk: Jameis Winston*
>
> *Top 100 Rankings ... #1 Jameis Winston* [153]

Draft Expert Walter Cherepinsky:

> *As a prospect from a pure football perspective and ignoring the off-the-field issues, Winston is elite and in Andrew Luck's ballpark as a quarterback prospect. Winston is a potential franchise quarterback who can lead his team to championships. Numerous sources from multiple teams agree that Winston is just a little bit behind Luck, but is a better prospect than Cam Newton, Sam Bradford or Matthew Stafford were when they came out and went No. 1 overall.* [154]

From Draft Scout Mark Schofield on Winston's release time:

> *331 milliseconds – very fast and much quicker than the time ascribed to Colin Kaepernick when ESPN's SportScience put him through testing during his NFL Combine. This would also put Winston on par with Dan Marino, known for having one of the quickest releases in NFL history.* [155]

From NFL.com Draft Profile:

Considered by scouting community to be advanced in ability to scan field and get through progressions. Has natural feel for throwing windows and anticipates openings that other college quarterbacks don't see. ... Big arm by NFL standards. ... Most teammates very trusting and protective of him, according to regional scouts. ... When pressure mounts, so does his focus. ... Fierce competitor and unafraid of mistakes. ... Will make throws and take chances others won't, which can be a special trait if properly harnessed. [156]

From Sportscaster Rich Eisen, recounting what former NFL Head Coach Steve Mariucci said about Winston:

the most astute X's and O's guy that he's ever put on the board [157]

Simply put, Jameis Winston was *the* franchise quarterback in the 2015 NFL draft and there was never any legitimate doubt that the Buccaneers were going to take him #1 overall. However, that didn't stop the main stream media from attempting to paint Jameis Winston in the most negative light it could, or from spinning the false narrative that the Buccaneers had an excruciating decision on their hands, and that such was the case because of off-the-field questions surrounding the golden armed gunslinger out of Florida State.

Media Slander Begins

Journalists Tom Pelissero, Rachel Axon and Jim Corbett writing for USA Today asked the question:

Who is the real Jameis Winston?

No player in this year's NFL draft has been picked apart like the Florida State quarterback, who is the favorite to go No. 1 overall to the Tampa Bay Buccaneers on Thursday night despite a string of poor decisions and allegations during Winston's college days. [158]

Journalist Kurt Streeter writing for ESPN asked:

> *WHAT DO WE make of this prodigy nicknamed Jaboo (pronounced Jay-Boo), a sobriquet from his mother?*
>
> *How do we square the man with the kid, reconcile his mature talent with the things he has done -- immature and entitled at least, inexcusable at worst?* [159]

Likewise, journalist Ian O'Connor writing for ESPN even wrote an article titled, *Why No. 1 pick Jameis Winston is monumental risk for Buccaneers,* which quoted super-agent Leigh Steinberg stating:

> *What's devilishly tricky with Winston is this: Did he learn from these experiences in a way that served as a cautionary tale for him in terms of how close he came to ruining a pro career he desperately wants? Or did he continue to retain the concepts that he is bigger than the system and the rules, and not subject to paying attention to them?* [160]

What O'Connor doesn't reveal however is that Leigh Steinberg's former partners Ryan and Bruce Tollner were representing Marcus Mariota [161] and that the above comment could therefore have been made for the express purpose of damaging Winston's draft stock while elevating Mariota's draft stock. This sort of thing goes over the head of many football fans, but when one recognizes that many – if not most – main stream sports media members are infected with *Winston Derangement Syndrome*, one gets used to spotting false narratives and misinformation.

For those of you reading this book who wonder why various members of the main stream sports media were attempting to torpedo Winston's draft stock and paint him in the most negative light they could, consider the following quote from author and radio show host, Clay Travis:

> *The left-wing sports media was using sports to advance their own political agendas and disguising it inside their sports coverage.* [162]

Simply put, such biased members of the media had decided that Jameis Winston was more deserving of a public stoning than being drafted #1 overall, and the fact that Winston had never even been arrested, let alone convicted of a crime at any time in his life, made no difference. To them, *Jaboo* was taboo, and if they could negatively impact his career prospects, they would be happy to do so.

A Voice of Reason Emerges

Regardless, Winston's former Florida State Head Coach Jimbo Fisher provided as good an answer as anyone to the supposed *questions* giving the Buccaneers pause in regards to Winston's character and off-the-field behavior, when he stated:

> *Why is there a question? Because of the character assassination that he's lived through in the media, and the misinformation that has been printed and half-truths that have been printed. What amazes me about this whole process is the unprofessionalism of a lot of major newspapers, a lot of major outlets that did not report the whole truth of the situation and only slanted it for their own opinion. And when you go through that you have to answer those questions. Jameis has great character. Did he make mistakes? Yes. Did he make silly mistakes? Yes. I mean, he's still a 20-year-old kid.* [163]

Fisher also stated before the draft:

> *Jameis, in football intellect, intelligence level, is as smart as anybody I've ever been around ... You can do so many different things with him and he grasps it. He just doesn't memorize plays, he understands the concepts of how to attack the coverage, how a play works, where his one-on-one matchups are. He just has a tremendous football intellect that way. Every night, Sunday, Monday, Tuesday, Wednesday, we get off the practice field, he eats his dinner at 6:45, and then he's up here in the offices until 9:30, 10, 10:30 at night. He would sit and watch every practice tape and then prepare for red zone, third down, whatever it might*

be. A lot of guys are very talented but he likes to understand the game. [164]

And, while many would discount the above comments as merely a coach giving love to a former player, such people would be mistaken.

According to NFL Insider Adam Schefter:

> *Buffalo certainly can't blame Florida St. coach Jimbo Fisher for overselling it on quarterback EJ Manuel. ... He was adamant throughout the pre-draft evaluation process that he didn't believe Manuel had the tools to be an NFL starter and he shouldn't be any better than a third-round pick. ... Fisher was extremely positive about Manuel as a person and as a hard worker, but he was very open and honest with teams about how limited he felt Manuel was as a quarterback prospect. Fisher also told teams that even if Manuel were eligible to return for another season, he had a redshirt freshman quarterback he had been developing waiting in the wings. A guy by the name of Jameis Winston.* [165]

While it may not be clear whether or not what Coach Fisher said about Winston contributed to him being drafted #1 overall by the Buccaneers, it's certainly clear that he wasn't merely blowing smoke when he spoke in glowing terms about Winston. However, what is extremely clear is that Buccaneers GM Jason Licht was thrilled to draft Jameis Winston with the #1 overall pick.

Jason Licht Sets the Record Straight and Exposes Fake News

Consider what Jason Licht stated after he drafted Jameis Winston during his post-draft press conference:

> *We wanted to take him (Winston, added). That was our plan. ... He's a franchise quarterback that we are thrilled to have.* [146]

As for the false narratives spun by the main stream sports media that the Buccaneers could pass on drafting Winston due to the so-called off-the-field questions surrounding him, consider what Licht also stated during the same press conference:

> *He (Winston, added) won us over. Um, he won a lot of people over in this building and around the league. ... We feel confident in Jameis. ... If we didn't feel like he was a great person, we wouldn't have drafted him. ... The players are excited about it, the coaches are excited about, this whole building, from, you know, everybody in the building, has, has, played a part in this, and, um, we're all very excited. ... It's not often, uh, a General Manager gets a chance to draft who he think is a, you know, he and coach, think are a franchise quarterback. And it felt, and I'm sure it's, it's similar for Lovie and you'll get a chance to talk to him now too, but, it was somebody asked me if it was like Christmas, and I said 'no, it's more like your wedding day.' And, ah, without the cold feet; I never had cold feet on my wedding day either. So, uh, it's, it, that's what it's like. ... We're beyond excited.* [146]

In fact, it wasn't revealed until after the draft just how enamored with, and determined to draft Winston, Licht was. However Sports Illustrated's Peter King revealed after the draft, that a full year earlier, during the 2014 NFL Draft, Licht's brother-in-law had sent him a text asking whether he preferred 2013 Heisman trophy winner Johnny Manziel or Louisville's Teddy Bridgewater. Licht replied to the text with one word: *Winston.* [166]

The simple truth, despite the false narratives spun by the media, was that there was never any real question which quarterback in the 2015 NFL Draft the Buccaneers were going to take, or wich quarterback they thought was, *the franchise.*

When Jason Licht was asked about what the process for deciding which quarterback to select was like, he stated:

> *Maybe 25 years from now I'll write a book.* [167]

Well Mr. Licht, you don't have to do that now. I've done it for you.

ROOKIE REVELATION

nobody — not in the entire history of FSU — has ever spun the ball like Winston did. The 6-4 QB was a revelation from the moment he walked on to the field at FSU. In his first year, as he was redshirting, he allegedly walked into his head coach's office and told him, "with all due respect, I can run this offense better than EJ Manuel does." [168]

Jameis Winston certainly was not an unknown commodity when he entered the NFL. The collegiate megastar known as *Famous Jameis* wasn't some 6th round draft pick that had been benched for a baseball player (i.e. Drew Henson) in college, ala Tom Brady. He wasn't even an obviously gifted but extremely unfamiliar gunslinger with a name nearly everyone mispronounced in his early NFL years, ala Brett Favre. Winston had went 26-1 at Florida State, won a National Title, won the Heisman trophy, had another top six Heisman finish, and thanks in large part to the media, was perhaps the most scrutinized prospect in NFL history.

However, while Winston may not have had any doubt in his own ability to start at quarterback for the Buccaneers from day one, the same way he believed he could have started from day one for the Seminoles, there was still an element of mystery with Winston. Unlike fellow draft-mate Marcus Mariota who had played 41 college games [169], Winston had only played 27 college games, had never been able to dedicate himself to football full-time as he had always split his time playing baseball, and many football fans and even one anonymous NFL Executive feared Winston would be a bust in the NFL on the level of JaMarcus Russell [170], who has been called the biggest draft bust in NFL history. [171]

Even many Buccaneers' fans seemed to be as fearful as they were hopeful about the team's future with Winston. They knew Winston was one of the greatest college quarterbacks of all-time but they had also been fed a steady diet of negative and false narratives about Winston for well over a year, from not only the national media but the local Tampa media as well.

Some Buccaneer fans weren't even sure Winston would be able to unseat former starting QB Mike Glennon, who the team had spent a 3rd round pick on just two years earlier. Various local Tampa websites were filled with posts from fans who felt the Bucs wasted the #1 overall draft pick on Winston.

Looking back, it is obvious such fans had an early strain of the disease that would come to be known as *Winston Derangement Syndrome*, as since Winston was drafted, Mike Glennon has thrown just 6 touchdown passes and is now on his fourth different team in as many seasons. However, that a large number of Buccaneer fans would be so illogical as to prefer Glennon to one of the greatest and most accomplished quarterbacks in the history of college football – a quarterback who accomplished all that he had just 250 or so miles from Tampa, Florida – makes one wonder if such fans caught said disease from their own local Tampa media, rather than the national media they could more easily overlook and consider mere outsiders.

It would take less than 24 hours from the time Winston was selected #1 overall to find the answer to such a question.

Who Needs Enemies When You Have Friends Like This?

It's one thing for a rookie to enter the NFL with negative national press. It's an entirely different thing for a #1 overall draft pick, a 21 year old that was drafted to be the savior of a moribund franchise, and a young man who was both a Heisman trophy winner and a National Champion in college no less, to be slandered by the local media in his new city and hated by a large number of his own team's fans before ever playing a single snap. Yet that is what Jameis Winston had to deal with from day one in Tampa, Florida.

The very day after Jameis Winston was drafted #1 overall in the 2015 NFL Draft, the *Tampa Bay Times* published a photo of Winston surrounded by nine words in all-caps:

LOVE HIM

OR HATE HIM

NOW HE'S A BUC [166]

Are you kidding me? What other #1 overall pick – let alone one as accomplished and decorated at the collegiate level as Winston was – in major sports history has ever had such a headline run about him the very day after he was drafted, and by his local newspaper no less?

Tampa Bay Times journalist Rick Stroud, who covers the Buccaneers, might as well have answered the above question when he was quoted as saying that Winston was the:

> *Most polarizing pick I've ever seen ... There is some division along racial and gender lines.* [166]

When Winston was shown the aforementioned article with the incendiary all-capped nine word headline and asked what he thought of it by Sports Illustrated's Peter King, his reply was simply:

> *Nothing. Just a newspaper article. Headlines.* [166]

At just 21 years of age Winston was obviously already aware that such a thing as *Winston Deranagment Syndrome* existed, and that such was propagated by a biased media. Nevertheless, he still had to perform on the field, to erase the doubts that lingered over his game, his personality and his future.

Game One:
The Favre Factor

Winston's first professional game – preseason excluded of course – and in fact his first professional pass, was an unmitigated disaster.

Just like Hall of Fame quarterback Brett Favre – a player Winston is often compared to for both his fun-loving nature as well as his penchant for taking risks on the field and thinking he can turn even the worse busted play into a big gain for his offense – Winston's very first NFL pass was not just intercepted but returned for a touchdown by the defense. In fact, Winston was the first QB since Brett Favre – 24 years prior – to throw a pick-six on his first NFL pass. [172] Strangely enough, just 3 years later, the New York Jets' Sam Darnold – a quarterback that is often compared to Winston (but who did not have even close to as good a rookie season as Winston had) – did the exact same thing. [173]

Despite throwing for 210 yards and two touchdowns in his NFL debut, Winston would be outplayed by #2 overall pick Marcus Mariota and the Buccaneers would be blown out 42-14. [174] After the game, journalist Samer Kalaf would write about Mariota's huge first game:

Mariota won't get to play Tampa Bay's defense every week [175]

Sadly, as Bucs fans know, the above statement was indeed a prescient one and one that could be repeated after nearly every single one of Winston's 56 games played to date.

The Winston vs. Mariota showdown was the first time quarterbacks selected #1 overall and #2 overall from the same draft class would play a head-to-head game since September 19, 1993, when gunslinger and historically under-rated #1 overall pick Drew Bledsoe would be outplayed and lose a home game to game-manager and draft bust, #2 overall pick Rick Mirer. [176]

Game Two:
On the Road against a Future Hall of Famer

Winston and the Bucs traveled to New Orleans in the second week of the 2015 season. It would be Winston's first game against a guaranteed future Hall of Fame quarterback – Drew Brees – the NFL's all-time leader in career passing yards. [177]

Winston would outplay Brees that Sunday and lead the Bucs to a 26-19 win on the road. When the game finished, Brees had a dismal 80.5 passer rating, while Winston would throw for 207 yards and a touchdown while accumulating a marvelous 114.6 passer rating, and even add 23 yards and a second touchdown on the ground. [178]

Games Three through Six:
It's Hard to Win Games with a Defense That Bad!

The next four games of Winston's career would feature individual highs and lows for the young gunslinger, such as when he set a career high in passing yards in back to back games in which he also had over a 122.5 passer rating each time, or when he threw four interceptions in a loss to the Panthers and completed under 50% of his passes against the Texans. However, despite throwing for 1,054 yards and the Bucs scoring 100 points in those 4 games, they went just 1-3 thanks to giving up a whopping 29.5 points per game over that span. [179] [180] [181] [182]

Game Seven:
Winning in Matty Ice's House

Jameis Winston's seventh professional game was against the Atlanta Falcons and quarterback Matt Ryan in Atlanta. Winston and the Bucs were up for the challenge.

While Ryan racked up 399 yards of total offense and two touchdowns, he threw a costly interception and fumbled twice, losing one. Winston on the other hand totalled just 201 yards, but also accounted for two touchdowns while playing mistake free football and ended up leading a game-winning drive in overtime, to give the Bucs a 23-20 victory and raising their record to 3-4 on the season. [183]

Games Eight and Nine:
More Peaks and Valleys

The next two games of Winston's rookie season featured more up and down individual and team play. Winston accounted for 538 yards, two touchdowns and two turnovers as the team split games with the Giants and Cowboys, despite Winston leading a clutch game-winning drive against the Cowboys and completely outplaying Eli Manning in the Giants game, a game in which three Buccaneers players not named Winston lost fumbles. [184] [185]

Game Ten:
The Greatest Rookie QB Performance of All Time?

Jameis Winston's rookie year magnum opus came in his 10th career game, on the road against the team he grew up rooting for, the Philadelphia Eagles. [186]

Both teams entered the game at 4-5 and desperately needing a victory. However, after the Buccaneers fell behind 7-0, Winston threw five touchdown passes over his next six drives and the team cruised to a 45-17 victory. Winston finished the game 19-29 for 246 yards, five touchdown passes, no turnovers, a magnificent 131.6 passer rating and an otherworldly 93.2 Raw QBR (based on a scale of 1-100) which many – including myself – consider the king of QB stats as it's truly comprehensive, far more than a stat like passer rating is. [187] [188]

After the game Winston stated:

> *It's just another day that I was blessed with ... I have a baseball mentality. Today, I went 5-for-5.* [189]

> *I ain't gonna cry, you know, but this, this is definitely a dream come true for me, uh, to play here,, you know I always wanted to play here. Uh, my whole life, since I was a little boy, I always wanted to be an Eagle. Uh, I was even signing the fight song out there, on the field.* [190]

In short, while the day may have been just another day the good Lord blessed Winton with on this earth, the game was anything but just another game for Winston. However, was it the greatest game a rookie quarterback has ever had in NFL history?

Other than Winston, there have been just two rookie quarterbacks in modern NFL history to throw five touchdown passes in a single game: Matthew Stafford and Deshaun Watson. [189] [191]

Below are the statistics each of the aforementioned three rookie quarterbacks compiled in their historic five touchdown pass games [188] [192] [193]:

Player	Comp %	Total Yards	TDs	TOs	Passer Rating	Raw QBR	W - L
Winston	**65.5**	**246**	**5**	**0**	**131.6**	**93.2**	**W**
Stafford	60.5	429	5	2	112.7	75.4	W
Watson	51.6	292	5	0	119.8	95.5	L

After viewing the above statistical table, it's quite clear that Winston did indeed have the greatest rookie quarterback performance in modern NFL history. Each of the three QBs totalled five touchdowns, but while the only category out of the six categories listed that Mattew Stafford led in was total yards, and the only category that Deshaun Watson led in was Raw QBR, Winston bested both Stafford and Watson in completion percentage and passer rating, while also never turning the ball over (unlike Stafford who threw two interceptions) and winning the game (unlike Watson whose Texans were down 23-7 at halftime and 39-20 in the 4th quarter before Watson threw two late garbage time touchdowns). [194]

All of the above said, there's really no doubt that when Jameis Winston shredded the Philadelphia Eagles on September 22, 2015, he did so while playing the single greatest game a rookie quarterback had and has ever played in modern NFL history!

Games Eleven and Twelve:
Playoffs Here We Come?

The next two games of Winston's rookie season once again featured more up and down individual and team play. Despite Winston accounting for 510 yards and three touchdowns against two turnovers, the Buccaneers split games with the Colts and Falcons. In the Colts game the Bucs held a 12-6 halftime lead, yet ended up losing thanks to veteran journeyman quarterback Matt Hasselbeck torching the Bucs porous defense. Hasselbeck posted a 100.8 passer rating and set his season highs in both passing yards and touchdown passes against the hapless Buccaneers defense. [195] However, the team bounced back against the Falcons with Winston leading the way and once again outplaying Matt Ryan. In that game, Winston threw the game winning touchdown pass with just 1:39 left in the game to give the Buccaneers a 23-19 victory. [196] [197]

Going into week 14 the Buccaneers had a 6-6 record, the 6th best *Power Ranking* in the NFC according to NFL.com [198] and were being talked about as a legitimate playoff team ... and then the NFL suspended star middle linebacker Kwon Alexander for the rest of the regular season for using *Performance Enhancing Drugs*. [199]

Games Thirteen through Sixteen:
Playoffs? There They Go!

After Kwon Alexander was suspended, the Buccaneers' already atrocious defense fell even further off the cliff, as they gave up 119 points in losing their last four games of the season en route to finishing the season with a 6-10 record. Winston himself however finished the season strong as he threw for more yards (1,165) in the last quarter of the season than he had during any other four game stretch in his rookie season. [200] [201] [202] [203] [204] However, as Hall of Fame quarterbacks like Dan Fouts and Warren Moon can tell you, a quarterback without a defense doesn't win many games in the ultimate team sport known as football, which Winston found out in his first season in the NFL.

Accolades and Achievements

After the Buccaneers' season ended, it became clear to many just how special a rookie season Jameis Winston had.

Winston was named to the Pro Football Writers of America All-Rookie Team [205] and finished second to Todd Gurley in the Associated Press' NFL Offensive Rookie of the Year voting. [206] Many felt the voting was a sham and that Winston obviously deserved to win the award. [207] [208] However, it's certainly possible Winston was punished by various voters who bought into the negative narratives the media spun regarding Winston in the past.

Regardless, Winston did win the Pepsi Rookie of the Year Award [209] and became the youngest quarterback in NFL history to earn a Pro Bowl nod! [210]

The Greatest 21 Year Old QB in NFL History?

Jameis Winston did not have the *greatest* rookie QB season in the Super Bowl era, as that title likely belongs to Ben Roethlisberger, thanks in large part to his Steelers going 13-0 during the regular season games he started, and then advancing to the AFC Title Game with him starting throughout the postseason as well. [211]

In fact, Winston did not have the *best* rookie QB season in the Super Bowl era either, as that title may belong to someone like Robert Griffin III, thanks to his finishing in the top 8 in the entire NFL in touchdown percentage and Raw QBR, the top 5 in completion percentage, interception percentage, yards per completion (Y/C), net yards gained per pass attempt (NY/A), adjusted net yards per pass attempt (ANY/A) and passer rating, and even finishing 1st in the entire league in yards per attempt (Y/A) and adjusted yards gained per attempt (AY/A). [212] Griffin III also managed to finish 20th in rushing yards (first among quarterbacks) in the entire NFL, tied for 15th in rushing touchdowns and even finished 1st in the entire league in yards per carry. [213]

However, Winston's rookie season can certainly be credibly ranked as one of the top 10 rookie seasons of all-time [214], which is quite marvelous considering he is generally the only quarterback on such lists to have been just 21 years old for his entire rookie season, let alone to have only played two years of college football and to have been a #1 overall draft pick playing for the worst team in the league from the previous season.

Nevertheless, what about comparing apples to apples? Does Winston's rookie season rank as the greatest ever for a 21 year old quarterback in NFL history?

To answer the above question, I will compare Winston with all nine quarterbacks in NFL history that started at least seven games while they were 21 years of age, namely: Fran Tarkenton, Dan Darragh, Drew Bledsoe, Alex Smith, Matthew Stafford, Josh Freeman, Sam Darnold, Lamar Jackson and Josh Rosen.

I will also adjust for era – as that is the only truly fair way to judge players from different eras – and simply list their league ranking in various statistical categories, adjusting for a 32 team league since that is what the current NFL has. For example, if a quarterback were to rank 5th in an 8 team league, that would translate to a ranking of 20th in a 32 team league, while a ranking of 2nd in a 16 team league would translate to a ranking of 4th in a 32 team league, etc. Also, under no circumstances will a quarterback be ranked lower than 32nd, even if – as in Lamar Jackson's case – he was 37th in passing yards during his rookie season.

In the following statistical table, I will examine each quarterbacks' league ranking in regards to passing yards, passing touchdowns, interception percentage (note that a rating of 1st, meaning the player had the highest INT % in the league, will actually be recorded as 32nd, so as not to confuse readers) as well as Raw QBR (if such was available in each respective players rookie season) or passer rating (if Raw QBR was not available in each respective players rookie season), and finally wins recorded as a starting quarterback, as such stats are rather undoubtedly considered the five most important factors in measuring great quarterback seasons.

Player	Pass Yds	Pass TDs	INT %	PR / QBR	Wins	Avg. Rank
Jameis Winston	**11th**	**16th**	**29th**	**12th**	**19th**	**17th**
Fran Tarkenton	21st	9th	27th	16th	32nd	21st
Dan Darragh	29th	32nd	21st	32nd	32nd	29th
Drew Bledsoe	18th	11th	21st	32nd	22nd	21st
Alex Smith	32nd	32nd	32nd	32nd	32nd	32nd
Matthew Stafford	25th	23rd	29th	25th	32nd	27th
Josh Freeman	28th	27th	32nd	24th	29th	28th
Sam Darnold	23rd	24th	28th	30th	25th	26th
Lamar Jackson	32nd	32nd	10th	29th	15th	24th
Josh Rosen	29th	30th	27th	32nd	32nd	30th

[215] [216] [217] [218] [219] [220] [221]

After viewing the above statistical table it's obvious that Jameis Winston absolutely did have the greatest rookie season in NFL history for a 21 year old quarterback. In fact, there isn't even a close second. Hall of Famer Fran Tarkenton and 1993 #1 overall draft pick Drew Bledsoe, who had a wonderful career himself, easily had the second and third best 21 year old rookie seasons, but Winston's rookie season easily bested both.

Jameis Winston on His Rookie Season

At the end of his rookie season – a season that saw him not only play the greatest game any rookie quarterback in the modern era had ever played, but have the greatest rookie season any 21 year old quarterback had ever had in NFL history – Winston was interviewed by Sports Illustrated's Peter King who asked what he learned through his rookie season. Winston stated:

> *I'm such a passionate player, I always want to make big plays and I always want to have excitement. It seems so cliché saying this, but do the simple things and you'll be OK. Don't overdo. It just sounds like, OK, it's like reading the Bible. The Bible tells you from right and wrong and you do that and you will have a good life. But it's really that easy: Make the simple decision. If you don't get too over-hyped, if you just make smart decisions and do the right thing, the sky is the limit. ... I got an opportunity to change lives and give people a sense of hope. That's something I like to do.* [222]

Winston certainly changed a lot of people's lives during his rookie campaign. His fantastic individual play got offensive coordinator Dirk Koetter hired as the Buccaneers' new head coach, as the Bucs were scared Koetter would accept the Miami Dolphins' head coaching position if they didn't offer him the job. [223] Winston also developed a marvelous rapport with undrafted rookie free agents Cameron Brate and Adam Humphries and turned them into young stars which led to both players receiving mega-contracts of their own in the future. However, if you were to ask Winston himself what his greatest achievement was, he'd likely say making an impact in the Tampa community, which he also did in spades during his rookie season. [224]

Many people don't like the idea of *tanking* in sports. However, the job of a General Manager is to do what's best for his team overall, not merely for one game, or even for one season, but for – at the very least – the life of his contract. Winning a meaningless game at the end of a losing season, rather than tanking to land one of the greatest quarterback prospects the NFL has ever seen, would not be respecting the game, or playing to win, it would simply be short-sighted lunacy. Buccaneers General Manager Jason Licht certainly understood that and many Bucs fans have no real doubt that the team tanked the final game of the 2014 NFL season to ensure they would receive the #1 overall pick and therefore earn the right to draft Jameis Winston, as the team pulled nearly every single one of its starters after the first half and lost a game they were comfortably leading at the half. [225]

The above said, congratulations Buccaneers fans; your GM had the foresight and common sense to order his team to *wilt for Winston* and *fail for Fameis*. That move paid off in the Bucs being able to draft a quarterback who would go on to have the greatest game in rookie quarterback Super Bowl era history, the greatest season a 21 year old rookie quarterback had ever had, and one of the greatest rookie quarterback seasons the NFL has ever seen!

JAMEIS WINSTON vs. THE GREATS

PART I

I think I could describe the perfect quarterback. Take a little piece of everybody. Take John Elway's arm, Dan Marino's release, maybe Troy Aikman's drop-back, Brett Favre's scrambling ability, Joe Montana's two-minute poise and, naturally, my speed.

– Peyton Manning [226]

There has obviously never been a perfect quarterback to step on a football field. Otto Graham may be the GOAT (Greatest of All Time), Tom Brady may be the GOTSBE (Greatest of the Super Bowl Era), Peyton Manning may be the *best* ever, Aaron Rodgers may be the most talented ever, Dan Marino may be the best pure passer ever and Michael Vick may be the best dual-threat ever. However, there has never been a truly perfect quarterback.

However, there have been Hall of Fame quarterbacks, and to be enshrined in Canton and earn a gold jacket is the closest thing to perfection that there is for an NFL quarterback. Rabid team fans may believe the goal of all quarterbacks should be to win a Super Bowl, but in reality, the highest goal any truly gifted quarterback has is likely to one day be enshrined in the Hall of Fame.

Hall of Fame > Super Bowl Championship

Counting the most recent eight individuals elected into the 2019 Pro Football Hall of Fame class, there are now a grand total of 326 individuals who have been elected into the Hall of Fame. [227] However, each and every season the NFL covers the cost of producing 150 Super Bowl rings for the winning team's players, coaches, executives and the like. [228] This said, it's very likely that are close to 20 times as many Super Bowl rings in existence as there are Hall of Fame busts!

There are thousands upon thousands of former NFL players that have won a Super Bowl ring who can't get into Canton without buying a ticket. However, some of the greatest individual players who have ever stepped on a football field and are now enshrined in Canton as Hall of Fame immortals never won a Super Bowl ring.

Simply put, while every journalist would love to win a nice little *journalist of the year* award plaque from his or her employer, truly gifted journalists strive to win a *Pulitzer*, as it's a more prestigious award. Likewise, while every NFL player would love to win a Super Bowl ring before his career ends, the truly great players strive to earn a spot in the Hall of Fame, as they know that receiving a bust in Canton is far more prestigious than merely winning one of 150 or so Super Bowl rings produced each and every year.

It's no wonder that before he was drafted, Jameis Winson said:

I dream of being a Hall of Famer one day. [229]

The 21 Current or Soon to Be
Super Bowl Era Hall of Fame Quarterbacks

All of the above said, there have been just 14 quarterbacks in NFL history who played their first game in the Super Bowl era and were later elected into the Hall of Fame: Troy Aikman, Terry Bradshaw, John Elway, Brett Favre, Dan Fouts, Bob Griese, Jim Kelly, Dan Marino, Joe Montana, Warren Moon, Ken Stabler, Roger Staubach, Kurt Warner and Steve Young.

There are also just seven quarterbacks that are currently playing in the NFL that seem like sure-fire locks to be elected to the Hall of Fame after they retire: Tom Brady, Drew Brees, Eli Manning, Peyton Manning, Philip Rivers, Aaron Rodgers and Ben Roethlisberger.

Therefore, there are just 21 quarterbacks that played their first game in the Super Bowl era that have ever been enshrined into Canton, been awarded a coveted gold jacket and became a Hall of Fame immortal, or are all but assured of being enshrined in the future. Now that is what you call an exclusive club and a rare award, unlike earning a mere Super Bowl ring which around 150 people earn every single year in the modern NFL.

We have already seen that it is Jameis Winston's goal to be elected to the Hall of Fame one day, and it is an absolute fact – whether anyone who has been infected with *Winston Derangement Syndrome* wants to admit it or not – that he is on a Hall of Fame statistical pace through the first four years of his career. Therefore, as it is my goal to combat the media-driven false narratives surrounding Winston's career, I will compare Winston's rookie season to all 21 of the aforementioned quarterbacks, and in doing so, you will clearly see that the media's narratives are false and that Winston is indeed on a Hall of Fame statistical pace.

There is no point – at least not in this book – in comparing Winston to anyone other than the aforementioned 21 current or soon to be Hall of Fame quarterbacks. It makes no difference if Winston surpassed or was surpassed in regards to his level of play as a rookie by former #1 overall picks like Tim Couch, JaMarcus Russell, or even Matthew Stafford or Andrew Luck, nor does it make any difference if Winston surpassed or was surpassed in regards to his level of play as a rookie by mere current starting quarterbacks like Matt Ryan or Jared Goff, as none of those players are sure-fire Hall of Famers … at least not yet.

Age Related Statistical Comparisons

The first way I will compare Jameis Winston to the 21 current or soon to be Hall of Fame quarterbacks who began their careers in the Super Bowl era, is to compare them by age. I will compare each player in four categories: passing yards, passing touchdowns, completion percentage and passer rating. Certainly there are other and even better stats to use to truly compare the on-field performance of multiple quarterbacks, and I will use such stats when I adjust for era and insert the league ranking statistical tables. However, yards, touchdowns, completion percentage and passer rating are perhaps the four most well-known stats amongst football fans today and very suitable to use in mere age related statistical comparisons.

Before Age 22 Stats	Pass Yards	Pass TDs	Comp %	Passer Rating
Jameis Winston	**4042**	**22**	**58.3**	**84.2**
Troy Aikman	0	0	DNP	DNP
Terry Bradshaw	0	0	DNP	DNP
Tom Brady	0	0	DNP	DNP
Drew Brees	0	0	DNP	DNP
John Elway	0	0	DNP	DNP
Brett Favre	0	0	DNP	DNP
Dan Fouts	0	0	DNP	DNP
Bob Griese	0	0	DNP	DNP
Jim Kelly	0	0	DNP	DNP
Eli Manning	0	0	DNP	DNP
Peyton Manning	0	0	DNP	DNP
Dan Marino	0	0	DNP	DNP
Joe Montana	0	0	DNP	DNP
Warren Moon	0	0	DNP	DNP
Philip Rivers	0	0	DNP	DNP
Aaron Rodgers	0	0	DNP	DNP
Ben Roethlisberger	0	0	DNP	DNP
Ken Stabler	0	0	DNP	DNP
Roger Staubach	0	0	DNP	DNP
Kurt Warner	0	0	DNP	DNP
Steve Young	0	0	DNP	DNP

[141] [230] [231] [232] [233] [234] [235] [236] [237] [238] [239] [240] [241] [242] [243] [244] [245] [211] [246] [247] [248] [249]

Obviously there's not much to glean from the above statistical table other than the fact that Jameis Winston was far more accomplished as an NFL quarterback before turning 22 years of age than any of the 21 current or soon to be Hall of Fame quarterbacks. However, that he was such is a fact, a fact many like to ignore and refuse to admit.

Rookie Season Statistical Comparisons

Despite the fact that Winston obviously compares favorably to all of the 21 quarterbacks when they are compared on an age related basis – not just at age 21 but through age 24, Winston's age when the 2019 regular season ended – the biased anti-Winston crowd who views the previous table often simply says, "The game was different in the past and players didn't enter the NFL at as young an age as Winston did, so those stats make Winston look better than he is". Such folks are simply ignorant of NFL quarterback history.

Fran Tarkenton entered the NFL in 1961, six years before the first Super Bowl was even played, and threw for 250 yards and 4 TD's in his first game [250], at a younger age than Jameis Winston was when he played his first game 54 years later in 2015. Also, Tarkenton wasn't even the first 21 year old starting quarterback in NFL history – that was Jacky Lee in 1960 [251] – and was just one of twelve 21 year old starting quarterbacks in the previous millennia. Along with the aforementioned Jacky Lee, the following 21 year old quarterbacks all played before the year 2000: Jack Concannon, Greg Landry, Dan Darrah, Terry Hanratty, Lynn Dickey, David Woodley, Mike Pagel, Bernie Kosar, Tommy Maddox and Drew Bledsoe [252]. Simply put, if a quarterback is good enough to be a starting quarterback in the NFL at the tender young age of 21, he can be a starting quarterback in the NFL at the tender young age of 21, whether his name is Jacky Lee or Jameis Winston. Most quarterbacks simply aren't that good that young.

Also, to the biased anti-Winston crowd that views the previous table and says, "Well, those are still just age-related stats so they don't mean anything; all that really matters are season stat comparisons", I will say two things.

Firstly, it is patently absurd to think that age-related stats are irrelevant as everyone knows that Hall of Fame careers are built upon accumulated Hall of Fame level stats. Dan Fouts and Warren Moon certainly weren't enshrined in Canton due to all the *team* success they experienced, as both quarterbacks won less career playoff games than Mark Sanchez – the man modern football fans refer to as *Buttfumble* and a guy who has about as good a shot of being elected to the Hall of Fame as yours truly does – and never even played in a single Super Bowl. In fact, Fouts and Moon combined to actually have a losing 194-196-1 career record including playoffs. That said, Dan Fouts and Warren Moon were undoubtedly enshrined in Canton as Hall of Fame immortals due to their career statistical accomplishments.

The same can be said for *ring-less* Hall of Fame quarterbacks like Fran Tarkenton, Dan Marino and Jim Kelly, not to mention non-quarterbacks a plenty, such as Gale Sayers, Dick Butkus, Floyd Little and Larry Wilson, all of whom never even played in a single playoff game, let alone won a playoff game or Super Bowl. [253]

The above said, the fact that Jameis Winston has accumulated more career passing yards and passing touchdowns than any of the aforementioned 21 quarterbacks before the age of 22 is obviously a pro and not a con when it comes to his compiling Hall of Fame level career stats.

Secondly, even when Jameis Winston is measured against the 21 aforementioned quarterbacks on a season basis rather than an age basis, he still shines.

The statistical table on the following page compares Winston's rookie season with the 21 legendary quarterbacks, regardless of each quarterbacks age. I will once again compare each player in the four prime categories: passing yards, passing touchdowns, completion percentage and passer rating.

Rookie Year Stats	Pass Yards	Pass TDs	Comp %	Passer Rating
Jameis Winston	**4042**	**22**	**58.3**	**84.2**
Troy Aikman	1749	9	52.9	55.7
Terry Bradshaw	1410	6	38.1	30.4
Tom Brady	6	0	33.3	42.4
Drew Brees	221	1	55.6	94.8
John Elway	1663	7	47.5	54.9
Brett Favre	0	0	0%	0.0
Dan Fouts	1126	6	44.8	46.0
Bob Griese	2005	15	50.2	61.6
Jim Kelly	3593	22	59.4	83.3
Eli Manning	1043	6	48.2	55.4
Peyton Manning	3739	26	56.7	71.2
Dan Marino	2210	20	58.4	96.0
Joe Montana	96	1	56.5	81.1
Warren Moon	3338	12	57.6	76.9
Philip Rivers	33	1	62.5	110.9
Aaron Rodgers	65	0	56.3	39.8
Ben Roethlisberger	2621	17	66.4	98.1
Ken Stabler	52	0	28.6	18.5
Roger Staubach	421	1	48.9	69.5
Kurt Warner	39	0	36.4	47.2
Steve Young	935	3	52.2	56.9

[141] [230] [231] [232] [233] [234] [235] [236] [237] [238] [239] [240] [241] [242] [243] [244] [245] [211] [246] [247] [248] [249]

After viewing the above statistical table, one quickly sees just what a great rookie season Jameis Winston had when compared to the other 21 quarterbacks, as he had the most passing yards, the second most touchdown passes, the fourth best completion percentage of any of the quarterbacks to throw for at least 34 passing yards, and the third best passer rating of any of the quarterbacks who had at least 222 yards passing.

However, to the biased anti-Winston crowd, even the above statistical table may not make them concede that Winston was on a Hall of Fame pace after his rookie season, as such individuals are famous for simply *moving the goalposts* when they debate. What I mean by this is that when such biased individuals encounter truthful stats they don't like, they simply demand *other* stats, hoping those *other* stats will fit the false narrative they presently believe regarding Winston.

Adjusted for Era Statistical Comparisons

Despite the previous two statistical tables proving that Jameis Winston is more statistically accomplished than any of the 21 legendary quarterbacks before the age of 22, and seeing that Winston also had the best statistical rookie season at any age when compared with the other 21 quarterbacks, individuals who are biased against Winston quickly *move the goalposts* and demand to see Winston compared with the other 21 quarterbacks on an adjusted for era basis.

Now, please do not misunderstand me. I am not saying that when one demands to see season stats instead of age-related stats, or when one demands to see era-adjusted stats instead of season stats, such proves that one is biased or a Winston-hater, as all three stat types are certainly relevant and beneficial to research. However, when one demands a certain stat thinking such a stat will prove their false narrative on Winston to be correct, only to find out such a stat proves the exact opposite, and then merely demands a different stat, followed by yet another different stat, that sort of behavior does prove one is infected with *confirmation bias* and is simply hoping that the next set of stats will confirm the false narrative they currently believe.

Regardless, I do personally think it's extremely obvious that the best and most accurate way to truly compare quarterbacks who played in different eras is to compare them in such a way where you can accurately and adequately adjust for era. In fact, if one doesn't do such, one could literally come away thinking that Baker Mayfield had a better 2018 season than Roman Gabriel had during the 1968 season, simply because Mayfield bested him in the *counting stats*, which would of course be absurd to anyone who knows NFL quarterback history.

The above said, the statistical table in this section comparing Winston's rookie season with the 21 legendary quarterbacks, will indeed adjust for era.

In this adjusted for era section, I will also forego the mere *counting stats* and focus on the advanced metrics of passing yards per attempt (Y/A), touchdown percentage (TD %), completion percentage (Comp %), and Raw QBR (if such stat was available in each respective players rookie season) or passer rating (if the Raw QBR stat was not available in each respective players rookie season) to really get an ultra-accurate picture of just how Jameis Winston compares to the 21 legendary quarterbacks.

Furthermore, rather than merely listing each player's Y/A, TD%, Comp % and Raw QBR / Passer Rating during his rookie season – which still does not adjust for era whatsoever – I will list where each player ranked across his league and even adjust said ranking for a 32 team league which the modern NFL has.

For example, if in a particular quarterbacks' rookie season there were only 16 teams and he finished 8th in the league in touchdown percentage, such would be akin to him finishing 16th in the modern 32 team NFL and therefore he will receive a ranking of 16th in the TD % category.

The formula I will use to determine each quarterback's league ranking in a particular category is: league rank, divided by qualifying quarterbacks, times 32. However, if there are more qualifying quarterbacks than there are teams, the formula would be league rank, divided by league teams, times 32.

Furthermore, if a particular quarterback did not qualify in all four statistical categories, it will say DNQ (i.e. Did Not Qualify) in all four of that quarterbacks' categories as well as in the *Average Rank* (Avg. Rank) category. However, if a quarterback qualifies in even one category, I will use his stats to rank him in the other categories, such as I did with Terry Bradshaw's fourth season (in *Jameis Winston vs. the Greats Part IV* chapter) in 1973, as in that season Bradshaw qualified in passer rating but not in completion percentage (where he was worse than the last place qualifier and would have therefore ranked 18th, but as there were only 17 quarterbacks who qualified he is ranked 34th, as his 18th ranking, divided by 17 qualifying quarterbacks, times 32 teams, equals 33.888 or a ranking of 34th in a 32 team league which the current NFL has). [254]

Also, if a quarterback started at least five games in a season, I will rank him even if he doesn't technically qualify in a specific category. Such is the case with Steve Young in his 1985 rookie season [255], as well as Eli Manning in his 2004 rookie season. [256]

Finally, I need to mention that while I have relied on pro-football-reference.com a great deal when researching for this book, and while such is an amazing website, it can be a little confusing for some when they are researching seasonal statistical *rankings* when two or more players *tie* to the decimal point in any particular category. For example, the site can at times show Dan Marino incorrectly ranked 2nd in TD % in his rookie season of 1983, when he was slight percentage points behind Neil Lomax and therefore truly should be ranked 3rd. However rest assured, I have done the math and made sure that every single one of the rankings I provide are absolutely correct. Please feel free to double-check my math for yourself in order to confirm that I am 100% correct each and every time.

All of the above said, the following table details how Jameis Winston compares to each of the 21 legendary quarterbacks when adjusted for era, as well as how each of those quarterbacks compare to each other.

Rookie Year Ranking	Y/A	TD %	Comp %	PR - QBR	Avg. Rank
Jameis Winston	**12th**	**22nd**	**32nd**	**12th**	**20th**
Troy Aikman	32nd	26th	27th	32nd	29th
Terry Bradshaw	23rd	27th	32nd	38th	30th
Tom Brady	DNQ	DNQ	DNQ	DNQ	DNQ
Drew Brees	DNQ	DNQ	DNQ	DNQ	DNQ
John Elway	29th	29th	32nd	31st	30th
Brett Favre	DNQ	DNQ	DNQ	DNQ	DNQ
Dan Fouts	28th	27th	32nd	32nd	30th
Bob Griese	25th	25th	18th	18th	22nd

Jim Kelly	9th	9th	8th	9th	9th
Jim Kelly	9th	9th	8th	9th	9th
Eli Manning	33rd	29th	34th	34th	33rd
Peyton Manning	20th	11th	20th	24th	19th
Dan Marino	11th	3rd	18th	3rd	9th
Joe Montana	DNQ	DNQ	DNQ	DNQ	DNQ
Warren Moon	15th	30th	14th	18th	19th
Philip Rivers	DNQ	DNQ	DNQ	DNQ	DNQ
Aaron Rodgers	DNQ	DNQ	DNQ	DNQ	DNQ
Ben Roethlisberger	2nd	7th	4th	5th	4th
Ken Stabler	DNQ	DNQ	DNQ	DNQ	DNQ
Roger Staubach	DNQ	DNQ	DNQ	DNQ	DNQ
Kurt Warner	DNQ	DNQ	DNQ	DNQ	DNQ
Steve Young	20th	31st	23rd	29th	26th

[215] [257] [258] [259] [260] [261] [262] [254] [263] [264] [256] [265] [261] [266] [267] [256] [219] [256] [258] [268] [265] [255]

After viewing the above statistical table, anyone who was infected with *Winston Derangement Syndrome* at any time in the past and has spun the narrative that Winston, even as a rookie, was a bust, should now know better than to ever spin such a false narrative again.

It's crystal clear that even when one adjusts for era, Jameis Winston had a better rookie season than all but five of the 21 legendary quarterbacks. And, of those five quarterbacks that did have better rookie seasons than Winston, all were also older than Winston, with Jim Kelly being nearly five full years older and Warren Moon over 6 full years older than Winston when they played in their first NFL game compared to Winston when he played in his first NFL game! [204] [269] [270] [271] [272] [273]

There simply is no way that anyone who has viewed the above table can still claim Winston had a poor rookie season unless they truly are infected with *Winston Derangement Syndrome* or are a mere illogical individual who simply has no interest in truth whatsoever.

The simple and irrefutable fact is that the hard data covered in this chapter proves that Jameis Winston is more statistically accomplished than any of the 21 legendary quarterbacks before the age of 22. Such hard data also proves that Winston had the best rookie season of said quarterbacks in regards to the counting stats. Finally, such hard data even confirms that Winston had, at worst, the 6th best rookie season of said quarterbacks even when adjusting for era!

Of course, one legendary season a career does not make, unless of course your name is Joe Namath. Therefore, let's proceed to detail and examine Winston's second NFL season in the next two chapters, shall we?

QBWINZ IS NOT A STAT ... HOWEVER

In football, it's the ultimate team sport. You have to have good people around you as a quarterback for things to happen.

— Warren Moon [274]

Especially in football, it is not a QB's game ... even though the media likes to make it into that - it takes the whole team.

— Joe Montana [275]

This chapter is for those readers who have been deceived by the media to believe that *team wins* are a legitimate *individual* quarterback stat. They are not. They never have been. To believe they are is idiotic. Can I be any clearer?

The term *QBWinz* is a popular term on social media and is used by people like me who enjoy educating low-football-IQ fans and leading them to the logical and obvious truth that teams win games in the ultimate team sport of football, and therefore wins – or *QBWinz* – is not a legitimate individual quarterback stat.

The above said, while I have been abundantly clear that I do not believe team wins are a legitimate individual quarterback stat, and while I will even go so far as to say that team wins have absolutely nothing to do with assessing individual talent at any position, I know there are many readers out there who either do view team wins as an individual quarterback stat, or would at least like to see team wins covered in this book to some extent. Therefore, I will do so in this chapter, as well as at various times throughout the remaining chapters in this book, in one way or another.

However before I do so, please consider one more quote, this time from the fun-loving, offense-carrying, wild gunslinger that Jameis Winston reminds many people of, the great Brett Favre:

I know it's not a one man team win or lose.

— Brett Favre [276]

Now, consider the even more illuminating facts of NFL history detailed in the table below:

Hall of Fame Quarterbacks That Never Won a Super Bowl	Non Hall of Fame QBs That Won a Super Bowl
Fran Tarkenton	Jim McMahon
Dan Fouts	Jeff Hostetler
Dan Marino	Trent Dilfer
Jim Kelly	Brad Johnson
Warren Moon	Doug Williams

The five quarterbacks on the left are not merely Hall of Famers, four of them were first ballot Hall of Famers and the fifth (i.e. Tarkenton) certainly could have and perhaps should have been as well. [277] However, the only way the five quarterbacks on the right are getting into the Hall of Fame is if they pay the price of admission just like your average Joe on the street. And, if there is anyone on earth that knows who the above ten named quarterbacks are and still cannot instantly come to the conclusion that judging quarterbacks on the basis of Super Bowl wins is absurd, such a person may need far more help than even this book can provide.

Hall of Fame (or Soon to be Hall of Fame) Quarterbacks That Never Even Played in a Super Bowl	Non Hall of Fame QBs That Played in a Super Bowl
Dan Fouts	Rex Grossman
Warren Moon	David Woodley
Philip Rivers	Stan Humphries

The table on the preceeding page is another fun little educational tool to use when one encounters the illogical *QBWinz* crowd. The three quarterbacks on the left were named to the Pro Bowl a combined 23 times yet never once played in a single Super Bowl in their combined 47 years in the NFL. [236] [243] [244] The three quarterbacks on the right however, were named to the Pro Bowl a combined zero times – that's right, zero times – yet played in a combined three Super Bowls in their combined mere 24 years in the NFL, and they are nowhere near the only non-Hall-of-Fame quarterbacks to play in the Super Bowl. [278] [279] [280]

However one doesn't have to compare various Hall of Fame quarterbacks and their lack of Super Bowl wins, with infinitely inferior quarterbacks and their Super Bowl wins, to understand just how silly the *QBWinz* concept is. One can merely consider the career of the *GOTSBE* (Greatest of the Super Bowl era), Tom Brady, as well as the career of perhaps the *best* quarterback in NFL history, Peyton Manning, as illustrated in the below table.

Quarterback	MVP Seasons	Super Bowl Winning Seasons
Tom Brady	2007 2010 2017	2001 2003 2004 2014 2016 2018
Peyton Manning	2003 2004 2008 2009 2013	2006 2015

[232] [240]

Just look at the above list. Two of the greatest quarterbacks who have ever stepped on a football field and who have combined to win eight regular season MVP trophies and eight Super Bowl rings, never once won a Super Bowl ring in the same season they won an MVP trophy! It doesn't take a great football mind to see that *QBWinz* is an absurd concept that deserves to be confined to the dustbin of history, alongside such discarded concepts as the drop kick field goal and leather helmets.

To those proponents of *QBWinz* that would say, "Well, maybe you have proved that Super Bowl wins is a silly metric by which to judge quarterbacks, but you haven't proved that playoff or even mere regular season wins are a useless metric by which to judge quarterbacks", I offer the following table.

Hall of Fame Quarterbacks	Career Playoff Wins	Non Hall of Fame Quarterbacks	Career Playoff Wins
Dan Marino	8	Joe Flacco	10
Steve Young	8	Donovan McNabb	9
Fran Tarkenton	6	Jim Plunkett	8
Len Dawson	5	Joe Theismann	6
Warren Moon	3	Danny White	5
Dan Fouts	3	Craig Morton	5
Joe Namath	2	Mark Brunell	5

[281]

How anyone that knows anything about NFL quarterback history could view the above table and still believe that while Super Bowl rings may be a silly metric by which to judge quarterbacks, playoff wins are a logical metric, is beyond me. There simply is no comparison whatsoever between the quarterbacks on the right and the unforgettable legends on the left, yet it's the comparatively forgettable quarterbacks that recorded more career playoff wins.

To those proponents of *QBWinz* that would say, "Well, okay, fine; maybe you have indeed proved that Super Bowl wins and playoff wins are both silly metrics by which to judge quarterbacks, but you haven't proved that regular season wins are a useless metric by which to judge quarterbacks", once again, I offer the table on the following page.

Hall of Fame Or Soon to be HOF Quarterbacks	Career Win %	Non Hall of Fame Quarterbacks	Career Win %
Drew Brees	.589	Tony Romo	.614
Troy Aikman	.570	Alex Smith	.587
Philip Rivers	.567	Brad Johnson	.576
Dan Fouts	.506	Andy Dalton	.575
Warren Moon	.502	Steve Grogan	.556

[282]

After viewing the above table, all the proponents of *QBWinz* should say is, "You've convinced me. QBWinz is never a legitimate stat and deserves to be ridiculed by everyone. Thank you for helping me become a high-football-IQ fan." And, to those individuals wise enough to say such, I merely say, "You're welcome."

In regards to silly *QBWinz* and Jameis Winston himself, he was one of, if not the, greatest winners at the quarterback position in the history of NCAA football, having gone 26-1 and having won a National Title. However, when you're that great in college, great enough to get selected #1 overall – and not by a team that traded up to the #1 spot – you are drafted by the worst team in the entire league 100% of the time.

The NFL isn't the NBA with its *lottery system*. The #1 overall pick – as long as there's not a trade of that pick – always goes to the worst team in the league. It also goes without saying that *team wins* don't always come easily, not even for great individual quarterbacks, especially when they happen to play for the worst team in the league, let alone for a hapless franchise like the Tampa Bay Buccaneers who had not only won just one Super Bowl in their 38 year team history at the time they drafted Winston, but had won just 17 games in the previous four seasons, for an abysmal .266 win percentage, before drafting Winston. [283]

However, the team tripled their previous season's win total with Winston starting every game during his 2015 rookie season. [283] And, while

Winston being credited with a 6-10 record as a rookie may be ridiculed by many of his detractors, when one considers that he, as a 21 year old *true rookie* (in the NBA sense of the phrase), quarterbacked a team that was 2-14 the year prior to a 6-10 season, and the fact that perhaps the most talented quarterback in NFL history and sure-fire future first ballot Hall of Famer, Aaron Rodgers, as a 25 year old *4th year rookie* (again, in the NBA sense of the phrase), quarterbacked a team that was 13-3 the year prior to the same 6-10 record [284] [245], one gets a new sense of appreciation for what Winston accomplished. Even from a purely team record perspective, Jameis Winston had a magnificent rookie season.

In fact, since the Super Bowl era began, other than Jameis Winston, there have only been a total of 17 quarterbacks that were drafted #1 overall that also played their first game for the worst NFL team from the previous year. [285] All other #1 overall picks in the Super Bowl era were either drafted by a team that traded up to land them, such as Jeff George in the 1990 draft [286], or were traded to a better team after being drafted but before they played their first game, such as Eli Manning in the 2004 draft. [287]

I will now examine each of those quarterbacks in regards to their rookie year win/loss record and win percentage in comparison to their team's win/loss record the previous year.

#1 Overall Draft Pick Quarterbacks	W	L	Rookie Year Win %	Prior Year Win %	Difference in Win %
Jameis Winston	**6**	**10**	**.375**	**.125**	**300%**
Terry Bradshaw	3	5	.375	.071	528%
Jim Plunkett	6	8	.429	.143	300%
Steve Bartkowski	4	7	.364	.214	170%
Vinny Testaverde	0	4	.000	.125	- 100%
Troy Aikman	0	11	.000	.188	- 100%
Drew Bledsoe	5	7	.417	.125	334%

Peyton Manning	3	13	.188	.188	0%
Tim Couch	2	12	.143	N/A*	N/A*
David Carr	4	12	.250	N/A*	N/A*
Carson Palmer	6	7	.462	.500	- 8 %
Alex Smith	2	5	.286	.125	229%
JaMarcus Russell	0	1	.000	.125	- 100%
Matthew Stafford	2	8	.200	.000	N/A**
Sam Bradford	7	9	.438	.067	654%
Cam Newton	6	10	.375	.125	300%
Andrew Luck	11	5	.688	.125	550%
Baker Mayfield	6	7	.462	.000	N/A**
Grand Totals	67	131	.338	.141	240%

[141] [288] [231] [289] [290] [291] [292] [293] [294] [295] [230] [296] [297] [298] [240] [299] [300] [301] [302] [303] [304] [305] [306] [307] [308] [309] [310] [311] [312] [313] [314] [315] [316]

* Tim Couch and David Carr were drafted by expansion teams and therefore their team did not have a win/loss record the year before they were drafted.

** The 2008 Detroit Lions and 2017 Cleveland Browns each went 0-16 therefore a percent increase cannot be calculated.

After viewing the above list, one can see that of the other 17 quarterbacks, only two won more games as a rookie than Jameis Winston did. Likewise, none of the three Hall of Fame quarterbacks on the list won as many games as a rookie as Winston did, and only one (i.e. Terry Bradshaw) accounted for a better difference in win percentage than Winston did.

Simply put, while Winston's rookie season was one for the ages on an individual statistical basis, it was also extremely impressive on a team basis. [317]

SOPHOMORE SENSATION

There is something about building up a comradeship - that I still believe is the greatest of all feats - and sharing in the dangers with your company of peers. It's the intense effort, the giving of everything you've got. It's really a very pleasant sensation.

– Edmund Hillary [318]

Just before the start of Jameis Winston's sophomore season in the NFL, head coach Dirk Koetter was asked about how Winston could improve his game and Koetter responded:

You're making it seem like there's so much more for him to do in his second year ... He already did it all ... there's nothing that we ask of him that he can't do. [319]

However, while Winston did indeed *do it all* in having one of the greatest rookie quarterback seasons in NFL history, the Buccaneers team had anything but a great season. And, after helping the Buccaneers triple their 2014 win total as a 21 year old rookie, Winston was on a mission to not just have a magnificent individual sophomore campaign but to lead his team to a magnificent season as well. In short, Winston wanted to win in the NFL the way he won in college, and to be the best leader of the best team possible, not just the best individual player he could be.

Those who knew Winston ... and even those who knew the great Tom Brady, had no doubt in Jameis' leadership qualities:

He is probably the best natural leader I've been around. I've dealt with a lot of college-aged guys. He is still a college-aged guy. He understands people. He is very perceptive, very observant; he sees things. Whether it is body language or things coming up, he sees it and reacts appropriately to it and says, 'That guy needs a pat on the butt,' or, 'That guy needs to be pushed a little more.' He's not afraid to do it. The No. 1 thing that makes him a good leader is he wants to win. He knows, to do that, he's got to get the most out of the guys around him.

– Bucs QB Coach Mike Bajakian [320]

He's the best leader I think I've ever been around -- in anything.

– Bucs GM Jason Licht [321]

To be called "the best leader ... in anything" is just about the highest praise a quarterback could ever receive from anyone. However, when one understands that the man who said that about Winston – Jason Licht – was a man who spent four years with Bill Bellichick, Tom Brady and the New England Patriots as either assistant director or director of player personnel, at a time when Brady won an MVP and the Patriots advanced to the Super Bowl [322] [323] [324], it becomes an even great compliment.

However, being a great leader doesn't automatically guarantee a great team season. Just ask Drew Brees if you don't believe me, as while former Super Bowl champion Brees was in the prime of his career and leading the league in passing yards for three straight seasons (2014-2016), he and his Saints had a losing record in all three seasons as well. [233]

Regardless, with the first game of the season on tap, and the future promising but uncertain, Winston was locked-in and ready to rock.

Game One: NFL Offensive Player of the Week

Winston and the Bucs traveled to Atlanta for the first game of the season, facing off against Matt Ryan and the Falcons who they went 2-0 against in 2015.

After falling behind 10-3 in the first quarter, Winston threw four touchdowns on his next five drives leading the Bucs to a 31-24 victory. [325]

Winston finished the game 23-32 for 281 yards and 4 touchdowns. It was a dominant performance and he was named NFC Offensive Player of the Week. [326]

Game Two:
On the Road against Future Coach Bruce Arians

Winston and the Bucs traveled to Arizona in the second week of the 2016 season to square off against the man who would later come out of retirement to become the head coach of the Buccaneers and to coach Jameis himself, Bruce Arians. However, the game would be over by half-time and Winston would have the worst game of his career, throwing four interceptions and losing a fumble while the Cardinals cruised to a 40-7 victory. [327]

There's not much more to say than that Winston played terrible. It happens. Hall of Famer Ken Stabler once threw seven interceptions in a single game, while Hall of Famers Brett Favre and Peyton Manning each had a six interception game during their careers. Even Russell Wilson, someone who has been considered one of the most efficient *game-managers* in NFL history, once threw a whopping five interceptions in a game. [328]

Game Three:
Bombs Away

Winston and the Bucs faced off in Tampa against the Los Angeles Rams in the third game of the season. Despite Winston having his first career 400 yard passing game and Rams quarterback Case Keenum passing for just 190 yards, the Rams were able to control the game thanks to their 137 yards rushing and two rushing touchdowns and pull out a 37-32 victory. The Bucs on the other hand provided Winston with just 70 yards rushing and their kicker – Roberto Aguayo – missed a field goal and an extra point, while Winston's last ditch scramble-attempt from the 15 yard line came up short. [329]

It was a tough loss for a young team, a loss that easily could have been a win, if not for the kicker, as had the kicker not left four points on the field, the team would never have needed to go for two 2-point conversions (both failed) and would actually have held a 38-37 lead while also having the ball in the Rams red zone to close to the game. [329]

However, as the great Vince Lombardi once said, "football is a game of inches" [330] and many times those inches are the difference between a win and a loss as Jameis Winston knows all too well.

Games Four through Eight:
No Run Game & Bad Defense Trumps Solid QB Play

After a rough game four for both Winston and the Buccaneers against the Broncos and their dominant defense [331], the following four games of Winston's career would feature magnificent individual play but result in a disappointing 2-2 record for the team. In those four games Winston threw for nine touchdowns against just one interception and compiled a 102.5 passer rating; however the Buccaneers gave up a whopping 73 points in the two losses and outside of the one game against the 49ers, provided Winston with an average of just 84 yards of run support on a paltry 3.4 yards per carry. [332] [333] [334] [335]

Game Nine:
A 5 Game Winning Streak Begins
and
Jameis Pulls Off the Best QB Play in NFL History?

The Buccaneers entered the second half of the season just 3-5 and looked destined for their sixth straight losing season as a franchise. Then Jameis Winston put on his Superman cape.

The Bucs were ahead just 17-10 early in the 3rd quarter against the Bears and faced a 3rd & 10 from their own 23 yard line. [336] At that point, Jameis Winston dropped back to pass and then inexplicably decided to see what it would feel like to pretend a real NFL game was akin to the original *Tecmo Bowl* video game – you know, the one where Bo Jackson could take one single handoff and run for an entire quarter, finishing the quarter with a 99 yard touchdown run where he actually ran perhaps 700 yards or so to score that 99 yard touchdown [337] – and pulled off perhaps the greatest and most unlikely single play from a quarterback in NFL history!

On the play, Winston received the hike in the shotgun and was almost immediately sacked by a blitzing linebacker who got his hands on Winston before Jameis shrugged him off. Winston then evaded another defender and started running backwards, and backwards, and backwards, until he was about 3 yards deep in his own end zone! Winston then started to work his way out of the end zone while evading three defenders before launching a perfect 54 yard pass over the outstretched hand of a Bears defender and right into the hands of star receiver Mike Evans. [338]

Not only did that play spark the Bucs, as Winston's very next pass was a 43 yard touchdown toss to backup receiver Freddie Martino, which gave the Bucs a 24-10 lead on the way to earning them a dominant 36-10 victory, but it also may very well have been the single greatest quarterback play in the history of the NFL. Simply put, you could try to repeat this exact play 100 times in *Madden NFL 20* and not be able to pull it off, the play truly was that spectacular!

In fact, I honestly believe if that exact play was pulled off by a winning quarterback – any quarterback – in a Super Bowl, it would undoubtedly be considered the greatest single play by a quarterback of all time. However, the play was pulled off by Jameis Winston – a quarterback the media loves to hate – in a week 10 regular season game, in Tampa Bay, at 1:00pm on a Sunday afternoon [336], so it never received the credit it should have, which is a shame.

The Letter

After the win versus the Bears, the Bucs sat at 4-5 and were still a long-shot to make the playoffs. And with their next four games being at the Alex Smith led Chiefs, home against the Russell Wilson led Seahawks, at the Philip Rivers led Chargers and home against the Drew Brees led Saints, it looked like a near sure thing that the Bucs would be sitting at 4-9 and headed for a top 5 pick in the 2017 NFL Draft.

Jameis Winston then decided to do one of those things superstars do that become part of their legend and get brought up at their Hall of Fame induction ceremonies. Winston went to head coach Dirk Koetter and asked permission to do something special for his teammates (yes, seriously, a 22 year old quarterback asked his coach for *permission* to do something special for his teammates). After receiving permission from his coach, Winston wrote hand-written letters to every single one of his teammates and then read them a typed letter he had written for the whole team as well, just before the team left Tampa to travel to Kansas City for their next game. [339]

It has never been revealed exactly what the team letter said, let alone what each of the individual letters said, but Winston as well as some in the know have stated the following:

> *It's team stuff; I'm not going to talk about it ... One thing I can say, I told them how grateful I was to be their quarterback.*

> – Jameis Winston [340]

> *It was a fantastic letter ... Jameis is a special guy.*

> – Head Coach Dirk Koetter [339]

> *That says a lot about him ... That letter kind of hit everybody. You always want to play for a quarterback like that. At a young age like that, to be a leader and stand up like that ... he's a born leader.*

> – Wide Receiver Cecil Shorts [339]

If the next four games were any indication, *The Letter* had a dramatic and extremely positive impact on the entire Buccaneers team.

Games Ten through Thirteen:
Winston + Good Defense = League Domination

The inspired Buccaneers arrived in Arrowhead Stadium and their young letter writing leader turned in one of the best games of his career. Winston led the Bucs to a tough 19-17 victory over the previously 7-2 Chiefs, in which he threw for 331 yards, one touchdown, no interceptions and had a 97.3 passer rating. [341]

After the game, Winston's head coach raved about his play:

> *Jameis was out of sight today ... That's as good a quarterback play as I've seen in however many years I've been in the league. He was awesome. .Jameis played a great, great game. We gave him the game ball already.* [340]

The Bucs' next game was against the 7-2-1 Seahawks [342], a team with Super Bowl aspirations who had won three straight games and just two weeks earlier had beat the eventual Super Bowl Champion New England Patriots on the road in Foxborough. [343]

The game would be an ugly one for one quarterback, but it wasn't Jameis Winston. While Winston had another fantastic game, completing 75% of his passes for 220 yards, 2 touchdowns and a 106.3 passer rating, Russell Wilson completed just 51.5% of his passes for a measly 151 yards, no touchdowns, 2 interceptions and a terrible 38.8 passer rating. The Bucs won the game 14-5 and improved to 6-5 on the season. [342]

The Buccaneers' next game would be against Philip Rivers and the Chargers in San Diego. The Chargers entered the 4th quarter with a 21-17 lead. Then *Clutch Jameis* showed up, went 5-6 for 59 yards and a touchdown plus a 2-point conversion and the Bucs pulled out a come from behind 28-20 victory. Winston outplayed Philip Rivers on the day and finished the game 20-30 for 280 yards, one touchdown and a 93.7 passer rating. [344]

The Buccaneers' next game would be a showdown with Drew Brees and the New Orleans Saints. The Bucs would jump out to a 13-0 lead, Winston would play an efficient and turnover free game and completely outplay Brees, and the Bucs would win a tough defensive game 16-11. [345]

In the five game win streak Winston outplayed legends Drew Brees, Philip Rivers and Russell Wilson, while accumulating a 97.9 passer rating over the 5 games, a number that would have been good for 7th in the NFL on the season. Likewise, despite the Bucs as a team giving Winston just 89.6 yards of run support, on an abysmal 3.1 yards per carry average, the defense stepped up and the team gave up just 12.8 points per game over the 5 games, and that was all Winston and the offense needed to lead the Bucs to five straight victories. [336] [341] [342] [344] [345]

The End of an Amazing Streak

Despite winning the Saints game the previous week – their fifth straight win as a team – one of the more remarkable records in NFL history was snapped. Going into that game, Jameis Winston had accounted for at least one touchdown in all 28 career games he had played since being drafted. In fact, dating back to college, Winston had accounted for at least one touchdown in all 55 NCAA/NFL games he had ever played in! [346]

Winston may not have been able to match Joe DiMaggio's 56 game MLB hit streak with a 56 game touchdown streak, but to put even his 28 game NFL streak in context, consider that the great Peyton Manning's streak was just two games. [270] In fact, many great quarterbacks didn't even account for a single touchdown in their very first game and two of the longest streaks for all-time great quarterbacks were Dan Marino's and Ben Roethlisberger's seven game streaks, a full twenty-one games less than Winston's streak! [271] [273]

The following table lists the career beginning touchdown streaks of each of the 21 legendary quarterbacks extensively covered in this book, compared to Winston's streak, which illustrates just how impressive Winston's streak was:

Quarterback	Games in a Row with at least One TD to Start NFL Career
Jameis Winston	**28**
Troy Aikman	0
Terry Bradshaw	0
Tom Brady	0
Drew Brees	3
John Elway	0
Brett Favre	0
Dan Fouts	2
Bob Griese	1
Jim Kelly	2
Eli Manning	0
Peyton Manning	2
Dan Marino	7
Joe Montana	0
Warren Moon	1
Philip Rivers	0
Aaron Rodgers	0
Ben Roethlisberger	7
Ken Stabler	0
Roger Staubach	1
Kurt Warner	0
Steve Young	0

[204] [347] [348] [349] [350] [351] [352] [353] [354] [355] [356] [269] [357] [270] [271] [358] [272] [359] [360] [273] [361] [362] [363] [364]

Games Fourteen through Fifteen:
End of the Winning Streak

The Buccaneers' next game was a road game against the 11-2 Dallas Cowboys. Despite being over-matched, the Bucs held a 20-17 lead going into the final quarter thanks in large part to Winston going 14-23 for 228 yards and two touchdowns up to that point. However after the Cowboys tied the game at 20 on the first drive of the 4th quarter, Bucs coach Dirk Koetter went completely one-dimensional and called 15 pass plays out of the team's 17 fourth quarter offensive plays. Winston went just 3-12 while having one pass batted down and while also being sacked three times in the quarter. The Bucs lost 26-20 and fell to 8-6 on the season. [365]

The next week the Buccaneers once again found themselves on the road, this time against Drew Brees and the New Orleans Saints, a team they had just beaten two weeks earlier [345]. This time however Drew Brees would play magnificent football and the Saints would jump out to a 20-7 lead before cruising to a 31-24 victory. [366]

Game Sixteen:
Jameis Winston's De Facto First Playoff Game

The Buccaneers entered the final game of the 2016 season with a solid shot at making the playoffs if they could get one last win. However, the opponent was the division rival Carolina Panthers, quarterbacked by defending league MVP Cam Newton, a quarterback Jameis Winston had yet to win a game against in his career.

The game was a tough defensive battle, a true de facto playoff game, and despite the Panthers outrushing the Buccaneers and winning the time of possession battle, the game was decided by the quarterbacks. Jameis Winston easily outplayed Cam Newton on the day and the Bucs escaped with a 17-16 victory, giving them a 9-7 winning record on the year. [367]

Tie-Breaker Heart Break

Despite the Buccaneers finishing the season with a playoff qualifying 9-7 record, the Detroit Lions won the NFL's *tiebreaker* and earned the 6th seed in the NFC despite the Buccaneers having a far better season resume. The Lions did not beat a single playoff team all season long, had lost their last three games of the season, and had been blow out by the #1 seed Cowboys in Dallas 42-21. The Bucs on the other hand had beaten three playoff teams, including the #2 AFC seed Kansas City Chiefs on the road, the #2 NFC seed Atlanta Falcons on the road, and the #4 NFC seed Seattle Seahawks at home. The Bucs also won their last game of the season and held a 20-17 lead in the fourth quarter before losing by less than a touchdown to the #1 NFC seed Dallas Cowboys in Dallas. [368] [369]

Had the Buccaneers made the playoffs as the #6 seed in the NFC they would have played the Seattle Seahawks in the wild card round, a team they defeated and even held to just 5 points earlier in the season. However the Lions were awarded the #6 seed, played the Seahawks, and were destroyed 26-6. [370]

If only the Buccaneers had had even a league average rushing attack in 2016. Instead, the team finished 24th in rushing yards, 29th in yards per carry, 31st in expected points contributed by rushing offense, and the only team with less team rushing touchdowns in the entire NFL was the New York Giants. [371]

In short, 22 year old Jameis Winston was asked to be an offense-carrier at an age and stage of his career when most quarterbacks are merely asked to be game-managers. Nevertheless, the Bucs still finished with a 9-7 winning record and only missed the playoffs on a tie-breaker; and, if not for some disastrous kicking in the Rams game would have finished 10-6 and easily earned the #6 seed and a first round matchup against a team they had already pummeled in the regular season.

Accolades and Achievements

Winston finished the season with 4,090 passing yards and 28 touchdown passes, both Tampa Bay Buccaneers team records. [372] And, while Winston failed to earn his second straight Pro Bowl nod since being drafted, despite having a better individual season and being part of a better team season than the year before, he was named to his first ever *NFL Top 100* list, being ranked ahead of both Philip Rivers and Kirk Cousins. [373]

And, while the Top 100 list is basically just a popularity contest, such an achievement is still considered a feather in a player's cap so to speak.

Strangely enough, it was Kirk Cousins that earned the Pro Bowl nod over Winston, depriving Winston of being the youngest two-time Pro Bowl quarterback in NFL history. However while Pro Bowl nods are nice, being regarded as the most accomplished 22 year old quarterback who ever lived is a whole lot nicer, and that is exactly what Winston was.

Also, according to the NFL and their *Next Gen Stats*, Winston finished the 2016 season:

2nd in the entire NFL in *Averaged Intended Air Yards* (IAY) [374] which is described as:

> *IAY shows the average Air Yards a passer throws on all attempts. This metric shows how far the ball is being thrown 'downfield'. Air Yards is recorded as a negative value when the pass is behind the Line of Scrimmage. Additionally Air Yards is calculated into the back of the end zone to better evaluate the true depth of the pass.* [375]

2nd in the entire NFL in *Air Yards to the Sticks* (AYTS) [374] which is described as:

> *Air Yards to the Sticks shows the amount of Air Yards ahead or behind the first down marker on all attempts for a passer. The metric indicates if the passer is attempting his passes past the 1st down marker, or if he is relying on his skill position players to make yards after catch.* [375]

3rd in the entire NFL in *Average Completed Air Yards* (CAY) [374] which is described as:

> *CAY shows the average Air Yards a passer throws on completions ... This metric shows how far the ball is being thrown 'downfield'. Air Yards is recorded as a negative value when the pass is behind the Line of Scrimmage. Additionally Air Yards is calculated into the back of the end zone to better evaluate the true depth of the pass.* [375]

And, for those of you who weren't incredibly impressed by the detailed *Next Gen Stats*, read the above section again. The accomplishments it details are absurdly impressive and paint a very clear picture of just how elite Jameis Winston's 2016 season was according to the advanced metrics.

The Most Accomplished
22 Year Old Quarterback in NFL History!

When Jameis Winston's second season concluded, he found himself atop the record books for quarterbacks of his age.

Winston became the first player in the history of the NFL to start his career with back to back 4,000 yard passing seasons [376] and while Winston-bashers like to downplay that achievement by saying all quarterbacks throw for 4,000 yards now-a-days, that simply is not the case at all. In fact, former #1 overall draft pick, NFL Offensive Player of the Year and league MVP Cam Newton has thrown for 4,000 yards just once in his eight NFL seasons [312] and perennial MVP candidate Russell Wilson has done so just two times in his seven NFL seasons. [377]

The simple fact is that Jameis Winston is the one and only quarterback in the history of the NFL to start his career with back to back 4,000 yard passing seasons. No matter how Winston-haters try to downplay such an accomplishment, the fact remains that no other quarterback in NFL history – not Fouts, Marino, Moon, Manning, Brady, Brees, Rodgers, et al. – has ever accomplished what Winston did, at any age, let alone the ripe young age of 22.

Not only did Winston become the first quarterback in NFL history to start his career with back to back 4,000 yard passing seasons, he also finished his second season #1 all-time in NFL history in both career passing yards and career passing touchdowns, before the age of 23.

Simply put, there has never been a more accomplished 22 year old quarterback in the history of the NFL, not a single one, and it's not even debatable.

JAMEIS WINSTON vs. THE GREATS

PART II

*there's only one reason for doing anything that you set out to do.
If you don't want to be the best, then there's no reason going out
and trying to accomplish anything.*

– Joe Montana [275]

Jameis Winston once signed a photo for me and inscribed it with the words, "The future G.O.A.T. God willing" [378] and from what I was told, his agent at that time wasn't happy as he felt the inscription was too brash. However, it's not brash to desire to be the best at something and Winston wants to be the best. In fact, anyone who knows Jameis Winston knows he wants to be the greatest quarterback that has ever played the game of football. [145] [229] [379]

No quarterback in history with a mere two years under his belt – let alone one who was also just 22 years of age – has ever amassed a resume that would guarantee he'd end up as one of the greatest quarterbacks ever. However, Jameis Winston's resume through his second season is one of the most impressive of all time; in fact it's absolutely indisputable that Winston was on a Hall of Fame pace through his sophomore season.

The above said and without further ado, I will jump right into comparing Winston with the 21 legendary quarterbacks I compared him to in the *Part I* version of this chapter previously.

Age Related Statistical Comparisons

As I did in the *Part I* version of this chapter, I will compare Winston to the 21 legendary quarterbacks, by age. Likewise, I will once again compare each quarterback in the following four categories: passing yards, passing touchdowns, completion percentage and passer rating.

Before Age 23 Stats	Pass Yards	Pass TDs	Comp %	Passer Rating
Jameis Winston	**8132**	**50**	**59.6**	**85.2**
Troy Aikman	1155	4	52.5	61.0
Terry Bradshaw	1410	6	38.1	30.4
Tom Brady	0	0	DNP	DNP
Drew Brees	221	1	55.6	94.8
John Elway	0	0	DNP	DNP
Brett Favre	848	5	64.7	85.7
Dan Fouts	1126	6	44.8	46.0
Bob Griese	2005	15	50.2	61.6
Jim Kelly	0	0	DNP	DNP
Eli Manning	0	0	DNP	DNP
Peyton Manning	3739	26	56.7	71.2
Dan Marino	2755	27	59.8	100.8
Joe Montana	0	0	DNP	DNP
Warren Moon	0	0	DNP	DNP
Philip Rivers	0	0	DNP	DNP
Aaron Rodgers	111	0	48.4	43.9
Ben Roethlisberger	2621	17	66.4	98.1
Ken Stabler	0	0	DNP	DNP
Roger Staubach	0	0	DNP	DNP
Kurt Warner	0	0	DNP	DNP
Steve Young	0	0	DNP	DNP

[141] [230] [348] [231] [232] [233] [234] [380] [236] [237] [238] [239] [240] [241] [381] [242] [243] [244] [245] [211] [246] [247] [248] [249]

Just as with the *Before Age 22 Stats* table detailed in the *Part 1* version of this chapter, there's not much to glean from the above statistical table, other than the fact that Jameis Winston was infinitely more accomplished as an NFL quarterback before turning 23 years of age than any of the legendary 21 quarterbacks. In fact, if one merely sets aside the passing yards and touchdown passes accumulated by Peyton Manning, Dan Marino and Terry Bradshaw, the fact is that Jameis Winston amassed more career passing yards and passing touchdowns than the other 18 quarterbacks amassed, all put together!

Sophomore Season Statistical Comparisons

While Jameis Winston has accumulated far more career passing yards and passing touchdowns than any of the 21 legendary quarterbacks before the age of 23, I will now compare Winston's second season alone, with each of their second seasons.

The below table compares Winston's second season with the second seasons of the other 21 legendary quarterbacks, regardless of each quarterbacks age. And, per the usual, I will compare each of the 22 quarterbacks in the four prime categories: passing yards, passing touchdowns, completion percentage and passer rating.

2nd Year Stats	Pass Yards	Pass TDs	Comp %	Passer Rating
Jameis Winston	**4090**	**28**	**60.8**	**86.1**
Troy Aikman	2579	11	56.6	66.6
Terry Bradshaw	2259	13	54.4	59.7
Tom Brady	2843	18	63.9	86.5
Drew Brees	3284	17	60.8	76.9
John Elway	2598	18	56.3	76.8
Brett Favre	3227	18	64.1	85.3
Dan Fouts	1732	8	48.5	61.4
Bob Griese	2473	21	52.4	75.7
Jim Kelly	2798	19	59.7	83.8
Eli Manning	3762	24	52.8	75.9
Peyton Manning	4135	26	62.1	90.7
Dan Marino	5084	48	64.2	108.9
Joe Montana	1795	15	64.5	87.8
Warren Moon	2709	15	53.1	68.5

Philip Rivers	115	0	54.5	50.4
Aaron Rodgers	46	0	71.4	48.2
Ben Roethlisberger	2385	17	62.7	98.6
Ken Stabler	268	1	50.0	39.2
Roger Staubach	542	2	53.7	42.9
Kurt Warner	2282	8	53.7	65.5
Steve Young	4353	41	65.1	109.2

[141] [230] [231] [232] [233] [234] [235] [236] [237] [238] [239] [240] [241] [242] [243] [244] [245] [211] [246] [247] [248] [249]

After viewing the above table, one can easily see how fantastic Jameis Winston's sophomore season in the NFL was when compared to the other 21 quarterbacks' sophomore seasons. Winston had the fourth most passing yards, the third most touchdown passes, the seventh best completion percentage of any of the quarterbacks to throw for at least 1,795 passing yards, and the seventh best passer rating of any of the quarterbacks as well.

Through Sophomore Season Statistical Comparisons

In this section, I will compare Jameis Winston's stats *through* his second season with the aforementioned 21 quarterbacks *through* their second seasons, irrespective of age. And, per the usual, in the below table I will compare each of the 22 quarterbacks in the four prime categories: passing yards, passing touchdowns, completion percentage and passer rating.

Through 2nd Year Stats	Pass Yards	Pass TDs	Comp %	Passer Rating
Jameis Winston	**8132**	**50**	**59.6**	**85.2**
Troy Aikman	4328	20	55.1	62.0
Terry Bradshaw	3669	19	48.4	46.6
Tom Brady	2849	18	63.7	86.1
Drew Brees	3505	18	60.6	77.8
John Elway	4261	25	52.7	68.0
Brett Favre	3227	18	63.6	82.9
Dan Fouts	2858	14	46.9	54.5
Bob Griese	4478	36	51.3	68.9

Jim Kelly	6391	41	59.5	83.5
Eli Manning	4805	30	51.6	70.5
Peyton Manning	7874	52	59.3	80.6
Dan Marino	7294	68	62.2	104.5
Joe Montana	1891	16	63.9	87.3
Warren Moon	6047	27	55.5	73.1
Philip Rivers	148	1	56.7	67.1
Aaron Rodgers	111	0	48.4	43.9
Ben Roethlisberger	5006	34	64.7	98.3
Ken Stabler	320	1	47.3	33.9
Roger Staubach	963	3	51.9	51.9
Kurt Warner	4392	41	64.5	107.9
Steve Young	3217	11	53.3	63.1

[141] [230] [231] [232] [233] [234] [235] [236] [237] [238] [239] [240] [241] [242] [243] [244] [245] [211] [246] [247] [248] [249]

After viewing the above statistical table, one can see that Jameis Winston, through his second season, had the most career passing yards, the third most career touchdown passes, the eighth best career completion percentage, and the sixth best career passer rating when compared to the other 21 legendary quarterbacks through their respective first two seasons in the NFL.

Likewise, of the other 21 quarterbacks, the only ones to best Jameis in at least two of the four categories were Tom Brady, Dan Marino, Joe Montana, Ben Roetlisberger and Kurt Warner, while the one and only quarterback to best Winston in three of the four categories was Dan Marino. No quarterback bested Winston in all four categories.

The above said, while Winston is undoubtedly the most statistically accomplished 22 year old passer in NFL history, it's also clear that he has a very strong claim to also having had one of very best first two seasons in quarterback history as well, irrespective of age.

Sophomore Season Adjusted for Era Statistical Comparisons

As I did in the *Part 1* version of this chapter, in this adjusted for era section I will forego the mere *counting stats* and focus on the advanced metrics of passing yards per attempt (Y/A), touchdown percentage (TD %), completion percentage (Comp %), as well as Raw QBR (if such was available in each respective players rookie season) or passer rating (if Raw QBR was not available in each respective players rookie season) to really get an ultra-accurate picture of just how Jameis Winston compares to the aforementioned 21 legendary quarterbacks.

Furthermore, rather than merely listing each player's Y/A, TD%, Comp % and Raw QBR / Passer Rating during his rookie season – which still does not adjust for era whatsoever – I will list where each player ranked across his league and even adjust said ranking for a 32 team league which the modern NFL has.

For example, if in a particular quarterback's sophomore season there were only 16 teams, and he finished 8th in the league in touchdown percentage, such would be akin to him finishing 16th in the modern 32 team NFL and therefore he will receive a ranking of 16th in the TD % category.

The formula I will use to determine each quarterback's league ranking in a particular category is: league rank, divided by qualifying quarterbacks, times 32. However, if there are more qualifying quarterbacks than there are teams, the formula would be league rank, divided by league teams, times 32.

Furthermore, if a particular quarterback did not qualify in all four statistical categories, it will say DNQ (i.e. Did Not Qualify) in all four of that quarterbacks' categories as well as in the *Average Rank* (Avg. Rank) category. However, if a quarterback qualifies in even one category, I will use his stats to rank him in the other categories, such as I did with Terry Bradshaw's fourth season (in *Jameis Winston vs. the Greats Part IV* chapter) in 1973, as in that season Bradshaw qualified in passer rating but not in completion percentage (where he was worse than the last place qualifier and would have therefore ranked 18th, but as there were only 17 quarterbacks who qualified he is ranked 34th, as his 18th ranking, divided by 17 qualifying quarterbacks, times 32 teams, equals 33.888 or a ranking of 34th in a 32 team league which the current NFL has). [254]

Also, if a quarterback started at least five games in a season, I will rank him even if he doesn't technically qualify in a specific category. Such is the case with Steve Young in his 1985 rookie season [255], as well as Eli Manning in his 2004 rookie season. [256]

Finally, I need to mention that while I have relied on pro-football-reference.com a great deal when researching for this book, and while such is an amazing website, it can be a little confusing for some when they are researching seasonal statistical *rankings* when two or more players *tie* to the decimal point in any particular category. For example, the site can at times show Dan Marino incorrectly ranked 2nd in TD % in his rookie season of 1983, when he was slight percentage points behind Neil Lomax and therefore truly should be ranked 3rd. However rest assured, I have done the math and made sure that every single one of the rankings I provide are absolutely correct. Please feel free to double-check my math for yourself in order to confirm that I am 100% correct each and every time.

All of the above said, the following table details how Jameis Winston compares to each of the 21 legendary quarterbacks when adjusted for era, as well as how each of those quarterbacks compare to each other.

2nd Year Ranking	Y/A	TD %	Comp %	PR / QBR	Avg. Rank
Jameis Winston	**15th**	**11th**	**23rd**	**11th**	**15th**
Troy Aikman	26th	30th	16th	30th	25th
Terry Bradshaw	29th	24th	11th	23rd	22nd
Tom Brady	16th	13th	4th	6th	10th
Drew Brees	26th	29th	18th	24th	24th
John Elway	25th	14th	16th	19th	18th
Brett Favre	24th	20th	5th	8th	14th
Dan Fouts	10th	20th	28th	26th	21st
Bob Griese	25th	18th	7th	11th	15th
Jim Kelly	27th	17th	5th	12th	15th
Eli Manning	17th	14th	31st	23rd	21st

Peyton Manning	4th	7th	2nd	4th	4th
Dan Marino	1st	1st	3rd	1st	1st
Joe Montana	25th	9th	1st	6th	10th
Warren Moon	12th	19th	23rd	23rd	19th
Philip Rivers	DNQ	DNQ	DNQ	DNQ	DNQ
Aaron Rodgers	DNQ	DNQ	DNQ	DNQ	DNQ
Ben Roethlisberger	1st	1st	9th	3rd	3rd
Ken Stabler	DNQ	DNQ	DNQ	DNQ	DNQ
Roger Staubach	DNQ	DNQ	DNQ	DNQ	DNQ
Kurt Warner	1st	1st	1st	1st	1st
Steve Young	26th	30th	21st	28th	26th

[382] [383] [384] [260] [385] [267] [386] [387] [388] [389] [219] [390] [267] [391] [255] [219] [392] [219] [384] [258] [390] [264]

After viewing the above statistical table, it's obvious to anyone other than those infected with *Winston Derangement Syndrome* that Winston's sophomore season compared favorably to the sophomore seasons of the 21 legendary quarterbacks, even when adjusted for era.

Winston had a better sophomore season than all but seven of the 21 legendary quarterbacks listed. The only quarterbacks who had a better average rank than Winston were Tom Brady, Joe Montana, Peyton Manning, Dan Marino, Ben Roethlisberger, Kurt Warner, and Brett Favre who just barely bested Winston.

And, of those seven quarterbacks that did have better sophomore seasons than Winston when adjusting for era, every single one of them were older than Winston, with Kurt Warner being nearly six full years older than Winston when each player was in their second season. [347] [392]

Through Sophomore Season
Adjusted for Era Statistical Comparisons

As I did in the previous section, I will now compare the adjusted for era statistics of Jameis Winston and the 21 legendary quarterbacks, this time comparing each quarterback's first two seasons, rather than merely their sophomore season alone.

In regards to how the rankings are calculated, it's a simple matter of adding and dividing. For example, if a quarterback ranked fourth in yards per attempt in his first season and sixth in the same category in his second season, he would receive a ranking of fifth in the following table in the yards per attempt category. And, as it's a matter of simple math that anyone can do, there are no citations following the table, as I do not assign a citation to my own original statistical tables.

Through 2nd Year Rankings	Y/A	TD %	Comp %	PR / QBR	Avg. Rank
Jameis Winston	**14th**	**17th**	**28th**	**12th**	**18th**
Troy Aikman	29th	28th	22nd	31st	28th
Terry Bradshaw	26th	26th	22nd	31st	26th
Tom Brady*	16th	13th	4th	6th	10th
Drew Brees*	26th	29th	18th	24th	24th
John Elway	27th	22nd	24th	25th	25th
Brett Favre*	24th	20th	5th	8th	14th
Dan Fouts	19th	24th	30th	29th	26th
Bob Griese	25th	22nd	13th	15th	19th
Jim Kelly	18th	13th	7th	11th	12th
Eli Manning	25th	22nd	32nd	29th	27th
Peyton Manning	12th	9th	11th	19th	13th
Dan Marino	6th	2nd	11th	2nd	5th
Joe Montana*	25th	9th	1st	6th	10th
Warren Moon	14th	25th	19th	21st	20th
Philip Rivers	DNQ	DNQ	DNQ	DNQ	DNQ
Aaron Rodgers	DNQ	DNQ	DNQ	DNQ	DNQ
Ben Roethlisberger	2nd	4th	7th	4th	4th
Ken Stabler	DNQ	DNQ	DNQ	DNQ	DNQ
Roger Staubach	DNQ	DNQ	DNQ	DNQ	DNQ
Kurt Warner*	1st	1st	1st	1st	1st
Steve Young	23rd	31st	22nd	29th	26th

* Quarterbacks with an asterisk next to their name did not qualify to be ranked as rookies and therefore have only their second year rankings included in their average rank.

After viewing the above statistical table, it's clear that Winston's first two NFL seasons compare favorably to the first two seasons of the 21 legendary quarterbacks, even when adjusted for era.

The only quarterbacks who had a better average rank than Winston who actually qualified to be ranked in both their rookie and second seasons were: Peyton Manning, Dan Marino, Jim Kelly, and Ben Roethlisberger who just barely bested Winston.

The indisputable fact is that the hard data covered in this chapter proves that Jameis Winston is more accomplished than any of the 21 legendary quarterbacks. Such hard data also proves that Winston had one of the best sophomore seasons of any such quarterback in regards to the counting stats. Such hard data also confirms that Winston had, at worst, the eighth best sophomore season of said quarterbacks even when adjusting for era. Finally, such hard data even confirms that Winston had the fifth best first two season start to his NFL career when compared to the 21 legendary quarterbacks and when adjusting for era!

Nevertheless, unless your name is Eli Manning, no modern quarterback's Hall of Fame resume will ever be boiled down to a mere two seasons, let alone their first two seasons in the league. Therefore, as legendary, statistically speaking, as Jameis Winston's first two seasons were, let's move on to examining his third season in the next two chapters.

JUNIOR JUXTAPOSITION

We live in a world of constant juxtaposition between joy that's possible and pain that's all too common. We hope for love and success and abundance, but we never quite forget that there is always lurking the possibility of disaster.

– Marianne Williamson [393]

After the individual success Winston had in his second season, and the Buccaneers team having its first winning season in six years [283], not to mention the signing of big-name free agent wide receiver DeSean Jackson [394], the Buccaneers were a sexy pick to make the playoffs in the 2017 season. [395]

However, whenever there are great expectations, or the hope for success, just as the above quote says, there is also the possibility for disaster. Remember the 2011 Philadelphia Eagles so-called *Super Team*? The Eagles had made the playoffs the previous three seasons, had won their division the previous year, had 10 Pro Bowler's on their roster, and had just finished going crazy signing big-name stars in free agency. Many felt they would win the Super Bowl. Instead, they started 4-8 on their way to missing the playoffs and finishing with a disappointing 8-8 record. [396] [397]

The Buccaneers – like the 2011 Eagles *Super Team* – would fail to live up to expectations. As for Jameis Winston himself, his junior season in the NFL would be a juxtaposition between his strong performances when he was healthy and his rather abysmal performances when he played through a severe throwing shoulder injury, the first major injury he had ever sustained in his life. [398]

However, before Winston suffered his serious injury, the Buccaneers had high hopes and a game against the Chicago Bears to kick off the 2017 season.

Game One: Domination

Winston and the Buccaneers hosted the Chicago Bears at Raymond James Stadium, jumped on them early, led 26-0 at halftime and cruised to a dominating 29-7 victory. Winston played an efficient game, finishing with 204 passing yards, a 91.5 passer rating and one touchdown while playing turnover free football. [399] In short, it was the type of all-around performance one would expect from a solid playoff contending team.

Game Two:
What Goes Up Must Come Down

Winston and the Bucs traveled to Minnesota in the second week of the season to square off against a legitimate Super Bowl contender. The Vikings would put a whooping on the Bucs and earn a 34-17 victory. For his part, Winston completed 70 percent of his passes for 328 yards and two touchdowns, however he also threw two interceptions in the fourth quarter when the game was all but over and finished with three picks on the day. [400]

Game Three:
Clutch Jameis

The Buccaneers squared off with the New York Giants in Tampa during week three, with the game coming down to the wire.

The Bucs were trailing mid-way through the 4th quarter and Winston – while throwing for 224 yards, two touchdowns and playing turnover free football – was just 15-30 passing. Then *Clutch Jameis* showed up. On the Bucs final two drives of the game Winston went 7-8 for 108 yards and one touchdown, scrambled for a first down and led the team to a game-winning field goal and a 25-23 comeback victory. [401]

Game Four:
Battling the GOTSBE

The Patriots and their golden-boy quarterback, Tom Brady, who I like to call *The Great GOTSBE* (i.e. Greatest of the Super Bowl Era) even though I rather despise F. Scott Fitzgerald's novel, *The Great Gatsby*, came to Tampa for a week four show down.

When the game ended the Patriots were victorious 19-14. However, Jameis Winston put on a show – especially in the fourth quarter, going 13-20 for 225 yards with one passing touchdown, and leading his team on what could have been three other scoring drives had it not been for kicker Nick Folk missing two field goals and the team therefore not being able to even attempt a third in field goal range, as they were down six points due to the earlier misses and therefore needed a touchdown – and finished the game with 345 total yards, one touchdown, no turnovers, and led four other drives that could have resulted in field goals, in the six point loss. [402]

Tom Brady finished the game with 308 total yards, one touchdown and two turnovers, but his field goal kicker (i.e. Stephen Gostkowski) made all four of his field goal attempts, while Winston's kicker missed all three of his attempts. [402]

To his credit, after the game, kicker Nick Folk stated:

> *I left points out there ... we should have won the game ... this one's on me.* [403]

However, the loss was a crushing one for the Buccaneers, not merely because they lost in such heart-breaking fashion, but more so because unbeknownst to them, Winston would soon suffer his first serious injury and the entire season would go down the tubes.

Game Five:
Knocked Out

The Buccaneers traveled to Arizona to face the Arizona Cardinals in week five, standing at 2-2 on the season. Half-way through the 2nd quarter the Cardinals were ahead 24-0 and old man Carson Palmer looked like 1984 Dan Marino, as he'd gone 13-14 for 211 yards and two touchdowns, while old man Adrian Peterson looked like 2012 Adrian Peterson, as he'd ran for 85 yards and a touchdown. [404]

As for Jameis Winston, he was knocked out of the game after taking a hard hit from Chandler Jones. [405] It was an injury that would affect him in one way or another for the much of the rest of the season.

Game Six:
Pain Killers and Pathetic Defense

After Jameis Winston was knocked out of the Buccaneers' last game with a nasty throwing shoulder injury, he returned to start against Buffalo in week six to face the 3-2 Bills, which surprised some folks, as Winston's throwing shoulder was in bad shape and there were rumblings that he'd have to miss the game entirely. [406] [407] [408] [409]

However, Jameis Winston is a soldier, and not only did he play, he came out firing! Winston started the game 9-12 for 115 yards on his first two drives, both of which ended with field goals and gave the Bucs a 6-3 lead at the end of the first quarter. Yet when the Bucs offense took the field in the fourth quarter for the first time, they were trailing 20-13 [410] and needed *Clutch Jameis* to show up once again. That's exactly what they got.

Winston went 9-10 passing for 115 yards with two touchdown passes over the Bucs two fourth quarter drives and with just 3:14 left in the game, the Bucs held a 27-20 lead and looked like they would even their season record at 3-3. [410] Then bad defenses do what bad defenses do, squander leads and wrestle losses from the jaws of victory.

The Bills marched right down the field and tied the game on a LeSean McCoy seven yard touchdown run. They then forced a fumble from Adam Humphries – after Winston completed his ninth straight pass of the quarter – and seven plays later kicked a game winning field goal to stun the Bucs and pull out a 30-27 win, sending the Bucs to a 2-4 record on the season. [410]

For his part, Winston completed his last 12 passes of the game, went 12-13 for 134 yards and two touchdowns in the fourth quarter alone, and finished the game 32-44 for 384 yards and three touchdowns with a 112.3 passer rating. [410]

In short, this was one of those games that is proof positive that football is the ultimate team sport, and that great quarterback play, even great quarterback play that features extremely clutch play with an almost perfect fourth quarter and a touchdown pass to give one's team a late lead, is often times not enough to actually win a game in the NFL.

Games Seven through Eight:
Who Knew a Throwing Shoulder
Could Be So Important for a Quarterback?

The next two weeks would be rough ones for the Buccaneers with Jameis Winston playing through pain thanks to having re-injured his throwing shoulder in the last game against Buffalo. [411] In fact, Winston's shoulder was so damaged that he seemingly had no real velocity on his passes and struggled to make simple passes that used to be as easy as breathing for him. [412]

The Bucs would get waxed in their next two games, the first at home against the Carolina Panthers and the second on the road against the New Orleans Saints, losing by a combined score of 47-13 with Winston throwing for a mere combined 277 yards with no touchdown passes and two interceptions and also getting knocked out in the first half of the Saints game after re-injurying his throwing shoulder, which he did not return to. [413] [414]

"Jameis Would Play with No Arm"

After the game, Buccaneers General Manager Jason Licht announced that Winston would be sidelined with his throwing shoulder injury, while also praising the 23 year old quarterback for his toughness and competitiveness:

> *This may be an extended period. There's no new information. It's still the same injury that we've diagnosed and had all of our doctors that do a great job with it. But this could be an extended situation. What is best for our future, because he is our future and we're going to make the best decisions we can medically to ensure that he is our future. ... First time in his career that he's going to be missing a game and that he's dealt with this ... This is a medical call we had to make. If it's up to Jameis, Jameis would play with no arm. He's an extreme competitor. I mean, I've never been around a guy like this guy. He can deal with more pain than most people. But medically, it was the decision we had to make.* [415]

Games Twelve through Thirteen: A Semi-Healthy Throwing Shoulder is a Beautiful Thing

Jameis Winston missed just three games due to his serious throwing shoulder injury and returned in week 13 of the 2017 NFL season. However, the team was 4-7, had a historically porous defense, and there was a great deal of speculation that coach Dirk Koetter had already lost the locker room and would likely be fired. [416] [417] [418]

Winston returned to face the Green Packers in Lambeau Field. He immediately proved his shoulder was back to full health and he was ready to be the gunslinger he always had been, as on the very first drive of the game he completed four passes to four different receivers and finished the drive 4-5 for 60 yards and threw a touchdown pass to tight end Cam Brate, giving the Bucs a quick 7-0 lead. [419]

After falling behind 17-7 shortly before halftime, Winston lead a long field goal drive on the Bucs last possession of the first half, another field goal drive that spanned the end of the third and start of the fourth quarter, and then a final touchdown drive in which he went 5-6 for 78 yards and threw his second touchdown pass of the game, once again to tight end Cam Brate. After that touchdown, the Bucs held a 20-17 lead with 6:02 left in the game. However, the lead didn't last as the Packers moved right down the field and kicked a game-tying field goal which ended up sending the game to overtime. The Packers then got the ball first in overtime and never gave it back to Winston and the Bucs offense, as they ran six times for a whopping 60 yards, including a walk-off 20 yard touchdown run. [419]

Despite Winston finishing the game 21-32 for 270 yards, two touchdowns and a magnificent 112.8 passer rating, and completely outplaying Packers quarterback Brett Hundley who passed for an abysmal 84 yards, no touchdowns, one interception and a terrible 48.3 passer rating, the Bucs lost and fell to 4-8 on the season, assuring they wouldn't make the playoffs. [419] At that point, many Buccaneer fans were hoping the team would *tank* the rest of the season, finish 4-12 and get the highest draft pick possible to provide Jameis Winston with the help he so obviously needed, either on the offensive line, or just about anywhere on the defensive side of the ball.

The next week Winston and the 4-8 Bucs would host the 6-6 Detroit Lions who had designs on earning a playoff berth. The game was an ugly one featuring eight combined turnovers and a mere 45 combined points despite the teams gaining a combined 834 yards of total offense. Winston threw for 285 yards and two touchdowns while counterpart Matthew

Stafford threw for 381 yards and one touchdown, with each quarterback tossing two interceptions and Stafford's tight end Eric Ebron losing a fumble while Winston's teammates lost two fumbles. [420]

However, despite the Bucs entering the fourth quarter down 21-7, Jameis Winston threw two quick fourth quarter touchdown passes and tied the game at 21-21 with just 8:05 remaining on the clock. Lions kicker Matt Prater would however break the tie and win the game on a 46 yard field goal with just 25 seconds remaining in the game, dropping the Buccaneers to 4-10 on the season. [420]

Game Fourteen:
Pitching a No-Hitter but Losing the Game

The next week the Buccaneers would square off with the 8-5 playoff bound Atlanta Falcons. Jameis would play a nearly perfect game, a game that would be the equivalent to a complete game no hitter loss for a pitcher in baseball. For those who say, "Oh come on, you must be exaggerating." All I can say is, "Watch the game for yourself; Jameis played near perfect football!"

And, for those who think a baseball pitcher can't pitch a no-hitter and still lose the game, tell that to Yankees pitcher Andy Hawkins who threw a complete game no-hitter and still lost. [421] In fact, you could also try to tell that to Matt Young, Ken Johnson, Steve Barber, Stu Miller, Jose Arredonodo and Jered Weaver as well, as all of those pitchers know what it feels like to pitch a no-hitter and still end up with a loss. [422]

Winston put on a marvelous performance on Monday Night Football, completely outplaying counterpart Matt Ryan and finishing the game 27-35 for 299 yards, three touchdown passes, no turnovers, and a 130.5 passer rating. Winston would also account for 82.8 percent of the offensive yards the Buccaneers gained as a team. Matt Ryan on the other hand would finish with just 212 passing yards, one touchdown, a passer rating of 87.0 and account for just 58.4 percent of his team's offensive yards. [423]

However the Falcons team would play turnover free football, while Buccaneers running back Peyton Barber would cough up a fumble inside the red zone and kicker Patrick Murray would miss a game-tying field goal as time expired, giving the Falcons a 24-21 victory and dropping the Buccaneers to 4-10 on the season. [423]

When the game ended, Winston praised the resilience of his teammates and stated:

> *It was the perfect example of the next man up ... like 46 guys on the roster, 9 people go down, like what are we, what are we gonna do? You know, we lose Cam Brate and OJ [Howard] and DeSean [Jackson] in the same quarter. We have Alan Cross come in and, and make a play for us, like, that's resilience man. ... That's only by the grace of God and that's all.* [424]

In fact, Winston even praised his embattled head coach Dirk Koetter and petitioned for his return in 2018. [425]

A Shockingly Unbiased Article
Amid the Usual Biased Tripe

After the Monday night Falcons game in which Winston put on a show in front of a national audience, the NY Times did the unthinkable; they wrote a glowing review of Winston with a perfectly appropriate title. The article was written by journalist Victor Mather and titled, *Jameis Winston Is Having a Great Season; the Bucs Are Not*. In it Mather accurately and unbiasedly stated:

> *Tampa Bay quarterback Jameis Winston was outstanding on Monday night ... The game was a microcosm of Winston's entire season, his third as the Bucs' quarterback. ... His completion*

percentage, interception percentage, adjusted yards per attempt, and quarterback rating are all at career bests. But because the Bucs are ... only 2-9 with Winston starting, few outside of Tampa have paid much attention. [426]

While one would think the above article would be the usual sort of article written for one of the young star quarterbacks in the NFL, that isn't the case when the young star quarterback's name is Jameis Winston. In fact, right around the time this NY Times article dropped, another article on the Washington Post dropped that was titled, *Bad Luck is plaguing Marcus Mariota. Poor play is ruining Jameis Winston.* [427] Yet another article dropped from The Atlanta Journal-Constitution titled, *Is Jameis Winston the next Josh Freeman?* The article actually posited that Winston appeared to be nothing more than another Josh Freeman [428] which is of course laughably absurd to anyone who actually watched both quarterbacks play football.

At the time the Washington Post article was penned, Marcus Mariota had thrown just 10 touchdown passes to 14 interceptions and had an abysmal passer rating of 76.9. Jameis Winston on the other hand had thrown 14 touchdowns to just eight interceptions and had an 89.7 passer rating, while also leading Mariota in most advanced metrics. However Mariota's *team* was 8-4 with him as starter while Winston's *team* was atrocious. Of course, the author of the article never seems to grasp the obvious fact that perhaps the Titan defense, offensive line, special teams and run support all being better than that of the Buccaneers could have something to do with each respective team's win/loss record. [429] [430] Either that or the author grasped such an obvious fact full well and merely needed to write a hit piece on Winston to balance the NY Times' glowing and accurate piece on Winston, because, well, it just wouldn't be fitting for accurate good news relating to Jameis Winston to go unchecked as that might cause the public to realize he's a far better quarterback than they were led to believe poreviously.

As for The Atlanta Journal-Constitution article, apparently the author forgot to even research Josh Freeman before comparing Jameis Winston to him, as in Freeman's third season he threw just 16 touchdown passes against a whopping 22 interceptions, had a pathetic 74.6 passer rating and also lagged behind Winston in most advanced metrics when comparing each quarterbacks' third season. [431] [430] But hey, no one can actually expect a journalist to do something as tedious as *research* before publishing an article slandering a quarterback like Jameis Winston, right?

Game Fifteen:
Media's Winston Derangement Syndrome in Full Effect

Winston and the Buccaneers next went on the road to Carolina to face the 10-4 playoff bound Panthers and entered the game as 10 point underdogs according to the Vegas line. [432]

The game was an ugly one right from the start, though the Bucs also dominated the game and should have won easily. However once again, the Bucs appalling defense managed to steal defeat from the jaws of victory, not that the fans who were in favor of tanking minded such one bit.

Despite Panthers quarterback Cam Newton throwing for just 160 yards, no touchdowns, one interception, and recording a dreadful 65.4 passer rating, and Winston looking like prime Dan Marino in completing nearly eighty percent of his passes for 367 yards, one touchdown, no interceptions and a remarkable 131.1 passer rating, and despite the Bucs holding a 19-15 lead with just 45 seconds remaining in the game, a win wasn't in the cards for Tampa Bay. With the Panthers facing a 4th and 3 from the Buccaneer five yard line, defensive end Chris *Swaggy* Baker inexplicably lunged offside and two plays later Cam Newton recovered his own fumble and scored on a two yard touchdown run which would be the final score in a 22-19 Panthers victory. [432]

However, one more noteworthy event happened before the game ended. After a touchback on the ensuing Panthers kickoff, the Buccaneers had the ball at their own 25 yard line with 35 seconds remaining in the game and one timeout to use. On 1st and 10 Winston dropped back to pass and was strip-sacked by Kawaan Short. Winston threw himself into the pile and came out of the pile with the ball; however the referee awarded the ball to the Panthers which effectively ended the game. Winston couldn't believe the referee ignored the fact that he had recovered the fumble, and he started screaming that he had the ball while showing the ball to the referee and his teammates and trying to get the referee to change the call as it obviously should have been the Buccaneers ball and 2nd down. [432] [433]

After the game ended, almost no one was talking about how Winston had drastically outplayed Cam Newton, how he had thrown for nearly 400 yards with an unreal 131.1 passer rating, or even how he had tied Dan Marino for the most touchdown passes before his 24th birthday. [434] Instead, all anyone wanted to talk about was the recovered, err, lost, fumble that effectively ended the game.

The headlines were typical *Winston Derangement Syndrome* drivel, such as:

CBS:

Jameis Winston loses his mind after fumble that sealed the Buccaneers' loss [433]

WASHINGTON POST:

Buccaneers' Jameis Winston loses his mind after losing fumble to Panthers [435]

SPORTS ILLUSTRATED:

Jameis Winston Flips Out On Sideline After Panthers Comeback [436]

USA TODAY:

Jameis Winston throws furious tantrum at ref after losing fumble late in loss [437]

SB NATION:

Jameis Winston had a meltdown on the sideline after a game-clinching fumble [438]

Even Deadspin ran an article titled, *Jameis Winston Melts Down After Panthers Comeback*, while at the same time acknowledging that Winston seemed to personally apologize to the official upon leaving the field at the end of the game. [439] And, anyone who actually watched the game can attest to the fact that Winston did indeed run over to the official as soon as the game ended and shake his hand and smooth things over. [440]

I mean, seriously, does anyone actually believe the media would replace the name *Jameis Winston* in the above headlines with *Tom Brady* or even 2018 rookie quarterback *Sam Darnold* or recent draft pick Dwayne Haskins for that matter, if the exact same event would've occurred? I for one highly doubt it. In fact, I believe the titles would read more as follows:

Fumble Gate: Tom Brady Indignant After Official Steals Final Possession from Patriots

Sam Darnold and Jets Cheated out of Fumble Recovery by Zebras

Dwayne Haskins Overcome with Emotion after Refs Rob Redskins

In all honesty, I loved when Jameis supposedly had a *meltdown, flipped out* and *lost his mind*, as to me, such a passionate reaction showed just how much Winston cares about his craft and about winning. In fact,

163

simply compare Jameis' diving into the pile and winning a wrestling match for the ball with future Hall of Famer and man-beast Julius Peppers, in a seemingly meaningless final game in a non-playoff season, with Cam Newton's effort or lack thereof when he coughed up a fumble against the Broncos in Super Bowl 50 [441] and I imagine you'll come to the same conclusion I did.

Game Sixteen:
Ignoring the Coach in order to Win the Game

The Buccaneers' final game of the 2017 season was a home game against the 11-4 New Orleans Saints and future first ballot Hall of Fame quarterback Drew Brees. The Saints were six point favorites according to the Vegas line [442] and if they could win the game they would lock up the #3 seed in the NFC Playoffs, while the Buccaneers were out of the playoff race and many of their fans were hoping the team would lose to assure the best draft ppick possible.

In short, the Saints had everything to play for while the Bucs had nothing to play for but pride. However, *pride* is Jameis Winston's middle name. Actually, his middle name is Lanaed, but still, you get the point; Winston is a young man who takes pride in his craft and wants to win at everything he attempts, even a meaningless regular season game in a lost season.

However, one thing Winston seems to like to do almost as much as *win* is help his teammates reach their goals, and coming into the game star receiver Mike Evans desperately wanted to reach 1,000 yards receiving as he had never missed that mark since being drafted in 2014. [45] However, Evans needed 54 yards to reach 1,000 on the season and when he had played the Saints earlier in the year he had a mere 13 receiving yards in the game [443], so Evans' personal goal was anything but a *given*.

As the game progressed it was obvious to anyone watching that Winston was forcing the ball to Mike Evans in an attempt to help him achieve his personal goal of reaching 1,000 receiving yards on the season. And, by the time the game ended Evans had received more targets – 13 – than he had in any other game during the season. [443] Despite Winston's personal stats taking a hit due to trying to force balls to Evans – as Winston threw two interceptions when forcing balls to Evans and ended up only completing 38.5% of his passes to Evans while completing 60.5% of his passes to all other receivers [442] – Winston did indeed get Evans his record, as Evans finished the game with 55 yards receiving and 1,001 on the season. [443]

As for the game itself, the Saints led at the end of the first, second and third quarters and held a 24-20 lead when Winston and the Bucs took the field with just 7:07 remaining in the game. Winston then led the Bucs on a 10 play, 51 yard drive that ended with a field goal, cutting the Saints lead to 24-23 with 4:31 remaining in the game. [442]

After the Buccaneers' defense forced the Saints to punt, Winston and the offense returned to the field with just 1:58 remaining in the game, with no timeouts and pinned deep at their own 5 yard line. [444] And, after three straight incompletions, *Clutch Jameis* showed up.

Winston completed a 12 yard pass to Cam Brate on 4th and 10, followed that up with a 9 yard completion to Mike Evans, and after another incompletion, hit Mike Evans for 9 yards and again for 16 yards, and after one last incompletion, Winston hit Adam Humphries for 10 yards. At that point there was just 15 seconds remaining in the game, and the Bucs were still 39 yards from the end zone. [442]

Buccaneers head coach Dirk Koetter then called for a pass to the left sideline to set up an attempt at a game-winning field goal. *Clutch Jameis* ignored Koetter, saw that rookie receiver Chris Godwin had one-on-one coverage and launched a gorgeous deep pass down the right sideline which dropped right into the hands of Godwin who crossed the goal-line giving the Bucs the victory and dropping the Saints from the #3 seed to the #4 seed. [445] [446]

On that final drive of the season, Winston led an 11 play – all pass plays by the way – 95 yard game-winning touchdown drive with less than 2 minutes remaining in the game. [442] Amazingly, this was the first time any quarterback in the past decade had led such a drive [447] and Winston did it without any timeouts to boot. That said, it can accurately be said that Jameis Winston led the most clutch game-winning drive in the NFL in the past 10 years that day!

The Statistical Juxtaposition between Healthy Jameis and Injured Jameis

The juxtaposition between Jameis Winston's healthy games – that is the 10 games he was able to start and finish with a healthy throwing shoulder – and his 3 injured games was dramatic.

In Winston's three unhealthy games he completed just 54.1% of his passes, threw zero touchdowns against two interceptions, and had a terrible 56.6 passer rating. However in his 10 healthy games, he completed 65.4% of his passes, threw 19 touchdowns against nine interceptions, and had a 98.0 passer rating [430] which would have ranked 8th in the NFL on the year. [448]

Likewise, Winston averaged 316.6 passing yards per game during those 10 healthy games. In fact, he even averaged 306.9 passing yards per full start, meaning any game he simply wasn't knocked out of with an injury. [430] Tom Brady won the passing yardage crown in 2017 and he averaged just 286.1 passing yards per game. [448]

The above said, Jameis Winston literally obliterated Tom Brady's league-leading passing yards per game mark in his healthy starts by over ten percent, and in all his full starts, even including ones where he played injured, by over seven percent.

In short, Jameis Winston was bad when he played injured, but to steal a phrase from Stephen A. Smith – an analyst infected with *Winston*

Derangement Syndrome sadly – he was also a baaaaaaaaaaaaaaaaaaaaaad man when he was healthy!

Accolades and Achievements

When the 2017 regular season ended, Jameis Winston was #1 all-time in NFL history in both career passing touchdowns and career passing yards before the age of 24. [449] However, it wasn't merely Winston's career numbers that moved him to the top of the class but his 2017 numbers as well.

Along with Winston throwing for 306.9 yards per full game and a whopping 316.6 yards per healthy full game, both of which would have easily earned Winston the passing yardage crown in the 2017 season [430] [448], Winston also led the NFL in total 300 yard passing games, despite only playing 11 full games, in a season in which 23 other quarterbacks started more games than Winston did. [448] [450]

Winston also finished 5th in the entire NFL in Passing Plus-Minus [451] which is a magnificent advanced metric that, according to Football Outsiders:

> *estimates how many passes a quarterback completed above or below what an average quarterback would have completed, given the location of those passes. It does not consider passes listed as "Thrown Away," "Tipped at Line," or "Quarterback Hit in Motion." Player performance is compared to a historical baseline of how often a pass is completed based on the pass distance, the distance required for a first down, and whether the ball was thrown to the left, middle, or right side of the field.* [451]

To finish 5th in the entire NFL in Passing Plus-Minus, especially at Winston's young age was remarkable. In fact, none of the other top 13 quarterbacks in the NFL were under the age of 29, while Winston finished the season at just 23 years of age!

Also, according to the NFL and their *Next Gen Stats*, Winston also finished the 2017 season:

2nd in the entire NFL in *Average Completed Air Yards* (CAY) [452] which is described as:

> *CAY shows the average Air Yards a passer throws on completions ... This metric shows how far the ball is being thrown 'downfield'. Air Yards is recorded as a negative value when the pass is behind the Line of Scrimmage. Additionally Air Yards is calculated into the back of the end zone to better evaluate the true depth of the pass.* [375]

3rd in the entire NFL in *Averaged Intended Air Yards* (IAY) [452] which is described as:

> *IAY shows the average Air Yards a passer throws on all attempts. This metric shows how far the ball is being thrown 'downfield'. Air Yards is recorded as a negative value when the pass is behind the Line of Scrimmage. Additionally Air Yards is calculated into the back of the end zone to better evaluate the true depth of the pass.* [375]

3rd in the entire NFL in *Air Yards to the Sticks* (AYTS) [452] which is described as:

> *Air Yards to the Sticks shows the amount of Air Yards ahead or behind the first down marker on all attempts for a passer. The metric indicates if the passer is attempting his passes past the 1st down marker, or if he is relying on his skill position players to make yards after catch.* [375]

5th in the entire NFL in *Completion Percentage Above Expectation* (+/-) [452] which is described as:

A passer's actual completion percentage compared to their Expected Completion Percentage. [375]

And, for those of you who weren't incredibly impressed by the detailed *Next Gen Stats*, read the above section again. The accomplishments it details are absurdly impressive and paint a very clear picture of just how elite Jameis Winston's 2016 season was according to the advanced metrics.

The Most Accomplished
23 Year Old Quarterback in NFL History!

When Jameis Winston's third season concluded, he once again found himself atop the record books for quarterbacks of his age, as no quarterback in NFL history had ever thrown for more career yards or touchdowns before the age of 24, not a single one, not Marino, not Manning, not Favre, not Tarkenton, no one! [449]

Simply put, there has never been a more statistically accomplished 23 year old quarterback in the history of the NFL than Jameis Winston, not a single one, and it's not even debatable.

JAMEIS WINSTON vs. THE GREATS

PART III

A lot of times I find that people who are blessed with the most talent don't ever develop that attitude, and the ones who aren't blessed in that way are the most competitive and have the biggest heart.

– Tom Brady [453]

Jameis Winston may be known for taking risks on the field other quarterbacks won't take and for never giving up on a play even when doing so would be the wise decision. However, no one who has ever played with or coached Jameis Winston would question his heart. [15] [415] [454]

Winston's third season was no exception as he played through a serious throwing shoulder injury and returned after missing just three games when many expected him to miss far more time. [405] [411] [412] [415] [419]

It's now time to jump into the comparisons between Winston and the 21 legendary quarterbacks I've compared him with throughout this book.

Age Related Statistical Comparisons

As I did in the previous *Part I* and *Part II* versions of this chapter, I will compare Winston to the 21 current or soon to be Hall of Fame quarterbacks who began their careers in the Super Bowl era, by age. Likewise, I will once again compare each player in the following four categories: passing yards, passing touchdowns, completion percentage and passer rating.

Before Age 24 Stats	Pass Yards	Pass TDs	Comp %	Passer Rating
Jameis Winston	**11636**	**69**	**60.8**	**87.2**
Troy Aikman	3765	17	53.8	59.2
Terry Bradshaw	3669	19	48.4	46.6
Tom Brady	6	0	33.3	42.4
Drew Brees	3505	18	60.6	77.8
John Elway	1663	7	47.5	54.9
Brett Favre	3926	22	62.8	80.2
Dan Fouts	2858	14	46.9	54.5
Bob Griese	4478	36	51.3	68.9
Jim Kelly	0	0	DNP	DNP
Eli Manning	1043	6	48.2	55.4
Peyton Manning	7874	52	59.3	80.6
Dan Marino	7453	68	62.0	102.7
Joe Montana	96	1	56.5	81.1
Warren Moon	0	0	DNP	DNP
Philip Rivers	33	1	62.5	110.9
Aaron Rodgers	329	1	59.3	73.3
Ben Roethlisberger	5006	34	64.7	98.3
Ken Stabler	0	0	DNP	DNP
Roger Staubach	0	0	DNP	DNP
Kurt Warner	0	0	DNP	DNP
Steve Young	0	0	DNP	DNP

[141] [230] [348.1] [231] [232] [233] [234] [235] [380.1] [236] [237] [238] [239] [240] [241] [381.1] [242] [243] [244] [245] [211] [246] [247] [248] [249]

Just as with the *Before Age 22 Stats* and *Before Age 23 Stats* tables detailed in the *Part 1* and *Part II* versions of this chapter, one can easily see that Jameis Winston is infinitely more statistically accomplished as an NFL passer before turning 24 years of age than any of the 21 legendary quarterbacks. In fact, Winston has more career passing yards and passing touchdowns by the age of 24 than any other quarterback in NFL history. [449]

171

Junior Season Statistical Comparisons

While Jameis Winston has accumulated more career passing yards and passing TDs than any of the 21 legendary quarterbacks before the age of 24, I will now compare his third season alone, with each of their third seasons.

Below is a statistical table comparing Winston's third season with the third seasons of the other 21 quarterbacks, regardless of each quarterbacks age. And, per the usual, I will compare each of the 22 quarterbacks in the four prime categories: passing yards, passing touchdowns, completion percentage and passer rating.

3rd Year Stats	Pass Yards	Pass TDs	Comp %	Passer Rating
Jameis Winston	**3504**	**19**	**63.8**	**92.2**
Troy Aikman	2754	11	65.3	86.7
Terry Bradshaw	1887	12	47.7	64.1
Tom Brady	3764	28	62.1	85.7
Drew Brees	2108	11	57.6	67.5
John Elway	3891	22	54.0	70.2
Brett Favre	3303	19	60.9	72.2
Dan Fouts	1396	2	54.4	59.3
Bob Griese	1695	10	48.0	56.9
Jim Kelly	3380	15	59.5	78.2
Eli Manning	3244	24	57.7	77.0
Peyton Manning	4413	33	62.5	94.7
Dan Marino	4137	30	59.3	84.1
Joe Montana	3565	19	63.7	88.4
Warren Moon	3489	13	52.5	62.3
Philip Rivers	3388	22	61.7	92.0
Aaron Rodgers	218	1	71.4	106.0
Ben Roethlisberger	3513	18	59.7	75.4
Ken Stabler	524	4	59.5	82.3
Roger Staubach	1882	15	59.7	104.8
Kurt Warner	3429	21	67.7	98.3

Steve Young	570	10	53.6	120.8

[141] [230] [231] [232] [233] [234] [235] [236] [237] [238] [239] [240] [241] [242] [243] [244] [245] [211] [246] [247] [248] [249]

After viewing the above statistical table, one can easily see how Jameis Winston – even while missing three full games and parts of two other games due to a serious throwing shoulder injury [412] – compared favorably to the other 21 quarterbacks in regards to the standard counting stats. Winston had the seventh most passing yards, eighth most touchdown passes and third best completion percentage of any of the quarterbacks, as well as the fifth best passer rating of any of the quarterbacks to throw for at least 219 passing yards.

Through Junior Season Statistical Comparisons

In this section, I will compare Jameis Winston's stats *through* his third season with the aforementioned 21 quarterbacks *through* their third seasons, irrespective of age. And, per the usual, in the below statistical table I will compare each of the 22 quarterbacks in the four prime categories: passing yards, passing touchdowns, completion percentage and passer rating.

Through 3rd Year Stats	Pass Yards	Pass TDs	Comp %	Passer Rating
Jameis Winston	**11636**	**69**	**60.8**	**87.2**
Troy Aikman	7082	31	58.6	70.5
Terry Bradshaw	5556	31	48.2	52.6
Tom Brady	6613	46	62.7	85.9
Drew Brees	5613	29	59.4	73.7
John Elway	8152	47	53.4	69.0
Brett Favre	6530	37	62.2	77.3
Dan Fouts	4254	16	49.2	56.0
Bob Griese	6173	46	50.4	65.7
Jim Kelly	9771	56	59.5	81.8
Eli Manning	8049	54	54.1	73.2
Peyton Manning	12287	85	60.4	85.4
Dan Marino	11431	98	61.0	96.4

Joe Montana	5456	35	63.8	88.0
Warren Moon	9536	40	54.4	69.1
Philip Rivers	3536	23	61.4	90.5
Aaron Rodgers	329	1	59.3	73.3
Ben Roethlisberger	8519	52	62.4	87.9
Ken Stabler	844	5	54.3	61.6
Roger Staubach	2845	18	56.8	84.7
Kurt Warner	7821	62	65.8	104.0
Steve Young	3787	21	53.3	71.1

[141] [230] [231] [232] [233] [234] [235] [236] [237] [238] [239] [240] [241] [242] [243] [244] [245] [211] [246] [247] [248] [249]

After viewing the above statistical table, one can see that Jameis Winston, through his third season, had the second most career passing yards, the third most career touchdown passes, the eighth best career completion percentage and the sixth best career passer rating when compared to the other 21 legendary quarterbacks through their respective first three seasons in the NFL.

Likewise, of the other 21 quarterbacks, the only ones to best Winston in at least two of the four categories were Peyton Manning, Dan Marino, Joe Montana, Philip Rivers, Ben Roetlisberger and Kurt Warner, and the only quarterback to best Winston in three of the four categories was Dan Marino. No quarterback bested Winston in all four categories.

The above said, while Winston is undoubtedly the most statistically accomplished 23 year old quarterback in NFL history, it's also clear that he has a very strong claim to also having had one of very best first three seasons in quarterback history as well, irrespective of age.

Adjusted for Era Statistical Comparisons

As I did in the *Part 1* and *Part II* versions of this chapter, in this adjusted for era section I will forego the mere *counting stats* and focus on the advanced metrics of passing yards per attempt (Y/A), touchdown percentage (TD %), completion percentage (Comp %), as well as Raw QBR (if such was available in each respective players rookie season) or passer rating (if Raw QBR was not available in each respective players rookie season) to really get an ultra-accurate picture of just how Jameis Winston compares to the aforementioned 21 legendary quarterbacks.

Furthermore, rather than merely listing each player's Y/A, TD%, Comp % and Raw QBR / Passer Rating during his junior season – which still does not adjust for era whatsoever – I will list where each player ranked across his league and even adjust said ranking for a 32 team league which the modern NFL has.

For example, if in a particular quarterback's junior season there were only 16 teams, and he finished 8th in the league in touchdown percentage, such would be akin to him finishing 16th in the modern 32 team NFL and therefore he will receive a ranking of 16th in the TD % category.

The formula I will use to determine each quarterback's league ranking in a particular category is: league rank, divided by qualifying quarterbacks, times 32. However, if there are more qualifying quarterbacks than there are teams, the formula would be league rank, divided by league teams, times 32.

Furthermore, if a particular quarterback did not qualify in all four statistical categories, it will say DNQ (i.e. Did Not Qualify) in all four of that quarterbacks' categories as well as in the *Average Rank* (Avg. Rank) category. However, if a quarterback qualifies in even one category, I will use his stats to rank him in the other categories, such as I did with Terry Bradshaw's fourth season (in *Jameis Winston vs. the Greats Part IV* chapter) in 1973, as in that season Bradshaw qualified in passer rating but not in completion percentage (where he was worse than the last place qualifier and would have therefore ranked 18th, but as there were only 17 quarterbacks who qualified he is ranked 34th, as his 18th ranking, divided by 17 qualifying quarterbacks, times 32 teams, equals 33.888 or a ranking of 34th in a 32 team league which the current NFL has). [254]

Also, if a quarterback started at least five games in a season, I will rank him even if he doesn't technically qualify in a specific category. Such is the case with Steve Young in his 1985 rookie season [255], as well as Eli Manning in his 2004 rookie season. [256]

Finally, I need to mention that while I have relied on pro-football-reference.com a great deal when researching for this book, and while such is an amazing website, it can be a little confusing for some when they are researching seasonal statistical *rankings* when two or more players *tie* to the decimal point in any particular category. For example, the site can at times show Dan Marino incorrectly ranked 2nd in TD % in his rookie season of 1983, when he was slight percentage points behind Neil Lomax and therefore truly should be ranked 3rd. However rest assured, I have done the math and made sure that every single one of the rankings I provide are absolutely correct. Please feel free to double-check my math for yourself in order to confirm that I am 100% correct each and every time.

All of the above said, the following table details how Jameis Winston compares to each of the 21 legendary quarterbacks when adjusted for era, as well as how each of those quarterbacks compare to each other.

3rd Year Ranking	Y/A	TD %	Comp %	PR / QBR	Avg. Rank
Jameis Winston	**4th**	**17th**	**12th**	**18th**	**13th**
Troy Aikman	4th	22nd	2nd	6th	8th
Terry Bradshaw	29th	24th	27th	20th	25th
Tom Brady	25th	9th	10th	9th	13th
Drew Brees	28th	26th	18th	29th	25th
John Elway	24th	24th	18th	19th	21st
Brett Favre	20th	16th	11th	21st	17th
Dan Fouts	14th	32nd	14th	28th	22nd
Bob Griese	21st	21st	28th	29th	25th
Jim Kelly	9th	24th	6th	15th	13th
Eli Manning	28th	11th	21st	17th	19th
Peyton Manning	5th	5th	6th	6th	5th
Dan Marino	9th	6th	6th	6th	7th
Joe Montana	11th	19th	1st	5th	9th
Warren Moon	18th	27th	25th	31st	25th
Philip Rivers	8th	8th	14th	4th	8th
Aaron Rodgers	DNQ	DNQ	DNQ	DNQ	DNQ
Ben Roethlisberger	7th	17th	19th	14th	14th

Ken Stabler	DNQ	DNQ	DNQ	DNQ	DNQ
Roger Staubach	1st	3rd	5th	1st	2nd
Kurt Warner	1st	3rd	1st	3rd	2nd
Steve Young	DNQ	DNQ	DNQ	DNQ	DNQ

[448] [262] [457] [385] [458] [255] [218] [459] [268] [460] [461] [259] [255] [462] [264] [461] [463] [461] [457] [384] [259] [389]

Note: Dan Fouts was tied for 22nd in a 26 team league in PR at 59.26 with Detroit's Joe Reed, so I used 22.5 / 26 x 32 to get a rank of 28th.

After viewing the above statistical table, it's obvious to anyone other than those infected with *Winston Derangement Syndrome* that Winston's junior season compared favorably to the 21 legendary quarterbacks, even when adjusted for era.

In fact, Winston had a better junior season than all but seven of the 21 legendary quarterbacks listed. The only quarterbacks who had a better average rank than Winston were Joe Montana, Dan Marino, Peyton Manning, Kurt Warner, Philip Rivers, Troy Aikman and Roger Staubach.

And, of those seven quarterbacks that did have better junior seasons than Winston, every single one of them was older than Winston, with both Kurt Warner and Roger Staubach being nearly six full years older than Winston when each player was in their third season. [430] [455] [456]

Through Junior Season
Adjusted for Era Statistical Comparisons

As I did in the previous section, I will now compare the adjusted for era statistics of Jameis Winston and the 21 legendary quarterbacks, this time comparing each quarterback's first three seasons, rather than merely their junior season alone.

In regards to how the rankings are calculated, it's a simple matter of adding and dividing. For example if a quarterback ranked third in yards per attempt in his first season, fourth in the same category in his second season and eighth in his third season, he would receive a ranking of fifth in the following table in the yards per attempt category. And, as it's a matter of simple math that anyone can do, there are no citations following the table, as I do not assign a citation to my own original statistical tables.

Through 3rd Year Rankings	Y/A	TD %	Comp %	PR / QBR	Avg. Rank
Jameis Winston	**10th**	**17th**	**22nd**	**14th**	**16th**
Troy Aikman	21st	26th	15th	23rd	21st
Terry Bradshaw	27th	25th	23rd	26th	25th
Tom Brady*	21st	11th	7th	8th	12th
Drew Brees*	27th	28th	18th	27th	25th
John Elway	26th	22nd	22nd	23rd	23rd
Brett Favre*	22nd	18th	8th	15th	16th
Dan Fouts	17th	26th	25th	29th	24th
Bob Griese	24th	21st	18th	19th	21st
Jim Kelly	15th	17th	6th	12th	13th
Eli Manning	26th	18th	29th	25th	25th
Peyton Manning	10th	8th	9th	11th	10th
Dan Marino	7th	3rd	9th	3rd	6th
Joe Montana*	18th	14th	1st	6th	10th
Warren Moon	15th	25th	21st	24th	21st
Philip Rivers**	8th	8th	14th	4th	9th
Aaron Rodgers***	DNQ	DNQ	DNQ	DNQ	DNQ
Ben Roethlisberger	3rd	8th	11th	7th	7th
Ken Stabler***	DNQ	DNQ	DNQ	DNQ	DNQ
Roger Staubach**	1st	3rd	5th	1st	3rd
Kurt Warner*	1st	2nd	1st	2nd	2nd
Steve Young*	23rd	31st	22nd	29th	26th

* Each asterisk represents one season that the respective quarterback did not qualify to be ranked. For example, Aaron Rodgers never qualified to be ranked in any of his first three seasons while Roger Staubach qualified just once and Joe Montana qualified twice.

After viewing the above statistical table, it's clear that Winston's first three NFL seasons compare favorably to the first three seasons of the 21 legendary quarterbacks, even when adjusted for era.

The only quarterbacks who had a better average rank than Winston, who actually qualified to be ranked in each of their first three seasons, were: Dan Marino, Peyton Manning, Ben Roethlisberger and Jim Kelly.

The indisputable fact is that the hard data covered in this chapter proves that Jameis Winston is more statistically accomplished than any of the 21 legendary quarterbacks, before the age of 24. Such hard data also proves that Winston had one of the best junior seasons of any such quarterback in regards to the counting stats. The data also confirms that Winston had, at worst, the 8th best junior season of said quarterbacks, even when adjusting for era! Finally, such hard data even confirms that Winston had the 5th best first three season start to his NFL career when compared to the 21 legendary quarterbacks and when adjusting for era!

#METOO & JABOO

It is proof of a base and low mind for one to wish to think with the masses or majority, merely because the majority is the majority. Truth does not change because it is, or is not, believed by a majority of the people.

– Giordano Bruno [464]

As stated in the *Personal Note from the Author* in the front matter of this book, any decent human being should denounce sexual harassment, assault and the like. In fact, such a statement should be a given in a civilized society. Likewise, any man or woman who has been convicted or been proven to have sexually assaulted another man or woman, deserves to not only be denounced by the public but to be punished for his or her crimes by the justice system.

I have personally witnessed the pain and suffering that envelops a woman who has reported a sexual assault and never received the justice she sought, as I took my own sister when she was in high school to the police when she filed her rape complaint, and to this day she has never received the justice she sought. I even know what it feels like to be the victim of – at the very least – an *attempted* sexual assault when I was still in grade school. However, I was able to escape the grasp of an adult male and run into and lock myself in my house when he tried to molest me.

The above said, please do not misinterpret anything written in this book as unsympathetic to any man, woman or child who has been sexually assaulted. Also, please do not misinterpret anything written in this book as a defense of assault of any kind.

Finally, please do not misinterpret anything written in this book as some sort of attack on the Democratic or Republican parties. I do not live in America, was not born in America and certainly do not vote in American elections. Also, as a Biblical Christian theologian that believes I owe 100% of my allegiance to my Lord and Savior Jesus Christ of Nazareth, no matter who the secular leader is at any given time I love and pray for that person whether I agree with their policies or not. In short, I'm probably unlike anyone you've ever met before, unless you know another theologian that has also studied NFL quarterbacks for decades, invests in high-end collectibles, quotes Tupac Shakur, Thomas Sowell and Gandhi, and gets mistaken for an Eastern Orthodox priest at times.

All of the above said, I do however strongly believe in the innocent until *proven* guilty concept. Likewise, I strongly believe that judging an innocent person to be guilty is just as reprehensible as judging a guilty person to be innocent. Furthermore, I do not believe in playing God, pretending to be omniscient, or judging individuals based on unknowable actions or events. I believe in hard data, proof, statistics and the like and in following the evidence wherever it leads. I hope you can respect these viewpoints of mine even if you don't agree with everything you read in the following pages of this chapter.

Regardless, it is never wise to simply believe the majority on any issue, especially when the known evidence and established truths do not fit with the majority's view on a particular issue. This said, my goal for this chapter is simply to relay factual information and to examine both sides of a he-said / she-said regarding an incident without witnesses, so that the reader may draw their own informed conclusion.

The Me Too Movement

The *Me Too Movement* is a largely social media based movement dedicated to denouncing sexual assault and harassment, two things any sane individual should support whether there is a *movement* about such or not. The movement became popular when the hashtag *#MeToo* spread virally on Twitter and Facebook in late 2017 [465] following sexual-abuse accusations against Hollywood director Harvey Weinstein [466] of *The Weinstein Company*, the same company founded by Harvey Weinstein himself, and which had distributed *The Hunting Ground* film [57] which had been exposed for having a bias against, and for slandering, Jameis Winston. [58] [63] [64]

The above said, the simple fact is that while the *Me Too Movement* has done good and has deserved much of the praise it has received at various times, it has also become more about social justice than legal justice. For example, it often lends itself to mob rule rather than the rule of law, and such never seems to work out well in the long run. Likewise, the movement has also been exposed for its blatant hypocrisy many times.

For example, actress Asia Argento, one of the first women to accuse Harvey Weinstein and therefore be identified with the *Me Too Movement*, was herself found to have settled a sexual assault case against her involving a child. [467] [468]

Further examples are actress Alyssa Milano – one of the leading figures of the *Me Too Movement* and a woman who helped popularize the phrase *believe all women* – as well as actress Whoopi Goldberg and even United States *Speaker of the House* Nancy Pelosi, each of whom made statements that many believed denigrated Lucy Flores. Flores is a former Democratic nominee for Lieutenant Governor of Nevada who called out former Vice President Joe Biden for demeaning her and for touching her in an intimate way uninvited. [469] [470]

Hypocritical or not, the *Me Too Movement* wielded a great deal of power at the time it was first reported on November 17, 2017 by *Buzzfeed News* that Jameis Winston had been accused by an *Uber* driver known only as *Kate P* of touching her uninvited back on March 13, 2016. [471] And, whether Winston was actually guilty of what he was originally accused of – let alone any of the accuser's three subsequent versions of her accusation – or whether he was in fact entirely innocent, wouldn't make much difference to those who believed in the *Me Too Movement*, the *believe all women* catchphrase, or those who simply disliked Winston for any reason whatsoever. To such folks, an accusation was as good as a conviction.

As Canadian author, journalist, broadcaster – and the person billed as *Canada's first female sports* columnist – Christie Blatchford [472] once wrote:

> *For #MeToo, there simply is no road back from an allegation of sexual assault. An accused man must pay forever. He will pay forever. ... Does one act define a man forever? if ... you have offended the little crazy children of #MeToo, the answer is yes.* [473]

The Uber Dilemma

The facts and timeline of the Kate P. vs. Jameis Winston in Arizona fiasco – which Winston will likely always be vilified for by many, whether innocent or guilty – will be detailed on the following pages.

Unsubstantiated Allegation – Version One

On March 13, 2016 in Arizona, Kate P. initially accused one of her *unknown* Uber passengers of putting his fingers on her crotch in a report she filed with Uber, which stated:

> *we stopped to get food at a Mexican drive thru. while we were stopped, out of the clear blue, this rider reached over and put his fingers on my crotch. It wasn't accidental, and it was only for a very brief moment. It wasn't my stomach or my thigh, it was my crotch and I want to be clear about that. I was totally shocked, and I shook him off and just said, what's up with that? ... the rest of the ride proceeded without incident.* [471]

The above wording, which Kate P. used in filing her incident report with Uber is quite serious. If Jameis Winston literally touched her crotch – as in made contact with her literal vagina, which is what the website

HollywoodLife.com falsely reported happened [474] – that is obviously far different than touching the outside of her pants over the crotch area.

Unsubstantiated Allegation – Version Two

However, that Kate P. was initially only accusing Winston of touching the outside of her pants can easily be understood by reading the text she sent to her personal friend later that same day, which stated:

> *I had a weird incident with a rider, an nfl qb named jameis Winston. I was getting food for him at a drive through and he totally touched my fu**ing (redaction added) crotch, like grazed his fingers over my pants while we were waiting. Like extremely inappropriate.* [471]

The above text being what it is, it is quite clear that Kate P. initially accused Winston of touching the outside of her pants and certainly not of touching her literal vagina, despite what HollywoodLife.com falsely reported. [474] In fact, Kate P. elaborated on her Uber report when texting her personal friend and made it clear that not only did Winston only touch the outside of her pants but that he merely grazed his fingers over her pants as well.

Now, do I believe that anyone – man or woman – should be allowed to graze their fingers over the outside of the crotch area of another's pants uninvited? Of course not! However, is doing such a thing *sexual assault*? No; it is not. That is just a fact, even if one does not like such a fact. If it were sexual assault, the Police would be called to nearly every bar, every night, to arrest multiple men and women who did such while attempting to make a pass at another individual.

Again, I am a Biblical Christian, so I don't even condone getting inebriated one single time in one's life, let alone trying to *hook up* with someone at a club, etc. I am merely pointing out that what Jameis Winston was initially accused of, is something that actually passes for acceptable behavior among many – and perhaps even most – these days.

The Rest of the Ride Proceeded Without Incident

It is also pertinent to draw attention to the fact that even in Kate P's initial report to Uber, she stated that "the rest of the ride proceeded without incident". That said, I find it strange that many of Winston's detractors like to portray him as some type of sexual predator, yet when he was alone in a vehicle, heavily inebriated, and after he allegedly had already made a pass and touched the crotch area of the outside of the driver's pants, all she had to say was "What's up with that?" and the ride then "proceeded without incident".

How many heavily inebriated sexual predators, who had already made a pass at an individual, touched them uninvited, and with no witnesses around, would fail to make a further advance, a lewd comment, etc., after merely being asked, "What's up with that?" I wonder if there is one such individual on earth.

Unsubstantiated Allegation – Version Three

Kate P. never filed a police report of any kind [475], seeing as what she had accused Winston of was not a crime. However, 20 months later, on November 17, 2017, *Buzzfeed News* published an article in which Kate P. embellished her initial and even her second clarified version of her accusation against Winston. This time she said that Winston *grabbed her crotch* and even that he held his hand on her crotch for 3-5 seconds [471], which amounted to her telling a new, third version of her story.

Kate P. further stated to *Buzzfeed News*:

> *I have been empowered by my sisters who have forged this path by speaking up, and I must do my part to make it a little more well traveled ... He sexually assaulted me, and I have every right to tell the d**n* [redaction added] *truth about it.* [471]

The problem with Kate P's above statement – other than that it was the third version she told of the alleged incident – is that it isn't true.

No Sexual Assault Occurred

According to the Criminal Code of Arizona – specifically *Criminal Code § 13-1406* – sexual assault can only be committed if one has engaged in actual intercourse or engaged in oral sexual contact [476]. Under no circumstances is touching the outside of one's pants, be it brushing one's fingers across the top of another's pants, holding one's fingers on top of another's pants for 3-5 seconds, or even grabbing the outside of another's pants over the crotch area – that is, any of Kate P's three different versions of the alleged event – considered *sexual assault* according to the law. Such a fact may offend you, but such is a fact nonetheless.

Initial Statements from Winston and Darby

After the *Buzzfeed News* article dropped, Jameis Winston released a statement that said:

> *A news organization has published a story about me regarding an alleged incident involving a female Uber driver from approximately two years ago. The story falsely accuses me of making inappropriate contact with this driver. I believe the driver was confused as to the number of passengers in the car and who was sitting next to her. The accusation is false, and given the nature of the allegation and increased awareness and consideration of these types of matters, I am addressing this false report immediately. ... I am supportive of the national movement to raise awareness and develop better responses to the concerns of parties who find themselves in these types of situations, but this accusation is false. While I am certain that I did not make any inappropriate contact, I don't want to engage in a battle with the driver and I regret if my demeanor or presence made her uncomfortable in any way.* [471]

Likewise, Eagles star cornerback Ronald Darby, who was with Winston on the night in question, also came forward and publicly stated:

> *I felt the need to come forward and clarify some inaccurate accounts of the evening of March 13, 2016 when myself, a friend and Jameis Winston took an Uber ride in Arizona ... There were three of us in the car, not just one as has been reported. Myself and Jameis were in the backseat. I am confident that nothing inappropriate in nature happened in the car that evening and Jameis did not have any physical contact with the Uber driver. The accusations are just not true.* [477]

Biased Main Stream Media Strikes Again

I do not know of one single media organization or even mainstream media member who pointed out the fact that Kate P told multiple versions of her allegation, or the fact that even had Winston done what he was accused of, such would not be sexual assault, which Kate P claimed it was. Not even the local Tampa, Florida media mentioned such facts in their articles, tweets and the like, even when I personally as well as other members of the general public alerted them to the fact that they were blatantly ignoring facts that called Kate P's allegation into question.

However, there were many main stream media organizations and members that did falsely report that a *friend* of Winston's went on the record to throw Winston under the bus.

On June 22, 2018, Ronald Darby's friend, Brandon Banks [478], through his attorney Mark Scruggs – who was appealing Banks' rape conviction at the time he talked about Winston [479] – detailed that while he and Darby and Winston were all in an Uber together on the night in question, later on, after Winston became inebriated and unruly, Winston was sent home alone in another Uber. This second Uber was apparently the one driven by Kate P, and therefore the alleged incident – at least one of Kate P's multiple versions of said alleged incident – at least potentially could have occurred. [478]

While it was obvious from Darby's original statement that Banks was *his* personal friend and not a friend of Winston's, and while Banks' own attorney made it explicitly clear that while Banks was a friend of Darby's, he was a mere *acquaintance* of Winston [480], various main stream and independent media outlets published articles stating that Banks was Winston's friend even though they knew such was entirely false. [479] [481] [482]

Proverbs 20:1

The NFL never spoke with Banks or with his attorney [480], possibly because they didn't view someone in prison on a rape conviction who was in the process of appealing said conviction as a credible witness. However, the league did determine that Winston was at least alone with the Uber driver for one leg of the trip. [483]

And, according to the NFL Network's Tom Pelissero, Winston had already told the NFL in the past that while he does not believe he did what he was accused of, he was inebriated and doesn't remember everything that happened that night. [484]

As a man who was raised by an alcoholic father who repented of his sins and bowed his knee to the Lord Jesus Christ about a year after I did the same, and who has now been sober for years and truly represents the *new creature* the Bible speaks of (see 2 Corinthians 5:17), I can certainly personally attest to how faulty his memory could be after he had been drinking heavily. In fact, not only did he often have no recollection of things he had done, but he also could have been convinced he did things he never did, as he simply didn't remember one way or the other.

Nevertheless, Pelissero also confirmed that from what he understood, Winston had indeed stopped drinking since the night in question and hadn't taken a drink of alcohol in over a year. Pelissero also said that when he spoke with Bucs team officials, they said that Winston was the person that they'd hoped he would be off the field. [484]

Suspension Announced

According to the original *Buzzfeed News* report, Kate P. said that she didn't want any money from Jameis Winston and that she merely came forward to tell the truth. [471] The NFL apparently took her at her word and conducted an extremely thorough investigation that did not end until June 28, 2018 when the NFL issued a three game suspension to Winston. [485]

The NFL's press release stated:

> *Based on the investigation, the NFL found that Winston had violated the NFL Personal Conduct Policy, which allows for discipline to be imposed even when criminal charges are not presented.*

> *In his letter advising Winston of the suspension, Jones stated after full consideration of the record, including a meeting with Winston and his representatives, and a written submission by his attorneys, that the driver's account of the incident was consistent and credible.* [485]

Consistent and Credible?

The NFL did not elaborate on how or why it found Kate P's account *consistent* considering the fact that she told three different versions of the alleged incident and did not have any actual *evidence* that such an incident even occurred. However, as the NFL has never needed actual evidence of any wrongdoing to suspend a player, the NFL's statement should not have shocked anyone.

As for the NFL finding Kate P *credible*, that isn't surprising either, especially considering that many attorneys and even full juries and judges have found various accusers so *credible* that they have believed their unsubstantiated accusations and jailed individuals who were later found to be innocent and to have been wrongly convicted, such as former Atlanta

Falcons' linebacker Brian Banks. [66] Of course, as Kate P. never even filed a police report [475] and as an NFL investigation is more about public perception than actual justice, and is in no way related to a true court of law, the NFL finding Kate P. *credible* is not proof whatsoever that any of the three versions of her accusation were actually credible in any legal sense of the word.

Simply put, an NFL investigation is not *credible* in regards to establishing whether or not any individual player actually committed a crime of any kind, or even in establishing whether any individual player committed a non-criminal act, especially a non-criminal act for which there was no witness and no evidence said act ever occurred.

Furthermore, I can't recall one single main stream media member asking whether Kate P could be trusted after giving three different versions of events. However, many main stream media members were more than happy to paint Winston as an absolute liar, simply because he stated that there were other passengers in the Uber. [486] [487] [488]

However, Winston did not lie. He may not have told the full truth – and that would be fitting if due to his intoxication on the night in question and lack of memory, he simply didn't know the full story – but there isn't a single sentence in his original statement that can justly be called a *lie*. The NFL itself confirmed that Winston was *not* the only passenger in the Uber on the night in question. And, the NFL certainly never established that there was any legitimate evidence that Winston did what he was accused of. Yes, the NFL did establish that during *one leg* of the Uber trip, Winston was alone with the driver for a time, but that information does not make even one single sentence of Winston's original statement a *lie*.

Regardless, I am not saying that Winston did not lie, just as I am not saying that Kate P. did lie about all the different versions she told of the alleged event, as one of them could be accurate. I absolutely refuse to play God and I am wise enough to acknowledge that as I wasn't in the Uber that night, I do not know for certain what happened. Therefore, I refuse to condemn or exonerate either Jameis Winston or Kate P. in this singular incident. I choose to simply let the actual *known* facts speak for themselves.

However, I do know that if a media member can feel confident in saying that Winston lied, simply because while every word of his original statement may have been true it may not have revealed additional information that media member wishes it revealed, that same media member most definitely could also, at the very least, question the truthfulness of Kate P., as it can absolutely be proven that she told multiple versions of her account of the alleged incident and that she accused Winston of sexual assault even though she never filed a police report and even though what she accused him of is not even considered sexual assault according to the law. [476] However, the media has never seemed to care about being logical or fair when it comes to Jameis Winston, so such questions about Kate P. and her multiple versions were covered up by the main stream media, and even by the local Tampa, Florida media.

An Optics Rather than Evidence Based Suspension

While the NFL did state that it found Kate P. consistent and credible, the fact is that the NFL only slapped Winston with a three game suspension. The three games were one less game than the NFL slapped Tom Brady with for "conduct detrimental to the integrity of the NFL" [489] due to his role in the infamous *Deflategate* when the New England Patriots were caught deflating footballs during the 2014 *AFC Championship Game* [490] [491] [492], but more specifically because according to the NFL there was:

> *substantial and credible evidence to conclude you were at least generally aware of the actions of the Patriots' employees involved in the deflation of the footballs and that it was unlikely that their actions were done without your knowledge. Moreover, the report documents your failure to cooperate fully and candidly with the investigation* [489]

Furthermore, Winston's three game suspension was also only half as long as the suspension Dallas Cowboys' running back Ezekiel Elliott received in 2017, also for violating the league Personal Conduct Policy [493] [494] [495] [496], but more specifically because according to the NFL there was:

> *substantial and persuasive evidence supporting a finding that [Elliott] engaged in physical violence against Ms. Thompson on multiple occasions during the week of July 16, 2016.* [497]

Do you notice anything different about the Brady and Elliott suspensions when copared with the Jameis Winston suspension? It's not something the main stream sports media wanted to make obvious. The difference is that in both the Brady and Elliott suspension letters, the NFL stated that they had "substantial evidence" as well as either *credible* or *persuasive* evidence against each player. [489] [497]

However, the NFL's letter to Winston merely says that the NFL "concluded that Winston violated the Personal Conduct Policy". There is absolutely no mention of the NFL having any *evidence* whatsoever that Winston actually did anything Kate P. accused him of doing – in any of her multiple versions – let alone *credible* or *persuasive* evidence. [485]

Simply put, while the NFL suspended Tom Brady for four games because they felt they had "substantial and credible evidence" against him, and suspended Ezekiel Elliott because they felt they had "substantial and persuasive evidence" against him, they suspended Winston three games after they merely *concluded* that he violated the Personal Conduct Policy.

The NFL simply didn't have a shred of evidence that Winston actually did what he was accused of – any of Kate P's multiple versions – and had no reason to suspend him other than the fact that doing so would appease the general public calling for Winston's head during the *#MeToo* phenomenon. In short, Winston's suspension was a suspension based on optics and public perception rather than any "substantial evidence" he actually did something wrong, unlike in the Tom Brady and Ezekiel Elliott cases.

Winston Disappointed in NFL's Decision, Says, "I Understand the NFL's Process"

After the suspension was announced, Winston almost immediately released his own statement, which read as follows:

The NFL informed me today that I will be suspended for the first three games of the season.

I'm sorry to the Uber driver for the position I put you in. It is uncharacteristic of me and I genuinely apologize. In the past 2 1/2 years my life has been filled with experiences, opportunities and events that have helped me grow, mature and learn, including the fact that I have eliminated alcohol from my life.

I know I have to hold myself to a higher standard on and off the field and that I have a responsibility to my family, community, and teammates to live above the platform with which God has blessed me. I apologize to my teammates, the Buccaneers organization and fans for letting them down and for not being able to be out there for the first three games of the season. Although I am disappointed in the NFL's decision, I understand the NFL's process, and I embrace this as an opportunity to take advantage of the resources available to help me achieve the goals that I have for myself.

I now look forward to putting this behind me and I will continue to work hard every day to be a positive influence in my community and be the best person, teammate and leader I can be. [498]

Media Freak Out

Almost as soon as Winston released his statement various media and the usual numbers of individual Winston haters on social media and the like pounced and began spinning the narrative that Jameis Winston admitted to doing what he was accused of doing [499] [500] [501] [502] even though such was obviously not the case. [484] USA Today even ran an article that unethically reiterated the absolute lie that Winston had committed sexual assault [503], even though they knew full well that such was not the case according to the law. [476]

Jameis Winston never apologized for doing what he was accused of doing – any of Kate P's multiple versions – because according to CBS Sports' John Breech, who also relayed a report from the NFL Network's Tom Pelissero, the:

> *Buccaneers quarterback doesn't believe that he did anything wrong. ... Winston refused to apologize for anything specific -- such as inappropriately touching the Uber driver -- because he doesn't believe the touching actually happened as it was alleged. ... Since Winston wouldn't admit guilt, the NFL negotiated a settlement with the Buccaneers quarterback that involved a three-game suspension, and Winston had to promise not to appeal it. Under the settlement, Winston wouldn't have to admit guilt, but he would have to admit that he was drinking, which is something he has apparently given up.* [504]

You may want to read the above again. Since Winston would not admit guilt, the NFL could not suspend him even the minimum baseline of 6 games. [505] Why? The obvious reason is simply because unlike with the Tom Brady and Ezekiel Elliott investigations the NFL had no "substantial evidence" that Jameis Winston had done anything wrong at all.

However, the NFL did have a general public influenced by the Me Too Movement to placate, and obviously seemed to figure that a three game suspension would do the trick. However, they should have known that, sadly, many in the *Me Too Movement*, let alone Winston-haters in general, would not be satisfied with anything short of a lifetime ban from the league.

Kate P. Goes for the $$$, Gives a New Fourth Version of the Alleged Incident and Gives a Shout Out to #MeToo

After Winston's three game suspension was announced, Kate P. filed a civil suit against Winston in hopes of winning a financial judgment. [506] Of course, such was something she previously said she had no interest in [471], which gained her extra credibility with the media and perhaps with the NFL as well. However, no one in the main stream media dared question her credibility, as the media would rather risk bearing false witness against an innocent man than be accused of *blaming the victim*, even if there is no true *victim* to speak of in any particular case.

In the civil suit, Kate P. told a new, fourth version of the alleged incident. This time, her suit alleged that Winston had, "placed his fingers between her legs and pressed them firmly against her vagina". [507]

The four versions of the alleged incident that Kate P. told are as follows:

> Firstly, Kate P. told Uber that Jameis "put his fingers on my crotch … for a very brief moment". [471]

> Secondly, Kate P. texted a personal friend that Winston "grazed his fingers over my pants". [471]

> Thirdly, Kate P. told *Buzzfeed News* over 20 months later, which article seemed to kick off the NFL investigation, that Winston "grabbed her crotch" and held his hand on her crotch for 3-5 seconds. [471]

> Fourthly, when Kate P. filed a civil suit in the hopes of securing a financial judgment, she increased the nastiness of her three previous unsubstantiated accusations. [507]

Regardless, Kate P. and Winston ended up settling out of court, and various NFL related media considered such a smart financial move by Winston. [508] [509] This was because Winston was in line to secure his 5th year contract option which had been picked up by the Buccaneers' brass but which was only guaranteed against injury for the following season

[510] and which was worth nearly $21,000,000. [511] Therefore, putting this sordid affair in the past rather than countersuing Kate P. for slander and/or libel and letting the case drag on and on and on, seemed like the prudent thing for Winston to do, and is in fact, exactly what he did.

Also, after Winston's post-suspension statement was released, Kate P. released her own statement – apparently irked that Winston did not admit to doing any of what she accused him of in any of her multiple versions – which included the following:

> *I am glad to see the NFL discipline Jameis Winston. I do appreciate his apology, even if it needs some work. ... My experience should highlight the importance of believing women when they have the courage to come forward about sexual assault. ... #MeToo* [498]

Kate P's statement makes it quite clear that she felt Winston should have apologized for more than merely being intoxicated and putting her in an uncomfortable situation, and she again referred to *sexual assault*, knowing full well that even what she accused Winston of doing was not *sexual assault* according to the law. [476] She then ended her statement with *#MeToo*, which as this chapter has detailed, was a very fitting way for her to end her statement … for a myriad of reasons.

GUILTY UNTIL PROVEN INNOCENT

None calleth for justice, nor any pleadeth for truth: they trust in vanity, and speak lies; they conceive mischief, and bring forth iniquity.

– Isaiah 59:4

To say that *Winston Derangement Syndrome* is drastically coloring the media's reporting on Jameis Winston's off-the-field activities and behaviour is more akin to an irrefutable fact than some wild conspiracy theory.

I could detail positive story after positive story about Winston that the vast majority of the main stream sports media refused to report on, as such stories would have painted Winston in a positive light, which wouldn't fit the narrative the main stream media is trying to spin to their audience. I could also detail the hypocrisy in how various media personalities speak about Winston, compared to how they speak about various politicians, Hollywood actors, musicians and other non-sports celebrities with sordid pasts.

I could question why the main stream sports media treats Winston like a criminal when he's never even been arrested, let alone convicted of a crime, at any time in his entire life, while players that have actually been arrested, such as Von Miller [512] [513], Jason Peters [514] and Marshawn Lynch [515] have had their sordid pasts forgiven and forgotten in short order. In fact, USA Today has a regularly updated online database of NFL player arrests that at the time of this writing, details 933 separate arrests, the vast majority of which have been largely ignored – or at the very least forgiven and forgotten – by the media. [516]

I could even question why the media continues to harp on Winston's suspension which was based on a mere unsubstantiated allegation, after quickly forgetting, forgiving, and now largely ignoring Tom Brady's and Ezeiel Elliott's longer suspensions that the NFL itself said were based on actual "substantial evidence". [489] [497] Even media darling Paul Hornung was suspended for the entire 1963 season for betting on games and he was elected into the *Pro Football Hall of Fame* [517] [518] and to this day is spoken of in glowing terms by just about everyone in the media.

Yet Jameis Winston is treated as guilty until proven innocent.

Go figure.

However, for the sake of brevity, in this chapter I will only mention the following NFL players: Peyton Manning, Larry Fitzgerald, Nigel Bradham and Dante Fowler, as they all play in the same league as Winston, and are routinely covered by the same media outlets that cover Winston himself.

Peyton Manning

Peyton Manning is not only known for being one of the greatest quarterbacks to ever play the game of football, he's also known for being in more commercials than every other player in the NFL combined, or at least it feels that way. Simply put, Peyton Manning is a media darling. And, as I've already stated, I personally consider Manning the *best* quarterback of all-time, not the greatest (i.e. Otto Graham), not the greatest of the Super Bowl era (i.e. Tom Brady), not the most talented (i.e. Aaron Rodgers), but the *best* to ever play.

However in late 2015, Al Jazeera reported that one of their sources had accused Manning of ordering HGH [519], considered a performance enhancing drug by the NFL. [520] Manning has always denied the allegations of course [521], but even now, many years later, the story refuses to die, as many believe the evidence points to Manning using the banned substance. [522] However, this story has been, for all intents and purposes, buried by the NFL and main stream media in a large cover-up that would make the creators of Project MK-Ultra blush. [523]

In 1996 Manning was accused by his female athletic trainer Jamie Naughtright of exposing his buttock to her, and while he denied any wrongdoing, the University of Tennessee did pay Nauhgtright $300,000 as part of a settlement. Later Naughtright sued Manning for defamation after he allegedly defamed her in a book he wrote and Manning settled that lawsuit as well in December of 2003. [524] The entire sordid affair was basically covered up by the NFL and the main stream media. [525] [526]

However, in 2016 Naughright appeared on CBS' *Inside Edition* and clarified her version of events when she stated:

> *I felt something on my face and Peyton had pulled his shorts down and sat his anus and his testicles on my face* [527]

If Naugright's allegations are accurate – and I am not saying they are either accurate or inaccurate – I don't know a single man or woman that isn't infected with the most virulent strain of *Winston Derangement Syndrome* that would say what Winston was alleged to have done by Kate P., namely grazing his fingers over the top of her pants uninvited, is worse than what Manning was accused of doing, namely sitting his naked anus and testicles on his female trainer's face uninvited.

However once again, the main stream sports media has helped shield one of their golden boys and basically buried said report. In fact, Peyton Manning was never suspended for one single game over his entire career and today Manning is seemingly as widely praised and revered as he was before Naughright's appearance on *Inside Edition*. [528] [529] [530] [531]

Maybe, just maybe, if Jameis Winston's last name was Manning and his daddy's name was Archie, rather than his last name being Winston and his daddy's name being Antonor, the NFL and the media would cover for him as well. As the legendary *C+C* Music Factory once sang, *things that make you go hmm.*

Larry Fitzgerald

Larry Fitzgerald is widely regarded as one of the greatest wide receivers to ever play the game of football and rightly so. The guy is a marvel, and I do firmly believe that Fitzgerald deserves to be a first ballot Hall of Famer in the future.

However in 2008, Angela Nazario, the mother of Fitzgerald's son, filed for an order of protection against Fitzgerald and claimed that he had violently assaulted her by pulling out chunks of her hair, throwing her across a room, grabbing her neck from behind and slamming her into a marble floor. [532]

There was also a witness – My-lihn French – to Fitzgerald's alleged assault, who stated:

> *I was afraid for Angie. He looked as if he didn't see me sitting there, glaring 'through' me. ... He wouldn't leave, he grabbed Angie's arms and pushed her on the ground forcefully ... he grabbed her head with both hands like a football and forcefully threw her across the room.* [533]

Perhaps most amazing is that while this story came to light just before the 2009 Super Bowl, which Fitzgerald was playing in, it was almost entirely covered up by not only the NFL and national media but by the local media in Arizona where Fitzgerald played as well! [534] [535]

Even the New York Times – the so-called *national paper of record -* wrote a feature piece of nearly 900 words on Fitzgerald shortly after the aforementioned incident. They spent just 43 words on the incident, yet spent two full paragraphs basically trying to besmirch his accuser. [536]

However, not only was Fitzgerald never suspended a single game, just four short years after the alleged incident he was named the *Arizona Cardinals/Walter Payton NFL Man of the Year* and was one of three finalists for the *Walter Payton NFL Man of the Year Award* [537], the most prestigious award in the league. And, just seven years after the alleged incident, Fitzgerald actually won the award! [538]

Can you imagine if Jameis Winston was playing in the Super Bowl at the end of this upcoming season, and shortly before media week his fiancé (i.e. the beautiful Breion Allen) as well as an eye witness came forward and Breion filed for a protection order against him and described the same sort of violent abuse that Angela Nazario said she suffered at the hands of Larry Fitzgerald? It's not at all unrealistic to believe that Winston would not only be crucified in the media for the rest of his natural life, but that the media as well as the masses would demand he receive a lifetime ban from the NFL as well.

Nigel Bradham

Nigel Bradham is not a household name. He was a member of the 2017 Philadelphia Eagles Super Bowl team and even started in the game and recorded 7 tackles [539], yet he is still a relative unknown to NFL fans outside of Philadelphia. However, even relative unknowns seem to receive more protection and benefit of the doubt from the NFL and media than Jameis Winston does, as the curious case of Nigel Bradham will prove.

Just one day after the NFL suspended Jameis Winston three games over an unsubstantiated allegation that he grazed his fingers over the outside of a woman's pants uninvited [471] the NFL suspended Nigel Bradham for a mere one game. [540]

Bradham had actually been arrested and charged with aggravated assault after breaking the nose of a hotel employee who Bradham felt took too long to serve his party [541] for which he accepted a deferred prosecution program. [542] Bradham had also previously been charged by the police for marijuana possession [541] and for bringing a weapon to an airport. [542] Yes, that guy – Nigel Bradham – received just a one game suspension, and the incident has since been basically forgotten by the main stream sports media.

Imagine if Jameis Winston had actually been arrested and charged with assault and admitted to the assault, after also being arrested for drug possession and bringing a weapon to an airport, rather than having been merely accused – without any actual evidence of any kind – of grazing his fingers across the top of a woman's pants and then immediately removing his hand and committing no further incident when the woman merely said, "what's up with that"? [471] It's not at all unrealistic to think Winston would have received a full 6 game suspension or more. However Winston isn't the little known Bradham, nor is Bradham the media whipping boy that Winston is.

Dante Fowler

Dante Fowler is a relatively unknown on a nationwide scale, former first round draft pick of the Jacksonville Jaguars. Just three weeks after Winston was suspended for three games, Fowler was suspended for one game.

What did Fowler do? Well, strangely enough the NFL did not ever say exactly what Fowler did to receive his one game suspension. However, in February 2016 TMZ released a video of Fowler watching and apparently *refereeing* a fight between his then girlfriend and the mother of his child. Yes, seriously. Then, in March 2016, Fowler was arrested and charged with assault against a police officer as well as with resisting arrest. Then, in March 2017, Fowler was arrested and charged with battery, criminal mischief and petit theft to which he pled no contest. [543]

How many games do you honestly believe Jameis Winston would be suspended by the NFL, if within a mere 17 month timeframe, he was caught on video refereeing a street fight between two women, then arrested and charged for assaulting a police officer, and then arrested and charged and pleading no contest to battery and theft? I doubt any honest person would say, "Just one game like Dante Fowler".

Jameis Lanaed Winston
vs.
Larry Nigel Dante Manning

What if Jameis Lanaed Winston was instead Larry Nigel Dante Manning? What if Winston wasn't the former Heisman winning, BCS National Title winning, Pepsi Rookie of the Year award winning, youngest NFL Pro Bowl quarterback in history? What if Winston were merely a wide receiver (Larry) that had just won a Super Bowl (Nigel) as a relative unknown despite being a former first round draft pick (Dante) and his dad was the revered father of a football family dynasty (Manning)?

The following table examines the real Jameis Lanaed Winston and the fictional Larry Nigel Dante Manning, which is a composite of Larry Fitzgerald, Nigel Bradham, Dante Fowler and Peyton Manning, in order to see what the differences are in what each player was accused of, arrested for, charged with, and how long each player was suspended by the NFL.

Accused's Name:	Jameis Lanaed Winston	Larry Nigel Dante Manning
Accused of:	Grazing fingers across the top of a woman's pants uninvited while inebriated	Pulling out chunks of hair, throwing across a room, grabbing the neck from behind and slamming into a marble floor, the mother of his child Refereeing a physical fight between his girlfriend and the mother of his child Sticking naked anus and testicles on the face of his female trainer uninvited

Arrested for:	Not arrested	Assault for breaking the nose of a hotel employee Marijuana possession Bringing a gun to an airport Petit theft, Criminal Mischief and Battery
Charged with:	Not charged	Assault for breaking the nose of a hotel employee Bringing a gun to an airport Marijuana possession Petit theft, Criminal Mischief and Battery
Games Suspended:	Three	Two

After viewing the previous table comparing the real Jameis Lanaed Winston with the fictional composite character of Larry Nigel Dante Manning, which of course was based on the exact actual allegations, arrests and charges that Larry Fitzgerald, Nigel Bradham, Dante Fowler and Peyton Manning all faced, combined, it's almost unthinkable to imagine that any logical individual or even relatively sane media member would feel Jameis Winston received fair and equal treatment from the NFL. However, many not only seem to believe that Winston received fair and equal treatment from the NFL, they actually think Winston received preferential treatment and should have been suspended even longer, or even cut from the Buccaneers team or banned from the league for life! [487] [503] [544] [545] [546] [547] [548] [549] [550]

All I can say to that is, while some players are treated as innocent until proven guilty, and then even when they are proven guilty, are quickly forgiven or even defended by the NFL and the media, Jameis Winston is obviously treated as guilty until proven innocent, even by those who claim to be interested in the truth and dedicated to accurate reporting.

Winston Derangement Syndrome must be one of the most diabolical and destructive brain diseases known to man. I can only hope and pray that those infected with such a disease will read this book and be cured once and for all.

However, just as a prosecuting attorney must first identify and expose a criminal if he wants to secure a conviction and rid the public of a dangerous menace, so too will I, in the next chapter, identify and expose some of the main stream media members infected with *Winston Derangement Syndrome* who consider Jameis Winston worthy of being considered guilty until proven innocent.

TALKING HEADS PLAYING GOD

The media's the most powerful entity on earth. They have the power to make the innocent guilty and to make the guilty innocent, and that's power. Because they control the minds of the masses.

– Malcolm X [2]

While current American President Donald Trump may be at war with the main stream media and even enjoying the battle, the concept of *Fake News* is most definitely not a Trumpian invention. Presidents Thomas Jefferson, Theodore Roosevelt, Woodrow Wilson, Harry Truman, and others have all went to war with the media at various times. [551] In fact, consider the following two remarkable statements by previous American Presidents:

Nothing can now be believed which is seen in a newspaper. Truth itself becomes suspicious by being put into that polluted vehicle.

– Thomas Jefferson [551]

Prostitutes of the mind (i.e. Journalists, added) have been the great menace to free government since freedom of speech and freedom of the press was first inaugurated. A prostitute of the mind is a much worse criminal in my opinion than a thief or a robber.

– Harry Truman [552]

However, it's not only the main stream political media or political journalists and talking heads, but the main stream sports media and sports journalists and talking heads, that deserve to be exposed and castigated at times. Right here and now, in this chapter of this book, is one of those times.

While I could name an inordinate amount of main stream sports media talking heads, journalists and the like that deserve to be called out for their obviously biased spoken or written statements regarding Jameis Winston, for the sake of brevity I will merely focus on four such individuals in this particular chapter, namely: Michelle Beadle, Max Kellerman, Keyshawn Johnson and Tom Jones. These four *Winston Derangement Syndrome* infected characters provide a well-rounded lineup to scrutinize, as one is a female reporter and hostess, one is a male talking head and commentator, one is a former NFL player and analyst, and one is a former newspaper columnist and current senior media writer.

Michelle Beadle

Michelle Beadle is a popular ESPN talking head who co-hosted the *Get Up* television show before being reassigned or demoted (depending on who one listens to) after the show drew an abysmal number of viewers and was widely panned. She now co-hosts *NBA Countdown*. [553] [554]

Beadle is also the same talking head that once landed in hot water after stating:

> *Not to stereotype, but I hear a lot from white men on these topics. You guys have a lot to say how black people should feel, about how women should feel. I gotta be honest with you guys. Shut up and listen for 5 minutes. Like, you will never know what I've been through, what he's been through. Just listen. God forbid, you learn something.* [555]

Now honestly, I don't care that she said the above as it doesn't bother me one bit. I'm not a speech Nazi nor do I have any interest in working for the word police. As long as a person's actions are not vile or illegal, I generally don't care what mere words are coming out of their mouth.

However, interestingly enough, after Beadle made the above statement, one of her main detractors was author and radio show host Clay Travis, who strangely enough also has one of the worst cases of *Winston Derangement Syndrome* one can imagine. After Beadle's statement, Travis tweeted:

> *What's funny about this @espn clip is if it's said about anyone other than white men MSESPN loses its mind* [555]

I find it quite amusing that Travis called out Beadle for her apparent bias towards white men, when his rabid bias toward Jameis Winston has been extremely evident for years.

On June 29, 2018, ESPN's Michelle Beadle, on a segment for the *Get Up* television program, stated:

> *This dude might not be a good dude. ... He has a fundamental problem with the way he views, I think, women, in general. ... There is an underlying idea for a lot of men in this world that women are to be conquered, and that is what we're here for, and that is it. And when you have that inherently in you, or subconsciously you think that way, then these types of problems don't just go away, and stopping to drink alcohol isn't going to make them go away. ... We give guys lots of chances ... this isn't the second chance, this is four, five and six at this point.* [556]

The above quote is obviously proof positive that Beadle chooses to believe – against all *evidence* by the way – or at the very least assumes that Winston actually did all the things that he was accused of in the past. It also means that Beadle believes she has the divine gift of being able to know the intent of one's heart, the super-power to be able to know what one thinks, as well as that she views Winston as *guilty until proven innocent*, as he has never even been arrested, let alone convicted of a crime, at any time in his entire life. However, in her mind, he's burned through six chances already.

Now, if you personally were accused of breaking an item that in fact your friend actually broke, and then you later get accused of stealing an item from a store that you didn't actually steal, would you believe you had burned through two chances and were now on your third strike? No, of course you wouldn't.

I mentioned a third strike as baseball provides a great analogy for just how insane Michelle Beadle's statement was. Can you imagine if a home plate umpire, during a world series game in the bottom of the ninth with the bases loaded and two outs, called the first two pitches thrown to Aaron Judge *balls*, and then on the third pitch – be it a ball or a strike – said, "steeeerrrrriiiiikeeee, you're out"? It wouldn't just be Judge himself but nearly every baseball fan across America that would want to see that ref fined, fired and publicly humiliated for his insanity.

Simply put, for a baseball player to be on his third strike, there needs to have been two previous actual strikes against him, not merely balls pitched that some people thought were strikes, but which were actually called balls by the umpire. The same principle holds true in normal modern life. For a person to be on their third strike there should be two actual convictions, or at least two actual criminal incidents that can be proven to have occurred, before such a person is considered to be on their third strike by anyone.

However, Michelle Beadle apparently believes she is omniscient, feels comfortable playing God, and has no qualms with risking bearing false witness against an innocent person. She simply apparently believes she has been gifted with the divine ability to pronounce someone who has never even been arrested, let alone convicted of a crime, at any time in his entire life, guilty.

Three years earlier, on May 12, 2015, Beadle stated on Twitter:

> *If FSU* [Florida State, added]*, in any form, is a part of your handle or bio, I thank you for making it easier for me to separate the filth.*
> [557]

Who needs things like evidence, truth, judges, or even courts of law when Michelle Beadle is gracing the earth with her presence and separating the wheat from the chaff, or the wheat from the *filth* to borrow her word?

All joking aside, I find it interesting that the female talking head who has chosen to spearhead the effort to publicly crucify Winston for things she simply chooses to believe he did in spite of the evidence, and the woman who said that stopping to drink alcohol will not change one's future behavior, is the same woman who was questioned by her bosses at ESPN after her own co-workers reported she was drinking heavily, using drugs, and that she sexually propositioned Packers' quarterback Aaron Rodgers at an ESPY's after-party! [558] [559]

Now, if all male sports fans were to judge Michelle Beadle by the same standards she used to judge Jameis Winston, we could all say:

> *This Michelle Beadle might not be a good lady. ... She has a fundamental problem with the way she views, I think, men, in general. ... There is an underlying idea for a lot of women in this world that men are to be conquered, and that is what we're here for, and that is it. And when you have that inherently in you, or subconsciously you think that way, then propositioning an NFL quarterback for sex at an ESPY's after-party just comes naturally to you, and ceasing to get drunk and high isn't going to make Michelle Beadle a good person. ... We give women lots of chances ... this isn't the second chance, this is four, five and six for Beadle at this point.*

Please understand, I do not have any ill will towards Michelle Beadle. She is paid to be provocative and to express a certain viewpoint and she does that relatively well, even if I don't agree with the particular viewpoint she expresses.

Regardless, I tend to feel that when a talking head like Beadle says something as foolish, biased, arrogant and absurd as what she said about Winston, the fact that she said such is punishment in and of itself, as she effectively exposed herself as someone who has been infected with *Winston Derangement Syndrome* and therefore as someone who should never be relied upon to provide a truthful narrative to her audience.

Max Kellerman

Max Kellerman is the co-host of the popular ESPN show *First Take* and a well-known boxing commentator. [560] Honestly, I love Max Kellerman. He's one of my favorite talking heads on television. He's obviously extremely intelligent, can debate better than almost any other sports media talking head around, has a magnificent voice, and once released a rap song with his brother Sam that was titled, *Young Man Rumble*, which is actually a solid song. [561]

Simply put, Kellerman seems like an interesting guy and someone I could have an entertaining and long talk with about a variety of issues, even if I may not agree with him on many of those issues, and even if my viewpoints and ability to debate may cause him to have a melt-down.

However, Kellerman is also a carrier of the infectious disease known as *Winston Derangement Syndrome*, or at least the *character* he plays on ESPN's *First Take* television program is, if in fact he is being paid to play a part and is taking his talking points from his bosses, which is always possible.

Regardless, Kellerman seems both skilled and comfortable passing off lies as truth to his audience, as he seems to know that his audience is unlikely to fact-check his statements and expose his errors. In short, Kellerman could certainly be called a rather dastardly purveyor of *fake news*.

Consider what Kellerman had to say about Jameis Winston on ESPN's *First Take* in 2018:

> *Jameis Winston is a bust. ... I said the team should move on from him already. ... If you look at the details of the Uber report and everything ... recidivist behavior.* [562]

Kellerman has long pretended to be one of the few sports talking heads that is truly impartial, more fact-based than emotion-based, and someone who has high morals and therefore has the right to not only moralize on any number of issues, but to be respected when he does so. However, the above quote proves such is not the case and that Kellerman is just another talking head that likes to pretend to be omniscient, play God, and someone who doesn't mind risking bearing false witness against an innocent individual.

Kellerman calling Winston a *bust* in regards to his on-field production is laughable and proof positive that he is biased against Winston. However, Kellerman bringing up the "details of the Uber report" and saying that Jameis has exhibited "recidivist behavior" is where he exposes himself as someone who thinks he has divine powers. The reason I say that is because nothing in the Uber report proved that Winston did anything wrong at all, not one single thing.

There was no police report to speak of [475], so it seems clear that Kellerman is referring to the NFL's actual statement regarding the alleged Uber incident. [485] However, as I have stated already, while the NFL stated their decisions to suspend both Tom Brady and Ezekiel Elliott were based on "substantial evidence" [489] [497] they did not use such wording in explaining why they decided to suspend Winston; they merely stated they "concluded that Winston violated the Personal Conduct Policy", that's it. [485]

Kellerman knows the above facts. He apparently just doesn't care enough to elucidate his audience on said facts, as doing so would weaken the false narrative he likes to spin against Jameis Winston.

Likewise, when Kellerman says that Winston is guilty of "recidivist behavior", he is in effect claiming – whether he knows it or not – that he has the divine power of omniscience. The reason I say this is because since Winston has never even been arrested, let alone convicted of a crime, at any time in his entire life, for Kellerman to say Winston is guilty of "recidivist behavior" means that Kellerman believes he knows that Winston is guilty of one or more things he has been accused of in the past, and that he is also guilty of the allegation levied against him by the Uber driver. However, of course, Max Kellerman cannot possibly know any of that unless he is the all-seeing God or has been blessed with the divine power of omniscience, and if that's the case, all-knowing Max should resign from ESPN and just set up shop as the new judge of all mankind.

Also, as with the woman – Michelle Beadle – who was accused by her own co-workers of being drunk, high and of sexually propositioning an NFL QB [558] [559] being the one to try and publicly chastise Jameis Winston over a completely unsubstantiated allegation, it strikes me as quite ironic that the man – Max Kellerman – who was suspended by ESPN for admitting he physically assaulted his girlfriend [563] is the one pretending to have the moral high-ground and to know that Jameis Winston committed various acts that have never been proven, and to have exhibited "recidivist behavior" despite having never even been arrested in his life.

Keyshawn Johnson

Keyshawn Johnson is a former #1 overall NFL draft pick who had a wonderful career and once even won a Super Bowl playing for the Tampa Bay Buccaneers. However, he was also traded three times in his career and was once deactivated for seven games for fighting with his coach. [564]

Johnson was also widely known as *Me-Shawn* and ranked 32nd on the Sporting News' 2018 list titled, *40 most hated NFL players of all-time: loudmouths, cheaters, criminals.* [565] And no, Jameis Winston does not appear on that list for those of you who are wondering. Regardless, after retiring from the NFL, Johnson was hired as an analyst by ESPN and continues to work for the company as of the time of this writing. [566] [567]

On the day Winston was suspended by the NFL, Johnso said on KSPN710:

> *I'm not a doctor, nor do I plan on being, but there's something wrong with you. If this is in fact true, the fact that you keep coming up with some type of sexual behavioral problems towards women, there's something wrong mentally. I don't care what anyone says. There's something wrong.* [568]

While it's nice that Johnson added the phrase, "if this is in fact true", such a caveat rings hollow considering that he follows that statement up with, "the fact that you keep coming up with some type of sexual behavioral problems towards women, there's something wrong mentally."

No Keyshawn, it's not a *fact* that Winston keeps coming up with sexual behavioral problems, not unless you too – like Michelle Beadle and Max Kellerman – are also omniscient and know that a man who has never even been arrested, let alone convicted for anything at any time in his entire life, was in fact guilty.

Now, while Johnson calls attention to the actual fact that he's not a doctor, he probably should also have called attention to the fact that he's not omnipotent, has no clue if what he's saying is true or merely slander, and probably isn't the best person to moralize about anyone's mental state, considering the reputation he had as a player, let alone the actual fact that he was arrested for misdemeanor domestic battery in 2014 as well, a crime for which he posted $20,000 to get out on bail. [569]

But hey, what's not to love about a former diva wide receiver with the nick-name *Me-Shawn* who was once deactivated for fighting with his coach, considered one of the 40 most hated NFL players of all-time, and who was arrested for domestic battery, who also likes to play God, feign omniscience, and pretends to have the moral high-ground over a 24 year old who has never been arrested in his life?

Tom Jones of the Tampa Bay Times

Before recently taking a post as a senior media writer for the liberal Poynter Institute [570] – the same institute that once published a list of 515 so-called *unreliable* websites, and the same institute that was accused of trying to blacklist conservative news sites [571] – Tom Jones was employed by the Tampa Bay Times as a columnist. However, it seemed his unofficial job title was *Jameis Winston hater in chief*, as he wrote hit piece after hit piece on the young quarterback and was called out by none other than former Buccaneers all-time great Ronde Barber [572] as well as hosts of other Buccaneer-connected indiviuals for doing such. [573]

In short, Tom Jones could literally be viewed as the type of person who could have his picture next to the phrase p*rostitutes of the mind*, coined by American President Harry Truman. Consider what President Truman stated regarding such *prostitutes of the mind*:

> *We have men, in this day and age, who are prostitutes of the mind. They sell their ability to write articles for sale, which will be so worded as to mislead people who read them as news. These articles or columns are most astute and plausible and unless the reader knows the facts are most misleading. ... Prostitutes of the mind are skillful purveyors of character assassination and the theft of good names of public men and private citizens too. They are the lowest form of thief & criminal.*
>
> – Harry Tuman [552]

The above could be said to be an almost perfect description of Tom Jones as he is indeed *skillfull* in the way he writes and spins false narratives. Now, I would not personally call Jones a *thief* or *criminal*, but words such as dishonest and even unethical certainly at least come to mind.

Regardless, the apparently omnipotent demigod known as Tom Jones penned three articles around the time the NFL suspended Jameis Winston. One article was published before Winston was suspended which exposed Jones' bias [574], one was published on the day Winston was suspended which exposed Jones' belief in his own omnipotence [575], and one was published about three months after Winston's suspension which exposed Jones' remarkable level of *Winston Derangement Syndrome* and just how much he personally dislikes Winston. [576]

On June 21, 2018, in his article titled, *Next move is simple for the Bucs: Get rid of Jameis Winston,* Jones wrote:

Trade him. Waive him. Cut him.

Whatever.

Just get rid of him.

Jameis Winston should never play another game for the Tampa Bay Bucs.

Plain and simple, he's a bad guy and the Bucs should have nothing more to do with him. [574]

Talk about bias! Not only had Jameis Winston not yet been suspended by the NFL when Jones wrote the above words, there certainly had not been one thing leaked by the media or the NFL stating that there was any evidence Winston had actually done what he was accused of doing. However, Jones didn't need something as obviously irrelevant as *evidence.* He simply *knew* that Jameis Winston was a "bad guy", and as an omnipotent demigod, he felt confident in condemning Jameis and calling for him to lose his job. Again, talk about bias!

A week later, on the day that the NFL announced its three game suspension, Jones followed that article up with another article titled, *Hey, Bucs, there's no more benefit of the doubt with Jameis Winston,* that once again called Jameis "a bad guy", falsely stated that what Winston was suspended for was "the exact definition of sexual assault" even though what Winston was accused of is not even considered sexual assault whatsoever according to the law [476], and even asked the absurd question:

> *If you don't cut him now, what kind of message are you sending to fans?* [575]

Well Tom, allow me to answer your ridiculous question. The message the team sent to its fans by not cutting Winston was that the team and its owners – unlike the omnipotent demigod Tom Jones of course – were not arrogant enough to believe they *knew* what had not been proven, that they actually believe in the *innocent until proven guilty* concept, and that they will not cut a player who not only has never even been arrested, let alone convicted of a crime at any time in his entire life, but whose suspension was not even based on "substantial evidence" as the suspensions levied against Tom Brady and Ezekiel Elliott were, according to the NFL. [489] [497] That is the message the Buccaneers' brass sent to its fans, and it was a beautiful and much needed message indeed, especially in this day and age of mob rule, group think, and the exaltation of social and internet justice rather than actual legal justice.

Jones followed the previous hit piece up with one more article titled, *Jameis Winston's Uber ride will never be forgotten, and shouldn't* on September 20, 2018 and in it stated:

> *Just as the good times have arrived, we are reminded of what a creep Jameis Winston is. ... If Winston had behaved like a responsible adult that night, this would not be a topic today. If Winston had respect for women that night, he would be getting ready to start Monday night's game against the Pittsburgh Steelers. ... Winston can visit all the schools he wants. He can pass out all the Thanksgiving turkeys he can. He can lob footballs to little kids until his right arm falls off. It doesn't excuse his behavior. ... There will come a time later this season, I predict, when Winston will again stand behind center for the Bucs. He will*

> *receive a standing ovation. He will do great things. He will win football games. But there will always be a stain on everything he does.* [576]

Wow. If you have ever searched high and low to find perhaps the most biased article ever written about an athlete, congratulations, you may have just found it in the above transparently biased and overtly malicious article written by Tom Jones.

Firstly, Jones opines that "If Winston had behaved like an adult that night, this wouldn't be a topic today", however that is an absurd statement, unless Jones believes he is omniscient and knows what he cannot know, namely that Winston actually did what he was accused of doing, which of course he does not *know*. Even if Winston was *falsely* accused – and it is still a very distinct possibility that such is exactly what happened – such would obviously still be a *topic*.

Likewise, if Winston did not do what he was accused of – and there's no hard evidence, or even "substantial evidence" to borrow a phrase from the NFL's suspension letters regarding both Tom Brady and Ezekiel Elliott [489] [497], to prove he did such – his actions on the night in question seem to be quite *adult* as it were. Winston admits he was inebriated and rather than attempting to drive home, he took an Uber. That is an adult thing to do, obviously.

Secondly, Jones states that "If Winston had respect for women that night, he would be getting ready to start Monday night's game against the Pittsburgh Steelers". However again, such is an absurd statement, unless Jones believes he is omniscient and knows that Winston actually did what he was accused of doing, which of course he does not *know*.

Finally, Jones finishes his sermon of hate so to speak, by basically saying that no matter what Winston does for the rest of his life, whether that is excelling on the football field, or being a blessing to the Tampa community off the field, it won't matter. Jones believes that no matter what happens, there will always be a stain on "everything he does", because, according to Jones' previous two articles, Jameis is a "bad guy".

Just imagine being told that at 24 years of age, your life is basically over and that nothing you will ever do from that point on will ever matter or change the fact that you're "a bad guy". Now imagine that you're not merely told such a disgusting thing in private by an abusive parent, psychotic teacher, or perverted doctor, but that such is published and told to the world. Seriously, imagine that!

Now imagine if what Tom Jones said were actually true, which of course, it is not. Every person who has ever even been merely accused of some incident past the age of 24, never mind actually charged and convicted of that incident, would have no reason to ever strive to be a better person, to accomplish anything of value, etc.

It seems Tom Jones feels he is a man who has never sinned and can therefore cast stones at others and even sentence them to a life of absolute uselessness unless they have a glowing reputation by the age of 24. It's as if he doesn't realize some of the greatest human lives ever lived were lived by people with incredibly sordid pasts.

In the interest of injecting just a bit of humor, I would love to ask Jones if he has ever watched a movie starring Mark Wahlberg with a family member, perhaps: *Patriot's Day*, *Lone Survivor* or *Invincible*. I also wonder if before or after watching such a film he took the time to stand on his custom-built soap-box, moralize about the evils of racism and violence, condemn Wahlberg for his extremely appalling past which has been reported to have included physically attacking black people – including children and a school teacher – simply for being black, and being arrested for beating a Vietnamese man unconscious. [577]

However, who knows, maybe Jones just reserves his outrage for quarterbacks he doesn't like that have never been arrested but who he'd arrest if he was able to function as the omnipotent demigod he knows he is? Maybe it's the rest of us mere humans that just don't understand how gloriously wise and so much better Jones is than all of us?

All joking aside, it literally freaks me out – I don't know what other phrase would better describe my current feeling – to think people like Tom Jones actually exist, let alone that such people hold positions of influence and actually are read by many on a regular basis. May God have mercy on all of us and keep us safe from the terrible and destructive advice of people such as Tom Jones.

Oh, and before I forget, I'd just like to say that I love many of Mark Wahlberg's movies and have no doubt people can change for the better, at any age. And, if you have never watched *The Lovely Bones*, do yourself a favor and watch it soon; just make sure you have a box of tissues nearby.

SENIOR SURVIVORSHIP

The greatest accomplishment is not in never failing, but in rising again after you fall.

– Vince Lombardi [578]

Jameis Winston's fourth NFL season obviously got off to a rough start thanks to the three game suspension levied against him by the NFL, who "concluded that Winston violated the Personal Conduct Policy" [485], though not on the basis of "substantial evidence" against him as was the case with the suspensions levied against Tom Brady and Ezekiel Elliott. [489] [497]

However, during the pre-season Winston played lights out. In about one full game's worth of action (i.e. 41 passes) he completed over 73 percent of his passes for 388 yards, 3 touchdowns, no interceptions and had a passer rating of 126.9. [579]

Coach Koetter stated the following when talking about Winston's complete pre-season performance:

> *I think performance-wise, you'd have to give Jameis an A for the preseason ... I don't think anybody in their right mind would say that wasn't an A performance on his part.* [579]

Koetter also stated before Winston made his first start of the 2018 season:

> *He's the same guy. Jameis has always been really good with how he approaches things mentally. I mean Jameis is the first guy here in the morning and the last guy to leave at night. He's always,*

since he came in as a rookie, he's always has been extremely well-prepared. [580]

However, despite Winston playing lights out during the entire pre-season, GM Jason Licht hinted that the Bucs' plan was not to start Winston until their fifth game of the season against the Falcons, rather than their fourth game of the season against the Bears, in part due to the Bears game coming on a short week, which would mean Winston would have very little practice time with the team, after not having been able to be with the team the previous three plus weeks. [579]

Likewise, coach Koetter also revealed later on that ever since he learned that Winston would be suspended the first three games, the plan was always to start him in the fifth game of the season rather than the fourth game, when he stated:

> *I was on vacation when we got the call, I got the call from Jason that Jameis would be suspended for three games, first thing I did was look at our schedule ... from that point on I had it in my head Fitz (Ryan Fitzpatrick) would start the first four games and Jameis would start in Atlanta.* [581]

However, the suspension still had to be carried out, and after Winston's final pre-season game, according to NFL suspension rules, he was not allowed to be at the team facilities or to have contact with teammates or coaches. Nevertheless, Winston did give what many of his teammates said was a *memorable speech* before leaving. [579]

As for Winston himself, he stated:

> *I'm just going to work my tail off ... Who knows how things will go? Hopefully they go great. I know it's going to be a tough situation for our coaches but I just want to get back with my team.* [579]

Winston was a man of his word, as work his tail off is exactly what he would do while on suspension, not that such surprised anyone in Buccaneers' headquarters, as Winston's work ethic was already legendary. For example, Bucs tight end Cameron Brate once spoke glowingly about Jameis renting a large house for all the Bucs players working out with him in the off-season and also personally scripting a complete 8-hour daily workout itinerary for each player in attendance. [582]

According to the NFL Network's Mike Garafolo, while Winston was suspended, he:

> *vowed to himself he wouldn't let his teammates outwork him during his three-game suspension for violating the league's personal-conduct policy. For that, he would need the help of about 20 to 25 players currently out of the NFL and looking for some good field work while trying to get their way back in the league. So Winston recruited those players, brought in his passing coach George Whitfield and longtime trainer Otis Leverette, scripted plays ... All of it in the name of being ready once he returned to the team* [583]

Former Buccaneers' wide receiver Louis Murphy was one of the players Winston recruited, and when recounting the training sessions, he stated:

> *Team drills, 7-on-7, plays and stuff the Bucs are working on, we did it all. It was intense ... I helped out with the receivers and concepts because I know a little bit about what the Bucs are doing from my time there, but it was Jameis leading the way and we all followed his lead.* [583]

Winston himself, when speaking about the experience, stated:

> *I did my best impersonation of what it would be like as an in-season schedule being here ... We did a lot of great things. After every practice I catered meals to my teammates just so I*

could have that team-building I missed here. ... I love those guys,
and I owe everything to them because they helped me prepare ...
It even boosted their confidence a little bit, getting a chance to
work in an NFL system, go out there and compete against each
other. [583]

There have been a lot of NFL players that have been suspended at one
time or another and what Winston did was anything but normal. However,
outside of Garafolo's article, Winston's professionalism and work ethic
during his suspension was almost entirely ignored by the national main
stream sports media, not that such should shock anyone.

Game One:
"A Terrible Situation"

Despite coach Koetter's aforementioned plan not to play Jameis Winston
until the fifth game of the season against the Falcons, Winston would see
his first action of the season in week four in Soldier Field against the
Chicago Bears and their vaunted defense. Starter Ryan Fitzpatrick had
thrown an interception and fumbled once and the Bucs were down 38-3 at
halftime [584] when coach Koetter decided to throw Winston to the wolves
so to speak. After the game Koetter confirmed as much when he stated:

We put Jameis in a terrible situation today, you know, uh, and I
told him that. I told him that right off the bat at halftime, that
we're putting him in a bad situation. And, uh, I mean, I knew
Jameis would go in and give us everything he had, and he did.
[585]

Winston finished his one half of action completing 80 percent of his
passes for 145 yards and one touchdown pass but had two passes
intercepted, one of which came on a deflection, and the Bears cruised to a
48-10 victory. [584]

Game Two:
Even Video-Game Stats
Can't Overcome Kicking and Defensive Woes

Winston's first start of the season would come in the following game, on the road against the division rival Atlanta Falcons. The Bucs offense would click and Winston would put on a magnificent show, throwing for 395 yards and four touchdowns with two interceptions (one on a ricochet that could have initially been caught for a touchdown) while recording a wonderful 115.4 passer rating and also adding 29 yards on the ground to finish with 414 yards of total offense. [586]

However, football is as much about defense as it is about offense, and as has generally been the case since Winston entered the league, his defense would have a rough game. The same defense that was torched for six touchdown passes the week before, by Mitchell Trubisky of all quarterbacks [584], would give up 355 passing yards and three touchdowns to Falcons quarterback Matt Ryan, and lose the game 34-29. [586]

In fact, the Bucs had a chance to win the game on the final play. After Falcons kicker and ageless wonder Matt Bryant drilled a remarkable 57 yard field goal to give the Falcons the five point lead (thanks to Bucs kicker Chandler Catanzaro missing an extra point and the team then needing and failing to convert a two-point conversion later in the game), Winston led the Bucs on a seven play, 68 yard drive that ended as time ran out at the Falcons eight yard line. And, had Catanzaro made the extra point he missed and also made the extra point that he could have attempted had the team not been forced to attempt a two-point conversion to try and make up for his earlier gaffe, he would have had a chance to kick a very makeable (for anyone but a Bucs kicker that is) 38 yard field goal to send the game to overtime knotted at 34-34. Such was not meant to be and the Bucs ended the game with a 2-3 record on the season. [586]

Game Three:
Jameis Puts On His Superman Cape
Yet is Treated like Lex Luthor by the Media

Winston's next game was his first home game of the season. The Buccaneers would square off with the Cleveland Browns and their sensational rookie quarterback Baker Mayfield. However it was the Browns ball-hawking defense that was carrying them as they had forced a whopping 16 turnovers in the season's first six games [587], including forcing future Hall of Fame Pittsburgh Steelers quarterback Ben Roethlisberger to commit an whopping five turnovers alone in a game that ended in a tie earlier in the season. [588]

Winston would turn the ball over against the Browns as well – three times to be precise – yet would also don his Superman cape, throw for 365 yards and gain another 55 yards on the ground while leading his team in rushing. Winston would also complete an absolutely brilliant and extremely clutch 14 yard pass on third down outside of field-goal range, to set up the game winning field goal that would give the Buccaneers a 26-23 victory and even their season record at 3-3. [589]

Winston was the only quarterback in the NFL that week to total over 400 yards of offense, lead his team in rushing and still win the game. [590] However, to my knowledge, I was the only person to mention that fact after the week concluded, when I did so on Twitter, and the national main stream sports media for the most part just ignored what Winston accomplished entirely.

By the way, many quarterbacks, including Ben Roethlisberger are often given credit for merely being trusted by their coach enough to call a high number of drop-backs in a game. Winston is asked to do such on the regular, yet the media barely notices. For example, in the aforementioned game against the Cleveland Browns, Roethlisberger attempted 41 passes, was sacked four times and ran the ball three times for a total of 48 drop-backs. The Steelers ran 80 offensive plays that game which also meant that Roethlisberger was asked to drop back on exactly 60 percent of the Steelers' offensive plays. [588]

In Jameis Winston's game against those same Cleveland Browns, he attempted 52 passes, was also sacked four times and scrambled 10 times, for an astonishing total of 66 drop-backs! Likewise, as the Buccaneers' only ran 88 plays that game, Winston was asked to drop-back on exactly 75 percent of his team's offensive plays, a full 25 percent higher than Roethlisberger was asked to do by the Steelers against the Browns! [589]

The media narrative for many quarterbacks – Roethlisberger included – when they turn the ball over, is that such is understandable as they were called upon by their coach to do so much. However, when Jameis Winston is called upon by his coach to do infinitely more, and does in fact do infinitely more, and even pulls out a win while totalling over 400 total yards and even leading his team in rushing, the media often either ignores his accomplishments or even finds a way to denigrate his performance by merely harping on his turnovers. The public then, trusting the media and likely not having the time to do their own research to fact-check said media, simply swallows the biased nonsense the media spouts.

Game Four:
Superman Gets Benched for Shazam

Going into their seventh game of the year against the Bengals in Cincinnati, and with the trade deadline right around the corner, many knowledgeable Bucs fans with foresight knew the team was not a playoff caliber team. Their defense was dreadful as usual, they didn't even have a league average rushing attack, their offensive line – especially the right side of the line – was getting abused on a regular basis, and their special teams were in shambles as well. They may have been 3-3 but could have just as easily been 0-6. Many fans were calling for the team to trade diva wide receiver DeSean Jackson for the highest draft pick they could get, as well as backup quarterback Ryan Fitzpatrick who was on the last year of his contract, for the same. However, the team decided to stand pat at the deadline and try to make a playoff push.

Jameis Winston was not up to the task in windy Cincinnati and had one of his worst games as a professional. Winston completed just 18-35 passes, though for a very respectable 276 yards and one touchdown, and tossed four interceptions. He was benched after throwing his fourth interception, a pick-six, in the third quarter and replaced by Ryan *Shazam* Fitzpatrick. Fitzpatrick would play fantastic in relief, though the Bucs would end up losing the game and drop to 3-4 on the season. [591]

Of course I know that Ryan Fitzpatrick's real nickname is *Fitzmagic*, which by the way is a very fitting nickname indeed, as Fitzpatrick has displayed *magic* at various times throughout his long NFL career. However, just one game after Winston put on his Superman cape, he was benched for Fitzpatrick, and therefore I'm calling Fitzpatrick *Shazam* in this chapter, as Shazam – also known as Captain Marvel – is one of the few comic book characters to ever defeat Superman in a battle. [592] If you don't appreciate a comic book reference, and believe me, I had to google it, just consider it a small tribute to former Buccaneer and comic book aficionado Gerald McCoy. [593] [594]

A Beneficial Benching?

Even yours truly was fine with Winston being benched during the Bengals game, as I am a firm believer that benchings, and even being traded or cut, can be extremely beneficial to almost any player in any sport, including quarterbacks in the NFL. History confirms the same.

For example, below is a list of just some of the quarterbacks enshrined in the *Pro Football Hall of Fame* that have been benched, traded or cut at some point during their careers, as well as a short summary of what transpired afterwards:

> Norm Van Brocklin: Van Brocklin was technically benched on a regular basis for years as he was platooned by his first team. He was later traded to the Philadelphia Eagles who he not only led to an NFL Championship as a full-time starter but where he also

made three straight Pro Bowls and won his one and only NFL MVP award. [595] [596]

Y.A. Tittle: Tittle was a good quarterback on his first team but was traded to the Giants where he won his one and only NFL MVP award, his only NFL Championship, and became a bona fide legend. [595] [597]

Johnny Unitas: Unitas was drafted by the Steelers but cut before ever playing in a single game, as the Steelers felt he wasn't intelligent enough to run a pro-style offense. He went on to be signed by the Colts and become one of the undisputed greatest quarterbacks who ever lived. [598]

Fran Tarkenton: Tarkenton was traded after six playoff-less seasons in Minnesota to the Giants, and after five playoff-less seasons in New York he was traded a second time, this time back to Minnesota. It wasn't until his 13th season in the league that he played in his first playoff game. However in the last six years of his NFL career, he won a division title in each and every season, advanced to three Super Bowls, made the Pro Bowl three times and won his one and only NFL MVP award. [595] [599]

Warren Moon: Moon was of course jettisoned to the CFL coming out of college, but even after he finally made his way to the NFL and turned into a superstar quarterback for the Houston Oilers, he was traded to the Vikings. After being traded he made the Pro Bowl three times and added a massive 15,640 passing yards and 95 touchdown passes to his career totals. [595] [243]

Kurt Warner: Warner was cut by his first team, the Green Bay Packers, and was later even benched by the Rams after winning two NFL MVP awards, a Super Bowl ring, Super Bowl MVP trophy, and becoming perhaps the greatest player in franchise history. He was later benched again, this time by the New York Giants. After that second benching he went on to sign with the

Arizona Cardinals, and after again being benched by them, ended up being named the NFL MVP by the *Newspaper Enterprise Association* and even led them to their first ever Super Bowl appearance which helped solidify his eventual enshrinement in Canton as a Hall of Fame immortal. [595] [600] [248]

A Minor Setback for a Major Comeback

Getting benched can be a death knell for a quarterback. Just ask Donovan McNabb and Drew Bledsoe, two quarterbacks that had a legitimate shot at ending up in the Hall of Fame at one time. However McNabb was benched by the Eagles, never played another game for them, was traded to the Redskins where he was benched again and traded again, this time to the Vikings where he was benched again, and then disappeared into the ether. As for Bledsoe, he was benched by the Dallas Cowboys and never played in another NFL game. [600]

However, as the previous section detailed, there have also been quarterbacks who seemed to benefit from being benched, or even traded or cut, and in hindsight such setbacks seemed to help those quarterbacks build a Hall of Fame resume.

Those who truly knew Jameis Winston had little doubt that he would respond to his benching the way Kurt Warner responded to his being benched by three different teams, rather than the way Donovan McNabb or Drew Bledsoe responded to their benchings.

The great philosopher Confucius originally coined a phrase that Vince Lombardi apparently enjoyed and re-phrased – as I used his version to open this chapter – which was:

> *Our greatest glory is not in never falling, but in rising every time we fall.* [601]

After being benched, Jameis Winston seemed to be in a mindset that would have made the great philosopher proud, as Winston stated:

> *I don't think I've ever been benched ... It's humbling, and it's definitely something I can grow from and learn from and you know what, it just adds to the story. I just have to keep working hard.* [602]

Hall of Fame quarterback Brett Favre once stated:

> *You have to play with the mentality that you are about to lose your job, and that they're going to talk about 'The Other Guy' first. You have to think, 'I want my name mentioned first.* [276]

And, while Favre was never technically *benched*, he was run out of Green Bay by Packers brass who wanted to hand the team over to "the other guy" also known as Aaron Rodgers. [603] Favre was also later released by the New York Jets [604] before having perhaps the best statistical season of his career in his 19th season playing for the Minnesota Vikings. [235]

As for Winston, he didn't seem at all worried that his benching would mean he'd lose his job long-term to "the other guy", let alone that it would mean anything close to a career death-knell, as he stated:

> *It's a setback ... But it's a minor setback for a major comeback.* [602]

Winston of course was right. He would return to the field just three games later and remain the starter for the rest of the season, while playing excellent as well. He would also have a literal major *comeback*, just as he said he would.

Game Five:
A Major Comeback Indeed

Jameis Winston's first game action since being benched came when coach Dirk Koetter inserted him into the week 11 game in MetLife Stadium against the New York Giants with 6:58 remaining in the 3rd quarter. The Buccaneers were already down 24-7, due in large part to the last three Bucs drives ending with Ryan Fitzpatrick throwing an interception. [605]

Winston entered the game and promptly led four straight TD drives, going 12-15 passing for 199 yards with two touchdown passes, another 16 rushing yards, no turnovers and a perfect 158.3 passer rating. However, the Bucs defense also gave up two more touchdowns and when Jameis and the Bucs took the field for the last time, they were down 38-35, and there was just 23 seconds remaining in the game and the Bucs had no timeouts left. Coach Koetter called for a Hail Mary type bomb to DeSean Jackson which was picked off, giving the Giants the victory and dropping the Bucs to 3-7 on the season. [605]

During Winston's postgame press conference, he never once boasted about how he played and instead stated:

> *I was just happy that uh, that God blessed me to have the opportunity to be out there again.* [606]

And, rather shockingly – at least to those who bought into the media's false narratives about Winston and a lack of *character* – when he was asked by a reporter in a roundabout way whether Coach Koetter – the coach that had benched him – should be fired if the Bucs had a second straight losing season, Winston stated:

> *No, I mean, I, I love my head coach. You know, he has to make some real tough decisions and I know that. ... My main focus is on the football field ... I'm trying so hard to find a way to win ... it*

*hurts me when I have to see my team lose a game ... it's not a time
to, to point fingers or blame anybody else.* [606]

Regardless of the final result, Jameis Winston was back! He had led a
major comeback indeed by leading the Bucs to 28 points in less than 22
minutes of game-time [605] and there was no question he would start the
next game. Coach Koetter confirmed the same the following day [607]
though everyone knew such would be the case when Koetter answered a
question as to how he thought Winston played against the Giants by
stating:

> *Fantastic, I mean, you didn't need to ask me that question. I mean
> it's pretty obvious he came in and lit it up.* [608]

Game Six:
"To God Be the Glory"

Jameis Winston started the week 11 game against the San Francisco 49ers
who boasted a top 10 pass defense. However, despite the Niners boasting
such a masterful pass defense, head coach and noted quarterback guru
Kyle Shanahan seemed fearful of his defense facing off against Winston,
as he stated before the game:

> *Jameis, some of the plays he's made over his career are
> unbelievable ... when nothing is there, he's made some plays that
> I didn't think people could make. He can be as good as anyone in
> this league and that's why we've got to play very well.* [609]

Shanahan's words were prophetic as Winston wouldn't just play "as good
as anyone in the league" had played against them all year; he would play
better than any other quarterback had played against them. Winston
shredded the 49ers defense to the tune of completing over 76 percent of
his passes for 312 yards, two touchdowns, no turnovers, a magnificent
passer rating of 117.3 [610] and an other-worldly QBR of 93.0 [611], which
just happened to be the highest QBR any quarterback – including Patrick

Mahomes, Aaron Rodgers, Russell Wilson and Philip Rivers – recorded against the 49ers all season. [612]

During Winston's post-game press conference he summed up his return game by stating:

> *To God be the glory; I'm so blessed to have the opportunity to be*
> *out there with my teammates again, and uh, and executing at a*
> *high level.* [613]

Jameis would start the next week, as well as every remaining game of the 2018 NFL season.

Game Seven:
Val-Zod Defeats Superman

Winston and the 4-7 Bucs hosted the 6-6 Carolina Panthers in week 13 and entered the game as 3.5 point underdogs despite being at home. [614] However, once again Jameis Winston would put on his Superman cape and this time lead his team to victory over the original Superman, Cam Newton. In short – and to borrow from the previous comic book theme and again to honor former Buccaneer Gerald McCoy – Jameis Winston became the second Superman in order to defeat the original superman, just like Val-Zod became the second Superman and defeated the original Superman, Clark Kent. [615]

Winston and the Buccaneers controlled the game from the get-go and led 10-0, then 17-7, then 24-10 on their way to a 24-17 victory. The original Superman – Cam Newton – threw four interceptions, finished with an abysmal 66.2 passer rating, and despite his teammates gaining a massive 135 rushing yards on just 13 carries, only led his team to 17 points on the day. Winston on the other hand received just 47 yards of run support despite his teammates getting 20 carries; however, he personally led the team in rushing with 48 yards on just five carries, added 249 passing yards and two passing touchdowns, played turnover-free football and posted an extremely impressive 114.4 passer rating on the day. [614]

Games Eight through Ten:
Three Losses to Three Heavily Favored Teams

The next three games were tough ones for both Winston and the Buccaneers. The Bucs entered their week 14 game against the Saints, week 15 game against the Ravens, and week 16 game against the Cowboys as heavy underdogs, yet led the Saints 14-3 at halftime and only trailed the Ravens 10-9 and Cowboys 17-13 at the half as well. The Bucs covered the spread in two of the three games, which made their gambling fans happy, but lost all three games and fell to 5-10 at the end of the stretch. [616] [617] [618]

As for Winston himself, over the three games he threw for just 706 yards and three touchdowns, pedestrian numbers by his own lofty standards. He also threw two interceptions over the three games, though one of them was a last-play Hail Mary, his second Hail Mary interception of the season. [616] [617] [618]

Strangely enough, Winston actually threw for more yards than the opposing team's quarterback (i.e. Drew Brees, Lamar Jackson and Dak Prescott) in each game. However, while Winston would once again lead the team in rushing – this time in the Saints game – the Bucs would give Jameis just 192 yards of run support over the three games, while the opposing team's quarterbacks would receive a combined total of 326 rushing yards over the same stretch. Likewise, the opposing team's kickers would go a combined 6-6 on their field goal attempts, while Bucs kicker Cairos Santos would hit on just four of seven attempts over the three games. [616] [617] [618]

Game Eleven:
Dirk Koetter's Farewell and Jameis Winston's Hello

The Buccaneers' final game of the year was against the Atlanta Falcons. [619] And, despite being a home game, there was a large segment of the fandom that were hoping the Bucs would lose the game so that they could get the highest draft pick possible in the 2019 NFL Draft. Those fans would get their wish.

The Bucs defense would find a way to once again snatch defeat from the jaws of victory by giving up 34 points and a game-winning field goal drive. [619] Jameis Winston however would put on an MVP level performance for the home fans, assure that Buccaneers brass would honor his 5th year nearly $21,000,000 option contract [511] that was only guaranteed against injury [510], and therefore keep his word that the benching he suffered earlier in the year was nothing more than a minor setback for a major comeback. [602]

Winston finished the game with 345 passing yards, four touchdown passes, one interception – which came off a dropped pass by Mike Evans that popped up into the air and was picked off – and an outstanding 121.7 passer rating. He also led back to back clutch fourth quarter touchdown drives, ending both with a touchdown pass, the second of which went to receiver Chris Godwin and gave the Bucs a 32-31 lead with just 5:10 left in the game. However, Winston wouldn't see the ball again, as the Bucs defense couldn't get the Falcons off the field and surrendered a game-ending field goal that gave the Falcons the two point victory. [619]

Nevertheless, there was a silver lining in the defeat, and that was that with the loss the Bucs locked up the fifth pick in the upcoming 2019 NFL Draft, which ended up being used on star linebacker Devin White, a player that many compare to Hall of Fame linebacker Ray Lewis. [620] [621] [622] [623]

Dirk Koetter Fired

Before the clock struck midnight after the Buccaneers' final game of the season, and despite Jameis Winston fighting for head coach Dirk Koetter to retain his job despite the team's poor record [624], Kotter was fired. [625] It seems that benching the quarterback whose historic rookie season was responsible for Koetter being hired in the first place [626], and whose third year progression despite playing much of the year with an injured throwing shoulder [398] [409] [411] [412] helped Koetter retain his job despite the team going 5-11 [627], may have been beneficial for Winston but disastrous for Koetter. Perhaps had Koetter merely benched Winston for the remainder of the Bengals game in which he threw four interceptions [591], rather than actually starting Ryan Fitzpatrick over Winston the next three weeks with the team losing all three of those games [628] [629] [605], Koetter could have retained his job.

However, the Buccaneer that many consider the team's current best player and the player that is undoubtedly the team's second most popular player behind Winston on a national scale – Mike Evans – stated something at the 2019 Pro Bowl that may have revealed that Koetter may have gone rogue and benched Winston against the team's wishes, and therefore lost the locker-room in the process, which of course is almost always a death knell for any coach. Evans was asked what he thought about Jameis Winston being "the guy" in 2019, and he simply stated:

That's what I thought all along. [630]

Regardless, Dirk Koetter was no longer Jameis Winston's coach, and while Winston fought for Koetter to retain his job [624] and always spoke highly of Koetter while he was still employed by the Buccaneers, he did make a very revealing comment after Koetter was fired that may explain why Koetter was fired.

During one post-season interview, Winston was asked how he turned things around after being benched. Winston answered that question by stating:

> *I had to look at myself in the mirror and say, 'Hey Jameis, what do you have to do?' And that was simply, 'Get back to playing Jameis Winston football. Be yourself. Have that swag. Don't try to be something that a coach is trying to get you to be.' You know, you gotta go and be you.* [631]

Wow. So basically Winston revealed that after he was benched, he realized he needed to ignore his coach and get back to being himself on the football field.

While the national media put a negative spin on Winston's statement and painted him out to be disrespectful to his coach [632], the simple fact is that Winston played so much better after being benched than he did before being benched. Therefore whatever he did – even if it was completely ignoring Dirk Koetter – worked beautifully!

Had Aaron Rodgers or another media darling quarterback said the exact same words that Jameis Winston said, and had their play improve the way Jameis' did, they would no doubt have been praised by the media for their personal fortitude and courage. However, Jameis Winston is anything but a media darling as we all know.

The Statistical Juxtaposition between
Pre-Benched Jameis and Post-Benched Jameis

The juxtaposition between Jameis Winston's pre-benching games and his post-benching games, or perhaps better said, his Koetter-coached games and his Winston-coached games was dramatic. Consider the statistical table on the following page:

Jameis Winston	TD %	INT %	Passer Rating
Pre-benching aka Koetter-coached	4.1	6.8	74.8
Post-benching aka Jameis-coached	5.7	1.7	100.1

[633]

To put the above statistics in perspective, had Winston finished the 2018 season with his pre-benching aka Koetter-coached stats, he would have ranked 23rd in the NFL in touchdown percentage, 33rd in interception percentage and 31st in passer rating. However, had Winston finished the 2018 season with his post-benching – aka Jameis-coached – stats, he would have ranked 11th in touchdown percentage, 9th in interception percentage and 10th in passer rating. And, if you were to discount Jameis' two Hail Mary interceptions, he actually would have ranked 2nd in the entire NFL in interception percentage, behind only Aaron Rodgers! [221]

There simply is no doubt that the Jameis-coached, post-benching Jameis Winston, was an elite NFL quarterback and performed infinitely better than the pre-benching, Koetter-coached Winston did. It isn't even debatable.

The above said, it's rather ironic that while Winston got Koetter hired in the first place [626] and while his statistical progression despite playing injured in his third season [398] [409] [411] [412] kept Koetter from getting fired [627], it just may have been the fact that Winston played far better after he decided to ignore his coach and simply "get back to playing Jameis Winston football" [631] that Koetter was ultimately canned.

Winston Thanks God for His Trials and Tribulations

Jameis Winston's fourth NFL season was certainly the most frustrating season of his career for him, as well as the most perplexing for his fans. It was filled with trials and tribulations, but like Kurt Warner before him, he overcame such trials and tribulations and turned his minor setback into a major comeback, just as he said he would.

After the year ended, Jameis Winston summed up his bizarre fourth season and tweeted:

> *God you get all the glory!!! Blessed for another year in the @nfl. You've taught me patience, perseverance humility and so much more through this game! Thank you!* [634]

> I can personally appreciate such a statement, as when I reflect back on my life, I fondly remember the trials and tribulations I was able to overcome with God's guidance and help, even more fondly than I remember my tangible successes. I can also sincerely understand why so many of Winston's family, friends, fans, teammates and coaches find him to be an extremely inspirational figure, no matter how hard the media tries to paint him as a villain in the modern day sports landscape.

Accolades and Achievements

When the 2018 regular season ended, Jameis Winston was second all-time in NFL history in both career passing touchdowns and career passing yards before the age of 25. [635] [636]

Likewise, according to the NFL and their *Next Gen Stats*, Winston also finished the 2018 season:

1st in the entire NFL in *Air Yards to the Sticks* (AYTS) [637] which is described as:

Air Yards to the Sticks shows the amount of Air Yards ahead or behind the first down marker on all attempts for a passer. The metric indicates if the passer is attempting his passes past the 1st down marker, or if he is relying on his skill position players to make yards after catch. [375]

2nd in the entire NFL in *Average Completed Air Yards* (CAY) [637] which is described as:

CAY shows the average Air Yards a passer throws on completions ... This metric shows how far the ball is being thrown 'downfield'. Air Yards is recorded as a negative value when the pass is behind the Line of Scrimmage. Additionally Air Yards is calculated into the back of the end zone to better evaluate the true depth of the pass. [375]

2nd in the entire NFL in *Averaged Intended Air Yards* (IAY) [637] which is described as:

IAY shows the average Air Yards a passer throws on all attempts. This metric shows how far the ball is being thrown 'downfield'. Air Yards is recorded as a negative value when the pass is behind the Line of Scrimmage. Additionally Air Yards is calculated into the back of the end zone to better evaluate the true depth of the pass. [375]

13th in the entire NFL in *Completion Percentage Above Expectation* (+/-) [637] which is described as:

A passer's actual completion percentage compared to their Expected Completion Percentage. [375]

And, while 13th may not sound all that impressive and certainly pales in comparison to his ranking of 5th in the entire NFL in both 2016 and 2017, he still finished higher than 2018 NFL MVP Patrick Mahomes, as well as higher than both Tom Brady and Aaron Rodgers, which is nothing to sneeze at. [637]

To put the above in perspective, let's simply compare Jameis Winston's expected completion percentage, actual completion percentage, and *Completion Percentage Above Expectation*, with the same stats for the GOTSBE, Tom Brady.

Player	Expected Completion %	Actual Completion %	+/-
Jameis Winston	62.7	64.6	+ 1.9
Jameis Winston (throwing the same passes as Brady)	67.7	69.6	+ 1.9
Tom Brady	67.7	65.8	- 1.9
Tom Brady (throwing the same passes as Winston)	62.7	60.8	- 1.9

The above is a fantastic statistical table as it shows why the lazy narratives spun by talking heads regarding completion percentage are so absurd. To the talking heads, Tom Brady is a much more accurate passer than Jameis Winston, simply because he had a 1.2 percent higher completion percentage on the season than Winston did. However, when one understands that Brady threw passes that should have resulted in a 5.0 percent higher completion rate than Winston, one realizes that Brady was actually far less accurate than Winston was during the 2018 season. In fact, had Winston been throwing the same passes Brady was throwing, he would have had a remarkable 69.6 percent completion percentage!

The way many media talking heads spin lazy narratives about completion percentage being identical to passing accuracy is akin to how some low-basketball-IQ fans say that Michael Jordan was a better *shooter* than Reggie Miller, simply because Jordan has a higher career field goal percentage than Miller. Anyone who actually watched Michael Jordan and Reggie Miller play knows that Miller was the far superior *shooter*. And, any stat-geek knows that Miller had the higher career 2-point field goal percentage, 3-point field goal percentage and free throw percentage, and the reason Jordan ended up with the higher career field goal percentage is simply because he took far less 3-point shots and got a great deal more easy shots at the rim than Miller ever dreamed of getting with his far inferior athleticism and strength.

Just as having a higher field goal percentage is not akin to being a better *shooter* in the NBA, so too is having a higher completion percentage not akin to being a more accurate passer in the NFL. In the case of the NBA player, it may be that he simply took less 3-pointers, or that he got more layups or dunks. In the case of the NFL quarterback, it may simply be that he threw less deep-balls and more short passes.

Regardless, it's time for sports fans to cast off the silly and lazy narratives spun by the media and to become more sophisticated in their understanding of the game, and a table like the one on the previous page can help make that happen.

Furthermore, on top of Winston's incredibly impressive Next Gen Stats, according to NFL Analyst Jonathan Kinsley of *Brick Wall Blitz*, Winston finished the 2018 season:

1st in the entire NFL in 3rd and long (eight plus yards) conversion percentage on pass plays. [638]

2nd in the entire NFL in 3rd down conversion percentage, behind only MVP Patrick Mahomes. [639]

Winston also finished 4th in the entire NFL in Raw QBR [221] ; in fact, he was the only quarterback other than Drew Brees to finish a season in the top five in Raw QBR on a losing team since 2015, the year he was drafted! That is an incredibly rare feat and a marvelous accomplishment for a quarterback on a team as bad as Tampa was, yet the media ignored it.

Finally, according to ESPN'S *NFL Matchup*, Winston also finished the 2018 season:

1st in the entire NFL in passer rating *under pressure*. [640]

1st in the entire NFL in passer rating *outside the pocket*. [641]

4th in the entire NFL in passer rating *on 3rd down*, behind only Russell Wilson, MVP Patrick Mahomes and future first ballot Hall of Famer Drew Brees. [642]

All of the above said, while Winston's fourth season may have been a disappointment when it came to the simple counting stats – due to him only playing around 9.5 games worth of plays – he was indisputably *elite* according to the advanced metrics – elite!

The Most Accomplished
24 Year Old Quarterback in NFL History?

When Jameis Winston's fourth season concluded, he found himself second all-time in NFL history in career passing touchdowns and career passing yards before the age of 25. [635]

However, the one quarterback ahead of him in career touchdown passes ranks just sixth in career passing yards before the age of 25, and the one quarterback ahead of him in career passing yards ranks just fourth in career passing touchdowns before the age of 25. [635] That said, there has never been a more statistically accomplished 24 year old passer in the history of the NFL than Jameis Winston, not a single one!

JAMEIS WINSTON vs. THE GREATS

PART IV

The great ones have the ability to focus and tune everything else out and see more than the others.

— Kurt Warner [643]

Jameis Winston's bizarre and trying fourth season could have broken any quarterback, let alone a 24 year old quarterback in a contract year like Winston. In fact, I challenge you the reader to find even one quarterback under 25 in the history of football that had as rough a first ten weeks of any season, as Winston had in 2018, yet came back to play as well as Winston did in the last seven weeks. I don't believe you'll find one, not a single one in the history of the NFL. Indeed Jameis Winston displayed amazing focus and the ability to tune everything else out, "get back to playing Jameis Winston football" [631] and make a major comeback [602] that was one for the ages in Tampa, Florida!

The above said, let's now jump into the comparisons between Winston and the 21 legendary quarterbacks we have compared him with throughout this book.

Age Related Statistical Comparisons

As I did in the previous *Part I*, *Part II* and *Part III* versions of this chapter, I will compare Winston to the 21 current or soon to be Hall of Fame quarterbacks who began their careers in the Super Bowl era, by age. Likewise, I will once again compare each player in the following four categories: passing yards, passing touchdowns, completion percentage and passer rating.

Before Age 25 Stats	Pass Yards	Pass TDs	Comp %	Passer Rating
Jameis Winston	**14628**	**88**	**61.6**	**87.8**
Troy Aikman	6878	30	58.5	70.0
Terry Bradshaw	5556	31	48.2	52.6
Tom Brady	2849	18	63.7	86.1
Drew Brees	5613	29	59.4	73.7
John Elway	4261	25	52.7	68.0
Brett Favre	8179	46	61.9	78.1
Dan Fouts	4254	16	49.2	56.0
Bob Griese	6173	46	50.4	65.7
Jim Kelly	0	0	DNP	DNP
Eli Manning	4805	30	51.6	70.5
Peyton Manning	12287	85	60.4	85.4
Dan Marino	11975	102	61.1	96.6
Joe Montana	1891	16	63.9	87.3
Warren Moon	0	0	DNP	DNP
Philip Rivers	2748	17	63.8	91.7
Aaron Rodgers	3226	21	63.1	88.9
Ben Roethlisberger	8519	52	62.4	87.9
Ken Stabler	52	0	28.6	18.5
Roger Staubach	0	0	DNP	DNP
Kurt Warner	0	0	DNP	DNP
Steve Young	1217	4	50.5	57.9

[141] [230] [644] [231] [232] [233] [234] [235] [645] [236] [237] [238] [239] [240] [241] [646] [242] [243] [244] [647] [245] [648] [211] [246] [247] [248] [249] [649]

Just as with the *Before Age 22* Stats, *Before Age 23 Stats* and *Before Age 24 Stats* tables detailed in the *Part 1*, *Part II* and *Part III* versions of this chapter, one can quickly see that Jameis Winston, at best, is the most statistically accomplished 24 year old quarterback out of all the 21 current or soon to be Hall of Fame quarterbacks, and at worst, is one of the two best along with Dan Marino. In fact, Winston has 2,341 more career passing yards than any other quarterback on the list, and is second to only Dan Marino in passing touchdowns.

Senior Season Statistical Comparisons

While Jameis Winston has accumulated the second most career passing yards and passing touchdowns of any of the aforementioned 21 legendary quarterbacks before the age of 25, I will now compare his fourth season alone, with each of their fourth seasons.

Below is a statistical table comparing Winston's fourth season with the fourth seasons of the other 21 quarterbacks, regardless of each quarterbacks age. And, per the usual, in the below statistical table I will compare each of the 22 quarterbacks in the four prime categories: passing yards, passing touchdowns, completion percentage and passer rating.

4th Year Stats	Pass Yards	Pass TDs	Comp %	Passer Rating
Jameis Winston	**2992**	**19**	**64.6**	**90.2**
Troy Aikman	3445	23	63.8	89.5
Terry Bradshaw	1183	10	49.4	54.5
Tom Brady	3620	23	60.2	85.9
Drew Brees	3159	27	65.5	104.8
John Elway	3485	19	55.6	79.0
Brett Favre	3882	33	62.4	90.7
Dan Fouts	2535	14	57.9	75.4
Bob Griese	2019	12	58.0	72.1
Jim Kelly	3130	25	58.3	86.2
Eli Manning	3336	23	56.1	73.9
Peyton Manning	4131	26	62.7	84.1
Dan Marino	4746	44	60.7	92.5
Joe Montana	2613	17	61.6	88.0
Warren Moon	2806	21	50.0	74.2
Philip Rivers	3152	21	60.2	82.4
Aaron Rodgers	4038	28	63.6	93.8
Ben Roethlisberger	3154	32	65.3	104.1
Ken Stabler	1997	14	62.7	88.3
Roger Staubach	98	0	45.0	20.4
Kurt Warner	4830	36	68.7	101.4

Steve Young	680	3	53.5	72.2

[141] [230] [231] [232] [233] [234] [235] [236] [237] [238] [239] [240] [241] [242] [243] [244] [245] [211] [246] [247] [248] [249]

After viewing the above statistical table, one can certainly see that Winston doesn't dominate this fourth season table the way he did the first three season tables. However, despite missing five full games and parts of three others, and therefore really only playing around 9.5 games worth of snaps, he still compares favorably across the board with the other 21 quarterbacks. In fact, Winston had the fourteenth most passing yards, fourteenth most touchdown passes, as well as the fourth best completion percentage and seventh best passer rating of any of the quarterbacks.

Through Fourth Season Statistical Comparisons

In this section, I will compare Jameis Winston's stats *through* his fourth season with the aforementioned 21 quarterbacks *through* their fourth seasons, irrespective of age. And, per the usual, in the below statistical table I will compare each of the 22 quarterbacks in the four prime categories: passing yards, passing touchdowns, completion percentage and passer rating.

Through 4th Year Stats	Pass Yards	Pass TDs	Comp %	Passer Rating
Jameis Winston	**14628**	**88**	**61.6**	**87.8**
Troy Aikman	10527	54	60.2	76.4
Terry Bradshaw	6739	41	48.4	52.9
Tom Brady	10233	69	61.9	85.9
Drew Brees	8772	56	61.3	83.2
John Elway	11637	66	54.0	71.9
Brett Favre	10412	70	62.3	82.2
Dan Fouts	6789	30	52.4	63.0
Bob Griese	8192	58	52.0	67.0
Jim Kelly	12901	81	59.2	82.7
Eli Manning	11385	77	54.7	73.4
Peyton Manning	16418	111	61.0	85.1
Dan Marino	16177	142	60.9	95.2

Joe Montana	8069	52	63.1	88.0
Warren Moon	12342	61	53.4	70.2
Philip Rivers	6688	44	60.8	86.6
Aaron Rodgers	4367	29	63.2	91.8
Ben Roethlisberger	11673	84	63.2	92.5
Ken Stabler	2841	19	59.9	79.4
Roger Staubach	2943	18	56.1	81.1
Steve Young	4467	24	53.4	71.3
Kurt Warner	12651	98	66.9	103.0

[141] [230] [231] [232] [233] [234] [235] [236] [237] [238] [239] [240] [241] [242] [243] [244] [245] [211] [246] [247] [248] [249]

After viewing the above statistical table, one can see that Jameis Winston, through his fourth season, had the third most career passing yards, the fourth most career touchdown passes, the seventh best career completion percentage, and the sixth best career passer rating when compared to the other 21 legendary quarterbacks through their respective first four seasons in the NFL.

Likewise, of the other 21 quarterbacks, the only ones to best Jameis in at least two of the four categories were Peyton Manning, Dan Marino, Joe Montana, Aaron Rodgers, Ben Roethlisberger and Kurt Warner. And, the only quarterbacks to best Winston in three of the four categories were Dan Marino and Kurt Warner. No quarterback bested Winston in all four categories.

The above said, while Winston is undoubtedly the most statistically accomplished 24 year old quarterback in NFL history, it's also clear that he has a very strong claim to also having had one of very best first four seasons in quarterback history as well, irrespective of age.

Adjusted for Era Statistical Comparisons

As I did in the *Part 1*, *Part II* and *Part III* versions of this chapter, in this adjusted for era section I will forego the mere *counting stats* and focus on the advanced metrics of passing yards per attempt (Y/A), touchdown percentage (TD %), completion percentage (Comp %), as well as Raw QBR (if such was available in each respective players rookie season) or passer rating (if Raw QBR was not available in each respective players rookie season) to really get an ultra-accurate picture of just how Jameis Winston compares to the aforementioned 21 legendary quarterbacks.

Furthermore, rather than merely listing each player's Y/A, TD%, Comp % and Raw QBR / Passer Rating during his junior season – which still does not adjust for era whatsoever – I will list where each player ranked across his league and even adjust said ranking for a 32 team league which the modern NFL has.

For example, if in a particular quarterback's junior season there were only 16 teams, and he finished 8th in the league in touchdown percentage, such would be akin to him finishing 16th in the modern 32 team NFL and therefore he will receive a ranking of 16th in the TD % category.

The formula I will use to determine each quarterback's league ranking in a particular category is: league rank, divided by qualifying quarterbacks, times 32. However, if there are more qualifying quarterbacks than there are teams, the formula would be league rank, divided by league teams, times 32.

Furthermore, if a particular quarterback did not qualify in all four statistical categories, it will say DNQ (i.e. Did Not Qualify) in all four of that quarterbacks' categories as well as in the *Average Rank* (Avg. Rank) category. However, if a quarterback qualifies in even one category, I will use his stats to rank him in the other categories, such as I did with Terry Bradshaw's fourth season (in *Jameis Winston vs. the Greats Part IV* chapter) in 1973, as in that season Bradshaw qualified in passer rating but not in completion percentage (where he was worse than the last place qualifier and would have therefore ranked 18th, but as there were only 17 quarterbacks who qualified he is ranked 34th, as his 18th ranking, divided by 17 qualifying quarterbacks, times 32 teams, equals 33.888 or a ranking of 34th in a 32 team league which the current NFL has). [254]

Also, if a quarterback started at least five games in a season, I will rank him even if he doesn't technically qualify in a specific category. Such is the case with Steve Young in his 1985 rookie season [255], as well as Eli Manning in his 2004 rookie season. [256]

Finally, I need to mention that while I have relied on pro-football-reference.com a great deal when researching for this book, and while such is an amazing website, it can be a little confusing for some when they are researching seasonal statistical *rankings* when two or more players *tie* to the decimal point in any particular category. For example, the site can at times show Dan Marino incorrectly ranked 2nd in TD % in his rookie season of 1983, when he was slight percentage points behind Neil Lomax and therefore truly should be ranked 3rd. However rest assured, I have done the math and made sure that every single one of the rankings I provide are absolutely correct. Please feel free to double-check my math for yourself in order to confirm that I am 100% correct each and every time.

All of the above said, the following table details how Jameis Winston compares to each of the 21 legendary quarterbacks when adjusted for era, as well as how each of those quarterbacks compare to each other.

4th Year Ranking	Y/A	TD %	Comp %	PR / QBR	Avg. Rank
Jameis Winston	**10th**	**18th**	**21st**	**5th**	**14th**
Troy Aikman	13th	8th	6th	4th	8th
Terry Bradshaw	21st	11th	34th	25th	23rd
Tom Brady	13th	13th	13th	10th	12th
Drew Brees	7th	3rd	7th	3rd	5th
John Elway	20th	15th	17th	13th	16th
Brett Favre	17th	2nd	7th	2nd	7th
Dan Fouts	13th	17th	6th	15th	13th
Bob Griese	3rd	12th	5th	12th	8th
Jim Kelly	4th	2nd	12th	7th	6th
Eli Manning	28th	13th	29th	18th	22nd
Peyton Manning	5th	9th	5th	9th	7th
Dan Marino	7th	1st	6th	2nd	4th
Joe Montana	9th	10th	8th	6th	8th
Warren Moon	10th	6th	30th	21st	17th
Philip Rivers	18th	11th	23rd	20th	18th
Aaron Rodgers	9th	4th	10th	10th	8th
Ben Roethlisberger	4th	2nd	7th	7th	5th

Ken Stabler	9th	15th	1st	5th	30th
Roger Staubach	DNQ	DNQ	DNQ	DNQ	DNQ
Kurt Warner	1st	1st	1st	1st	1st
Steve Young	DNQ	DNQ	DNQ	DNQ	DNQ

[221] [386] [254] [458] [256] [264] [650] [651] [258] [257] [463] [260] [264] [652] [389]
[463] [653] [463] [254] [457] [260] [460]

Note: Bradshaw did not technically qualify in the completion percentage category, however he was worse than the last place qualifier and would therefore have ranked 18th, but as there were only 17 quarterbacks who qualified he is ranked 34th, as I used 18 / 17 x 32 to get a rank of 34th.

After viewing the above statistical table it's obvious that while Winston's senior season did not compare to the 21 legendary quarterbacks' senior seasons as favorably as his first three seasons did, it still compared favorably indeed, even when adjusted for era.

Winston had the fourteenth best average ranking of the 21 legendary quarterbacks listed above. In fact, Winston ranked in between the Tom Brady and Dan Fouts duo and the John Elway and Warren Moon duo.

Through Senior Season
Adjusted for Era Statistical Comparisons

As I did in the previous section, I will now compare the adjusted for era statistics of Jameis Winston and the 21 legendary quarterbacks, this time comparing each quarterback's first four seasons, rather than merely their senior season alone.

In regards to how the rankings are calculated, it's a simple matter of adding and dividing. For example if a quarterback ranked third in yards per attempt in his first season, fourth in the same category in his second season and eighth in his third season, he would receive a ranking of fifth in the following table in the yards per attempt category. And, as it's a matter of simple math that anyone can do, there are no citations following the table on the following page, as I do not assign citations to my own original statistical research.

Through 4th Year Rankings	Y/A	TD %	Comp %	PR / QBR	Avg. Rank
Jameis Winston	**10th**	**17th**	**22nd**	**12th**	**15th**
Troy Aikman	19th	22nd	13th	18th	18th
Terry Bradshaw	26th	22nd	26th	26th	25th
Tom Brady*	18th	12th	9th	8th	12th
Drew Brees*	20th	19th	14th	19th	18th
John Elway	25th	21st	21st	21st	22nd
Brett Favre*	20th	13th	8th	10th	13th
Dan Fouts	16th	24th	20th	25th	21st
Bob Griese	19th	19th	15th	18th	18th
Jim Kelly	12th	13th	8th	11th	11th
Eli Manning	27th	17th	29th	23rd	24th
Peyton Manning	9th	8th	8th	11th	9th
Dan Marino	7th	3rd	8th	3rd	5th
Joe Montana*	15th	13th	3rd	6th	9th
Warren Moon	14th	21st	23rd	23rd	20th
Philip Rivers**	13th	10th	19th	12th	14th
Aaron Rodgers***	9th	4th	10th	10th	8th
Ben Roethlisberger	4th	7th	10th	7th	7th
Ken Stabler***	9th	15th	1st	5th	8th
Roger Staubach***	1st	3rd	5th	1st	3rd
Kurt Warner*	1st	2nd	1st	2nd	2nd
Steve Young**	23rd	31st	22nd	29th	26th

* Each asterisk represents one season that the respective quarterback did not qualify to be ranked. For example, Aaron Rodgers failed to qualify to be ranked in three of his first four season, while Steve Young failed to qualify in two of his first four season and Tom Brady failed to qualify in one of his first four seasons.

After viewing the above statistical table, it's clear that Winston's first four NFL seasons compare favorably to the first four seasons of the 21 legendary quarterbacks, even when adjusted for era.

In fact, the only quarterbacks who had a better average rank than Winston who actually qualified to be ranked in all four of their first four seasons in the league were: Peyton Manning, Ben Roethlisberger, Jim Kelly and Dan Marino.

The indisputable fact is that the hard data covered in this chapter proves that Jameis Winston is more statistically accomplished than any of the 21 legendary quarterbacks – other than perhaps Dan Marino – before the age of 25. Such hard data also proves that Winston had a solid senior season when compared to the 21 legendary quarterbacks in regards to the counting stats, and even confirms that Winston had, at worst, the 14th best senior season of said quarterbacks, even when adjusting for era. Finally, such hard data even confirms that Winston had the fifth best, first four season start to his NFL career, when compared to the 21 legendary quarterbacks and when adjusting for era!

EXPOSING MEDIA FALSE NARRATIVES

Propaganda is as powerful as heroin; it surreptitiously dissolves all capacity to think.

– Gil Courtemanche [654]

Today the world is the victim of propaganda because people are not intellectually competent.

– William Mather Lewis [3.1]

The two quotes above present a sort of chicken and egg situation when it comes to propaganda and intellectual competency or the ability to think. Are modern sports fans so intellectually incompetent that they cannot discern between actual truth and biased propaganda, or have they been so poisoned by biased propaganda that they have been made intellectually incompetent? Such may be a question that will never be answered, however as the great philosophical television show – G.I. Joe – was known to conclude each episode, *knowing is half the battle*. Therefore, while we may never be able to answer such a question we can at least *know* that propaganda exists, even in the sports world, and through this chapter *know* how to combat such propaganda with truth.

The above said, many media members have personal biases against various NFL quarterbacks, such as Stephen A. Smith with Jay Cutler or Skip Bayless with Carson Wentz. Likewise, many media members have personal biases in favor of various quarterbacks, such as Max Kellerman with Aaron Rodgers or Colin Cowherd with Sam Darnold. However, such obvious biases are usually light-hearted and even forced for effect devices to generate audience interaction or to stir the pot as it were. They are harmless idiosyncrasies of various talking heads that add spice to silly little sports debates.

The media bias against Jameis Winston is entirely different. It is unbelievably widespread, supremely coordinated, incredibly vicious, and even extraordinarily constant. It is as if Jameis Winston is a politician rather than an athlete, and as if the main stream sports media talking heads are literally being ordered by their bosses to slander Winston every chance they get, and to stealthily spread *Winston Derangement Syndrome* to their audience en masse.

While Winston certainly is not a politician, I do believe that many main stream sports media talking heads and journalists are indeed receiving their talking points from, and slandering Winston under the instruction of, their corporate higher ups. Believing such is simply more logical and rational than actually believing that so many otherwise intelligent and conscientious media personalities each went insane around the exact same time and decided that the former youngest Heisman winner in NCAA history, the quarterback who went 26-1 and won a National Title along with a National Title Game MVP award, the only quarterback in NFL history to start his career with back to back 4,000 yard passing seasons, the youngest Pro Bowl quarterback in the history of the NFL, the quarterback who led the entire NFL in 300 yard passing games in 2017 despite missing all or part of five different games due to injury, and the 24 year old quarterback who in 2018 led the entire NFL in passer rating under pressure, as well as led the entire NFL in a number of other advanced metrics, is a bust and should be nothing more than a backup somewhere, or even out of the NFL altogether. It seems to me that, that sort of mass insanity amongst media members simply must be orchestrated rather than accidental.

However, I suppose if the talking heads want to claim that such a belief is crazy, and that they truly all did lose their minds at the same time, and that such was simply pure coincidence, we can take them at their word, right?

Regardless, if you were to go on a solo nature hike and stumble upon a group of people all dressed alike, singing the same song, dancing and having a cook-out in the middle of the woods, would you believe that such a group of people planned such a gathering, or would you believe that such a group of people just accidentally put on the same clothes and happened to bump into each other in the middle of the woods? If you're honest, you'd obviously believe the former. Likewise, I believe it's obvious that the false media narratives surrounding Jameis Winston that are parroted and furthered by talking heads coast to coast, were planned by corporate higher ups and then carried out by the talking heads and journalists in their charge, as I believe such is by far the most logical conclusion one can reach, and the one conclusion that fits the evidence at hand.

Could I be wrong? Sure. Could the media really all have just become deranged at the same time when it comes to Jameis Winston? I suppose that's possible. However, again, I do believe the evidence points to an *orchestrated* rather than a *coincidental* outbreak of *Winston Derangement Syndrome*.

Speaking of the evidence at hand, in the following pages of this chapter I will expose no less than thirteen different false narratives the main stream sports media has spun about Jameis Winston. I will also refute such false narratives with actual truth, because as the great author George Orwell once said:

> *The very concept of objective truth is fading out of the world. Lies will pass into history.* [655]

And:

> *We have now sunk to a depth at which the restatement of the obvious is the first duty of intelligent men.* [655]

I will now expose false narratives, search for objective truth and restate obvious facts so that we can all become more intelligent sports fans.

False Narrative #1:
Main Stream Sports Media is not Biased

Many folks assume that main stream sports media members are just like the general public, relatively unbiased, merely interested in reporting on sports independent of politics, and therefore nothing like the talking heads that work for political news networks. Such folks are wrong.

Journalist Michael Brendan Dougherty of *The Week* wrote the following about liberal sports media members:

> *They proudly admit that they are at a remove from their readers. ... sports writers seem to be appealing to the general manager or team HR departments to enforce liberal norms on their highly paid assets. The smaller portion of athletes who happen to share cultural affinities or political commitments with liberal sports writers are given glowing, intimate, get-to-know-you portraits.* [656]

Journalist Bryan Curtis of *The Ringer* went even further when he wrote:

> *Today, sports writing is basically a liberal profession, practiced by liberals who enforce an unapologetically liberal code ... There was a time when filling your column with liberal ideas on race, class, gender, and labor policy got you dubbed a "sociologist." These days, such views are more likely to get you a job.* [657]

Radio show host Clay Travis agreed with Curtis when he wrote in his book, *Republicans Buy Sneakers Too: How the Left Is Ruining Sports with Politics*:

> *ESPN decided that combining sports and politics would make it matter in the modern era ... The network made the decision not just to embrace sports and politics, they decided to marry sports to left-wing politics.*
>
> *A big part of this decision came via Jon Skipper, the president ... Skipper was a far-left-wing liberal, and his values immediately*

rolled throughout the company ... elevating the talent that most fervently connected left-wing politics and sports. Max Kellerman ... Michelle Beadle ... the more left-wing your politics, the more you got on television. [162]

Travis also made it clear that it wasn't just ESPN that was involved in such a propaganda operation, when he wrote:

Far too often in America today, companies of all stripes, but particularly in sports media, want people who look different but think the same. ... ESPN has cultivated that exact kind of groupthink. ... Frankly, most media entities in sports have too. [162]

Even Jim Brady, ESPN's very own Public Editor, confessed:

Many ESPN employees I talked to -- including liberals and conservatives, most of whom preferred to speak on background -- worry that the company's politics have become a little too obvious, empowering those who feel as if they're in line with the company's position and driving underground those who don't. ... "If you're a Republican or conservative, you feel the need to talk in whispers," one conservative ESPN employee said. "There's even a fear of putting Fox News on a TV [in the office]." [658]

Approximately nine months later Brady wrote a follow-up piece which stated:

the personalities the network has promoted into high-profile positions tend to be more liberal, and as their voices are amplified, the overall voice has shifted with it. ...if ESPN ... wants to hold onto a larger share of its audience ... the answer is improved ideological diversity in ESPN's overall products. [659]

However, improved ideological diversity is not something the main stream sports media seems to have any interest in whatsoever. According to a poll conducted by *The Big Lead*, just 6% of all sports media members polled identified as *Republican* and less than 4% said they voted for American President Donald Trump in the 2016 Presidential election. [660] When one compares that with the Gallup Poll conducted near the same time that found 31% of Americans identify as Republicans [661], one quickly ascertains that the main stream sports media may be over 500% more liberal than the American public! Also, when one considers Trump received over 46% of the popular vote in the Presidential election [662], one realizes the main stream sports media does not even come remotely close to representing the American voting public's various factions equally. Not even close.

However, perhaps things will change in the near future. Former ESPN President John Skipper, the man author and radio show host Clay Travis called a "far left-wing liberal" [162] recently resigned from the company after a cocaine extortion scandal [663] and new President Jimmy Pitaro recently stated:

> *Without question our data tells us our fans do not want us to cover politics ... My job is to provide clarity. I really believe that some of our talent was confused on what was expected of them. If you fast-forward to today, I don't believe they are confused.* [664]

The above is good news indeed. However, even if all ESPN employees, let alone all the employees at the other main stream sports media outlets, were counseled to avoid political talk, if those employees by and large still lean to only one side politically, they will still be able to slander someone like Jameis Winston who wears his Christian faith on his sleeve and doesn't have a politically correct reputation, without specifically speaking about politics. They can just continue to spin false narratives about his on-field play that lead their audience to think negatively about Winston, as they have done for years.

The greatest rap artist and true prophet of the streets once summed up the media with a quote that easily could come out of the mouth of Jameis Winston today, when he stated:

As far as the media ... they don't care about my resume ... it's just another story ... they don't have to pay for it and they gonna milk it for all it's worth.

– Tupac Shakur aka 2PAC [665]

Likewise, the great musician Jim Morrison powerfully contrasted the media's position of power with the ovious weakness of the public's positon, when he stated:

Whoever controls the media, controls the mind.

– Jim Morrison [665.1]

False Narrative #2:
Jameis Winston Was a Criminal
Who Shouldn't Have Been Drafted

I have discussed in great detail how the media treated Jameis Winston like a convicted criminal long before he even entered the 2015 NFL Draft. It's as if the media was run by Cade Cothren – the Chief of Staff for the current Speaker of the Tennessee House of Representatives, Glen Casada – who was caught referring to Jameis Winston as "thug nigg*r [redaction added]". [666]

While no main stream media member dared refer to Winston in such a way in print or on the radio or air waves, it was quite clear that many viewed him as a criminal. However, as I have previously detailed, the fact of the matter is that Jameis Winston has never even been arrested, let alone convicted for a crime, at any time in his entire life. Therefore, the narrative that Winston is a criminal is a false one that deserves to be repudiated by anyone who hears such, just as much as the false narrative that former U.S. President Bill Clinton was never impeached. [667] Again, it is just as wrong to judge someone who is innocent, as guilty, as it is to judge someone who is guilty, as innocent.

Before I move on to dealing with the next false narrative surrounding Jameis Winston, I'd like to mention that I find it extremely interesting that

I could not find one single main stream news article that mentioned Jameis Winston in the title, relating to the racist comments of the aforementioned Cade Cothren, not one. Can you imagine how many articles would have named Russell Wilson or Dak Prescott or Deshaun Watson in the title, had they been the player called a *thug nigg*r*?

However, it seems clear that had the media used Jameis Winston's name in their article titles, such would have functioned to cause the public to feel sorry for Winston and to view him as a player in need of their support, and that is not what the media desires anyone's reaction to be when they hear the name Jameis Winston. Again, the media decided long ago that portraying Jameis Winston as a villain is what sells and generates the most buzz, and they generally stick to their playbook without fail.

False Narrative #3:
Jameis Winston Doesn't Have the Mental Makeup to Be a Star NFL QB

There was a common false narrative about Jameis Winston before he was drafted into the NFL, namely that he didn't have the mental make-up to thrive as an NFL quarterback. In fact, the narrative was that he was someone with severe psychological issues, as well as a plain and simple idiot.

Dr. Richard Lustberg who has been featured by the New York Times, ESPN and CBS' Sportsline wrote:

> *We should not be debating whether Winston can play football and baseball at the same time, or where he is going to be selected in the draft. Winston needs treatment and he needs it now! ... It has been my experience that people commit crimes for a myriad of reasons. ... It is my guess that Winston who is too valuable a property will not get the full mental health services he requires, and that would be one huge mistake. It is a mistake that those in the world of sport continue to make at the peril of those who are left untreated– but why should they care?* [668]

Good ol' omniscient Dr. Lustberg thought it was crazy that Winston could be drafted into the NFL. He was sure Winston was a criminal, and not just any criminal, but a criminal who needed immediate psychiatric treatment. Never mind the fact that Winston had not – and still has not – ever even been arrested, let alone convicted of a crime, at any time in his entire life; the young man must be insane to supposedly leave a store with unpaid for crab legs that he said an employee hooked him up with, insane I tell you!

Dr. Lustberg even wrote that because Winston is such a valuable piece of property due to his athletic excellence, he will likely never receive the mental help he needs because whoever drafts him won't care to provide such. My guess is that critical thinking, logic, rationale and common sense are not among Dr. Lustberg's strong points, as obviously, it is specifically because Winston is such a valuable player that any team considering drafting him would have done extensive background research on him before drafting him. And of course, that is exactly what Jason Licht and Buccaneers' brass did as I detailed earlier in this book.

Many also remember Alabama quarterback A.J. McCarron's mother publicly asking if Jameis Winston was even speaking English when he gave his famous post-game speech after leading a game-winning drive that won Florida State University the 2014 BCS National Title. In fact, how could anyone forget, as it seemed nearly every national main stream media site ran an article regarding the insult? And, while LeBron James tweeted out that Winston's speech was unbelievable and showed why Jameis was so special, Dee Dee McCarron took a dig at Jameis' intelligence. She later apologized *if* she offended anyone and claimed she wasn't racist, but never actually apologized for, or said a word about, Jameis' actual intelligence which she had called into question. [669]

Shortly after the above incident, *The Arkansas Travler* ran an article titled:

Winston May be Idiot, but He's Smarter Than You [670]

Honestly, despite the incendiary and insulting title of the article, I honestly believe it was one of the best articles written regarding the incident, which says a lot, as any article titled that way and which starts out with the sentence; "Jameis Winston is an idiot." is at the very least, extremely distasteful.

However, to the author's credit the article does go on to point out the fact that, despite what the general public may think about Winston, he was successfully academically admitted to Stanford, something most students around the country are not capable of. The author also points out that Winston had a 4.0 GPA in high school while juggling multiple honors courses. He even included a quote in the article from Coach Matt Scott about Winston's on-field intelligence as well, which stated:

> *I've never seen anything like that guy. I'm not even talking about his talent ... There's a lot of people that can throw the ball. What people don't understand is the difference with him. His football IQ is through the roof. If they had some kind of scientific study for it they'd have to do a special on CNN. It's unbelievable.* [670]

While we're on the subject of Winston's mental makeup, I'd also like to mention Michael Pasatieri's extremely original and truly interesting *NFL Personality Analysis Method*, as well as the profile he created on Winston leading up to the 2015 NFL Draft. In the profile Pasatieri detailed how Winston had:

> *The NFL Personality Analysis Method ranks Jameis as a 10RsT-Wa. ...*

> *Jameis' historical precedent analysis show an almost exact mental makeup match with Bart Starr and Ken Stabler. Sharing a near exact correlation with 2 SB winning QBs is very rare. This bodes well for Jameis' NFL career prospects. ...*

> *Jameis' Personality Family leans toward the gunslinger mindset and definitely are not 'game managers'. Ken Stabler threw more*

INTs (222) than TDs (194) and Brett Farve is the all time leader of throwing INTs (336). Those with high mental makeup correlation to Jameis generally throw lots of picks, almost a 1:1 career ratio. Expect Jameis to throw his share of interceptions. It typically takes 3-5 years for these folks to become solid NFL QBs in which he'll have his best year for yardage and TD:INT ratio. ...

He comes from a lineage of successful NFL QBs and the historical success of this Pf/Pt combination is rare. In spite of lacking physical prowess, he has a winning mental makeup for NFL success and the historical precedent to back it up. Combined with the right system, he has the necessary tools to win a Super Bowl. ... you heard it here first, congrats to Jameis Winston on at least one Super Bowl win. [671]

Likewise, while we're on the subject of Jameis Winston's intelligence, let us consider the Wonderlic Test (the standard intelligence test given to NFL prospects) scores of various quarterbacks. Below is a list of various Hall of Fame as well as other past or present big name quarterbacks – and one benchwarmer who is included for obvious reasons, thanks to his mother – listed with their respective test score and the non-NFL equivalent job that coincides with such a test score according to recognized standards, starting with Winston:

Quarterback	Wonderlic Test Score	Non-NFL Equivalent Job
Jameis Winston	**27**	**Investment Analyst**
Ben Roethlisberger	25	Salesperson
Baker Mayfield	25	Salesperson
Patrick Mahomes	24	Secretary
Brett Favre	22	Bank Teller
A.J. McCarron	22	Bank Teller
Cam Newton	21	Cashier
Deshaun Watson	20	Craftsman
Dan Marino	16	Warehouseman
Jim Kelly	15	Warehouseman

Donovan McNabb	14	Janitor
Lamar Jackson	13	N/A below a "14"
Jeff George	10	N/A below a "14"
Vince Young	6	N/A below a "14"

[672] [673] [674]

The lowest Wonderlic Test score ever recorded by someone who actually played a game in the NFL was recorded by Morris Claiborne [672] while the only perfect score ever recorded by an NFL player was recorded by Harvard cum laude graduate and later Pro Bowl and All-Pro punter, Pat McInally.

McInally, like yours truly, graduated cum laude, worked as a writer amongst other things, was employed by a Christian school, and is even an avid collector of rare items such as original handwritten music lyrics from the Beatles and Bob Dylan [675] as well as rare books. [676] While I've had a main stream sports journalist attempt to dox me on Twitter and have had many folks accuse me of being Jameis Winston's agent, father, or even Jameis Winston himself, it's rather surprising no one has ever accused me of being Pat McInally yet. Of course, when I took the Wonderlic years ago I only scored a 43, though even McInally himself was quoted as saying:

> *It was definitely a once-in-a-lifetime thing ... I could probably take it 100 more times and never do it again.* [675]

Once again, as the legendary *C+C* Music Factory sang, *things that make you go hmm.*

False Narrative #4:
Jameis Winston's Record Setting
First Two Seasons Weren't Impressive

As detailed earlier in this book, Jameis Winston is the:

- Only quarterback in NFL history to start his career with back to back 4,000 yard passing seasons. [376]

- Youngest Pro Bowl quarterback in the history of the NFL. [210]

However, many people have no knowledge of the above facts, as the main stream sports media for the most part either never reported on either fact, or never made much of an effort to promote such remarkable facts, which they certainly would have done for many other quarterbacks not named Jameis Winston. For those who don't believe such is the case, go to Google and see how much media praise Baker Mayfield received for breaking the rookie touchdown pass record, a far less impressive accomplishment, especially when considering Winston's was a two year accomplishment, and when realizing that superstar quarterbacks Cam Newton and Russell Wilson *combined* to throw for 4,000 yards in a season just three times in a combined 15 NFL seasons! [312] [377]

False Narrative #5:
Jameis Winston Gave a Sexist Speech to School Children

During the offseason between Winston's second and third NFL season he went to Melrose Elementary in Saint Petersburg, Florida to give an inspirational speech to the young students. And, while his speech lasted around 40 minutes, a veritable eternity with which to slip up in this day and age where speech-police are lurking around every corner, even one of the most well-known Jameis-haters in existence at the time – the Tampa Bay Times' Tom Jones – wrote in an article that Winston:

> *delivered a good message — a heartfelt, you-can-do-anything message to young kids who probably can't imagine that even being close to true. For many, it might have been the first time anyone ever told them such things.* [677]

However, the above didn't stop Jones from also publicly crucifying Winston in the exact same article, simply because he didn't like literally three seconds of the speech – three seconds! Three seconds out of 40 minutes is the mathematical equivalent of 36 seconds in an eight hour work day – 36 seconds!

Can you imagine going to work and doing an absolutely praiseworthy job for your full 7.5 hours on the clock, then taking a lunch break, and instead of eating lunch, volunteering to help the janitor clean the bathrooms – a praiseworthy act indeed – and during that half hour helping the janitor clean the bathroom, you take 36 seconds to say something to inspire him but which some nosey co-worker hears and gets offended by, and then get publicly condemned across the entire country because some liberal writer somewhere who thought he was really the speech-police also took offense to what you said when he heard about it? Jameis Winston knows exactly what that feels like.

So, what did Winston say that got Tom Jones so riled up that he wrote a hit piece meant to shame Winston? When some of the boys in the audience were apparently horsing around and not paying attention, Winston got their attention by asking them – the boys only – to all stand up and for the girls to sit down. He then talked about how boys are expected to be strong rather than soft-spoken and he asked them to scream, "I can do anything I put my mind to" [677] which for a professing Christian like Winston, is obviously a reference to the Bible verse Philippians 4:13 which he has displayed on his own personal Twitter biography [678] and which states:

I can do all things through Christ which strengtheneth me.

Winston then continued by explaining how ladies are viewed. Please note he did not say that he personally viewed ladies any specific way; in context he merely stated that there is a difference in how men and ladies are viewed in general, which of course is absolutely true, even if the liberal media wishes such were not the case. Winston stated:

But the ladies, they're supposed to be silent, polite, gentle. [677]

There you have it, ten words. Ten words that caused Tom Jones to start typing up a hit piece on Jameis Winston. The speech-police are real folks.

Never mind the fact, that again, Winston was not saying that he personally felt ladies are supposed to be silent, polite and gentle, as he was clearly stating how ladies are viewed by people in general. However, even if he was stating that he personally believes such, so what?

Jameis Winston is a baptized Christian that is engaged to a baptized Christian [679] and who named his first born child after his family's favorite book in the Bible, Malachi. [680] So, would anyone be surprised, or have any right to try to publicly shame him for believing the following Bible verses:

> *study to be quiet, and to do your own business, and to work with your own hands, as we commanded you*

> - 1 Thessalonians 4:11b

> *And be ye kind one to another*

> – Ephesians 4:32a

> *And the servant of the Lord must not strive; but be gentle unto all*

> – 2 Timothy 2:24a

Millions, perhaps billions around the world believe the above verses should be adhered to in one's daily life. And, while strength in numbers, and truth, are certainly not synonymous, neither is the mind of one liberal writer synonymous with truth, even when that writer's name is Tom Jones.

The above said, even if Jameis Winston were stating that he personally believes – which he was not doing – that ladies should be *silent, polite* and *gentle,* or *quiet, kind* and *gentle* in King James parlance, good for him! What sensible parent on earth would object to such? What loving parent does not want their daughter, or son for that matter, to be such, when such is a wonderful description of Jesus Christ Himself?

Nevertheless, it wasn't just the Tampa Bay Times' resident chief Jameis-basher – Tom Jones – who wrote a hit piece on Winston after he sacrificed his free time to inspire school children. USA Today also joined in on the public stoning with its own hit piece [681] just to name one more main stream media outlet.

However, one independent local Tampa website published an article filled with various quotes from individuals supportive of Winston, and even included an audio clip of Winston's lovely mother Loretta defending Jameis as well. [682] And, even journalist Roy Peter Clark of *The Undefeated* published a piece that stuck up for Winston to a point, and which I would recommend reading as it's a well-written and very informative article. [683]

Even the leader of the public mob calling for Winston's blood, the aforementioned Tom Jones, snuck in a tiny snippet in his larger hit piece – possibly because he knew his article was slanderous rubbish and was ashamed of himself for writing it – that stated:

> *The principal said it was a really good day for Melrose* [677]

However, it seemed that even the rare media members that were defending Winston did so half-heartedly while still saying that he made a *mistake* in his choice of words.

For his part, Winston issued a public apology, and stated:

> *I was making an effort to interact with a young male in the audience who didn't seem to be paying attention, and I didn't want to single him out so I asked all the boys to stand up ... During my talk, I used a poor word choice that may have overshadowed that positive message for some.* [681]

However, I don't believe Winston needed to apologize at all. Just as when he says something like, "I can't turn the ball over and need to do better" in a post-game press conference where his only interception came on a ball that one of his receivers bobbled up into the air, I believe he merely apologized because that is the sort of person he is, and taking responsibility and accepting blame, even for something he doesn't deserve to be blamed for, is something he's used to doing.

However, I believe Winston would have been fully justified to issue the following public statement:

> *I was making an effort to interact with a young male in the audience who didn't seem to be paying attention, and I didn't want to single him out so I asked all the boys to stand up. I then explained what many people expect from boys and girls and told those standing boys that they can be strong and accomplish anything they put their mind too, which of course is a reference to Philippians 4:13, one of my favorite Bible verses. However, I did not say that I personally feel girls should be silent, polite and gentle and am not going to be bullied into apologizing for giving an inspirational speech to school children on my off-day, or for saying words that the media wants to pretend were bad. I am used to the media spinning false narratives about me and writing hit pieces on me; it doesn't bother me. However, those biased media members need to understand that I'm not going to be bullied into pretending I did something wrong when I know such isn't the case, nor am I going to be bullied into ignoring what I consider my God-given duties to help my community and inspire the youth in my community. Giving motivational speeches to school children is one of the ways God allows me to make a difference and I'm going to continue doing that whether anyone in the media likes it or not.*

Now, of course the main stream media would have published hit pieces galore against Winston if he would have said the above, but that doesn't mean he would have been wrong for saying such. It only means that the speech-police would have taken offence and exacted their form of revenge against one of their favorite whipping boys, by running slanderous articles and television segments calling Winston *unhinged* and saying he needs *help* of one kind or another.

Author and radio show host Clay Travis once wrote in his book, *Republicans Buy Sneakers Too: How the Left Is Ruining Sports with Politics*:

> *Race rarely, if ever, impacts the way a story is covered in sports media ... But when race is involved it's far more likely that white athletes ... receive more criticism than black athletes would today for doing the same thing. That's because most members of the sports media are so hypersensitive to racism allegations that white players are attacked far more aggressively than their black counterparts. Far from being penalized by the media based on their race, the reverse is true. Black athletes are much less likely to be challenged because of their race because the media either supports them or is afraid of being called racist.* [162]

Travis may have a point as he could certainly point to various black athletes that have seemed to get a pass from the media, and he does in fact do just that in his book. However, Jameis Winston is most definitely not one of those black athletes that get a pass from the media, which Travis himself knows as he has a severe strain of *Winston Derangement Syndrome*.

In fact, if what Travis wrote above is true, such would point to my hypothesis that the rabid attacks on Winston carried out by the media, are so constant, vicious and synchronized, that they must be orchestrated by media higher-ups, being 100 percent accurate.

Perhaps Mr. Travis should write a more accurate book in the future, one that says the media separates current athletes into three classes, namely: blacks, whites and Jameis Winston, and that while whites are treated more harshly than blacks, Jameis Winston is treated infinitely more harshly than both.

However, don't hold your breath waiting for Travis to write such a book as he himself is incredibly biased against Winston, so much so that he attempted to engage me in a Twitter debate, lied about Winston's statistics, and then blocked me and ran away when I exposed his lies and deceitful debate tactics.

That brief engagement with Clay Travis was extremely amusing for me, though it exposed him as an absolute hypocrite considering he is the author who wrote:

> *I resolved to investigate every story on my own and not allow media misperceptions to ever drive my opinions again. If sometimes that lead to me being called names or attacked for my opinions, I could handle that. ... I'd become a First Amendment warrior ... She (Jemele Hill, added) unfollowed me and even blocked me on Twitter ... Sadly, this is exactly what I've come to expect from many left-wing sports media figures. They don't want to engage in debate. [162]*

One would think that if someone is going to be a public figure and even a published author who brags about being a "First Amendment warrior" and calls out another media member for blocking him on Twitter rather than engaging in a debate, that said public figure and author would actually value the First Amendment, engage rather than run from debate, and not block someone simply because they can't win a mere Twitter debate against that person. Maybe I'm asking too much though, as hypocrisy is all the rage these days for many main stream sports media members.

Regardless, even the self-proclaimed "First Amendment warrior" is so infected with *Winston Derangement Syndrome* that for him, the First Amendment is only sacrosanct when it's being used to slander, rather than to expose false narratives surrounding, Jameis Winston.

Regardless, and with all of the above said, I'll end this subsection with an apropos quote from abolitionist and statesman Frederick Douglass, as I believe it sums up just how Jameis Winston sincerely feels and lives his life, even if he won't come right out and say so as he knows such would provoke a media firestorm ... even from First Amendment warriors:

> *I prefer to be true to myself, even at the hazard of incurring the ridicule of others, rather than to be false, and to incur my own abhorrence.* [70]

False Narrative #6:
Jameis Winston Regressed in His Third Season

A common and almost constant media narrative following the 2017 season was that Jameis Winston regressed from his second to his third season. Allow me to fact-check that false narrative and blow it out of the water by posting a simple statistical table below that compares Jameis Winston's 2016 and 2017 seasons:

Year	Comp %	Y/G	Y/A	Y/C	ANY/A	AY/A	NY/A	TD %	INT %	Passer Rating
2017	63.8	269.5	7.9	12.4	6.70	7.7	6.94	4.3	2.5	92.2
2016	60.8	255.6	7.2	11.9	5.98	6.8	6.40	4.9	3.2	86.1

[141]

It takes all of 30 seconds viewing the above table to realize that Winston progressed, not regressed, from his second to his third season in the NFL. Winston literally improved in nine of the ten above listed statistical categories! And, when one considers that he did that while playing many of his 2017 games with a seriously injured throwing shoulder, it becomes even more clear that the media's narrative that Winston regressed in 2017 was the worst kind of *fake* news, as it was an absolute lie that could have been disproven in a matter of seconds with even a modicum of statistical research.

Now, one could say that the main stream sports media simply glanced at the final 2017 league standings, saw the Bucs as a team regressed, and then just decided to report that Jameis Winston regressed as an individual. However, while I do not believe such is the case, as journalists are required to do research and even clueless talking heads who have their jobs due to their personality and popularity rather than their ability to research and pay attention to detail, all have researchers that work for them. When *fake news* is spread about Jameis Winston, I do believe that most of the time, such fake news is spread because the media higher-ups want it spread, period.

False Narrative #7:
Jameis Winston Should Have Been Suspended Six Games Over the Alleged Uber Incident

I already discussed Winston's three game suspension in depth earlier in this book and explained in detail why he likely should not have been suspended for even a single game, nor the three games he was suspended for, let alone the six games many in the media were calling for. This is because, while the NFL stated that they had "substantial evidence" against both Tom Brady and Ezekiel Elliott when they suspended those two players [489] [497] the league merely "concluded that Winston violated the Personal Conduct Policy" [485] as there was not one shred of hard evidence that Winston actually did what he was accused of – any of the accuser's multiple versions of the alleged incident – and still isn't.

However, I wanted to list this false narrative, as it deserves to be listed seeing as such a false narrative did a great deal of damage to Winston's reputation, and also so that I could point out two specific articles that perfectly illustrate just how biased the main stream sports media is against Winston.

On July 5, 2018, ESPN's Jenna Laine wrote an article that I found reprehensible. [680] Please don't misunderstand me; I personally like Jenna, have cited a great deal of her articles in this book, have praised her multiple times on Twitter, and do not personally think she is one of the media members that is infected with *Winston Derangement Syndrome* per se. Honestly, it wouldn't surprise me one bit to hear that her editor or another higher up asked her to include the reprehensible portion in her article. On the other hand, I have also called her out many times for writing shoddy articles and drawing absurd conclusions that do make it at least seem like she has *Winston Derangement Syndrome*; so, who knows?

Regardless, the article I am referring to was titled, *Buccaneers QB Jameis Winston's fiancee delivers baby boy* and it's first five paragraphs were lovely and served as a mere announcement of the birth of Jameis Winston's first child, Antonor Malachi Winston, who was named after his father and the family's favorite book in the Bible. [680] However, it was the final two paragraphs that I found extremely tasteless and worthy of rebuke, which stated:

> *Winston was suspended the first three games of the 2018 season after the NFL determined that he inappropriately touched a female Uber driver in March 2016.*

> *He also just recently parted ways with his agents, Greg Genske and Kenny Felder, who had represented him since the start of his NFL career.* [680]

Can you imagine an ESPN journalist writing an article announcing the birth of Tom Brady and Gisele Bundchen's next child and concluding the article with a paragraph mentioning that Brady dumped the mother of his first child, and then closing the article with another paragraph mentioning that Brady was once suspended four games for cheating? However, Jameis Winston isn't Tom Brady and the media isn't fair in its treatment of all NFL players, just most of them not named Jameis Winston.

Furthermore, on July 29, 2018, the Tampa Bay Times journalist Martin Fennelly – a known Jameis Winston hater – published an article titled, *Bucs fans wear Jameis Winston's No. 3, some uneasily,* in which he *quoted* many Bucs fans and attempted to spin the narrative that such fans were ready to turn on Winston due to the three game suspension. [684] The only problem with that – other than that the article was a despicable hit piece – was that many of those supposedly *quoted* fans came out publicly and stated that Fennelly had *misquoted* them in an attempt to slander Winston!

For example, Fennelly stated:

> *Lastly, there was Antonio Hill, 34, a hotel worker from Tampa. He sat in his Winston jersey with his friends.*
>
> *"I'm with Jameis until the wheels fall off," Hill said. "But if he does one more thing, I'll be done. I already got two backups, a Mike Evans jersey and a Lavonte (David). I'm ready for whatever happens."* [684]

However, Antonio Hill quickly went on Twitter and tweeted:

> *I'm Antonio Hill. I did tell em I was riding with @Jaboowins until the walls fall off. But I never said if he messes up again I have a Mike Evans and Lavonta David Jersey ready* [685]

It was also revealed on a local podcast that two other individuals mentioned in the article also revealed that Fennelly had misquoted them, which I reported as well. [686]

Likewise, popular Tampa media outlet *Bucs Nation* stated in reply to this scandal:

> *So the Tampa Bay Times misquoted this Bucs fan while at practice on Sunday. This is a bad look. Only drives the notion of a potential narrative by the outlet. The Times said it's up to the editor to fix the quote. As of the time of this tweet, it's still not fixed.* [687]

Attorney Felix G. Montanez agreed with Bucs Nation and stated:

> *Seems to me the Times has decided that trashing Jameis drives traffic. How many ways can they write the same hit piece?* [688]

What the tasteless Jenna Laine article and seemingly unethical Martin Fennelly article shows, is that the main stream media is dedicated to taking even the most innocent and the most beautiful news involving Jameis Winston and putting a negative spin on it. It's obvious the media does not want their audience to even feel mere indifference towards Winston, if leading them to feel anger and outrage towards Winston is a possibility. Simply put, *Winston Derangement Syndrome* exists and it's a plague upon sports fans everywhere!

False Narrative #8:
Jameis Winston was Benched for a Bum

When Ryan Fitzpatrick was lighting up the NFL in the first three weeks of the 2017 NFL season and becoming the first player in NFL history to throw for at least 400 yards in three straight games [689], the prevailing media narrative was that Fitzpatrick was playing at an MVP level [690] which showed he was a better quarterback than Jameis Winston, as Winston hadn't done the same in the previous season, on an entirely different team, while playing with a seriously injured throwing shoulder. [691] Yeah, I know, what a fair and unbiased narrative right?

However, strangely enough, the media and fan narrative at the exact same time was that Jameis Winston had been benched for a bum. Talk about playing both sides of the fence or trying to eat your cake and have it too!

By the way, for those of you who think I said the above idiomatic proverb the wrong way, watch the magnificent show *Manhunt: Unabomber*, or better yet read Ted Kaczynski's own riveting, yet often disturbing manifesto titled, *Industrial Society and Its Future*, and pay special attention to paragraph 185. [692]

Simply put, the media wanted to play both sides of the fence when it came to Winston being benched for Ryan Fitzpatrick. They wanted to pretend that Fitzpatrick was a terrible quarterback and therefore Winston had been benched for a bum, as that would definitely damage Winston's reputation, which they love to do; however they also wanted to pretend that Fitzpatrick had played at an MVP level, and that such proved he was infinitely better than Winston, which would also damage Winston's reputation.

However, the real fact was that Winston was not *benched* for Fitzpatrick in the Bears game, even though the media and fans believed he was, as his head coach was extremely clear that the plan was always to start Winston in the following game rather than in his first game back. [581] The one and only time Winston was truly *benched* in the 2018 season was in the week eight Bengals game when he was pulled after throwing his fourth interception of the game. [591] Fitzpatrick would play lights out for the remainder of that game and start the next three games on the strength of that performance, as well as the strength of his historic performance in the first three weeks of the season.

The above said, when Winston was *benched*, he was benched for a quarterback who up to that time had thrown for over 400 yards in three of his first four starts and had a magnificent 114.4 passer rating on the season. [693] Honestly, there were probably 25 or more starting quarterbacks that could have been benched if a backup quarterback with those numbers was sitting behind them! Therefore, when Winston was benched, he certainly wasn't benched for a bum, but for a guy with MVP level numbers on the season. There's no shame in that, which even his head coach made clear when he stated:

> *I think all quarterbacks -- like pro golfers -- why do some of the best golfers in the world struggle from time to time? I think Jameis is one of the best quarterbacks in the world and I think he will be back. For right now -- we went over this the other day, all this stuff. A lot of teams don't switch because they have an untested backup or they're afraid to put their backup in there and we don't have either of those. Right now, we just have to stop*

turning the ball over and so we're going to go with Fitz. I still have plenty of confidence in Jameis moving forward. [694]

Read that above quote again, seriously. That is not a quote the main stream sports media talking heads repeated when they were trashing Winston. Why? Because it didn't fit the narrative they wanted to spin, namely that Winston was benched for a bum and that his head coach had given up on him, which of course was an entirely false narrative.

Simply put, a young Jameis Winston being benched for three games for a veteran quarterback who had been playing MVP level football is not remotely close to the same thing as a prime Kurt Warner being benched for a second year backup with just 14 career touchdown passes, and then kept on the bench for 15 straight games, despite that young backup throwing just as many interceptions as touchdowns over those 15 games. And yes, that actually happened to Hall of Famer Kurt Warner. [695] [696] Yet the media wanted everyone to believe that Jameis Winston had flamed out, turned into a bust, and was done in Tampa, and they didn't mind spinning a false narrative to convince their audience such was the case.

False Narrative #9:
Jameis Winston was Outplayed by Ryan Fitzpatrick

The media-driven narrative that Jameis Winston was benched for a bum – when in reality he was benched for a guy who had played MVP level ball and could have replaced 25 plus starting NFL quarterbacks at the time he replaced Winston – was a dud as it was so easily disproven. However, the media-driven narrative that Jameis Winston was outplayed by Ryan Fitzpatrick at least had a basis in truth, namely that Fitzpatrick's first three games of 2018 at least made for a more impressive three game stretch – at least statistically speaking – than almost any Hall of Fame quarterback had ever had in his career. Simply put, *Fitzmagic* did indeed happen, and while it may have turned into *Fitztragic*, the magic happened nonetheless.

If all it took was a monster statistical game or three for a backup quarterback to outplay in totality, or prove he is better in general than a starting quarterback, Matt Flynn and Billy Volek were better quarterbacks than Aaron Rodgers and Steve McNair as well.

In the greatest season of Aaron Rodgers' magnificent career (2011), the year he won his first MVP award and set a record for the highest season passer rating in NFL history [245], his backup Matt Flynn actually had a higher passer rating on the season than he did [697] and had a better game than Rodgers has ever had in his entire storied career, when Flynn threw for 480 yards and 6 touchdown passes in a 45-41 victory over the 10-5 playoff bound Detroit Lions. [698]

Likewise, in the greatest season (2003) of Tennessee Titans legendary quarterback Steve McNair's career, the year he won his one and only MVP award and recorded his highest ever season passer rating [699], his backup Billy Volek actually had a higher passer rating on the season than he did. [700] And, the very next season when McNair was injured, Volek replaced him and had back to back 400 yard passing games in which he totalled a whopping 918 yards and 8 touchdown passes [701] – a better two game stretch than even Fitzpatrick had in 2018 – though after that season Volek would start just one more game over the next 7 years before retiring. [702] As for the great Steve *Air* McNair, he had just one 400 yard passing game in his entire 13 year career.

However, no sane football fan or even typically biased media member was spinning the narrative that Billy Volek was a better quarterback than Steve McNair, or that Matt Flynn was a better quarterback than Aaron Rodgers back then. Of course, there's never been a widespread media cabal dedicated to destroying Steve McNair, nor has there even been such a thing as *Rodgers Derangement Syndrome*, like there have been with Jameis Winston.

As for comparing Jameis Winston with his former backup Ryan Fitzpatrick, Winston has played just four years in the NFL, has two 4,000 yard passing seasons and one Pro Bowl, while Fitzpatrick has played 14 years in the NFL, has never had a 4,000 yard passing season and never made a Pro Bowl. [703] Honestly, other than those infected with the most virulent strain of *Winston Derangement Syndrome*, there may not be one single individual on earth that actually believes Fitzpatrick is a better quarterback than Winston, as he simply isn't. [704]

Furthermore, one prominent main stream sports media outlet – NBC's *Pro Football Talk*, an outlet known for being infected with *Winston Derangement Syndrome* – literally took Ryan Fitzpatrick's stats from the three games he played when he replaced an injured Winston in 2017, combined them with the stats he put up in his first three games of 2018, and then claimed that since they were better than the last 6 games Jameis Winston played in 2017 – one of which he was knocked out of after re-injuring his throwing shoulder and after throwing just 13 passes – such proved that Fitzpatrick was a better quarterback than Winston. [691]

Are you kidding me? That sort of biased tripe and mangling of statistics to fit an absurd narrative passes for accurate reporting these days? It must be, because those same pieced-together stats started popping up on other main stream sports media outlets in no time. The main stream sports media doesn't even try to cover-up their bias against Jameis Winston, yet many fans still don't seem to understand that such a bias even exists. Unbelieveable.

It's not at all difficult to see which quarterback was better in the 2017 season – you know, when both Winston and Fitzpatrick played on the same exact team, with the same exact players, in the same exact season – as it was Winston by a mile. Consider the following statistical table:

Player	Comp %	Y/G	Y/A	Y/C	ANY/A	AY/A	NY/A	TD %	INT %	Passer Rating
JW	63.8	269.5	7.9	12.4	6.70	7.7	6.94	4.3	2.5	92.2
RF	58.9	183.8	6.8	11.5	6.32	6.8	6.29	4.3	1.8	86.0

[705]

Once again, it takes all of 30 seconds viewing the above table, to realize this time that Jameis Winston was unquestionably better than Ryan Fitzpatrick in the 2017 season. Winston bested Fitzpatrick in eight of the ten above listed statistical categories and tied him in another! And, when one considers that Winston did such while playing many of his 2017 games with a seriously injured throwing shoulder, while Fitzpatrick was healthy during his games, it becomes even more clear that the media's narrative that Fitzpatrick outplayed Winston in 2017 was an outright lie.

In regards to the 2018 season, Fitzpatrick certainly fared better than Winsston in various non counting number stats, thanks in large part to his wonderful first three starts and fourth quarter coming off the bench in Cincinnati, and Winston's rougher first three starts coming off his suspension and one half coming off the bench in Chicago.

However, let us compare Fitzpatrick's last four 2018 starts – which caused him to be benched once for three games and then again for the final six games of the season – and Jameis Winston's last six starts after returning from his one and only benching when he was pulled from the Bengals game after throwing his fourth interception.

Player	Comp %	TD %	INT %	Passer Rating	Team Record
Jameis Winston	63.6	5.1	1.4	97.7	2-4
Ryan Fitzpatrick	62.5	3.3	6.7	70.2	0-4

[706]

All of the above said, Ryan Fitzpatrick deserves credit for what he was able to do in the 2018 season. His first three games of the season were the stuff of legend, and Jameis Winston's first three games before being benched were not, and due to those two things being true it is fair to say that Fitzpatrick may have had a better overall statistical season than Winston. I wouldn't argue that such is at least debatable, though I would not agree with such. To see why, simply pay special attention to the *False Narrative #11* subsection of this chapter as it details just how elite Winston's 2018 season was according to the advanced metrics.

However, Jameis Winston deserves credit for what he was able to do after returning from his benching. And, it is a fact that while Winston was benched in a game once, Fitzpatrick was benched in a game twice, during the 2018 season. Likewise, it is a fact that while Fitzpatrick was only able to hold onto the starting position for no more than three games in a row, after Winston returned as the starter he was never benched again and started the last six games of the 2018 season, playing wonderfully as well. [703]

It's also a fact that after the season ended Jameis Winston was rewarded with a nearly $21,000,000 contract being honored for the upcoming 2019 season [511] whereas Ryan Fitzpatrick was let go entirely by the team and ended up signing with the Miami Dolphins to a two year contract averaging just $5,500,000 annually. [707] The Dolphins even later traded for Josh Rosen with an eye towards replacing Fitzpatrick in Miami as well. [708]

All things considered, I doubt there's a single quarterback on earth that would trade Jameis Winston's 2018 season for Ryan Fitzpatrick's 2018 season, not one.

False Narrative #10:
Jameis Winston Would Never Start for the Buccaneers Again After Getting Benched

When Jameis Winston was benched after throwing his fourth interception against the Cincinnati Bengals, it didn't take long for the main stream sports media to start spinning the narrative that Winston not only wouldn't start another game for the Buccaneers during the 2018 season, but that he should never start another game for the team and should be cut once the season ended. [709] [710] [711] [712] Never mind the fact that Winston was just 24 years old, or that he was coming off his best season as a professional in 2017 according to the advanced metrics, or that he was still a flamethrower who could push the ball down the field better than almost any quarterback in the entire NFL. No, the media wanted everyone to believe that Winston was done in Tampa.

Sports Illustrated, still one of the most respected and supposedly unbiased main stream sports outlets around, ran an obviously biased and literally absurd in hindsight article written by journalist Conor Orr titled, *Will Jameis Winston Be on the Tampa Bay Buccaneers in 2019?* The article ridiculously stated:

> *Winston is in the final year of his rookie deal ... they will most likely be starting over at the quarterback position. ... Barring a catastrophically bizarre decision, Winston will probably ride the bench for the remainder of this season.* [709]

Mr. Orr was of course entirely wrong. However, journalists can be a great deal like false prophets in a religious cult. When they miss on a prophecy, they just quickly make another one and hope their acolytes forget about the failed one; and, if they're good at it, they can keep doing so in perpetuity, knowing their devotees will never hold them accountable for fear of missing out on an accurate prophesy in the future.

Sportsnet journalist Donnovan Bennett wrote an absurd article as well. It was titled, *Why it's time for Buccaneers to move on from Jameis Winston* and in it he sounded even more deranged than Orr by stating:

> *The Buccaneers should cut ties with Jameis Winston. Winston's talent is unquestioned. The 24-year-old can make all the throws and has been the top quarterback prospect of his age class since he began playing the position. ... This season he has 10 interceptions – the same number as rookie Sam Darnold and Winston missed three games due to suspension and was pulled from two games for bad play. ... Winston has shown us who he is countless times. Tampa Bay needs to believe him and say goodbye.* [710]

I won't even dwell on the obvious absurdity of mentioning Winston's remarkable talent and the fact that he has always been a phenom, whilst also recommending he be cut from the team. I will however absolutely call attention to the fact that one of the reasons Bennett provides for why Winston should be cut, is that he was "pulled from two games for bad play". The problem with that statement is that it is entirely false!

When Bennett wrote this article, Winston had only played in four games, so it's not like Winston was some NBA player, deep into an 82 game season schedule and Bennett had to watch numerous games and the like to determine how many times he had been pulled from a game for bad play. Winston had only played in a mere four games. He was pulled just one time – once – not twice, once.

When a journalist writes an article literally calling for a 24 year old phenom who he admits has remarkable talent, to be flat out cut from a team, and can't even bother to watch the mere four games he played in or to know how many games he was pulled from, there's little doubt that the journalist was simply writing a biased hit piece, period.

False Narrative #11:
Jameis Winston Had a Terrible Fourth Season

The common narrative surrounding Jameis Winston's fourth NFL season was that he had a terrible season. However, such is not even close to the truth.

The actual fact is that Winston finished the 2018 season:

- 1st in the entire NFL in passer rating *under pressure.* [640]
- 1st in the entire NFL in passer rating *outside the pocket.* [641]
- 1st in the entire NFL in *Air Yards to the Sticks* (AYTS) [637]
- 1st in the entire NFL in 3rd and long (eight plus yards) conversion percentage on pass plays. [638]
- 2nd in the entire NFL in 3rd down conversion percentage behind only Patrick Mahomes. [639]
- 2nd in the entire NFL in *Average Completed Air Yards* (CAY) [637]
- 2nd in the entire NFL in *Averaged Intended Air Yards* (IAY) [637]

- 4th in the entire NFL in passer rating *on 3rd down* behind only Russell Wilson, Patrick Mahomes and Drew Brees. [642]
- 4th in the entire NFL in Raw QBR [221], which also made Winston the only quarterback other than Drew Brees to finish a season in the top five in Raw QBR on a losing team since 2015, the year he was drafted!

All of the above said, while Winston's fourth season may have been a disappointment when it comes to the simple counting stats – due to him only playing around 9.5 games worth of plays – he was indisputably *elite* according to the advanced metrics – elite!

The real truth is that the popular main stream media personalities and even journalists are so incredibly lazy that they don't do any legitimate research and therefore are simply ignorant of the truth. Instead, they spend 5 minutes looking at the league standings, stare at some website containing mere counting stats, and then just spin whatever narrative their biased minds concoct. It's all rather juvenile and sad to be honest.

Now, I'd like to compare Winston's fourth season, which the media says was terrible, with two of the truly terrible fourth seasons for Hall of Fame or soon to be Hall of Fame quarterbacks. I will adjust for era and simply show their league ranking in an equivalent 32 team league so that you can fully grasp just how good or bad each quarterback was in comparison to just how good or bad Jameis Winston was during his fourth season.

4th Year Ranking	Y/A	TD %	Comp %	PR / QBR	Avg. Rank	Team Record	Rush Offense Yards Gained	Team Defense Points Against
Jameis Winston	10th	18th	21st	5th	14th	3-6	29th	31st
Terry Bradshaw	21st	11th	34th	25th	23rd	8-1	10th	10th
Eli Manning	28th	13th	29th	18th	22nd	10-6	4th	17th

[221] [141] [706] [254] [231] [713] [463] [239] [714]

287

Jameis Winston had a far better individual fourth season than either Hall of Famer Terry Bradshaw or soon to be Hall of Famer Eli Manning had. However, Bradshaw's season was considered a success and Manning's season was considered a colossal success and the main reason he will end up in the Hall of Fame. Why? Because despite Bradshaw playing terrible individually, he was carried to a magnificent 8-1 record by his dominant run game and defense. And, because despite Eli Manning playing terrible individually, he was also carried by a dominant run game and decent defense, all the way to a Super Bowl victory!

Winston on the other hand, played far better individually than both Bradshaw and Manning, but was saddled with a dreadful defense and bad run game. Who would think that having a terrible run game and an absolutely awful defense would affect a quarterback's win/loss record? Apparently not the *Winston Derangement Syndrome* infected biased media.

False Narrative #12:
Winston Would Not Have His Contract Option Honored and the Bucs Would Draft a Quarterback in the 2019 NFL Draft

One of the most ridiculous yet popular false media narratives surrounding Jameis Winston during and succeeding his fourth season, was that the Buccaneers would cut him rather than honor his fifth year, nearly $21,000,000 contract, and that the team would use their first round draft pick on a new franchise quarterback.

I already detailed the fact – in *False Narrative #10* – that the media spun the absurd and malicious narrative that Jameis Winston should not and would not ever start another game for the Buccaneers during the 2018 season, and that he should be cut once the season ended. [709] [710] [711] [712] However, the media also spun the illogical and even laughable narrative that the Buccaneers would spend a high 2019 draft pick – even their first rounder – on a new starting quarterback. [715] [716] [717] [718]

Before Winston had even played his first game in the 2018 season, journalist Henry McKenna, writing for *The Big Lead*, advocated trading Winston before the trade deadline, because as he put it:

> *The Bucs could re-sign Winston and find out they've got Joe Flacco 2.0 — but without Flacco's Super Bowl win* [715]

What McKenna failed to point out is that Winston didn't just best Flacco in passer rating, Raw QBR, yards per attempt, yards per completion and touchdown percentage in the 2017 season, but in every season since entering the league. In fact, the absolute worst season number Winston accumulated in each of those stats in the previous three years, was better than the best season number Flacco had accumulated in the past three years. Likewise, while Winston made the Pro Bowl as a 21 year old rookie, Joe Flacco had never made the Pro Bowl – and still hasn't – in his entire career. In short, there was and is no real comparison between Jameis Winston and Joe Flacco, which McKenna would have known had he done even cursory statistical research. [141] [719]

Even more embarrassing for McKenna is that the two quarterbacks that entered the 2019 NFL Draft that he called *elite* and said the Buccaneers could draft and replace Winston with, were Drew Lock – a quarterback that wasn't drafted until the second round of the 2019 NFL Draft and was drafted to be ... wait for it ... Joe Flacco's backup – and Will Grier, a quarterback that wasn't drafted until late in the third round and to be a backup as well. [715] [720] Buccaneers fans can thank God that Henry McKenna isn't the team's General Manager!

Likewise, *Bleacher Report's* Matt Miller wrote:

> *The Jameis Winston era should come to an end in four weeks, no matter what the product on the field looks like, if the Tampa Bay Buccaneers are smart.* [716]

I suppose there's nothing like just admitting your biased and not hiding it at all, which is basically what Miller did when he said that "no matter what the product on the field looks like" the Bucs should move on from Winston. How can any quarterback change the mind of someone in the media that is that biased? Apparently it's not even possible if you take Miller's words at face value.

Journalist Chris Trapasso, writing for *CBS Sports*, may have had the worst take of all, when he wrote:

> *The Jameis Winston era might be over in Tampa Bay. With Fitzpatrick clearly not being the long-term plan at the signal-caller position, either GM Jason Licht or the next GM in Tampa will likely turn their attention to a quarterback who doesn't have a propensity to make bad decisions and give the ball to the other team often. That's NC State's Ryan Finley.* [717]

What makes the above take so terrible isn't just that Trapasso foolishly predicted the Buccaneers would move on from Winston, nor that they would move on from him for the uninspiring Ryan Finley of all people, but that they would actually spend their first round draft pick on Finley. For those who aren't aware, Ryan Finley was drafted in the fourth and to be a backup for Andy Dalton. [720] It's almost as if the main stream sports media is completely clueless, because, well, many times they are.

However, the majority of the media isn't just clueless when it comes to Jameis Winston, many of its members are also biased and even malevolent. Consider the following statement from the popular website WalterFootball.com, which predicted the Bucs would draft a new quarterback to replace Winston and wrote:

> *The Buccaneers are another team that will have to think about a new quarterback, as they'll have to replace their crotch-grabbing interception machine soon.* [718]

There isn't another quarterback on earth that deals with the literal hatred from the media that Winston does, yet he never calls them out on it and has always handled it with class.

I can only imagine what a quarterback like Derek Carr – who recently threatened to fight ESPN's Max Kellerman over spinning what Carr believed was a false narrative that he had quit on his team [721] – would say or do if the media was even 1/10th as hard on him as it is on Jameis Winston.

I wonder the same thing about a quarterback like Baker Mayfield – who has been in a long-running verbal war with popular sports host Colin Cowherd, also seemingly over perceived false narratives Cowherd has spun about him [722] [723] [724] – who much of the media fawns over and who has certainly never experienced the amount of bias, let alone abject hatred Jameis Winston has faced.

Even the headlines the media runs for other quarterbacks are so markedly different than the ones they run and would run when it comes to Jameis Winston. For example, when Derek Carr threatened to fight Max Kellerman, the title of the CBS Sports article was:

> *Raiders GM Mike Mayock on Derek Carr's proposal to fight ESPN host: 'I like the attitude'* [721]

What would the article have been had Winston threatened to fight a member of the media? Probably something like:

> *Jameis Winston Should be Banned from the NFL for Life After Threatening Physical Violence Against Member of the Media*

Likewise, when Baker Mayfield first went to war with Colin Cowherd, the Washington Post ran an article supporting Mayfield with the following title:

> *Baker Mayfield took on Colin Cowherd and 'won the interview' with more than just his shirt* [722]

It would not have surprised me in the least, if the same publication would have used the following article title, if Jameis Winston had done the exact same thing that Baker Mayfield did:

> *Jameis Winston Comes Unhinged and Attacks Colin Cowherd During Interview*

Regardless, as we all now know, the Tampa Bay Buccaneers did honor Jameis Winston's fifth year option contract, worth nearly $21,000,000, and did not draft a quarterback at all in the 2019 draft, not in the first round or even in the seventh round. As usual, the narrative the media spun regarding Jameis Winston, his contract, and the 2019 NFL Draft, had absolutely no basis in truth whatsoever, no connection to reality, and was nothing more than yet another attempt to slander the young man and lead casual football fans to think less of Winston.

False Narrative #13:
The Buccaneers Would Have a Hard Time Hiring a Top Coaching Candidate due to Winston Being Their Quarterback

The thirteenth and final false narrative to be dealt with in this chapter is the biased media-driven fake news that not only was the Buccaneers head coaching job one of the least attractive head coaching jobs on the market following the 2018 season, but that the reason it was such, was because Jameis Winston was the team's quarterback.

The biased media literally tried to get their audiences to believe that a former Heisman winning, National Title winning, #1 overall draft pick who would be just 25 years old during the upcoming 2019 NFL season and was also the youngest Pro Bowl quarterback in NFL history, and already second all-time in NFL history in both career passing yards and passing touchdowns, would be the main reason his team would struggle to land a suitable head coach.

Whoever said *NFL* stood for *No Fun League* [725] obviously hadn't yet read any articles from the *Winston Derangement Syndrome* infected media, as had they done so, they may have said NFL stood for *Never Forgive Lanaed* – as in Jameis Lanaed Winston – and realized just how hilarious the NFL, or at least the NFL media, could be when spinning their unbelievably preposterous false narratives.

ESPN's Bill Barnwell wrote an article titled, *Ranking the best and worst potential NFL head-coaching openings*. In said article, he ranked the Green Bay Packers as the best potential job opening and the Buccaneers as the second worst potential opening in the entire NFL, while listing their biggest weakness as the *QB situation* and stating:

> *The Bucs seem set on sitting Winston before releasing him this offseason to avoid his fifth-year option in 2019. ... This is going to be a tough sell.* [726]

NFL.com reporter Judy Battista wrote an article titled, *Ranking NFL coaching vacancies: Browns, Packers most alluring*. In said article, she ranked the Cleveland Browns and Green Bay Packers as the best job openings, and, like Barnwell, ranked the Buccaneers as the second worst opening, specifically asking the question:

> *do you believe in Winston, on the field and off?* [727]

Hilariously, Battista actually ranked the Arizona Cardinals as a better job opening, specifically stating that quarterback Josh Rosen – who had one of the worst rookie quarterback seasons in recent memory and was traded to the Miami Dolphins shortly after her article was written [708] – made the job alluring. [727] I know there are hot takes that don't age well, but it's not often you see such an outrageously bad take written in a supposedly researched article from a main stream media outlet, unless of course said bad take is in an article that deals with Jameis Winston that is.

Brothers Dan and Todd Salem, writing for *Fan Sided*, wrote an article titled, *NFL Offseason 2019: Ranking the 8 coaching vacancies worst to first*. In said article, both brothers ranked the Green Bay Packers job as one of the two best openings, while also ranking the Buccaneers job as the absolute worst opening in the entire NFL. [728]

Todd Salem justified his ranking the Bucs opening dead last by writing:

> *TB is committed to Jameis Winston, which is a major issue for any new head coach.* [728]

And, Dan Salem justified his ranking the Bucs opening dead last by writing:

> *This job would be better if the GM did not publicly declare Winston as their starting quarterback. ... Tampa Bay is the only team on this list with a real question mark at quarterback.* [728]

Like the aforementioned Judy Battista, Dan Salem's above words read like a bad hot take's bad hot take, as, like Battista, he believed the Cardinals' quarterback Josh Rosen and even the Dolphins' quarterback Ryan Tannehill would be a better draw for a head coaching candidate than Winston would be. And, like Josh Rosen who was dumped by the Cardinals shortly after Battista's article was written, so too was Ryan Tannehil dumped by the Dolphins shortly after Dan Salem's article was written. [729]

John Clayton writing for the *Washington Post* and Tyler Lauletta writing for *Business Insider* wrote perhaps the two least biased and absurd articles on this topic, though both ranked the Packers job as one of the top two openings and Lauletta also ranked the Buccaneers job as a less attractive opening than the Arizona Cardinals job, and like the aforementioned Judy Battista and the Salem brothers, mentioned the soon to be traded Josh Rosen in a good light. [730] [731]

Per the norm, what transpired in reality with Winston and the Buccaneers was nothing at all like what the media had predicted.

The Cardinals ended up hiring a recently fired college coach with a career losing record. [732] [733] The media darling Packers – after Aaron Rodgers was outed by former teammates and team executives as what could most accurately be described as a *diva* [734] – seemed to be ignored by all the top head coaching candidates, until they were finally able to hire former Tennessee Titans offensive coordinator Matt LaFleur after he coached one of the worst offenses in the entire NFL in 2018. [735]

As for the Buccaneers, it turned out that not only did Jameis Winston not impair the team from hiring a new head coach, he was the main reason that the team was able to sign the head coaching candidate with by far the best resume of any of the available head coachinf candidates, the man, the myth, the legend, Bruce Arians. Arians was a man who had won two Super Bowl rings as an assistant coach and two NFL Coach of the Year awards as a head coach with two different franchises! [736] [737]

Back in 2016, when Arians was still coaching the Arizona Cardinals, he spoke of how he knew *Jaboo* during his childhood years and made it clear that he would love to coach him one day:

> *Jaboo' is legend in Birmingham ... We had a little football camp back then in Birmingham, and he threw one day. We had a bunch of local kids there and one of his high school coaches was a good friend of mine, so we've known him and watched him grow and we're very, very proud of him. ... He would be fun to coach, there's no doubt about it ... He's a winner and a great leader and obviously a heck of a young quarterback.* [738]

And, after officially being hired by the Buccaneers to be their new head coach, Arians was intereviewed by team reporter Casey Philips who asked him, now that he was the coach what he was most excited about, to which Arians replied:

> *Our quarterback here, we can win with, we can win the championship with.* [739]

Arians was also interviewed after being hired, by Rich Eisen – a popular talking head that was infected with *Winston Derangement Syndrome* long ago – and elaborated on his thoughts about Winston:

> *I've got a great feel for him, his excitement for the game. His willingness to work is unbelievable. He's in the office at 5 o'clock in the morning. ... Everything is going to be built around him. I think he can win it all. He has the intelligence, the toughness and obviously the arm ability to lead a team.* [740]

It's clear that Bruce Arians has been a colossal fan of Jameis Winston for many years, and that he specifically came out of retirement to coach Winston.

Likewise, Scott Reynolds – Vice President of the fantastic *PewterReport.com* website – wrote a wonderful article detailing how Winston actually fits the description of exactly what Bruce Arians said he looks for in a quarterback in his book, *The Quarterback Whisperer: How to Build an Elite NFL Quarterback.* [741]

In short, Jameis Winston is everything Bruce Arians has always looked for in a true superstar quarterback, and is *the reason* that the Buccaneers were able to hire the top head coaching candidate available.

The above said, the main stream sports media should literally feel personally ashamed of themselves as well as professionally embarrassed for spinning the absurd false narratives they did. However, Buccaneers fans can thank the much maligned Jameis Winston for making the Bucs head coaching job the most attractive opening in the entire NFL following the 2018 season, and for landing two-time Super Bowl champion and two-time NFL coach of the year, Bruce Arians!

WHAT ABOUT THOSE #QBWINZ AGAIN?

I've lost almost 300 games. 26 times, I've been trusted to take the game winning shot and missed. I've failed over and over and over again in my life. And that is why I succeed.

– Michael Jordan [742]

Winning is not always the barometer of getting better.

– Tiger Woods [743]

Winning isn't always championships.

– Michael Jordan [742]

I already detailed exactly why I do not believe team wins are a legitimate individual quarterback stat, as well as why I'd even go so far as to say that team wins have absolutely nothing to do with assessing individual talent at any position, in the previous chapter titled, *QBWINZ IS NOT A STAT ... HOWEVER.*

Nevertheless, as I know many NFL fans consider *team* wins an important *individual* quarterback statistic, and in the interest of being thorough, I will now compare Jameis Winston's career win/loss record accumulated in his four years in the league to date, to the 21 Hall of Fame or soon to be Hall of Fame Super Bowl era quarterbacks covered extensively in this book.

There certainly is no *perfect* way to compare quarterback win/loss records as every quarterback is in a unique situation. However, in the statistical tables in this chapter I will at least attempt to accurately depict the situation each of the 22 quarterbacks – including Winston – were in during their first four seasons as a starting NFL quarterback. I will do so by listing their win/loss record and corresponding win percentage, followed by their team's average rushing yards gained rank in an equivalent 32 team league, as well as their team's average points against defense rank in an equivalent 32 team league. Doing so should give a very accurate picture of just how much help each quarterback received from their surrounding cast, and also just how much responsibility each quarterback had to *carry* their team to victory, something that is of course an impossibility in the ultimate team sport that is football.

Through First Four Years as a QB1*	W/L Record	Win %	Average Rushing Yards Gained Rank in 32 Team League	Average Points Against Defense Rank in 32 Team League
Jameis Winston	**21-33**	**.389**	**21st**	**24th**
Troy Aikman	27-27	.500	19th	17th
Terry Bradshaw	27-17	.613	11th	13th
Tom Brady	48-14	.774	19th	7th
Drew Brees	30-28	.517	7th	19th
John Elway	38-18	.679	20th	11th
Brett Favre	37-24	.607	25th	9th
Dan Fouts	10-28-1	.269	18th	25th
Bob Griese	20-24-2	.457	18th	20th
Jim Kelly	28-29	.491	14th	14th
Eli Manning	30-25	.545	7th	18th
Peyton Manning	32-32	.500	18th	24th
Dan Marino	41-16	.719	21st	13th
Joe Montana	18-15	.545	26th	22nd
Warren Moon	19-38	.333	23rd	24th
Philip Rivers	46-18	.719	15th	10th
Aaron Rodgers	41-21	.661	21st	13th
Ben Roethlisberger	39-16	.709	5th	4th
Ken Stabler	20-5-1	.788	6th	11th
Roger Staubach	23-5	.821	3rd	8th
Kurt Warner	35-14	.714	15th	17th
Steve Young	7-18	.280	23rd	27th

[141][744] [369] [705] [706] [230] [745] [746] [747] [748] [231] [749] [750] [751] [713] [232] [752] [753] [754] [755] [233] [756] [757] [758] [759] [234] [760] [761] [762] [763] [235] [764] [765] [766] [767] [236] [768] [769] [770] [771] [237] [772] [773] [774] [775] [238] [776] [777] [778] [779] [239] [780] [781] [782] [714] [240] [783] [784] [785] [786] [241] [787] [788] [789] [790] [242] [791] [792] [793] [794] [243] [795] [796] [797] [798] [244] [799] [800] [801] [802] [245] [803] [804] [805] [697] [211] [806] [807] [808] [809] [246] [810] [811] [812] [813] [247] [814] [815] [816] [817] [248] [818] [819] [820] [821] [249] [822] [295] [823] [824]

* At least one start in a season.

As can be seen from the table on the previous page, just six of the legendary quarterbacks had less career wins than Jameis Winston did in their first four years as a starting quarterback, and just three had a worse win percentage at the same stage. However, you can also clearly see that just four quarterbacks received less run support than Jameis Winston received, just two quarterbacks were saddled with a worse team defense than Winston had, and just three quarterbacks had worse combined run support and team defense than Winston had.

The above said, Winston had the fourth worst combined run support and team defense of all the quarterbacks and also had the fourth worst win percentage of all the quarterbacks. It's almost as if an NFL quarterback's win percentage is somehow tied to the amount of run support he receives and whether his defense is any good or not. What a shocking revelation!

Perhaps those who have never played a single football game in their entire life – even a backyard game of two-hand-touch with extended family on Thanksgiving – will find such a fact alarming. However, there is no excuse for anyone in the main stream sports media that covers the NFL to be ignorant of such an obvious fact.

Nevertheless, the way much of the media talks about one quarterback beating another quarterback, as if the two quarterbacks were playing a game of 1-on-1 basketball, would lead one to believe such media figures actually are ignorant of such an obvious fact. The truth of the matter is far worse. Such media figures are not at all ignorant of said fact, they merely only promote said fact when they want to spin a positive narrative about a golden boy quarterback they like such as Aaron Rodgers, and completely ignore said fact when they want to spin a negative narrative against a quarterback they dislike such as Jameis Winston.

Now, let's take the same statistical table but simply arrange it so that it's ranked from top to bottom based on how much help each quarterback received, so that we can accurately assess which of the quarterbacks truly exceeded where they should have ranked on such a list based on how much help they received, which quarterbacks failed to even match what their ranking should have been, and which quarterbacks broke even.

Through First Four Years as a QB1*	W/L Record	Win %	Combined Average Rank of Run Support and Points Against Defense in 32 Team League	Score Highest is Best
Ben Roethlisberger	39-16	.709	9th	- 6
Roger Staubach	23-5	.821	11th	+ 1
Ken Stabler	20-5-1	.788	17th	+ 1
Terry Bradshaw	27-17	.613	24th	- 6
Philip Rivers	46-18	.719	25th	+ 1
Eli Manning	30-25	.545	25th	- 7
Tom Brady	48-14	.774	26th	+ 4
Drew Brees	30-28	.517	26th	- 6
Jim Kelly	28-29	.491	28th	- 8
John Elway	38-18	.679	31st	+ 2
Kurt Warner	35-14	.714	32nd	+ 5
Dan Marino	41-16	.719	34th	+ 8
Aaron Rodgers	41-21	.661	34th	+ 4
Brett Favre	37-24	.607	34th	+ 3
Troy Aikman	27-27	.500	36th	- 1
Bob Griese	20-24-2	.457	38th	- 2
Peyton Manning	32-32	.500	42nd	+ 2
Dan Fouts	10-28-1	.269	43rd	- 4
Jameis Winston	**21-33**	**.389**	**45th**	**Even**
Warren Moon	19-38	.333	47th	Even
Joe Montana	18-15	.545	48th	+ 8

| Steve Young | 7-18 | .280 | 50th | + 1 |

* At least one start in a season.

Starting from the top of the list we see that Ben Roethlisberger had the most help. However, looking at his win percentage and comparing it to all the other quarterbacks, we see that six other quarterbacks who had less help than Roethlisberger did actually had better win percentages. Therefore Roethlisberger would receive a - 6 score, meaning he finished with a win percentage that was six slots lower – namely in 7th place – than it should have been – namely in 1st place – based on the help he received.

In fact, while Big Ben received the most help and did in fact finish with the seventh highest win percentage of the 22 quarterbacks listed, only Eli Manning and Jim Kelly finished with a worse +- rank, with Manning finishing seven slots below where he should have based on help received, and Kelly finishing eight slots below where he should have.

As for Jameis Winston, one can see that he exactly *broke even*, as only three quarterbacks received less help than he did and only three quarterbacks had a worse win percentage than he did.

Finally, let's take the same table but simply arrange it so that the 22 quarterbacks are ranked, in order from best to worst in regards to their +- rating from the previous table. Doing so will show which quarterbacks truly accounted for the most team wins, independent of the amount of help they received, and therefore which quarterbacks were truly contributing the most to their team's wins on an individual basis.

Through First Four Years as a QB1*	W/L Record	Win %	Combined Average Rank of Run Support and Points Against Defense in 32 Team League	Score Highest is Best
Dan Marino	41-16	.719	34th	+ 8
Joe Montana	18-15	.545	48th	+ 8
Kurt Warner	35-14	.714	32nd	+ 5

Tom Brady	48-14	.774	26th	+ 4
Aaron Rodgers	41-21	.661	34th	+ 4
Brett Favre	37-24	.607	34th	+ 3
John Elway	38-18	.679	31st	+ 2
Peyton Manning	32-32	.500	42nd	+ 2
Philip Rivers	46-18	.719	25th	+ 1
Roger Staubach	23-5	.821	11th	+ 1
Ken Stabler	20-5-1	.788	17th	+ 1
Steve Young	7-18	.280	50th	+ 1
Jameis Winston	**21-33**	**.389**	**45th**	**Even**
Warren Moon	19-38	.333	47th	Even
Troy Aikman	27-27	.500	36th	- 1
Bob Griese	20-24-2	.457	38th	- 2
Dan Fouts	10-28-1	.269	43rd	- 4
Ben Roethlisberger	39-16	.709	9th	- 6
Drew Brees	30-28	.517	26th	- 6
Terry Bradshaw	27-17	.613	24th	- 6
Eli Manning	30-25	.545	25th	- 7
Jim Kelly	28-29	.491	28th	- 8

* At least one start in a season.

When we view the above table, a few things become extremely clear.

Firstly, as has been pretty clear throughout this book, Dan Marino was a quarterback god right from the beginning of his career.

Secondly, Joe Montana – even before Jerry Rice came to town – was a guy that excelled at leading his team to more wins than should have been expected.

Thirdly, Kurt Warner had one of the strongest starts to a career in NFL history, even if his career went downhill and almost flamed out entirely, before being resurrected in Arizona in his quarterback golden years.

Fourthly, Ben Roethlisberger, Drew Brees, Terry Bradshaw, Eli Manning and Jim Kelly, while solid individual statistical quarterbacks in their first four starting seasons – at least in the case of all except Manning – really hurt their teams chances of winning, even if their teams all experienced a great deal of success at times. In fact, all five of those quarterbacks made the playoffs at least one time in their first four seasons as a starting quarterback, and actually combined to go to the playoffs 11 times and win two Super Bowls in those mere 20 combined seasons.

Fifthly, Jameis Winston and Warren Moon – two quarterbacks who know what it's like to be slandered and even hated by a biased media from the time they left college and declared for the NFL draft – despite having two of the lowest win percentages on the above list, actually ranked higher than eight of the other 20 quarterbacks, many of whom had even won a Super Bowl in their first four years!

As for Winston, he – despite being infinitely better statistically over his first four years as a starting quarterback than Terry Bradshaw, Eli Manning and even Drew Brees and arguably better than Roethlisberger and Kelly as well, and who ranked higher as a winner on this list, in regards to win percentage measured against the amount of help he received from his run game and defense – has never made it to the playoffs yet in four NFL seasons.

Those five inferior statistical quarterbacks played in a combined 20 playoff games in a combined 20 seasons over their first four years as starting quarterbacks, for an average of one playoff game every season [231] [239] [233] [211] [238] yet Jameis Winston, who has been markedly better than three of them and arguably better than the remaining two, has never been on a team that has made the playoffs yet.

Once again, who would have thought that a quarterback actually needs some help from his run game and defense to win games at a high level in the ultimate team sport that is football? Only every football fan on earth that hasn't been infected with *Winston Derangement Syndrome*, that's who.

All of the above said, it should be extremely obvious that in his first four seasons in the NFL, Jameis Winston – while being bashed by the media for not single-handedly carrying his team that has had a terrible run game and dreadful defense to more wins – has won games at a higher clip above what should have been realistically expected of him considering his lack of support in the run game and from his defense, than eight other Hall of Fame or soon to be Hall of Fame quarterbacks over their first four years as starting quarterbacks in the NFL. This being the case, the next time you hear that Jameis Winston didn't win enough in his first four years, or that he should have won more, you'll be able to refute such a false narrative with hard data that the media is clueless about.

You're welcome.

WHAT ABOUT TURNOVERS?

I live life and call plays the same way, no risk it, no biscuit

– Bruce Arians [825]

You can't be Superman on every throw, which he [Jameis Winston] can be, and when you have great ones, they think they can be. But you've just got to pick and choose sometimes when you want to be Superman.

– Bruce Arians [826]

Perhaps the biggest knock on Jameis Winston is that he turns the ball over too much due to the supreme confidence he has in his own ability, as well as his hyper competitiveness and belief that he can make magic happen on each and every play, which of course just isn't possible on the NFL level. I suppose one could say that Winston's greatest weakness, namely having a Superman complex, is a byproduct of his greatest strength, namely the ability to literally be Superman from time to time on a football field.

However, the same exact thing could be said about some of the greatest quarterbacks of all time when they were young, such as Terry Bradshaw, John Elway and Peyton Manning. It's also the same exact thing that was said about Brett Favre throughout his entire career. However, just as shooters will shoot in basketball, gunslingers will sling in football. It's just who they are and what they do.

Of the 26 highest interceptions thrown seasons in NFL history, 12 came from quarterbacks already in the Hall of Fame with two more coming from soon tobe Hall of Famers: Peyton and Eli Manning. [827] Likewise, of the 20 quarterbacks that have thrown the most career interceptions, 12 are Hall of Famers with three more being soon to be Hall of Famers: Peyton Manning, Drew Brees and Eli Manning. [828]

Simply put, a great many Hall of Fame quarterbacks have turned the ball over a great deal, primarily because most Hall of Fame quarterbacks were *gunslingers* whose coaches expected them to be *offense-carriers* rather than mere *game-managers*. And, while it may be easy to complete a high percentage of passes and rarely throw interceptions when you are throwing screen-passes, dumping off short throws to your running backs and tight ends, and rarely even being asked to throw a 15 yard pass, let alone a 30 plus yard pass, it's extremely common to throw a relatively high number of interceptions when you're asked to *air it out*.

For example, consider the stat known as *Averaged Intended Air Yards* (IAY) which originated in 2016 and is described as:

> *IAY shows the average Air Yards a passer throws on all attempts. This metric shows how far the ball is being thrown 'downfield'. Air Yards is recorded as a negative value when the pass is behind the Line of Scrimmage. Additionally Air Yards is calculated into the back of the end zone to better evaluate the true depth of the pass.* [375]

Now, consider the fact that since 2016, Jameis Winston ranked:

- 2nd in the entire NFL in 2016 [374]
- 3rd in the entire NFL in 2017 [452]
- 2nd in the entire NFL in 2018 [637]

Likewise, consider the fact that Drew Brees, in the same stat, ranked:

- 36th in the entire NFL in 2016 [374]
- 41st in the entire NFL in 2017 [452]
- 32nd in the entire NFL in 2018 [637]

The fact is that over the past three seasons, according to the simple math based on the stats cited above, Jameis Winston has been asked by his coaches to literally throw every single pass on average 52.4% further than Drew Brees – 52.4%!

If you don't think that a gunslinger quarterback who is asked by his coaches to throw every single pass on average 52.4% farther than a competing game-manager quarterback will negatively impact said gunslingers completion percentage and the amount of interceptions he throws, you can call me George Parker as I'm going to sell you the Brooklyn Bridge! [829]

Regardless, I believe Aaron Rodgers' mastery when it comes to avoiding interceptions, coupled with the fact that he's one of the media's golden boys, and the fact that the vast majority of the media doesn't seem to grasp advanced metrics like *IAY* and lacks the common sense needed to understand a quarterback's *IAY* can have a huge impact on his interception total, has made throwing interceptions the one thing the media likes to harp on the most.

Never mind the fact that the NFL's all-time leader in interceptions thrown – Brett Favre – is a quarterback god, or that Terry Bradshaw with his four Super Bowl rings was known as an interception machine in his day, or that Peyton Manning threw a whopping 100 hundred interceptions in just his first 5 years in the NFL – yes, one hundred! In fact, you might as well forget that even the GOTSBE himself – Tom Brady – didn't just throw an interception but a dreaded pick-six in Super Bowl LI, and then threw another easily interceptable pass with the game on the line in the fourth quarter, which the same defender who pick-sixed him earlier – Robert Alford – simply dropped, yet Brady's *team* still won the game. [539] The media has simply decided that throwing interceptions is now an unpardonable sin for quarterbacks, and that Jameis Winston deserves to be crucified whenever he throws one.

Likewise, fumbling the ball is considered another mortal sin for quarterbacks, though many quarterbacks not named Jameis Winston do seem to get a pass when it comes to fumbles. Regardless, fumbles certainly contribute to a quarterback's total turnovers and therefore deserve to be factored into the narrative surrounding any quarterback, as to whether or not he is a turnover prone quarterback.

Furthermore, just as with interceptions, the all-time career fumbles list is also loaded with Hall of Fame quarterbacks. In fact, of the 14 quarterbacks that have recorded the most career fumbles, five of them are Hall of Famers with three more being soon to be Hall of Famers: Tom Brady, Eli Manning and Drew Brees. [830]

However, while there is a stat called interception percentage that is quite useful, there is no such stat for fumbles, let alone for *total* turnovers, which is a shame, as to truly measure a quarterback's penchant for turning the ball over one would need to know their *total turnover percentage*.

The above said, in this chapter I will create such a stat, which I will term *Total Turnover Percentage* and which I will abbreviate as *TTO %*. This *Total Turnover Percentage* statistic will be calculated as follows:

Total Turnovers
(Interceptions + Fumbles - Fumbles Recovered)

÷

Total touches
(Attempted Passes + Rushes + Receptions + Times Sacked)

=

Total Turnover Percentage

For example, if a quarterback throws one interception, fumbles the ball twice, but also recovers one fumble, he would have two *total turnovers* as they are defined by this stat. And, if he attempts 34 passes, catches a pass on some gadget play, records three rushing attempts and is sacked two times, he would have 40 *total touches* as such is defined by this stat. Therefore, one would simply divide the number two (i.e. the number of total turnovers) by the number 40 (i.e. the number of total touches) which would give one a total turnover percentage of .05 or five percent (5.0%) for that particular quarterback in that particular game.

All of the above said and without further ado, let's look at how Jameis Winston compares to all 21 legendary quarterbacks by viewing the below *Total Turnover Percentage* (TTO%) table:

Through First Four Years as a QB1*	Total Touches: Attempted Passes + Rushes + Receptions + Times Sacked	Interceptions Plus Fumbles Minus Fumbles Recovered	Total Turnover Percentage (TTO %)
Jameis Winston	**2,233**	**80**	**3.6**
Troy Aikman	1,774	74	4.2
Terry Bradshaw	1,367	83	6.1
Tom Brady	2,309	82	3.6
Drew Brees	2,007	70	3.5
John Elway	2,058	89	4.3
Brett Favre	2,460	99	4.0
Dan Fouts	1,142	62	5.4
Bob Griese	1,443**	76	5.3**
Jim Kelly	2,008	80	4.0
Eli Manning	1,987	93	4.7
Peyton Manning	2,433	96	3.9
Dan Marino	2,202	85	3.9
Joe Montana	1,864	54	2.9
Warren Moon	2,015	104	5.2
Philip Rivers	2,117	69	3.3
Aaron Rodgers	2,443	54	2.2
Ben Roethlisberger	1,736	67	3.9
Ken Stabler	1,290	75	5.8
Roger Staubach	1,231	59	4.8
Kurt Warner	1,797	91	5.1
Steve Young	922	38	4.1

[141] [230] [231] [232] [233] [234] [235] [236] [237] [238] [239] [240] [241] [242] [243] [244] [245] [211] [246] [247] [248] [249]

* At least 3 starts in a season

** Sack stats were not recorded in Griese's first two seasons, so I took the average amount of times he was sacked in his 3rd-4th seasons and multiplied that by the amount of games he played in his first two seasons to add his estimated sack totals to his *total touches*.

After viewing the *Total Turnover Percentage* (TTO%) table on the following page, three things become clear almost immediately.

Firstly, Jameis Winston has the exact same TTO% through his first four years as a starting quarterback in the NFL as the GOTSBE Tom Brady, someone who has never really been accused by the media of being a turnover prone quarterback, had at the same stage of his career.

Secondly, it does appear that some form of adjusting for era may be called for, even if such would be a gargantuan task for a statistician. That said, I will leave such a task either to a greater mind than my own, or at least to a mind belonging to someone that has a great deal more spare time than I currently do.

Thirdly, while some form of adjusting for era may be called for, it does not appear that a quarterback's era has as much of a factor in regards to *Total Turnover Percentage* as it does to merely interceptions alone, let alone a stat like passing yards or completion perentage. This is probably do to fumble totals – unlike interception totals – being more of a constant throughout the different eras and even escalating in the modern eras, likely due to there being less running plays called as the NFL has become a pass-first league, and therefore there are simply many more opportunities in each game for a modern quarterback to fumble than their were in past eras.

Also, simply looking at the TTO% of various quarterbacks on the table shows that era adjustment is less needed for TTO% than for something like INT % alone.

Warren Moon played his first game 15 years after Roger Staubach played his first game, yet Staubach has a markedly better TTO% despite playing in the earlier era. Likewise, Joe Montana started his first game 22 years before Tom Brady started his first game, yet Montana has a markedly better TTO% than Brady, despite playing in the earlier era where interceptions were more prevalent.

All of that said, it seems extremely clear that Jameis Winston – with the exact same Total Turnover Percentage as the GOTSBE Tom Brady – has gotten a bit of a bad rap when it comes to being a turnover machine. Now, don't get me wrong, every player has a greatest weakness, whether it's arm strength for Joe Montana or foot speed for Dan Marino or personality for Ben Roethlisberger or height for Drew Brees or leadership for Aaron Rodgers, and it is more than fair to say that Jameis Winston's greatest weakness – ala Brett Favre – is that he seems averse to giving up on any play, trusts his arm too much, and therefore turns the ball over more than many other quarterbacks. Nevertheless, one can turn the ball over more than many other quarterbacks and still be a great quarterback, and the *Total Turnover Percentage* statistic is proof of that.

In fact, of the three best known quarterbacks in the legendary 1983 NFL Draft class – Dan Marino, John Elway and Ken O'Brien – it was Ken O'Brien that had the best career *Total Turnover Percentage*, that's right, Ken O'Brien! O'Brien had a career 3.5 TTO% while Marino had a 3.6 TTO% and Elway had a 3.8 TTO%. By the way, O'Brien also had a better career interception percentage and even a better career passer rating then John Elway did; yes, I'm serious. [241] [234] [831]

If the above wasn't shocking enough for you, also consider the fact that in the past eight years, Philip Rivers, a sure-fire future Hall of Famer has recorded a 3.1 TTO%, while Alex Smith, someone who will have to buy a ticket like the general public to get into Canton, has recorded an otherworldly 1.7 TTO%. [244] [304]

No NFL owner, General Manager, or coach in their right mind, would rather have had Ken O'Brien over John Elway, or Alex Smith over Philip Rivers, yet Elway and especially Rivers turned the ball over at a higher clip than did O'Brien and Smith. That said, it should be obvious to everyone reading this book that while the media may be in love with efficient game-manager quarterbacks at present, a gunslinger that turns the ball over more than another quarterback does not make that gunslinger a worse quarterback by any stretch of the imagination.

As for how some of Jameis Winston's *Total Turnover Percentages* stack up with some of his contemporaries, consider the following:

In Winston's rookie season – the last time he had solid run support – he recorded a 2.8 TTO%. In that same exact season (i.e. 2015) future Hall of Famer Ben Roethlisberger recorded a 3.4 TTO% and Peyton Manning – who won the Super Bowl that season – recorded a 5.1 TTO%. [141] [211] [240]

In Winston's 22 year old sophomore season he recorded a 3.3 TTO%. In that same exact season (i.e. 2016) future Hall of Famer Philip Rivers recorded a 4.3 TTO%. [141] [244]

In Winston's third season, he played nearly half of his games with a severly injured throwing shoulder, fumbled like crazy and finished with a 3.7 TTO%, a career worst but still better than what Philip Rivers had put up the year prior. [141]

And, in Winston's fourth season, he had a disastrous 4.2 TTO%, though again, that was far better than Peyton Manning's 5.1 TTO% in 2015 when he won the Super Bowl, proving just how much of a *team* sport football is. However, after Winston returned to the starting lineup for the final six games of the season, he put up an absolutely remarkable 1.97 TTO% to be extra specific. [633] Yes, the gunslinger kept slinging while also protecting the ball like an efficient game-manager!

I feel I should also state that, like the great gunslinger himself – Brett Favre, who once threw six interceptions in a single playoff game [832] – Jameis Winston tends to throw his interceptions in bunches. In fact, he has thrown 41 of his 58 career interceptions in just 16 games. Yes, that's horrible. However, what that also means is that in his other 40 career games Winston has thrown just 17 interceptions – on 1,288 pass attempts – which if extrapolated over a full 16 game season would work out to just

7 interceptions and a magnificent 1.3 interception percentage, which would have been good for fourth best in the entire NFL in 2018, behind only Aaron Rodgers, Drew Brees and Matt Ryan! [204] [347] [430] [633] [221]

In closing, if there's one thing that stands out about all the statsitics covered in this chapter, it's that while turning the ball over may currently be viewed by the media as an unforgiveable sin, nearly all of the greatest quarterbacks throughout NFL history have turned the ball over at a fairly high rate, as most were true risk-taking gunslingers, rather than mere efficient game-managers. That said, while Jameis Winston may be more Brett Favre than Aaron Rodgers and more Warren Moon than Joe Montana, his *Total Turnover Percentage* through four years is on par, and even better than, many of the greatest quarterbacks to have ever played in the NFL.

WHERE DOES JAMEIS WINSTON RANK?

If you ask any great player or great quarterback, there's a certain inner confidence that you're as good as anybody. But you can't say who is the absolute best. To be considered is special in itself.

– Dan Marino [833]

Ever since I created my Jameis1of1 pseudonym years ago, with its corresponding Twitter account, Sports Card Forum account and the like, the one statement that I have made more than any other and the one that has incensed people more than any other is simply that Jameis Winston is the most statistically accomplished passer of his age in the history of the NFL. Such was an irrefutable fact through Winston's age 23 season, his third in the league. And, as this book has proven, such is still a logical statement backed by a great deal of hard data, even if such is now more debatable, as depending on the parameters one uses to evaluate quarterbacks, a solid case can be made to support the claim that Jameis Winston is the greatest 24 year old quarterback in the history of the NFL.

However, depending on the parameters used, one could also make a strong case for a handful of other quarterbacks being the NFL's 24 year old GOAT. Regardless, after Winston finished his fourth season, Buccaneers General Manager Jason Licht publicly stated:

> *Jameis ... He has done some amazing things for a young 24, turns 25 in a week, quarterback. He's accomplished more than most of the elite quarterbacks have at his age throughout that time span.* [834]

When I heard Licht make those statements, it was literally as if he was reading aloud from one of my tweets when he spoke, which is great, as if anyone has the authority to put the media in their place and to refute the false narratives surrounding Jameis Winston, it's the General Manager of the Tampa Bay Buccaneers.

Of course, I don't expect Licht to go on a crusade – Jameis1of1 style – combatting the false narratives surrounding Winston, but it was wonderful to see him state facts about his young quarterback rather than just allowing the media to control the narrative as many General Managers do. I sincerely applaud Jason Licht for speaking truth to power (and you better believe the media has a great deal of power in this day and age) in the way that he did.

Who is the GOAT 24 Year Old NFL Quarterback?

Is Jameis Winston truly the *greatest* 24 year old quarterback in the history of the NFL, and if he's not, who is, and where does Winston rank on such a list when compared with the 21 Super Bowl era Hall of Fame or soon to be Hall of Fame quarterbacks extensively covered in this book?

The Difference between *Best* and *Greatest*

As I explained earlier in this book, when most football fans debate which players are the *best* at their respective positions, they generally mean which players have accomplished the most on an individual basis, meaning which players have won the most individual awards or accumulated the best individual stats, independent of team success.

For example, many people – myself included – believe that Barry Sanders was the the *best* pure runner in NFL history. However, Sanders won just one single playoff game in his 10 year NFL career and therefore is not generally considered the *greatest* NFL running back of all time, as that title is generally reserved for Jim Brown.

On the flip side, when most football fans debate which players are the *greatest* at their respective positions, they generally mean which players have accomplished the most on both an individual and team basis.

For example, many people – myself included – believe that Terry Bradshaw deserves to be ranked higher on an NFL quarterback GOAT list than Dan Fouts, thanks in large part to the massive amount of team success he experienced, especially when compared to Fouts' utter lack of team success. However, many of those same people – myself included again – do not believe Bradshaw was a better individual quarterback than Fouts was, which the statistics and individual accolades Fouts amassed attest to.

The Parameters

When debating who the *greatest* – not the *best* – 24 year old quarterback in the history of the NFL is, I believe it's fair to give equal weight to career passing yards, career passing touchdowns, regular season wins, individual accolades, as well as season playoff appearances plus Super Bowl rings as a starting quarterback, as those are literally the only things fans and even so-called experts really discuss when engaging in GOAT debates.

The above said, in regards to individual accolades, each player will receive one point for a rookie of the year award, NFL All-Rookie Team selection, Pro Bowl selection, All-Pro selection, regular season MVP Award, Offensive Player of the Year Award or Super Bowl MVP Award, through their 24 year old season and as long as they played at least half their regular season games before turning 25 years of age.

Also, in regards to the playoff appearances plus Super Bowl wins category, each player will receive one point for each season playoff appearance in a season he was his team's QB1, plus one point for each Super Bowl win through their 24 year old season and as long as they played at least half their regular season games before turning 25 years of age.

That said, before I detail where each quarterback ranks in comparison to each other using such parameters, I will first provide a table showing their accumulated career totals in each of the five statistical categories, before the age of 25.

Career Totals Before the Age of 25	Passing Yards	Passing TDs	Regular Season Wins	Indiv. Awards	Playoff Apps + SB Wins
Jameis Winston	**14628**	**88**	**21**	**2**	**0**
Troy Aikman	6878	30	12	2	1
Terry Bradshaw	5556	31	19	0	1
Tom Brady	2849	18	11	2*	2**
Drew Brees	5613	29	10	0	0
John Elway	4261	25	16	0	2
Brett Favre	8179	46	20	2	1
Dan Fouts	4254	16	5	0	0
Bob Griese	6173	46	10	2	0
Jim Kelly	0	0	0	0	0
Eli Manning	4805	30	12	0	1
Peyton Manning	12287	85	26	3	2
Dan Marino	11975	102	34	8	3
Joe Montana	1891	16	2	0	0
Warren Moon	0	0	0	0	0
Philip Rivers	2748	17	10	1	1
Aaron Rodgers	3226	21	5	0	0
Ben Roethlisberger	8519	52	29	2	3**
Ken Stabler	52	0	0	0	0
Roger Staubach	0	0	0	0	0
Kurt Warner	0	0	0	0	0
Steve Young	1217	4	2	0	0

* Tom Brady is the only quarterback in this table to win a Super Bowl MVP award before the age of 25.

** Tom Brady and Ben Roethlisberger are the only quarterbacks in this table to win a Super Bowl before the age of 25.

Now that you have seen the career totals of each quarterback through age 24, I will rank each quarterback from 1st to worst in each individual statistical category. Those individual category rankings will then be totalled up and the players will then be assigned a final ranking, to see how – using these parameters – each of the 22 quarterbacks stack up on a 24 year old GOAT NFL quarterback list.

317

Please note that both Tom Brady and Ben Roethlisberger will win a ranking tie with other players with the same amount of playoff appearances plus Super Bowl wins as they are the only two quarterbacks in the table that won a Super Bowl before the age of 25. Likewise Tom Brady will win a ranking tie with other players with the same amount of individual awards as he is the only quarterback in the table that won a Super Bowl MVP award before the age of 25.

Finally, please note that no citations will be given following the table, as the ranks are generated from previous tables in this book and previously cited statistical webpages from pro-football-referece.com; therefore not a single new source or citation is necessary. However, by all means, feel free to spend a few solid weeks fact-checking each and every ranking if you'd like, before ultimately coming to the realization that my research, math, and therefore the ranks assigned to each quarterback are beyond reproach.

All of the above said and without further ado, the GOAT 24 Year Old NFL Quarterback table is as follows.

GOAT 24 YEAR OLD NFL QUARTERBACK

Rankings Before the Age of 25	Career Pass Yards Rank	Career Pass TDs Rank	Regular Season Wins Rank	Indiv. Awards Rank	Playoff Apps + SB Wins Rank	Final Rank
Dan Marino	3	1	1	1	2	1st
Peyton Manning	2	3	3	2	4	2nd
Ben Roethlisberger	4	4	2	4	1**	3rd
Jameis Winston	1	2	4	4	11	4th
Brett Favre	5	5	5	4	6	5th
Troy Aikman	6	8	8	4	6	6th
Bob Griese	7	5	11	4	11	7th
Terry Bradshaw	9	7	6	11	6	8th
Tom Brady	14	13	10	3*	3**	9th
Eli Manning	10	8	8	11	6	10th
John Elway	11	11	7	11	4	11th
Drew Brees	8	10	11	11	11	12th
Philip Rivers	15	14	11	9	6	13th

Aaron Rodgers	13	12	14	11	11	14th
Dan Fouts	12	15	14	11	11	15th
Joe Montana	16	15	16	11	11	16th
Steve Young	17	17	16	11	11	17th
Warren Moon	19	18	18	9	11	18th
Ken Stabler	18	18	18	11	11	19th
Jim Kelly	19	18	18	11	11	20th
Roger Staubach	19	18	18	11	11	20th
Kurt Warner	19	18	18	11	11	20th

* Tom Brady is the only quarterback in this table to win a Super Bowl MVP award before the age of 25.

** Tom Brady and Ben Roethlisberger are the only quarterbacks in this table to win a Super Bowl before the age of 25.

After viewing the final rankings, we see that Dan Marino – when using these parameters – is not only the GOAT 24 year old NFL quarterback, but that there really isn't even a close second when totalling up the ranks of each quarterback in each of the five statistical categories. Marino basically laps the field!

As for the subject of this book – Jameis Winston – he finishes in a strong fourth place, behind only the GOAT 24 year old Dan Marino, Peyton Manning and Ben Roethlisberger. Not too shabby for a young man that nearly the entire main stream media wants everyone to believe is a *bust* and someone that will be out of the league or at the very least a backup by the time the 2020 NFL season rolls around.

Who is the GOAT NFL Quarterback Through Four Seasons?

While Jameis Winston ranked 4th on the previous GOAT 24 year old quarterback list, where does he rank on a GOAT list for quarterbacks that have played four *seasons* in the league? View the statistical tables on the following pages to find out.

Totals Through First 4 Seasons	Career Pass Yards	Career Pass TDs	Regular Season Wins	Indiv. Awards	Playoff Apps + SB Wins
Jameis Winston	**14628**	**88**	**21**	**2**	**0**
Troy Aikman	10527	54	27	4***	3*
Terry Bradshaw	6739	41	27	0	2
Tom Brady	10233	69	34	3****	4**
Drew Brees	8772	56	21	1	1
John Elway	11637	66	38	1	3
Brett Favre	10412	70	26	2	2
Dan Fouts	6789	30	10	0	0
Bob Griese	8192	58	20	3	1
Jim Kelly	12901	81	28	2	2
Eli Manning	11385	77	30	1***	4*
Peyton Manning	16418	111	32	3	2
Dan Marino	16177	142	41	10	3
Joe Montana	8069	52	18	2***	2*
Warren Moon	12342	61	19	1	1
Philip Rivers	6688	44	25	1	2
Aaron Rodgers	4367	29	6	0	0
Ben Roethlisberger	11673	84	39	3	4
Ken Stabler	2841	19	9	1	1
Roger Staubach	2943	18	13	2***	2*
Kurt Warner	12651	98	35	8	4
Steve Young	4467	24	7	0	0

* Troy Aikman, Eli Manning, Joe Montana and Roger Staubach are the only quarterbacks in this table to win a Super Bowl through first four seasons.

** Tom Brady is the only quarterback in this table to win two Super Bowls through first four seasons.

*** Troy Aikman, Eli Manning, Joe Montana and Roger Staubach are the only quarterbacks in this table to win a Super Bowl MVP award through first four seasons.

**** Tom Brady is the only quarterback in this table to win two Super Bowl MVP awards through first four seasons.

Now that you have seen the career totals of each quarterback through their first four seasons in the league, I will rank each quarterback from 1st to worst in each individual statistical category. Those individual category rankings will then be totalled up and the players will then be assigned a final ranking, to see how – using these parameters – each of the 22 quarterbacks stack up on a GOAT NFL quarterback through four seasons list.

Once again, please note that no citations will be given following the table, as the ranks are generated from previous tables in this book and previously cited statistical webpages from pro-football-referece.com; therefore not a single new source or citation is necessary. However, by all means, feel free to spend a few solid weeks fact-checking each and every ranking if you'd like, before ultimately coming to the realization that my research, math, and therefore the ranks assigned to each quarterback are beyond reproach.

Also, please note that the higher number of playoff appearances will break ties in the *Regular Season Wins* category. Therefore Drew Brees trumped Jameis Winston in that one statistical category, as Brees had one playoff appearance while Winston did not.

Likewise, Super Bowl wins trump ties in the *Regular Season Wins* category that are also tied in the *Playoff Appearances Plus Super Bowl Wins* category. Therefore Troy Aikman trumped Terry Bradshaw, as Aikman won a Super Bowl unlike Bradshaw.

Furthermore, Eli Manning's Super Bowl MVP award trumps all other players that tied with him in the *Individual Awards* category. Likewise, while Brady, Eli Manning, Kurt Warner and Ben Roethlisberger all recorded four playoff appearances plus Super Bowl wins, Brady trumps all of them as he is the only one with two Super Bowl wins, while Manning and Warner tie each other but trump Roethlisberger, as while all three of those quarterbacks won one Super Bowl, only Manning and Warner won a Super Bowl MVP award. In the same way, Aikman trumps Marino and Elway though the three quarterbacks tied in said category, as Aikman was the only one who won a Super Bowl.

Finally, in calculating the final ranking for each quarterback, there were just two pairs of quarterbacks that tied after all five statistical categories were factored in. The first was Troy Aikman and John Elway – who had a cumulative total ranking of 41 across the five categories – though Aikman trumped Elway as only he had won a Super Bowl. The second pair – who had a cumulative total ranking of 68 across the five categories – was Drew Brees and Philip Rivers, which is interesting as Brees is the quarterback Rivers replaced in San Diego.

All of the above said and without further ado, the final statistical table in this entire book, the *GOAT NFL Quarterback Through Four Seasons* table is as follows:

GOAT NFL QUARTERBACK THROUGH FOUR SEASONS

Rankings Through First 4 Seasons	Career Pass Yards	Career Pass TDs	Regular Season Wins	Indiv. Awards	Playoff Apps + SB Wins	Final Rank Based on Totals
Dan Marino	2	1	1	1	6	1
Kurt Warner	5	3	4	2	2	2
Peyton Manning	1	2	6	5	8	3
Ben Roethlisberger	7	5	2	5	4	4
Tom Brady	12	9	5	4	1	5
Jim Kelly	4	6	8	10	8	6
Eli Manning	9	7	7	13	2	7
Troy Aikman	10	14	9	3	5	8
John Elway	8	10	3	14	6	9
Brett Favre	11	8	11	10	8	10
Jameis Winston	**3**	**4**	**14**	**10**	**19**	**11**
Bob Griese	14	12	15	5	15	12
Warren Moon	6	11	16	14	15	13
Joe Montana	15	15	17	8	8	14
Drew Brees	13	13	13	14	15	15
Philip Rivers	18	16	12	14	8	15
Terry Bradshaw	17	17	10	19	8	17
Roger Staubach	21	22	18	8	8	18
Dan Fouts	16	18	19	19	19	19
Ken Stabler	22	21	20	14	15	20
Aaron Rodgers	19	19	22	19	19	21
Steve Young	20	20	21	19	19	22

* Troy Aikman, Eli Manning, Joe Montana and Roger Staubach are the only quarterbacks in this table to win a Super Bowl through first four seasons.

** Tom Brady is the only quarterback in this table to win two Super Bowls through first four seasons.

*** Troy Aikman, Eli Manning, Joe Montana and Roger Staubach are the only quarterbacks in this table to win a Super Bowl MVP award through first four seasons.

**** Tom Brady is the only quarterback in this table to win two Super Bowl MVP awards through first four seasons.

After viewing the final rankings on the previous page, we see that just as Dan Marino – when using these parameters – was the GOAT 24 year old NFL quarterback, he is also the GOAT NFL quarterback through four seasons. However, this time he is at least given a bit of a run for his money by Kurt Warner, a man who had one of the strangest careers in NFL history, as he played like a quarterback god through his first four years, then won just 13 total games over the following six seasons, while getting benched four different times by three different teams [835], before having two final glory years with the Arizona Cardinals that helped cement his case to be enshrined in the Hall of Fame, which he ultimately was in 2017. [836] [837]

As for the subject of this book – Jameis Winston – he finishes ranked eleventh in the GOAT NFL quarterback through four seasons debate, with ten Hall of Fame or soon to be Hall of Fame quarterbacks ranked above him and eleven such quarterbacks ranked below him.

That is a very strong ranking for Winston, especially considering he is not only the youngest of any of the 22 quarterbacks, but was also drafted #1 overall and started his career on the worst team in the entire NFL from the year prior, as only two other quarterbacks – Peyton Manning and Troy Aikman – that ranked higher than Winston, can say the same. Every other quarterback that ranked higher than Winston was drafted into a better – sometimes a much better – situation than he was. Not bad for the most maligned young quarterback in the history of the NFL!

Conclusion

In conclusion, this book has shown that:

- Of the seven quarterbacks in the conversation for being considered the greatest NCAA QB of all-time, there is a great case for Jameis Winston to be ranked 3rd behind only Tim Tebow and the NCAA QB GOAT, Matt Leinart.

- Jameis Winston had – by far – the greatest 21 year old rookie quarterback season in NFL history.

- There is a great case to be made that Jameis Winston not only had the 6th best rookie season of any of the 21 legendary Super Bowl era quarterbacks extensively detailed in this book but one of the 10 greatest rookie quarterback seasons in NFL history, irrespective of age and even when adjusting for era.

- Jameis Winston was – by far – the most statistically accomplished 22 year old quarterback in the history of the NFL.

- There is a great case to be made that Jameis Winston had – at worst – the 8th best sophomore season of any of the 21 legendary Super Bowl era quarterbacks extensively detailed in this book, irrespective of age and even when adjusting for era.

- There is a great case to be made that Jameis Winston had – at worst – the 5th best first two seasons of any of the 21 legendary Super Bowl era quarterbacks extensively detailed in this book, irrespective of age and even when adjusting for era.

- Jameis Winston was – by far – the most statistically accomplished 23 year old quarterback in the history of the NFL.

- There is a great case to be made that Jameis Winston had – at worst – the 8th best junior season of any of the 21 legendary Super Bowl era quarterbacks extensively detailed in this book, irrespective of age and even when adjusting for era.

- There is a great case to be made that Jameis Winston had – at worst – the 5th best first three seasons of any of the 21 legendary Super Bowl era quarterbacks extensively detailed in this book, irrespective of age and even when adjusting for era.

- Jameis Winston is – at worst – the 2nd most statistically accomplished 24 year old quarterback in the history of the NFL.

- There is a great case to be made that Jameis Winston had – at worst – the 14th best senior season of any of the 21 legendary Super Bowl era quarterbacks extensively detailed in this book, irrespective of age and even when adjusting for era.

- There is a great case to be made that Jameis Winston had – at worst – the 5th best first four seasons of any of the 21 legendary Super Bowl era quarterbacks extensively detailed in this book, irrespective of age and even when adjusting for era, statistically speaking.

- There is a great case to be made that Jameis Winston ranks 4th when compared to the 21 legendary Super Bowl era quarterbacks extensively detailed in this book, on a *GOAT 24 Year Old Quarterback* list.

- There is a great case to be made that Jameis Winston ranks 11th when compared to the 21 legendary Super Bowl era quarterbacks extensively detailed in this book, on a *GOAT NFL Quarterback Through Four Seasons* list.

All of the above said, it's extremely clear that the only people on this earth that know all the above information and yet still claim that Jameis

Winston is on anything other than a Hall of Fame pace, are those individuals that are either infected with the most severe form of *Winston Derangement Syndrome* imaginable, or are simply obeying orders from higher-ups to slander Winston. There simply is no other logical or rational reason that I can think of, that anyone could know all of the above information and still claim Winston isn't on a Hall of Fame pace.

Of course, there will almost certainly always be Jameis-haters, as like Warren Sapp, Randy Moss, Ray Lewis and others, while Winston is obviously a Hall of Fame talent he also may always be an extremely polarizing figure. In fact, consider what both Otis Leverette and Jon Gruden said about both Winston's talent as well as his polarizing nature:

I see Jameis as being that ... polarizing figure. I think he's that rare guy who only comes along every so often.

– Otis Leverette [13]

He's polarizing for some people, but he's a rare talent.

– Jon Gruden [149]

However, the Warren Sapp, Randy Moss and Ray Lewis haters didn't keep any of those three players from being enshrined in the Pro Football Hall of Fame, and I have a feeling the same thing will be true where Jameis Winston is concerned. One day – say around AD 2039 – look for Jameis Winston to be inducted into the Pro Football Hall of Fame whether or not rabid Jameis-haters who never watched him play one full game in his entire career take to social media to rant and rave, and biased *Winston Derangement Syndrome* infected media members write articles nationwide ridiculing his selection.

And, if his old Florida State coach Jimbo Fisher – who is not one to blow smoke just because he coached someone, which was made clear when he told teams that the quarterback Winston replaced (E.J. Manuel) wasn't worthy of being drafted before the 3rd round – knows what he's talking about, the Hall of Fame is exactly where Winston will end up when all is said and done.

> *A lot of people think it's because I've coached him. But I've been around him. I know ... He is a student of the game. His demeanor and personality is so infectious that you can't be around him and not play hard and practice hard and not want to do it. And his drive and expectations for himself. I know the physical talent, but I know the mental and physiological disposition of him. ... You don't want to jinx the guy, but I think he'll be a Hall of Fame guy, and be one of the great guys. I really do.*
>
> – Jimbo Fisher [838]

The above said, allow me to be the first person to say congratulations to Jameis Winston in advance, on being elected to the Pro Football Hall of Fame sometime around AD 2039.

However, in reality, Jameis Winston has his sights set even higher than being enshrined in Canton.

> *I want to be the greatest of all time one day.*
>
> – Jameis Winston [379]

To that, I simply say, God's will be done!

FINAL WORD

Fortunately for serious minds, a bias recognized is a bias sterilized.

– Benjamin Haydon [839]

All truth passes through three stages. First, it is ridiculed. Second, it is violently opposed. Third, it is accepted as being self-evident.

– Arthur Schopenhauer [840]

The two quotes above perfectly illustrate my goals for this book.

Firstly, I desire to see sports fans worldwide – at least those with *serious minds* who care about truth – recognize the mainstream sports media *bias* against Jameis Winston, so that the effect of such bias – *Winston Derangement Syndrome* – may be *sterilized* and one day entirely eradicated.

Secondly, I desire to see the truths as well as the overall truth presented in this book ultimately accepted by such serious minded sports fans as *self-evident*.

There is evidence that my first goal is coming to fruition, as a great many serious minded sports fans, website owners, statisticians and the like, have begun to recognize just how elite Jameis Winston is according to the advanced metrics, along with just how well he stacks up to many of the all-time great quarterbacks in NFL history, both at his current age and through his first four seasons in the league. In order for them to recognize such facts, they had to already have cast aside the media's erroneous narratives regarding Winston and done their own research, so even if they may not publicly admit that they know there is a main stream media bias against Winston, their actions reveal they know such to be true.

In fact, two well known statisticians offered me wonderful words of support while I was writing this book, and know that this book deserves to be read by anyone interested in the truth regarding Jameis Winston. However, neither wanted to be publicly linked to this book in any way, as they also know just how polarizing Winston is and that *Winston Derangement Syndrome* is real, and they'd rather not be bombarded with messages from Jameis-haters and social justice warriors, attacking them for merely promoting a book due to it containing truthful statistics and exposing false narratives. That said, there is obviously still work to be done before the majority of the news surrounding Jameis Winston is accurate news, rather than mere negative *spin*.

As far as my second goal of having the truths as well as the overall truth presented in this book ultimately accepted by serious minded sports fans as *self-evident*, I can at least say that the first two of the three stages Schopenhauer described have certainly already passed.

When I first started posting on various sports sites, writing for two Tampa Bay Buccaneer-centric media organizations, and tweeting the various 100 percent accurate Jameis Winston statistics I was known for, I was heavily derided by football fans and even Tampa Bay Buccaneers fans who had been infected with *Winston Derangement Syndrome*. Such individuals knew full well that I was conveying truth, but simply didn't like the truth I was conveying and therefore ridiculed it.

Likewise, it didn't take long before the truthful statistics and logical statements I was conveying became popular amongst many Buccaneer fans; however when that happened, it also didn't take long before said truthful statistics and logical statements were fiercely opposed by various members of the main stream media. As I previously mentioned in the *Personal Note from the Author* chapter of this book, various main stream sports media members, a former CEO of an NFL team, and even one Hollywood actor have personally insulted, cursed, muted, blocked and even threatened and attempted to dox me, simply for tweeting 100 percent accurate statistics that refute the false narratives surrounding Jameis Winston, and using logical, rational and common sense arguments to refute the seemingly all-pervasive *Winston Derangement Syndrome* that infects said individuals.

Therefore as I see it, Schopenhauer's first two stages have already come to pass, and there is even evidence the third and final stage may come to pass once this book hits the marketplace.

Regardless, Jameis Winston isn't about to just rest on his laurels and the salary and endorsements he's earned to date. He remains about his Father's business, even if the media and general public like to pretend only those with an absolutely angelic reputation – as if anyone on earth had such a thing – can possibly be doing God's work.

However, as former Buccaneers coach and legendary Hall of Famer Tony Dungy stated:

> *The Lord doesn't always take you in a straight line. He tests you sometimes.* [841]

And:

> *Sometimes I think God wants there to be a circus so we can show there's another way to respond.* [841]

The simple – yet generally ridiculed by modern mankind – truth is that Jameis Winston is exactly the type of person God has often used throughout history to do His work and fulfill His will.

Consider the following passage of Scripture:

Where is the wise? where is the scribe? where is the disputer of this world? hath not God made foolish the wisdom of this world? For after that in the wisdom of God the world by wisdom knew not God, it pleased God by the foolishness of preaching to save them that believe. For the Jews require a sign, and the Greeks seek after wisdom: But we preach Christ crucified, unto the Jews a stumblingblock, and unto the Greeks foolishness; But unto them which are called, both Jews and Greeks, Christ the power of God, and the wisdom of God. Because the foolishness of God is wiser than men; and the weakness of God is stronger than men. For ye see your calling, brethren, how that not many wise men after the flesh, not many mighty, not many noble, are called: But God hath chosen the foolish things of the world to confound the wise; and God hath chosen the weak things of the world to confound the things which are mighty; And base things of the world, and things which are despised, hath God chosen, yea, and things which are not, to bring to nought things that are: That no flesh should glory in his presence.

– 1 Corinthians 1: 20-29

In fact, while Winston is literally *despised* by much of the media and may often be ridiculed by the media and the masses alike as *foolish*, *base* and *ignoble*, he actually has a sterling reputation compared to many of the men and women God has used to do His work throughout history.

The Biblical Joseph was convicted and imprisoned for rape before saving his family as well as all of Egypt through his foresight and wisdom.

The Israelite King David was a literal adulterer and murderer, yet is now remembered more for his repentance, for being called a man after God's own heart, and even for being perhaps the greatest Israelite King of all time.

The apostle Paul was also a murderer – at least according to Jesus Christ's New Covenant standard – yet he was the man God chose to write much of the New Testament.

It's also certainly not only in the Bible where one can find the lives of literal sinners who became actual saints.

The Orthodox Christian Church (before 1054 AD there was just one universal Orthodox Cristian Church, unlike the literally thousands of denominations and off-shoots we have today due mostly to the Bishop of Rome splitting from the Orthodox Church first, and Martin Luther splitting from the Bishop of Rome second) uses a massive seven volume Synaxarion containing nearly 4,000 pages of text detailing the lives of thousands of sinners turned saints, in their public worship. The complete seven volume series can be purchased from *Alexander Press* and is a series I would personally heartily recommend.

In fact, I would venture to guess that every single person reading this book – whether religious or entirely irreligious – likely personally knows multiple individuals who used to live wicked lives, that after merely giving up alcohol or drugs – let alone actually repenting of their sins and dedicating their life to Jesus Christ as Jameis Winston has done – turned into upstanding men and women. Therefore, for anyone to pretend that Jameis Winston is somehow incapable of becoming an inspiration, good role model, and even a literal hero to many, is preposterous and actual proof positive that such an individual has been infected with *Winston Derangement Syndrome*.

Simply put, the main stream sports media seems to have decided that Jameis Winston's role in their sports coverage is to play the villain. Reporting on his charitable foundation, community involvement and the like isn't conducive to maintaining, let alone further developing, his villain character.

For much of the media, Jameis Winston isn't the revered *Black Mamba* Kobe Bryant but the young Colorado Kobe Bryant. He isn't the young

Pirate Barry Bonds but the swollen-headed Giant Barry Bonds. He isn't the Buffalo Bill O.J. Simpson but the Ford Bronco O.J. Simpson. It isn't right, it isn't ethical, it isn't fair, but it is what it is and it's not likely to change until sports fans recognize the media bias against Winston, refuse to become infected with *Winston Derangement Syndrome* and start trusting the irrefutable stats, advanced metrics and even their own eyes, rather than simply believing what they're told by a biased media. Aside from that happening, the only way the media may start reporting accurately on Jameis Winston is if Winston wins an MVP trophy, or Super Bowl trophy, or climbs up the all-time passing yardage or touchdown ranks, etc., and the media simply can't sell him as a villain anymore.

Regardless, as I stated above, despite the media's incessant attacks and false narratives following him like a plague, Jameis Winston remains about his father's business, as he stated shortly after his fourth season ended:

> *I'm a man of God, you know, and to chase Him every single day, I have to do my, my work, my Christ work, and live a great life.* [68]

And, as Hall of Fame coach Tony Dungy stated:

> *The best leaders are following Christ. That's the best leader you can follow.* [841]

The above said, after Winston and his fiancé Breion Allen were both baptized during a Christian retreat hosted by Pro Athletes Outreach [679], Winston started his non-profit *Dream Forever Foundation* on October 24, 2017. At the launch party Winston told the audience:

> *I don't want to sit back and watch other people give back and try their best to help others without helping. ... I wanted to know how I could use my passion for learning and transfer it to learning opportunities for kids. ... We want to help kids have the decision to explore their greatest dreams, to achieve whatever they want to achieve.* [842]

According to the official website for the foundation, it states:

> *The purpose of his* [Winston's] *foundation is to have a positive impact on the lives of financially disadvantaged children by providing encouragement, opportunities, and resources which enable the discovery, development, and eventually the achievement of their dreams.* [843]

One of the main ways the foundation serves children is through creating state-of-the-art technology centers called *Dream Rooms* in financially disadvantaged Title 1 schools. Such Dream Rooms include 3D printers, robotics and more, and the first one was unveiled at Alexander Elementary School. [844]

Winston also organized what's called the *Famous Jameis Jamboree* where each December he hosts 20 children selected by the Boys & Girls Clubs of Tampa Bay – Nuccio Center, and spends the day taking them to Busch Gardens, the zoo, etc., while also giving them Christmas presents. [844]

Likewise Winston, along with former Buccaneer teammate Gerald McCoy and WWE wrestler Titus O'Neil, teamed up to arrange a free screening of the film *Black Panther* for nearly 2,000 local children. Winston and O'Neil also teamed up to spend the day personally seeing the film with 130 children, each of whom had to submit an essay to Winston on which African-American leaders inspired them the most. [845]

The above is just a brief overview of Winston's charitable efforts and the time and energy he enjoys expending on his off days to serve his community. He's also hosted many *An Evening with Jameis Winston* events to raise awareness as well as funds for the foundation, taken children from disadvantaged schools on educational trips and shopping sprees and the like. [846] [847]

When interviewed about what he personally communicates to the children, Winston stated:

I have a little sit-down with them and talk about the influence God has had on my life and how important their faith is ... The second message being school, so education and continuing to learn and grow mentally. The third thing is to dream forever. [847]

Winston also hosts various free youth football camps and even started the *Dream Forever Exposure Camp*, which is a free football camp for top high school recruits which is streamed live to college coaches across the country, and which also features seminars focused on NCAA rules and regulations, social justice, character building and the like. [847]

Furthermore, even before Jameis Winston started his foundation, he was seeking for ways to be a blessing to others. For example, for the past four straight years Winston has covered the cost for 75 Special Olympic athletes (300 in total) to attend his *Dream Forever Foundational Football Camp*. When interviewed about such, Winston stated:

I just wanted to take that extra step to invite them every year to this camp and just to show the kids, we're all on the same page ... That's what my foundation is all about -- evening the playing grounds for everybody to be successful and everybody to learn how to dream, and instilling in every one of these kids that they can do whatever they want to, whatever they put their mind to, they really can dream forever. [848]

The manager of Unified Champion Schools with Special Olympics Florida – Herley Pellew – also was quoted as saying:

Having someone like Jameis who treats them like everyone else -- it shows them that not only do their families and the Special Olympics organization care about them, someone of Jameis' caliber cares about them as well. That sends a tremendous message to our group. Everyone wants to be included, everyone wants to be part of everything, so if someone like Jameis can speak up on their behalf, it's tremendous to their confidence overall. ... Jameis is just such a tremendous ambassador for the organization overall. He is always very lively with our group of kids and very welcoming to them. [848]

As any parent knows, when you have a child that loves you, looks up to you, and receives inspiration from you, it really doesn't matter whether some co-worker or even friend or extended family member dislikes you or even slanders you, as they can't steal your joy as you're already blessed. In the same way, the biased media and *Winston Derangement Syndrome* infected individuals – most of whom will never impact their community anywhere near as much as Jameis Winston impacts his – can pretend Winston is a villain all they want and can slander him until the day he dies; such actions won't change who he is and won't keep him from being about his Father's business.

Conclusion

The great philosopher Confucius stated long ago:

The object of the superior man is truth. [601]

Likewise, the great African-American abolitionist and women's rights activist Sojourner Truth stated:

I feel safe in the midst of my enemies, for the truth is all powerful and will prevail. [849]

While I do not claim to be superior to anyone on earth, I certainly do consider myself a seeker of truth, be it religious, historical, or even mere sports-centric statistical truth. Likewise, the goal of this book was to combat the false narratives surrounding Jameis Winston with truth, powerful truth that will indeed prevail!

However, I will say that while this book is filled with a myriad of statistical truths as well as an overall message of truth, let us not forget that the ultimate truth isn't a mere factoid or even an ideology, but a Creator and Savior named Jesus Christ of Nazareth.

And, what better way to end a book written by a Biblical Christian theologian about an athlete who has bowed the knee to Christ and is not ashamed of the Gospel, than to allow that athlete to speak for himself, and to then close with a quote from his Savior and mine?

The above said, below are the words of Jameis Winston, which he spoke while being interviewed by *Sports Spectrum* podcast host and author of the book *Live to Forgive*, Jason Romano:

> *I knew that, that I was saved by Jesus Christ and I knew who my Lord and Savior was. ... I was a born again Christian in November of 2014. ... I got baptized when I was young, when I was like eight, nine years old and then my first year in the NFL, that next year, I got baptized with my now fiancé in Colorado. So, I've been through ups and downs, but one thing about me is I always knew that my identity wasn't in football, that it wasn't in baseball, I knew that my identity always has been in Christ. And, just my upbringing has always led me to have a tremendous faith that God was going to see me through, and that He would not put too much, give me too much that I couldn't bear.*
>
> *So, I've always had that solid foundation of whose child I really was, no matter who my parents were and no matter who my father was, I knew who was my Savior and I knew who I was in His kingdom. So, that always just instilled in me a great confidence.*
>
> *But actually, actually living by the word instead of you know, knowing the word, of knowing of the word, has really been a great change in not only the way that I live but really the way that I carry myself.*
>
> *Just growing up, you know, I always was a guy that wanted to be liked, that wanted to be like everyone else, not really*

understanding that the platform that I had was different than others, not really understanding that, you know, God expects more from His leaders than he does of people that are not really committed to Him.

I recently got engaged, had my first son, and it kind of overshadows, once I had my son, it kind of gave me a new perspective on life because his birth really overshadowed all the good and the bad, no matter about the accomplishments I had in college, the accomplishments that I had in high school, or you know, the adversity that I faced in college, or the adversity that I faced in high school. His birth really just showed me a glimpse of what it really meant for God to love us. You know, because, He knows that we will never live up to what, to His satisfaction. But He loves us no matter what, He is forgiving of us; His grace is so sufficient. ...

Your source has to be in God and not yourself or not in any other human being; God has to be your ultimate source. ...

God is teaching me to really just take small increments towards Him every single day. You know, one thing about Jesus, He's always walking towards us because He wants to guide us. But all we have to do is, we have to be willing to be vulnerable and take steps towards Him.

So, when I talk about leading my family, when I talk about my fiancé and my son, me taking small steps towards Christ has allowed me to be free from, you know, having to support my friends through their initiatives, be from, you know, having to respond to family members calling me asking me for money. You know, because that's not, I'm not their source. I'm the head of my home and I have to get my daily bread by chasing Christ, and as long as I'm chasing Christ every single step of the day, then I'm leading my family towards Christ. And, if I can lead my family towards Christ then I'm doing something that is right, I'm doing what His great commission is, I'm going and creating more disciples of Him.

And, I know my son is eight months now but just him seeing me pray with his mom ... and he's seeing me pray over him at night ... he's witnessing this. It's just really got me in a good place man, so, that's what God's just teaching me, just take small steps towards Him and rely on Him.

– Jameis Winston [850]

I am the way, the truth, and the life: no man cometh unto the Father, but by me.

– Jesus Christ, from John 14:6

POSTFACE

Publishing a book is a very different thing than writing one.

−Tara Westover [851]

When I finished writing this book I was elated. Then again, I'm a writer at heart. I am not however an editor, formatter, publicist and the like, nor do I particularly enjoy functioning in any of those roles. Regardless, when I finished the fun work of writing this book, I jumped into the hard work of getting it ready for publication, knowing I had no time to spare as this book needed to be published before the start of the 2019 season.

I tracked down *Team Winston* – a common moniker used for Jameis Winston's inner circle – and was pleased to hear they had been following me via social media and the like for a long time. And, after being vetted by Winston's trainer and mentor – Otis Leverette – I was able to receive a wonderful foreword for this book from him.

I also was able to contact and receive a great many marvelous blurbs from various media members, authors, former players as well as Buccaneer and Jameis Winston fans alike, each one of whom I am very appreciative of.

In short, everything about this project has been extremely fulfilling on every level. I'm thankful that I felt the *call* to write it, thrilled that I was able to meet so many amazing individuals while working on it, and blessed that God allowed me to finish it and get it into your hands!

While I'm not sure I will ever write another book on Jameis Winston – at least, not until he enters the Hall of Fame in AD 2039 or so – it wouldn't surprise me to see many books written about him in the future, as he truly is one of the most polarizing players to ever grace an NFL field, yet also has the God-given talent, as well as the drive and determination, to end up as one of the greatest quarterbacks to ever play the game of football.

In short, Jameis Winston is the type of athlete books should be written about. However, there's one particular passage of Scripture that I read at regular intervals, as it applies to both my professional and personal life and keeps me on the straight and narrow. I will quote such below as it also seems perfectly apropos for this book.

> *And further, by these, my son, be admonished: of making many books there is no end; and much study is a weariness of the flesh. Let us hear the conclusion of the whole matter: Fear God, and keep his commandments: for this is the whole duty of man. For God shall bring every work into judgment, with every secret thing, whether it be good, or whether it be evil.*
>
> – Ecclesiastes 12: 12-14

Finally, to those who after reading this book still find themselves infected with *Winston Derangement Syndrome* and cursing Jameis Winston or even myself, I'll simply close with one final verse from God's word and let you meditate upon such:

> *Am I therefore become your enemy, because I tell you the truth?*
>
> – Galatians 4:16

NOTE TO READERS

I, Jameis1of1, want to personally thank you for reading this book and to invite you to contact me via Twitter. One of the most fulfilling parts of writing a book is engaging with the readers of said book and I'd love to hear from each and every one of you at your convenience.

I'd even like to request that if you really enjoyed this book, that you promote it by recommending it on whatever social media platforms you are on, and that you rate and write a review for it on Amazon, Barnes & Noble, Apple Books, etc.

Multiple conventional publishers refused to publish this book, not because of the quality of the book – as it's obviously superbly written and meticulously researched if I do say so myself – but because of the content of the book, and more specifically, the subject of the book, namely, Jameis Winston. Therefore, I decided that in order to tell the truth, and to give you the reader the *straight dope* as they say, I needed to retain full creative control of the content and therefore needed to self-publish.

However, self-publishing also means self-promoting, and as I am just one man, one man without a great deal of *free time* as a theologian, businessman, freelance writer, author, investor, and home-schooling father of eight, I could really use your help in promoting this book.

Jameis Winston's story deserves to be told. Football fans coast to coast require truthful narratives and accurate reporting. *Winston Derangement Syndrome* needs to be exposed and eliminated. And, because all three of those things are true, this book deserves to be read and promoted, as doing so can help change the tide of anti-Winston sentiment and replace such with actual truth. Therefore, buy as many copies as you can, give them to your local libraries, friends and co-workers.

Spread the truth!

Sincerely,

Jameis1of1

REFERENCES

[I] BrainyMedia Inc 2019. John Steinbeck quotes. Online article. Retrieved from www.brainyquote.com.

[II] BrainyMedia Inc 2019. David Lagercrantz quotes. Online article. Retrieved from www.brainyquote.com.

[III] BrainyMedia Inc 2019. Terry Tempest Williams quotes. Online article. Retrieved from www.brainyquote.com.

[IV] BrainyMedia Inc 2019. Ann Patchett quotes. Online article. Retrieved from www.brainyquote.com.

[1] BrainyMedia Inc 2019. Thomas Sowell quotes. Online article. Retrieved from www.brainyquote.com.

[2] BrainyMedia Inc 2019. Malcolm X quotes. Online article. Retrieved from www.brainyquote.com.

[3] BrainyMedia Inc 2019. George Washington quotes. Online article. Retrieved from www.brainyquote.com.

[3.1] BrainyMedia Inc 2019. William Mather Lewis quotes. Online article. Retrieved from www.brainyquote.com.

[4] BrainyMedia Inc 2019. Albert Einstein quotes. Online article. Retrieved from www.brainyquote.com.

[5] BrainyMedia Inc 2019. E.B. White quotes. Online article. Retrieved from www.brainyquote.com.

[6] BrainyMedia Inc 2019. Karl Pearson quotes. Online article. Retrieved from www.brainyquote.com.

[7] BrainyMedia Inc 2019. George Bernard Shaw quotes. Online article. Retrieved from www.brainyquote.com.

[8] BrainyMedia Inc 2019. W. Clement Stone quotes. Online article. Retrieved from www.brainyquote.com.

[9] BrainyMedia Inc 2019. Gandhi quotes. Online article. Retrieved from www.brainyquote.com.

[10] BrainyMedia Inc 2019. Miguel de Cervantes quotes. Online article. Retrieved from www.brainyquote.com.

[11] Winston J 2017. Online article. Retrieved from www.twitter.com, posted by Jameis Winston aka @Jaboowins on 2017-02-20

[12] Dictionary.com, LLC 2019. Entry for 'Phenom'. *Dictionary.com.* Online article. Retrieved from www.dictionary.com.

[13] Kirpalani S 2015. The Jameis Winston You Don't Know – According to Childhood Mentor Otis Leverette. Online article. Retrieved from www.bleacherreport.com.

[14] Wiltfong S 2011. Elite 11: Winston got in early. Online article. Retrieved from www.247sorts.com.

[15] Hale D 2013. The legend of Jameis Winston. Online article. Retrieved from www.espn.com.

[16] Anderson L 2014. Jameis Winston has 'embarrassed' Hueytown, residents say. Online article. Retrieved from www.al.com.

[17] Muldowney C 2013. Jameis Winston's Pop Warner Highlights Will Make You Drool. Online article. Retrieved from www.rantsports.com.

[18] Lombardi M 2004. Gridiron Genius: A Master Class in Winning Championships and Building Dynasties in the NFL. New York, NY, USA: Crown Archetype

[19] Somers K 2016. Buccaneers' Jameis Winston Loves Bruce Arians – and Vice Versa. Online article. Retrieved from www.azcentral.com.

[20] Beaudry P 2009. Hueytown Gophers Reloading for 2009. Online article. Retrieved from www.highschoolsports.al.com.

[21] Alabama High School Football Historical Society 2018. Hueytown Yearly Summary. Online article. Retrieved from www.ahsfhs.org.

[22] Alabama High School Football Historical Society 2018. Spanish Fort Football Team History. Online article. Retrieved from www.ahsfhs.org.

[23] Alabama High School Football Historical Society 2018. Hueytown Football Team History – Year 2011. Online article. Retrieved from www.ahsfhs.org.

[24] Alabama High School Football Historical Society 2018. Alabama High School Football Players – Jameis Winston. Online article. Retrieved from www.ahsfhs.org.

[25] CBS Interactive Inc. 2019. Player – Jameis Winston. Online article. Retrieved from www.247sports.com.

[26] Hale D 2014. Winston the same despite opinion. Online article. Retrieved from www.espn.com.

[27] Student Sports LLC 2019. Elite 11 History. Online article. Retrieved from www.elite11.com.

[28] CBS Interactive Inc. 2019. All-Time Football Players- Quarterback. Online article. Retrieved from www.247sports.com.

[29] CBS Interactive Inc. 2019. 2012 Top Football Recruits. Online article. Retrieved from www.247sports.com.

[30] Lewis CS 1954. *Mere Christianity: A Revised and Amplified Edition, with a New Introduction, of the Three Books, Broadcast Talks, Christian Behaviour, and Beyond Personality*. London, UK: The Macmillan Company

[31] Newberg J 2011. Jameis Winston picks Noles over Tide. Online article. Retrieved from www.espn.com.

[32] Axon R 2014. As incidents mount for Jameis Winston, so does concern. Online article. Retrieved from www.usatoday.com.

[33] ESPN.com news services 2013. Jameis Winston in 2 minor incidents. Online article. Retrieved from www.espn.com.

[34] Elliott B 2014. Jameis Winston, squirrel hunter: The important stuff and some Florida State laughs. Online article. Retrieved from www.tomahawknation.com.

[35] Axon R 2014. Jameis Winston stopped by police at gunpoint in 2012 incident. Online article. Retrieved from www.usatoday.com.

[36] ESPN.com news services 2013. Jameis Winston: Store employee "hooked us up" with crab legs. Online article. Retrieved from www.espn.com.

[37] Fornelli T 2014. VIDEO: Jameis Winston leaving Publix with crab legs. Online article. Retrieved from www.cbssports.com.

[38] BrainyMedia Inc 2019. Charles Spurgeon quotes. Online article. Retrieved from www.brainyquote.com.

[39] Pierre N 2014. Florida State admin has "no further comment" on Jameis Winston's full-game suspension. Online article. Retrieved from www.tallahassee.com.

[40] Tracy M 2014. Jameis Winston Suspended for First Half of Florida State-Clemson Game. Online article. Retrieved from www.nytimes.com.

[41] Van Denburg H 2010. Brett Favre 'We Want Somme Pussy' video surfaces. Online article. Retrieved from www.citypages.com.

[42] Elliott B 2012. The Jameis Winston Experience: Seminoles Sign Top Quarterback. Online article. Retrieved from www.tomahawknation.com.

[43] ESPN Enterprises, Inc. 2019. NFL – Player – Cam Newton. Online article. Retrieved from www.espn.com.

[44] ESPN Enterprises, Inc. 2019. NFL – Player – Russell Wilson. Online article. Retrieved from www.espn.com.

[45] Sports Reference, LLC. 2019. Player – Mike Evans. Online article. Retrieved from www.pro-football-reference.com.

[46] Sports Reference, LLC. 2019. Player – Brent Grimes. Online article. Retrieved from www.pro-football-reference.com.

[47] Schlabach M 2013. FSU's Jameis Winston not charged. Online article. Retrieved from www.espn.com.

[48] BrethalyzerAlcoholTester 2016. Blood Alcohol Chart For Estimation. Online article. Retrieved from www.breathalyzeralcoholtester.com.

[49] Schlabach M 2014. Winston hearing pushed to Dec. 1. Online article. Retrieved from www.espn.com.

[50] Wikimedia Foundation Inc. 2019. Major B. Harding. Online article. Retrieved from www.en.wikipedia.org.

[51] Fox Sports Interactive Media, LLC. 2019. Full copy of Jameis Winston hearing decision. Online article. Retrieved from www.foxsports.com.

[52] Axon R 2015. Judge dismisses one of Jameis Winston's counterclaims, upholds defamation claim. Online article. Retrieved from www.usatoday.com.

[53] Over The Cap 2019. Player – Jameis Winston. Online article. Retrieved from www.overthecap.com.

[54] Kinsman v. Winston, Case 6:15-cv-00696-ACC-GJK, Document 7, Filed 2015-05-15

[55] Reedy J 2016. Jameis Winston, rape accuser settle lawsuit. Online article. Retrieved from www.orlandosentinel.com.

[56] Mcelroy W 2015. Is 'the Hunting Ground' documentary or propaganda? Online article. Retrieved from www.thehill.com.

[57] Hendershott A 2017. Hollywood's dishonest campus rape panic. Online article. Retrieved from www.washingtontimes.com.

[58] Taylor Jr. S 2015. The Cinematic Railroading of Jameis Winston. Online article. Retrieved from www.nationalreview.com.

[59] Soave R 2015. How the Hunting Ground Spreads Myths About Campus Rape. Online article. Retrieved from www.reason.com.

[60] Shammas M 2015. Harvard Law Professors Defend Law Student Brandon Winston, Denouncing His Portrayal in "The Hunting Ground". Online article. Retrieved from variety.com.

[61] Variety Media, LLC 2015. Variety Critics Pick Their Least Favorite Films of 2015 – Ella Taylor. Online article. Retrieved from www.variety.com.

[62] Yoffe E 2015. The Hunting Ground: The failures of a new documentary about rape on college campuses. Online article. Retrieved from www.slate.com.

[63] Schow A 2015. 'The Hunting Ground' crew caught editing Wikipedia to make facts conform to film. Online article. Retrieved from www.washingtonexaminer.com.

[64] Taylor Jr. S 2015. A Smoking-Gun E-mail Exposes the Bias of The Hunting Ground. Online article. Retrieved from www.nationalreview.com.

[65] Schow A 2016. Ten years after Duke Lacrosse rape hoax, media has learned nothing. Online article. Retrieved from www.washingtonexaminer.com.

[66] California Innocent Project 2019. Freed Clients – Brian Banks. Online Article. Retrieved from www.californiainnocenceproject.org.

[67] BrainyMedia Inc 2019. Vladimir Lenin quotes. Online article. Retrieved from www.brainyquote.com.

[68] Jameis Winston 2019. Tiki and Tierney 2-1-19 Hour 2. Online interview. Retrieved from www.omny.fm.

[69] Jameis Winston 2017. Online article. Retrieved from www.instagram.com, posted by Jameis Winston on 2019-02-04

[70] BrainyMedia Inc 2019. Frederick Douglass quotes. Online article. Retrieved from www.brainyquote.com.

[71] Sports Reference, LLC. 2019. Florida State at Pitt Box Score, September 2, 2013. Online article. Retrieved from www.sports-reference.com.

[72] Clark C 2013. Jameis Winston dazzles as No. 12 Florida State routs Pitt. Online article. Retrieved from www.usatoday.com.

[73] Sports Reference, LLC. 2019. 2013 Florida State Seminoles Schedule and Results. Online article. Retrieved from www.sports-reference.com.

[74] Sports Reference, LLC. 2019. Nevada at Florida State Box Score, September 14, 2013. Online article. Retrieved from www.sports-reference.com.

[75] Sports Reference, LLC. 2019. Bethune-Cookman at Florida State Box Score, September 21, 2013. Online article. Retrieved from www.sports-reference.com.

[76] Sports Reference, LLC. 2019. Florida State at Boston College Box Score, September 28, 2013. Online article. Retrieved from www.sports-reference.com.

[77] Sports Reference, LLC. 2019. Maryland at Florida State Box Score, October 5, 2013. Online article. Retrieved from www.sports-reference.com.

[78] McGarry T 2013. Jameis Winston is chasing the Heisman trophy. Online article. Retrieved from www.ftw.usatoday.com.

[79] Bradley K 2013. Jameis Winston: Take notice, FSU quarterback is the real deal. Online article. Retrieved from www.sportingnews.com.

[80] Associated Press 2013. No. 3 Clemson handed worst Death Valley defeat by No. 5 Florida State, QB Winston. Online article. Retrieved from www.foxnews.com.

[81] Sports Reference, LLC. 2019. Florida State at Clemson Box Score, October 19, 2013. Online article. Retrieved from www.sports-reference.com.

[82] Rohan T 2013. Winston Solidifies Stardom by Overwhelming Clemson. Online article. Retrieved from www.nytimes.com.

[83] Sports Reference, LLC. 2019. North Carolina State at Florida State Box Score, October 26, 2013. Online article. Retrieved from www.sports-reference.com.

[84] Sports Reference, LLC. 2019. Miami (FL) at Florida State Box Score, November 2, 2013. Online article. Retrieved from www.sports-reference.com.

[85] Sports Reference, LLC. 2019. Florida State at Wake Forest Box Score, November 9, 2013. Online article. Retrieved from www.sports-reference.com.

[86] Sports Reference, LLC. 2019. Syracuse at Florida State Box Score, November 16, 2013. Online article. Retrieved from www.sports-reference.com.

[87] Sports Reference, LLC. 2019. Idaho at Florida State Box Score, November 23, 2013. Online article. Retrieved from www.sports-reference.com.

[88] Sports Reference, LLC. 2019. Florida State at Florida Box Score, November 30, 2013. Online article. Retrieved from www.sports-reference.com.

[89] Associated Press 2013. Jameis Winston (4 total TDs) helps No. 1 FSU to 2nd straight ACC Title. Online article. Retrieved from www.espn.com.

[90] Sports Reference, LLC. 2019. Duke vs Florida State Box Score, December 7, 2013. Online article. Retrieved from www.sports-reference.com.

[91] Ward R 2014. Lakers News: Kobe Bryant Reveals Origin of 'Black Mamba' Nickname. Online article. Retrieved from www.lakersnation.com.

[92] Sports Reference, LLC 2019. ACC Offensive Player of the Year Winners. Online article. Retrieved from www.sports-reference.com.

[93] Sports Reference, LLC 2019. ACC Player of the Year Winners. Online article. Retrieved from www.sports-reference.com.

[94] Sports Reference, LLC 2019. Consensus All-America Teams (2010-2018). Online article. Retrieved from www.sports-reference.com.

[95] Sports Reference, LLC 2019. AP Player of the Year Award Winners. Online article. Retrieved from www.sports-reference.com.

[96] Sports Reference, LLC 2019. Davey O'Brien Award Winners. Online article. Retrieved from www.sports-reference.com.

[97] Sports Reference, LLC 2019. Manning Award Winners. Online article. Retrieved from www.sports-reference.com.

[98] Sports Reference, LLC 2019. Walter Camp Player of the Year Award Winners. Online article. Retrieved from www.sports-reference.com.

[99] Sports Reference, LLC 2019. 2013 Heisman Trophy Voting. Online article. Retrieved from www.sports-reference.com.

[100] ESPN.com news services 2013. Jameis Winston wins Heisman. Online article. Retrieved from www.espn.com.

[101] Alex Friedman 2013. Jameis Winston Heisman Trophy Speech. Online Video. Retrieved from www.youtube.com.

[102] Jameis Winston 2013. Jameis Winston Heisman Trophy Acceptance Address. Online Audio with Transcript. Retrieved from www.americanrhetoric.com.

[103] ESPN Enterprises, Inc. 2019. VIZIO BCS NATIONAL CHAMPIONSHIP - Gamecast. Online article. Retrieved from www.espn.com.

[104] ESPN Enterprises, Inc. 2019. VIZIO BCS NATIONAL CHAMPIONSHIP – Play-by-Play. Online article. Retrieved from www.espn.com.

[105] All State Sugar Bowl 2019. 66th Annual Sugar Bowl Classic – January 4, 2000. Online article. Retrieved from www.allstatesugarbowl.org.

[106] Skybox 360 Media, LLC. 2019. Montana drives 49ers past Bengals in Super Bowl XXIII. Online article. Retrieved from www.49erswebzone.com.

[107] Sports Reference, LLC 2019. Passing Efficiency Rating Single Season Leaders and Records. Online article. Retrieved from www.sports-reference.com.

[108] Wkipedia 2019. List of NCAA major college football yearly passing leaders. Online article. Retrieved from www.en.wikipedia.org.

[109] USA Today Sports Digital Properties 2019. Aaron Rodgers' 2011 season ranked among best ever from NFL QB. Online article. Retrieved from www.packerswire.usatoday.com.

[110] Brooke T 2014. Jameis Winston Named MVP of 2014 BCS National Championship Game. Online article. Retrieved from www.bleacherreport.com.

[111] Associated Press 2014. Florida State wins national title with touchdown in final seconds. Online article. Retrieved from www.foxnews.com.

[112] Dufresne C 2014. A Seminole moment: Florida State wins thrilling BCS finale, 34-31. Online article. Retrieved from www.articles.latimes.com.

[113] Todd's TV 2014. Jameis Winston Post-Game Interview BCS Championship Game. Online Video. Retrieved from www.youtube.com.

[114] BrainyMedia Inc 2019. William Shakespeare quotes. Online article. Retrieved from www.brainyquote.com.

[115] Abdul-Jabbar K 2019. Kareem Abdul-Jabbar: LeBron James Is Bigger Than the 'GOAT' Debate, He's a Hero for Our Time. Online article. Retrieved from www.newsweek.com.

[116] Wikimedia Foundation Inc. 2019. Tommie Frazier. Online article. Retrieved from www.en.wikipedia.org.

[117] Sports Reference, LLC 2019. 1995 Heisman Trophy Voting. Online article. Retrieved from www.sports-reference.com.

[118] Wikimedia Foundation Inc. 2019. A.J. McCarron. Online article. Retrieved from www.en.wikipedia.org.

[119] Miller D n.d. Report: Newton Faced Possible Expulsion Upon Leaving Florida. Online article. Retrieved from www.nationalfootballpost.com.

[120] Sports Reference, LLC 2019. 2003 Heisman Trophy Voting. Online article. Retrieved from www.sports-reference.com.

[121] Sports Reference, LLC 2019. 2004 Heisman Trophy Voting. Online article. Retrieved from www.sports-reference.com.

[122] Sports Reference, LLC 2019. 2005 Heisman Trophy Voting. Online article. Retrieved from www.sports-reference.com.

[123] Sports Reference, LLC 2019. 2007 Heisman Trophy Voting. Online article. Retrieved from www.sports-reference.com.

[124] Sports Reference, LLC 2019. 2008 Heisman Trophy Voting. Online article. Retrieved from www.sports-reference.com.

[125] Sports Reference, LLC 2019. 2009 Heisman Trophy Voting. Online article. Retrieved from www.sports-reference.com.

[126] Wikimedia Foundation Inc. 2019. Matt Leinart. Online article. Retrieved from www.en.wikipedia.org.

[127] Wikimedia Foundation Inc. 2019. Tim Tebow. Online article. Retrieved from www.en.wikipedia.org.

[128] Sports Reference, LLC 2019. 2006 Florida Gators Stats. Online article. Retrieved from www.sports-reference.com.

[129] Sports Reference, LLC 2019. 2005 USC Trojans Stats. Online article. Retrieved from www.sports-reference.com.

[130] Sports Reference, LLC 2019. 2007 Florida Gators Stats. Online article. Retrieved from www.sports-reference.com.

[131] Wikimedia Foundation Inc. 2019. 1994 Orange Bowl. Online article. Retrieved from www.en.wikipedia.org.

[132] Wikimedia Foundation Inc. 2019. 1997 Sugar Bowl. Online article. Retrieved from www.en.wikipedia.org.

[133] Wikimedia Foundation Inc. 2019. 2014 BCA National Championship Game. Online article. Retrieved from www.en.wikipedia.org.

[134] Sports Reference, LLC 2019. 1992 Heisman Trophy Voting. Online article. Retrieved from www.sports-reference.com.

[135] Sports Reference, LLC 2019. 1993 Heisman Trophy Voting. Online article. Retrieved from www.sports-reference.com.

[136] Sports Reference, LLC 2019. 1996 Heisman Trophy Voting. Online article. Retrieved from www.sports-reference.com.

[137] Sports Reference, LLC 2019. 2014 Heisman Trophy Voting. Online article. Retrieved from www.sports-reference.com.

[138] SI Wire 2015. Florida State quarterback Jameis Winston to enter NFL draft. Online article. Retrieved from www.si.com.

[139] Sports Reference, LLC 2019. Player – Charlie Ward. Online article. Retrieved from www.sports-reference.com.

[140] Sports Reference, LLC 2019. Player – Danny Wuerffel. Online article. Retrieved from www.sports-reference.com.

[141] Sports Reference, LLC 2019. Player – Jameis Winston. Online article. Retrieved from www.sports-reference.com.

[142] Graham T 2011. Tom Brady first unanimous MVP. Online article. Retrieved from www.espn.com.

[143] Barnwell B 2015. The Year the NFL Went Insane and Gave a Kicker the MVP Award. Online article. Retrieved from www.grantland.com.

[144] Sports Reference, LLC. 2019. Super Bowl XL - Seattle Seahawks vs. Pittsburgh Steelers - February 5th, 2006. Online article. Retrieved from www.pro-football-reference.com.

[145] King P 2015. The Bucs Start Here. Online article. Retrieved from www.si.com.

[146] Sports Talk Florida 2015. Tampa Bay Buccaneers 2015 NFL Draft: GM Jason Licht Press Conference. Online Video. Retrieved from www.youtube.com.

[147] Gaines C 2015. NFL Draft expert says Jameis Winston is the 2nd-best quarterback prospect of the past 10 years. Online article. Retrieved from www.businessinsider.com.

[148] Huguenin M 2015. Mayock on Florida State's Jameis Winston: 'He scares me'. Online article. Retrieved from www.nfl.com.

[149] BrainyMedia Inc 2019. Jon Gruden quotes. Online article. Retrieved from www.brainyquote.com.

[150] Philipse S 2015. Mel Kiper, Todd McShay call Jameis Winston best on-field prospect. Online article. Retrieved from www.bucsnation.com.

[151] Schrager P 2015. Online article. Retrieved from www.twitter.com, posted by Peter Schrager aka @PSchrags on 2015-04-22

[152] Klemko R 2015. T-Minus 7 Days: The Draft's QB's, Now and Then. Online article. Retrieved from www.si.com.

[153] Miller M 2015. NFL Draft Big Boards 2015: Matt Miller's Final Rankings. Online article. Retrieved from www.bleacherreport.com.

[154] Cherepinsky W 2019. 2015 NFL Draft Scouting Report: Jameis Winston. Online article. Retrieved from www.walterfootball.com.

[155] Schofield M 2015. Getting To Know Jameis Winston. Online article. Retrieved from www.insidethepylon.com.

[156] Zierlein L 2015. Prospects – Jameis Winston. Online article. Retrieved from www.nfl.com.

[157] Huguenin M 2015. Steve Mariucci: Jameis Winston 'most astute X's and O's guy'. Online article. Retrieved from www.nfl.com.

[158] Pelissero T, Axon R and Corbett J 2015. Jameis Winston: The personal insiders' view of his past, present, future. Online article. Retrieved from www.usatoday.com.

[159] Streeter K 2015. JAMEIS WINSTON IS ON THE CLOCK. Online article. Retrieved from www.espn.com.

[160] O'Connor I 2015. Why No.1 pick Jameis Winston is monumental risk for Buccaneers. Online article. Retrieved from www.espn.com.

[161] Sports 1 Marketing, n.d. Top NFL Sports Agents Create a Legacy. Online article. Retrieved from www.sports1marketing.com.

[162] Travis C 2018. *Republicans Buy Sneakers Too: How the Left Is Ruining Sports with Politics.* New York, NY, USA: Broadside Books

[163] Smith M D 2015. Jimbo doesn't understand why there is a question about Jameis. Online article. Retrieved from www.profootballtalk.nbcsports.com.

[164] Wilson R 2015. Jimbo Fisher: Jameis Winston 'is as smart as anybody I've been around'. Online article. Retrieved from www.cbssports.com.

[165] Wilson R 2015. Report: Jimbo Fisher said EJ Manuel didn't have tools to be NFL starter. Online article. Retrieved from www.cbssports.com.

[166] King P 2015. How Winston Became the Buccaneers' No. 1 Hope. Online article. Retrieved from www.si.com.

[167] Fischer B 2015. Bucs GM: We spoke with over 75 people vetting Jameis Winston. Online article. Retrieved from www.nfl.com.

[168] Nohe P 2015. NFL Combine Review: QB Jameis Wiinston. Online article. Retrieved from www.chopchat.com.

[169] Sports Reference, LLC 2019. Player – Marcus Mariota. Online article. Retrieved from www.sports-reference.com.

[170] Goodbread C 2015. Ex-GM blasts Jameis Winston –JaMarcus Russell comparison. Online article. Retrieved from www.nfl.com.

[171] Farrar D 2019. The biggest draft bust in the history of every NFL team. Online article. Retrieved from www.touchdownwire.usatoday.com.

[172] Bleacher Report Inc. 2019. Winston Becomes First Player Since Favre to Throw Pick-6 on 1st Pass. Online article. Retrieved from www.bleacherreport.com.

[173] Reineking J 2018. Jets rookie QB Sam Darnold throws pick-six on first pass in NFL debut vs. Lions. Online article. Retrieved from www.usatoday.com.

[174] Sports Reference, LLC. 2019. Tennessee Titans at Tampa Bay Buccaneers – September 13th, 2015. Online article. Retrieved from www.pro-football-reference.com.

[175] Kalaf S 2015. Marcus Mariota Looked Fantastic. Online article. Retrieved from www.nfl.com.

[176] Sports Reference, LLC. 2019. Seattle Seahawks at New England Patriots – September 19th, 1993. Online article. Retrieved from www.pro-football-reference.com.

[177] ESPN Internet Ventures 2019. NFL History – Passing Yardage Leaders. Online article. Retrieved from www.espn.com.

[178] Sports Reference, LLC. 2019. Tampa Bay Buccaneers at New Orleans Saints – September 20th, 2015. Online article. Retrieved from www.pro-football-reference.com.

[179] Sports Reference, LLC. 2019. Tampa Bay Buccaneers at Houston Texans – September 27th, 2015. Online article. Retrieved from www.pro-football-reference.com.

[180] Sports Reference, LLC. 2019. Carolina Panthers at Tampa Bay Buccaneers – October 4th, 2015. Online article. Retrieved from www.pro-football-reference.com.

[181] Sports Reference, LLC. 2019. Jacksonville Jaguars at Tampa Bay Buccaneers – October 11th, 2015. Online article. Retrieved from www.pro-football-reference.com.

[182] Sports Reference, LLC. 2019. Tampa Bay Buccaneers at Washington Redskins – October 25th, 2015. Online article. Retrieved from www.pro-football-reference.com.

[183] Sports Reference, LLC. 2019. Tampa Bay Buccaneers at Atlanta Falcons – November 1st, 2015. Online article. Retrieved from www.pro-football-reference.com.

[184] Sports Reference, LLC. 2019. New York Giants at Tampa Bay Buccaneers – November 8th, 2015. Online article. Retrieved from www.pro-football-reference.com.

[185] Sports Reference, LLC. 2019. Dallas Cowboys at Tampa Bay Buccaneers – November 15th, 2015. Online article. Retrieved from www.pro-football-reference.com.

[186] Frank R 2015. Big Eagles fan Jameis Winston 'so excited' for trip to Linc. Online article. Retrieved from www.nbcsports.com.

[187] Sports Reference, LLC. 2019. Tampa Bay Buccaneers at Philadelphia Eagles – November 22nd, 2015. Online article. Retrieved from www.pro-football-reference.com.

[188] ESPN Enterprises, Inc. 2019. Tampa Bay Buccaneers at Philadelphia Eagles, November 22nd, 2015 – Box Score. Online article. Retrieved from www.espn.com.

[189] Jasner A 2015. Bucs QB Jameis Winston ties NFL rookie record with 5 TD passes. Online article. Retrieved from www.espn.com.

[190] NFL Enterprises LLC 2019. Jameis Winston almost comes to tears after beating Eagles. Online Video. Retrieved from www.nfl.com.

[191] Bleacher Report Inc. 2019. Deshaun Watson Becomes 4th Rookie Quarterback with 5 TD Passes in a Game. Online article. Retrieved from www.bleacherreport.com.

[192] ESPN Enterprises, Inc. 2019. Cleveland Browns at Detroit Lions, November 22nd, 2009 – Box Score. Online article. Retrieved from www.espn.com.

[193] ESPN Enterprises, Inc. 2019. Kansas City Chiefs at Houston Texans, October 8th, 2017 – Box Score. Online article. Retrieved from www.espn.com.

[194] Sports Reference, LLC. 2019. Kansas City Chiefs at Houston Texans – October 8th, 2017. Online article. Retrieved from www.pro-football-reference.com.

[195] Sports Reference, LLC. 2019. Player – Matt Hasselbeck – 2015 Game Log. Online article. Retrieved from www.pro-football-reference.com.

[196] Sports Reference, LLC. 2019. Tampa Bay Buccaneers at Indianapolis Colts – November 29th, 2015. Online article. Retrieved from www.pro-football-reference.com.

[197] Sports Reference, LLC. 2019. Atlanta Falcons at Tampa Bay Buccaneers – December 6th, 2015. Online article. Retrieved from www.pro-football-reference.com.

[198] Harrison E 2015. NFL Power Rankings, Week 14: Seahawks climb; Patriots drop. Online article. Retrieved from www.nfl.com.

[199] Reimer A 2015. Bucs rookie LB Kwon Alexander suspended 4 games for PED violation. Online article. Retrieved from www.sbnation.com.

[200] Sports Reference, LLC. 2019. New Orleans Saints at Tampa Bay Buccaneers – December 13th, 2015. Online article. Retrieved from www.pro-football-reference.com.

[201] Sports Reference, LLC. 2019. Tampa Bay Buccaneers at St. Louis Rams – December 17th, 2015. Online article. Retrieved from www.pro-football-reference.com.

[202] Sports Reference, LLC. 2019. Chicago Bears at Tampa Bay Buccaneers – December 27th, 2015. Online article. Retrieved from www.pro-football-reference.com.

[203] Sports Reference, LLC. 2019. Tampa Bay Buccaneers at Carolina Panthers – January 3rd, 2015. Online article. Retrieved from www.pro-football-reference.com.

[204] Sports Reference, LLC. 2019. Player – Jameis Winston – 2015 Game Log. Online article. Retrieved from www.pro-football-reference.com.

[205] Pro Football Writers of America 2019. Rams' Gurley PFWA Rookie/Offensive Rookie of the Year, Chiefs' Peters Defensive Rookie of the Year; 2015 All-Rookie Team named. Online article. Retrieved from www.profootballwriters.org.

[206] Nathan A 2016. NFL Rookie of the Year 2015-16: Award Winners, Voting Results, Twitter Reaction. Online article. Retrieved from www.bleacherreport.com.

[207] Philipse S 2016. Jameis Winston snubbed for Offensive Rookie of the Year. Online article. Retrieved from www.bucsnation.com.

[208] Brown R 2016. How Jameis Winston compares to QBs who have been Rookie of the Year. Online article. Retrieved from www.espn.com.

[209] Lam Q M 2016. Jameis Winston wins Pepsi Rookie of the Year award. Online article. Retrieved from www.nfl.com.

[210] Norris M 2016. Jameis Winston Replaces Tom Brady at 2016 NFL Pro Bowl. Online article. Retrieved from www.bleacherreport.com.

[211] Sports Reference, LLC. 2019. Player – Ben Roethlisberger. Online article. Retrieved from www.pro-football-reference.com.

[212] Sports Reference, LLC. 2019. 2012 NFL Passing. Online article. Retrieved from www.pro-football-reference.com.

[213] Sports Reference, LLC. 2019. 2012 NFL Rushing. Online article. Retrieved from www.pro-football-reference.com.

[214] T.I. Gotham Inc. 2019. Best Rookie Quarterback Seasons in NFL History. Online article. Retrieved from www.si.com.

[215] Sports Reference, LLC. 2019. 2015 NFL Passing. Online article. Retrieved from www.pro-football-reference.com.

[216] Sports Reference, LLC. 2019. 1961 NFL Passing. Online article. Retrieved from www.pro-football-reference.com.

[217] Sports Reference, LLC. 2019. 1968 AFL Passing. Online article. Retrieved from www.pro-football-reference.com.

[218] Sports Reference, LLC. 2019. 1993 NFL Passing. Online article. Retrieved from www.pro-football-reference.com.

[219] Sports Reference, LLC. 2019. 2005 NFL Passing. Online article. Retrieved from www.pro-football-reference.com.

[220] Sports Reference, LLC. 2019. 2009 NFL Passing. Online article. Retrieved from www.pro-football-reference.com.

[221] Sports Reference, LLC. 2019. 2018 NFL Passing. Online article. Retrieved from www.pro-football-reference.com.

[222] King P 2016. Jameis Winston: What I Learned. Online article. Retrieved from www.si.com.

[223] Hanzus D 2016. Buccaneers promote OC Dirk Koetter to head coach. Online article. Retrieved from www.nfl.com.

[224] Stroud R 2015. Bucs' Jameis Winston off the field: So far, so very good. Online article. Retrieved from www.tampabay.com.

[225] Philipse S 2015. Why no one is talking about the Buccaneers tanking for Jameis Winston. Online article. Retrieved from www.bucsnation.com.

[226] BrainyMedia Inc 2019. Peyton Manning quotes. Online article. Retrieved from www.brainyquote.com.

[227] PRO FOOTBALL HALL OF FAME 2019. Measurement Monday Class of 2019. Online article. Retrieved from www.profootballhofl.com.

[228] Barrabi T 2019. Super Bowl rings: Fun facts on cost, history and more. Online article. Retrieved from www.foxbusiness.com.

[229] Williams N 2015. 2015 NFL Draft: Jameis Winston's rots helped shape him for the storms. Online article. Retrieved from www.al.com.

[230] Sports Reference, LLC. 2019. Player – Troy Aikman. Online article. Retrieved from www.pro-football-reference.com.

[231] Sports Reference, LLC. 2019. Player – Terry Bradshaw. Online article. Retrieved from www.pro-football-reference.com.

[232] Sports Reference, LLC. 2019. Player – Tom Brady. Online article. Retrieved from www.pro-football-reference.com.

[233] Sports Reference, LLC. 2019. Player – Drew Brees. Online article. Retrieved from www.pro-football-reference.com.

[234] Sports Reference, LLC. 2019. Player – John Elway. Online article. Retrieved from www.pro-football-reference.com.

[235] Sports Reference, LLC. 2019. Player – Brett Favre. Online article. Retrieved from www.pro-football-reference.com.

[236] Sports Reference, LLC. 2019. Player – Dan Fouts. Online article. Retrieved from www.pro-football-reference.com.

[237] Sports Reference, LLC. 2019. Player – Bob Griese. Online article. Retrieved from www.pro-football-reference.com.

[238] Sports Reference, LLC. 2019. Player – Jim Kelly. Online article. Retrieved from www.pro-football-reference.com.

[239] Sports Reference, LLC. 2019. Player – Eli Manning. Online article. Retrieved from www.pro-football-reference.com.

[240] Sports Reference, LLC. 2019. Player – Peyton Manning. Online article. Retrieved from www.pro-football-reference.com.

[241] Sports Reference, LLC. 2019. Player – Dan Marino. Online article. Retrieved from www.pro-football-reference.com.

[242] Sports Reference, LLC. 2019. Player – Joe Montana. Online article. Retrieved from www.pro-football-reference.com.

[243] Sports Reference, LLC. 2019. Player – Warren Moon. Online article. Retrieved from www.pro-football-reference.com.

[244] Sports Reference, LLC. 2019. Player – Philip Rivers. Online article. Retrieved from www.pro-football-reference.com.

[245] Sports Reference, LLC. 2019. Player – Aaron Rodgers. Online article. Retrieved from www.pro-football-reference.com.

[246] Sports Reference, LLC. 2019. Player – Ken Stabler. Online article. Retrieved from www.pro-football-reference.com.

[247] Sports Reference, LLC. 2019. Player – Roger Staubach. Online article. Retrieved from www.pro-football-reference.com.

[248] Sports Reference, LLC. 2019. Player – Kurt Warner. Online article. Retrieved from www.pro-football-reference.com.

[249] Sports Reference, LLC. 2019. Player – Steve Young. Online article. Retrieved from www.pro-football-reference.com.

[250] Sports Reference, LLC. 2019. Chicago Bears at Minnesota Vikings – September 17th, 1961. Online article. Retrieved from www.pro-football-reference.com.

[251] Sports Reference, LLC. 2019. Player – Jacky Lee – 1960 Game Log. Online article. Retrieved from www.pro-football-reference.com.

[252] McIntyre J and Lisk J 2014. The List of Successful Starting NFL QBs at Age 21 is Very Short, and Johnny Manziel is 21. Online article. Retrieved from www.al.com.

[253] Patsko S 2018. How many Pro Football Hall of Famers are like Joe Thomas and never played a playoff game? Online article. Retrieved from www.cleveland.com.

[254] Sports Reference, LLC. 2019. 1973 NFL Passing. Online article. Retrieved from www.pro-football-reference.com.

[255] Sports Reference, LLC. 2019. 1985 NFL Passing. Online article. Retrieved from www.pro-football-reference.com.

[256] Sports Reference, LLC. 2019. 2004 NFL Passing. Online article. Retrieved from www.pro-football-reference.com.

[257] Sports Reference, LLC. 2019. 1989 NFL Passing. Online article. Retrieved from www.pro-football-reference.com.

[258] Sports Reference, LLC. 2019. 1970 NFL Passing. Online article. Retrieved from www.pro-football-reference.com.

[259] Sports Reference, LLC. 2019. 2000 NFL Passing. Online article. Retrieved from www.pro-football-reference.com.

[260] Sports Reference, LLC. 2019. 2001 NFL Passing. Online article. Retrieved from www.pro-football-reference.com.

[261] Sports Reference, LLC. 2019. 1983 NFL Passing. Online article. Retrieved from www.pro-football-reference.com.

[262] Sports Reference, LLC. 2019. 1991 NFL Passing. Online article. Retrieved from www.pro-football-reference.com.

[263] Sports Reference, LLC. 2019. 1967 NFL Passing. Online article. Retrieved from www.pro-football-reference.com.

[264] Sports Reference, LLC. 2019. 1986 NFL Passing. Online article. Retrieved from www.pro-football-reference.com.

[265] Sports Reference, LLC. 2019. 1998 NFL Passing. Online article. Retrieved from www.pro-football-reference.com.

[266] Sports Reference, LLC. 2019. 1979 NFL Passing. Online article. Retrieved from www.pro-football-reference.com.

[267] Sports Reference, LLC. 2019. 1984 NFL Passing. Online article. Retrieved from www.pro-football-reference.com.

[268] Sports Reference, LLC. 2019. 1969 NFL Passing. Online article. Retrieved from www.pro-football-reference.com.

[269] Sports Reference, LLC. 2019. Player – Jim Kelly – 1986 Game Log. Online article. Retrieved from www.pro-football-reference.com.

[270] Sports Reference, LLC. 2019. Player – Peyton Manning – 1998 Game Log. Online article. Retrieved from www.pro-football-reference.com.

[271] Sports Reference, LLC. 2019. Player – Dan Marino – 1983 Game Log. Online article. Retrieved from www.pro-football-reference.com.

[272] Sports Reference, LLC. 2019. Player – Warren Moon – 1984 Game Log. Online article. Retrieved from www.pro-football-reference.com.

[273] Sports Reference, LLC. 2019. Player – Ben Roethlisberger – 2004 Game Log. Online article. Retrieved from www.pro-football-reference.com.

[274] BrainyMedia Inc 2019. Warren Moon quotes. Online article. Retrieved from www.brainyquote.com.

[275] BrainyMedia Inc 2019. Joe Montana quotes. Online article. Retrieved from www.brainyquote.com.

[276] BrainyMedia Inc 2019. Brett Favre quotes. Online article. Retrieved from www.brainyquote.com.

[277] Wikimedia Foundation Inc. 2019. List of Pro Football Hall of Fame inductees. Online article. Retrieved from www.en.wikipedia.org.

[278] Sports Reference, LLC. 2019. Player – Rex Grossman. Online article. Retrieved from www.pro-football-reference.com.

[279] Sports Reference, LLC. 2019. Player – David Woodley. Online article. Retrieved from www.pro-football-reference.com.

[280] Sports Reference, LLC. 2019. Player – Stan Humphries. Online article. Retrieved from www.pro-football-reference.com.

[281] 6th Ring. NFL QB playoff records, stats. Online article. Retrieved from www.6thring.com.

[282] The Football Database, LLC. 2019. NFL Regular Season Quarterback Win/Loss Records. Online article. Retrieved from www.pro-football-reference.com.

[283] Wikimedia Foundation Inc. 2019. List of Tampa Bay Buccaneers seasons. Online article. Retrieved from www.en.wikipedia.org.

[284] Sports Reference, LLC. 2019. 2007 Green Bay Packers Statistics & Players. Online article. Retrieved from www.pro-football-reference.com.

[285] Werner B 2019. NFL Draft 2019: Kyler Murray becomes the 24th QB to be picked first in the Super Bowl era. Online article. Retrieved from www.msn.com.

[286] Wikimedia Foundation Inc. 2019. 1990 NFL Draft. Online article. Retrieved from www.en.wikipedia.org.

[287] Wikimedia Foundation Inc. 2019. 2004 NFL Draft. Online article. Retrieved from www.en.wikipedia.org.

[288] Sports Reference, LLC. 2019. 2014 Tampa Bay Buccaneers Statistics & Players. Online article. Retrieved from www.pro-football-reference.com.

[289] Sports Reference, LLC. 2019. 1969 Pittsburgh Steelers Statistics & Players. Online article. Retrieved from www.pro-football-reference.com.

[290] Sports Reference, LLC. 2019. Player – Jim Plunkett. Online article. Retrieved from www.pro-football-reference.com.

[291] Sports Reference, LLC. 2019. 1970 New England Patriots Statistics & Players. Online article. Retrieved from www.pro-football-reference.com.

[292] Sports Reference, LLC. 2019. Player – Steve Bartkowski. Online article. Retrieved from www.pro-football-reference.com.

[293] Sports Reference, LLC. 2019. 1974 Atlanta Falcons Statistics & Players. Online article. Retrieved from www.pro-football-reference.com.

[294] Sports Reference, LLC. 2019. Player – Vinny Testaverde. Online article. Retrieved from www.pro-football-reference.com.

[295] Sports Reference, LLC. 2019. 1986 Tampa Bay Buccaneers Statistics & Players. Online article. Retrieved from www.pro-football-reference.com.

[296] Sports Reference, LLC. 2019. 1988 Dallas Cowboys Statistics & Players. Online article. Retrieved from www.pro-football-reference.com.

[297] Sports Reference, LLC. 2019. Player – Drew Bledsoe. Online article. Retrieved from www.pro-football-reference.com.

[298] Sports Reference, LLC. 2019. 1992 New England Patriots Statistics & Players. Online article. Retrieved from www.pro-football-reference.com.

[299] Sports Reference, LLC. 2019. 1997 Indianapolis Colts Statistics & Players. Online article. Retrieved from www.pro-football-reference.com.

[300] Sports Reference, LLC. 2019. Player – Tim Couch. Online article. Retrieved from www.pro-football-reference.com.

[301] Sports Reference, LLC. 2019. Player – David Carr. Online article. Retrieved from www.pro-football-reference.com.

[302] Sports Reference, LLC. 2019. Player – Carson Palmer. Online article. Retrieved from www.pro-football-reference.com.

[303] Sports Reference, LLC. 2019. 2003 Cincinnati Bengals Statistics & Players. Online article. Retrieved from www.pro-football-reference.com.

[304] Sports Reference, LLC. 2019. Player – Alex Smith. Online article. Retrieved from www.pro-football-reference.com.

[305] Sports Reference, LLC. 2019. 2004 San Francisco 49ers Statistics & Players. Online article. Retrieved from www.pro-football-reference.com.

[306] Sports Reference, LLC. 2019. Player – JaMarcus Russell. Online article. Retrieved from www.pro-football-reference.com.

[307] Sports Reference, LLC. 2019. 2006 Oakland Raiders Statistics & Players. Online article. Retrieved from www.pro-football-reference.com.

[308] Sports Reference, LLC. 2019. Player – Matthew Stafford. Online article. Retrieved from www.pro-football-reference.com.

[309] Sports Reference, LLC. 2019. 2008 Detroit Lions Statistics & Players. Online article. Retrieved from www.pro-football-reference.com.

[310] Sports Reference, LLC. 2019. Player – Sam Bradford. Online article. Retrieved from www.pro-football-reference.com.

[311] Sports Reference, LLC. 2019. 2009 St. Louis Rams Statistics & Players. Online article. Retrieved from www.pro-football-reference.com.

[312] Sports Reference, LLC. 2019. Player – Cam Newton. Online article. Retrieved from www.pro-football-reference.com.

[313] Sports Reference, LLC. 2019. 2010 Carolina Panthers Statistics & Players. Online article. Retrieved from www.pro-football-reference.com.

[314] Sports Reference, LLC. 2019. Player – Andrew Luck. Online article. Retrieved from www.pro-football-reference.com.

[315] Sports Reference, LLC. 2019. 2011 Indianapolis Colts Statistics & Players. Online article. Retrieved from www.pro-football-reference.com.

[316] Sports Reference, LLC. 2019. Player – Baker Mayfield. Online article. Retrieved from www.pro-football-reference.com.

[317] Hunt K 2016. Jameis Winston Is Changing The Culture In Tampa Bay. Online article. Retrieved from www.chopchat.com.

[318] BrainyMedia Inc 2019. Edmund Hillary quotes. Online article. Retrieved from www.brainyquote.com.

[319] Reyes L 2016. In Jameis Winston, Buccaneers see limitless potential. Online article. Retrieved from www.usatoday.com.

[320] Battista J 2016. SOPHOMORE YEAR: THE PROGRESSION OF JAMEIS WINSTON. Online article. Retrieved from www.nfl.com.

[321] ESPN Enterprises, Inc. 2017. Bucs GM: Jameis Winston is 'best leader I think I've ever been around'. Online article. Retrieved from www.espn.com.

[322] Wikimedia Foundation Inc. 2019. Jason Licht. Online article. Retrieved from www.en.wikipedia.org.

[323] Sports Reference, LLC. 2019. 2010 NFL Standings & Team Stats. Online article. Retrieved from www.pro-football-reference.com.

[324] Sports Reference, LLC. 2019. 2011 New England Patriots Statistics & Players. Online article. Retrieved from www.pro-football-reference.com.

[325] Sports Reference, LLC. 2019. Tampa Bay Buccaneers at Atlanta Falcons – September 11th, 2016. Online article. Retrieved from www.pro-football-reference.com.

[326] Fox Media LLC and Fox Sports Interactive Media, LLC. 2017. Jameis Winston Named NFC Offensive Player Of The Week. Online article. Retrieved from www.foxsports.com.

[327] Sports Reference, LLC. 2019. Tampa Bay Buccaneers at Arizona Cardinals – September 18th, 2016. Online article. Retrieved from www.pro-football-reference.com.

[328] Sports Reference, LLC. 2019. NFL Passes Intercepted Single Game Leaders. Online article. Retrieved from www.pro-football-reference.com.

[329] Sports Reference, LLC. 2019. Los Angeles Rams at Tampa Bay Buccaneers – September 25th, 2016. Online article. Retrieved from www.pro-football-reference.com.

[330] Goodreads, Inc. 2019. Vince Lombardi Jr. quotes. Online article. Retrieved from www.goodreads.com.

[331] Sports Reference, LLC. 2019. Denver Broncos at Tampa Bay Buccaneers – October 2nd, 2016. Online article. Retrieved from www.pro-football-reference.com.

[332] Sports Reference, LLC. 2019. Tampa Bay Buccaneers at Carolina Panthers – October 10th, 2016. Online article. Retrieved from www.pro-football-reference.com.

[333] Sports Reference, LLC. 2019. Tampa Bay Buccaneers at San Francisco 49ers – October 23rd, 2016. Online article. Retrieved from www.pro-football-reference.com.

[334] Sports Reference, LLC. 2019. Oakland Raiders at Tampa Bay Buccaneers – October 30th, 2016. Online article. Retrieved from www.pro-football-reference.com.

[335] Sports Reference, LLC. 2019. Atlanta Falcons at Tampa Bay Buccaneers – November 3rd, 2016. Online article. Retrieved from www.pro-football-reference.com.

[336] Sports Reference, LLC. 2019. Chicago Bears at Tampa Bay Buccaneers – November 13th, 2016. Online article. Retrieved from www.pro-football-reference.com.

[337] raidergirlsdotcom 2011. Amazing Bo Jackson Recmo Bowl Run – 1 quarter long! Online Video. Retrieved from www.youtube.com.

[338] Roling C 2016. Jameis Winston escapes defenders, completes bomb to Mike Evans (video). Online article with video. Retrieved from www.thesportsdaily.com.

[339] Mott B 2016. Jameis Winston's inspiring letter to teammates guides Bucs to big win. Online article. Retrieved from www.bucswire.usatoday.com.

[340] Gretz B 2016. Jameis Winston plays letter-perfect game in Tampa Bay Buccaneers' win. Online article. Retrieved from www.bucswire.upi.com.

[341] Sports Reference, LLC. 2019. Tampa Bay Buccaneers at Kansas City Chiefs – November 20th, 2016. Online article. Retrieved from www.pro-football-reference.com.

[342] Sports Reference, LLC. 2019. Seattle Seahawks at Tampa Bay Buccaneers – November 27th, 2016. Online article. Retrieved from www.pro-football-reference.com.

[343] Sports Reference, LLC. 2019. 2016 Seattle Seahawks Statistics & Players. Online article. Retrieved from www.pro-football-reference.com.

[344] Sports Reference, LLC. 2019. Tampa Bay Buccaneers at San Diego Chargers – December 4th, 2016. Online article. Retrieved from www.pro-football-reference.com, 2019-02-25

[345] Sports Reference, LLC. 2019. New Orleans Saints at Tampa Bay Buccaneers – December 11th, 2016. Online article. Retrieved from www.pro-football-reference.com.

[346] DaSilva C 2016. Jameis Winston had a remarkable 55-game streak snapped Sunday. Online article. Retrieved from www.foxsports.com.

[347] Sports Reference, LLC. 2019. Player – Jameis Winston – 2016 Game Log. Online article. Retrieved from www.pro-football-reference.com.

[348] Sports Reference, LLC. 2019. Player – Troy Aikman – 1989 Game Log. Online article. Retrieved from www.pro-football-reference.com.

[348.1] Sports Reference, LLC. 2019. Player – Troy Aikman – 1990 Game Log. Online article. Retrieved from www.pro-football-reference.com.

[349] Sports Reference, LLC. 2019. Player – Terry Bradshaw – 1970 Game Log. Online article. Retrieved from www.pro-football-reference.com.

[350] Sports Reference, LLC. 2019. Player – Tom Brady – 2001 Game Log. Online article. Retrieved from www.pro-football-reference.com.

[351] Sports Reference, LLC. 2019. Player – Drew Brees – 2001 Game Log. Online article. Retrieved from www.pro-football-reference.com.

[352] Sports Reference, LLC. 2019. Player – Drew Brees – 2002 Game Log. Online article. Retrieved from www.pro-football-reference.com.

[353] Sports Reference, LLC. 2019. Player – John Elway – 1983 Game Log. Online article. Retrieved from www.pro-football-reference.com.

[354] Sports Reference, LLC. 2019. Player – Brett Favre – 1991 Game Log. Online article. Retrieved from www.pro-football-reference.com.

[355] Sports Reference, LLC. 2019. Player – Dan Fouts – 1973 Game Log. Online article. Retrieved from www.pro-football-reference.com.

[356] Sports Reference, LLC. 2019. Player – Bob Griese – 1967 Game Log. Online article. Retrieved from www.pro-football-reference.com.

[357] Sports Reference, LLC. 2019. Player – Eli Manning – 2004 Game Log. Online article. Retrieved from www.pro-football-reference.com.

[358] Sports Reference, LLC. 2019. Player – Joe Montana – 1979 Game Log. Online article. Retrieved from www.pro-football-reference.com.

[359] Sports Reference, LLC. 2019. Player – Philip Rivers – 2004 Game Log. Online article. Retrieved from www.pro-football-reference.com.

[360] Sports Reference, LLC. 2019. Player – Aaron Rodgers – 2005 Game Log. Online article. Retrieved from www.pro-football-reference.com.

[361] Sports Reference, LLC. 2019. Player – Ken Stabler– 1970 Game Log. Online article. Retrieved from www.pro-football-reference.com.

[362] Sports Reference, LLC. 2019. Player – Roger Staubach – 1969 Game Log. Online article. Retrieved from www.pro-football-reference.com.

[363] Sports Reference, LLC. 2019. Player – Kurt Warner – 1998 Game Log. Online article. Retrieved from www.pro-football-reference.com.

[364] Sports Reference, LLC. 2019. Player – Steve Young – 1985 Game Log. Online article. Retrieved from www.pro-football-reference.com.

[365] Sports Reference, LLC. 2019. Tampa Bay Buccaneers at Dallas Cowboys – December 18th, 2016. Online article. Retrieved from www.pro-football-reference.com.

[366] Sports Reference, LLC. 2019. Tampa Bay Buccaneers at New Orleans Saints – December 24th, 2016. Online article. Retrieved from www.pro-football-reference.com.

[367] Sports Reference, LLC. 2019. Carolina Panthers at Tampa Bay Buccaneers – January 1st, 2017. Online article. Retrieved from www.pro-football-reference.com.

[368] Sports Reference, LLC. 2019. 2016 Detroit Lions Statistics & Players. Online article. Retrieved from www.pro-football-reference.com.

[369] Sports Reference, LLC. 2019. 2016 Tampa Bay Buccaneers Statistics & Players. Online article. Retrieved from www.pro-football-reference.com.

[370] Sports Reference, LLC. 2019. Wild Card – Detroit Lions at Seattle Seahawks – January 7th, 2017. Online article. Retrieved from www.pro-football-reference.com.

[371] Sports Reference, LLC. 2019. 2016 NFL Standings & Team Stats – Rushing Offense. Online article. Retrieved from www.pro-football-reference.com.

[372] Philipse S 2017. Jameis Winston sets league and team records in week 17. Online article. Retrieved from www.bucsnation.com.

[373] Sports Reference, LLC. 2019. 2017 NFL Top 100. Online article. Retrieved from www.pro-football-reference.com.

[374] NFL Enterprises LLC 2019. Next Gen Stats – Passing Leaders – 2016 – Regular Season. Online article. Retrieved from www.nextgenstats.nfl.com.

[375] NFL Enterprises LLC 2019. Next Gen Stats – Glossary. Online article. Retrieved from www.nextgenstats.nfl.com.

[376] Laine J 2017. Jameis Winston 1st in NFL history with consecutive 4,000-yard passing seasons to start career. Online article. Retrieved from www.espn.com.

[377] Sports Reference, LLC. 2019. Player – Russell Wilson. Online article. Retrieved from www.pro-football-reference.com.

[378] Jameis1of1 2018. Online article. Retrieved from www.twitter.com, posted by @Jameis1of1 on 2018-8-05

[379] Hunt K 2017. Jameis Winston: 'I want to be the greatest of all time one day'. Online article. Retrieved from www.chopchat.com.

[380] Sports Reference, LLC. 2019. Player – Brett Favre – 1992 Game Log. Online article. Retrieved from www.pro-football-reference.com.

[380.1] Sports Reference, LLC. 2019. Player – Brett Favre – 1993 Game Log. Online article. Retrieved from www.pro-football-reference.com.

[381] Sports Reference, LLC. 2019. Player – Dan Marino – 1984 Game Log. Online article. Retrieved from www.pro-football-reference.com.

[381.1] Sports Reference, LLC. 2019. Player – Dan Marino – 1985 Game Log. Online article. Retrieved from www.pro-football-reference.com.

[382] Sports Reference, LLC. 2019. 2016 NFL Passing. Online article. Retrieved from www.pro-football-reference.com.

[383] Sports Reference, LLC. 2019. 1990 NFL Passing. Online article. Retrieved from www.pro-football-reference.com.

[384] Sports Reference, LLC. 2019. 1971 NFL Passing. Online article. Retrieved from www.pro-football-reference.com.

[385] Sports Reference, LLC. 2019. 2002 NFL Passing. Online article. Retrieved from www.pro-football-reference.com.

[386] Sports Reference, LLC. 2019. 1992 NFL Passing. Online article. Retrieved from www.pro-football-reference.com.

[387] Sports Reference, LLC. 2019. 1974 NFL Passing. Online article. Retrieved from www.pro-football-reference.com.

[388] Sports Reference, LLC. 2019. 1968 NFL Passing. Online article. Retrieved from www.pro-football-reference.com.

[389] Sports Reference, LLC. 2019. 1987 NFL Passing. Online article. Retrieved from www.pro-football-reference.com.

[390] Sports Reference, LLC. 2019. 1999 NFL Passing. Online article. Retrieved from www.pro-football-reference.com.

[391] Sports Reference, LLC. 2019. 1980 NFL Passing. Online article. Retrieved from www.pro-football-reference.com.

[392] Sports Reference, LLC. 2019. Player – Kurt Warner – 1999 Game Log. Online article. Retrieved from www.pro-football-reference.com.

[393] BrainyMedia Inc 2019. Marianne Williamson quotes. Online article. Retrieved from www.brainyquote.com.

[394] Orr C 2017. DeSean Jackson agrees to three-year deal with Bucs. Online article. Retrieved from www.nfl.com.

[395] The SI Staff 2017. NFL Predictions: Playoff Picks, Super Bowl LII Winner, Awards and More. Online article. Retrieved from www.si.com.

[396] Pompei D 2016. The Dream Team That Wasn't: A Cautionary Tale for Free Agency. Online article. Retrieved from www.bleacherreport.com.

[397] Wikimedia Foundation Inc. 2019. 2011 Philadelphia Eagles season. Online article. Retrieved from www.en.wikipedia.org.

[398] Boren C 2017. Jameis Winston's shoulder injury may keep him out 'an extended period,' not just a few weeks. Online article. Retrieved from www.washingtonpost.com.

[399] Sports Reference, LLC. 2019. Chicago Bears at Tampa Bay Buccaneers – September 17th, 2017. Online article. Retrieved from www.pro-football-reference.com.

[400] Sports Reference, LLC. 2019. Tampa Bay Buccaneers at Minnesota Vikings – September 24th, 2017. Online article. Retrieved from www.pro-football-reference.com.

[401] Sports Reference, LLC. 2019. New York Giants at Tampa Bay Buccaneers – October 1st, 2017. Online article. Retrieved from www.pro-football-reference.com.

[402] Sports Reference, LLC. 2019. New England Patriots at Tampa Bay Buccaneers – October 5th, 2017. Online article. Retrieved from www.pro-football-reference.com.

[403] Associated Press 2017. Brady throws for 303 yards, Patriots hold off Bucs 19-14. Online article. Retrieved from www.espn.com.

[404] Sports Reference, LLC. 2019. Tampa Bay Buccaneers at Arizona Cardinals – October 15th, 2017. Online article. Retrieved from www.pro-football-reference.com.

[405] Laine J 2017. Bucs QB Jameis Winston exits game with shoulder injury. Online article. Retrieved from www.abcnews.go.com.

[406] Silagyi K 2017. Jameis Winston is injured, but Bills know Bucs' QB presents huge challenge. Online article. Retrieved from www.billswire.usatoday.com.

[407] Kennedy W 2017. Jameis Winston injury: status uncertain for Buffalo Bills game. Online article. Retrieved from www.buffalorumblings.com.

[408] Associated Press 2017. Bucs: Injured QB Jameis Winston will start against Bills. Online article. Retrieved from www.usatoday.com.

[409] Chiari M 2017. Jameis Winston to Start vs. Bills Despite Shoulder Injury. Online article. Retrieved from www.bleacherreport.com.

[410] Sports Reference, LLC. 2019. Tampa Bay Buccaneers at Buffalo Bills – October 22nd, 2017. Online article. Retrieved from www.pro-football-reference.com.

[411] Howard Chelsea 2017. Buccaneers QB Jameis Winston re-injured shoulder in Buffalo. Online article. Retrieved from www.sportingnews.com.

[412] PROFOOTBALLDOC 2017. UPDATE: Jameis Winston showing signs of rotator cuff injury. Online article. Retrieved from www.sandiegouniontribune.com.

[413] Sports Reference, LLC. 2019. Carolina Panthers at Tampa Bay Buccaneers – October 29th, 2017. Online article. Retrieved from www.pro-football-reference.com.

[414] Sports Reference, LLC. 2019. Tampa Bay Buccaneers at New Orleans Saints – November 5th, 2017. Online article. Retrieved from www.pro-football-reference.com.

[415] Boren C 2017. UPDATE: Jameis Winston's shoulder injury may keep him out 'an extended period', not just a few weeks. Online article. Retrieved from www.washingtonpost.com.

[416] NBC Universal 2019. PROFOOTBALLTALK Bucs' Koetter has seven-week audition to save job. Online Video. Retrieved from www.nbcsports.com.

[417] Belden S 2017. Jon Gruden says he may return to coaching, and 2 teams appear to be the most likely destinations. Online article. Retrieved from www.businessinsider.com.

[418] Rauf B 2017. These Are The 6 NFL Teams That Will Fire Their Coach This Season. Online article. Retrieved from www.chatsports.com.

[419] Sports Reference, LLC. 2019. Tampa Bay Buccaneers at Green Bay Packers – December 3rd, 2017. Online article. Retrieved from www.pro-football-reference.com.

[420] Sports Reference, LLC. 2019. Detroit Lions at Tampa Bay Buccaneers – December 10th, 2017. Online article. Retrieved from www.pro-football-reference.com.

[421] Brisbee G 2015. How to throw a no-hitter and lose by 4 runs. Online article. Retrieved from www.sbnation.com.

[422] MLB Advanced Media, LP 2018. No-hit games in losing effort. Online article. Retrieved from www.mlb.mlb.com.

[423] Sports Reference, LLC. 2019. Atlanta Falcons at Tampa Bay Buccaneers – December 18th, 2017. Online article. Retrieved from www.pro-football-reference.com.

[424] NFL Enterprises LLC 2019. Jameis Winston gets philosophical in postgame press conference. Online Video. Retrieved from www.nfl.com.

[425] Stroud R 2017. Jameis Winston restores the Bucs faith, then lobbies for the return of head coach Dirk Koetter. Online article. Retrieved from www.tampabay.com.

[426] Mather V 2017. Jameis Winston Is Having a Great Season; the Bucs Are Not. Online article. Retrieved from www.nytimes.com.

[427] Renner M 2017. Bad luck is plaguing Marcus Mariota. Poor play is ruining Jameis Winston. Online article. Retrieved from www.washingtonpost.com.

[428] Ledbetter D O 2017. Is Jameis Winston the next Josh Freeman? Online article. Retrieved from www.ajc.com.

[429] Sports Reference, LLC. 2019. Player – Marcus Mariota – 2017 Game Log. Online article. Retrieved from www.pro-football-reference.com.

[430] Sports Reference, LLC. 2019. Player – Jameis Winston – 2017 Game Log. Online article. Retrieved from www.pro-football-reference.com.

[431] Sports Reference, LLC. 2019. Player – Josh Freeman – 2011 Game Log. Online article. Retrieved from www.pro-football-reference.com.

[432] Sports Reference, LLC. 2019. Tampa Bay Buccaneers at Carolina Panthers – December 24th, 2017. Online article. Retrieved from www.pro-football-reference.com.

[433] Wagner-McGough S 2017. Jameis Winston loses his mind after fumble that sealed the Buccaneers' loss. Online article. Retrieved from www.cbssports.com.

[434] Reed S 2017. Bucs QB Jameis Winston joins Dan Marino in elite company. Online article. Retrieved from www.chicagotribune.com.

[435] Bieler D 2017. Buccaneers' Jameis Winston loses his mind after losing fumble to Panthers. Online article. Retrieved from www.washingtonpost.com.

[436] Chavez C 2017. Watch: Jameis Winston Flips Out On Sideline After Panthers Comeback. Online article. Retrieved from www.si.com.

[437] Ruiz S 2017. Jameis Winston throws furious tantrum at ref after losing fumble late in loss. Online article. Retrieved from www.ftw.usatoday.com.

[438] Stites A 2017. Jameis Winston had a meltdown on the sideline after a game-clinching fumble. Online article. Retrieved from www.sbnation.com.

[439] McQuade D 2017. Jameis Winston Melts Down After Panthers Comeback. Online article. Retrieved from www.deadspin.com.

[440] Wantitall MG 2017. Jameis Winston Goes Off On Official!! Online Video. Retrieved from www.youtube.com.

[441] Denver Broncos 2016. Miller sacks Newton forcing a fumble for the second time | Plays of the Week | SuperBowl 50. Online Video. Retrieved from www.youtube.com.

[442] Sports Reference, LLC. 2019. New Orleans Saints at Tampa Bay Buccaneers – December 31st, 2017. Online article. Retrieved from www.pro-football-reference.com.

[443] Sports Reference, LLC. 2019. Player – Mike Evans – 2017 Game Log. Online article. Retrieved from www.pro-football-reference.com.

[444] Johnston J 2017. Jameis Winston guides Tampa Bay Bucs to improbable win over New Orleans Saints. Online article. Retrieved from www.upi.com.

[445] Associated Press 2017. Winston throws late TD pass, Buccaneers beat Saints 31-24. Online article. Retrieved from www.usatoday.com.

[446] NFL 2017. Jameis Winston Tosses Game-Winning TD Pass vs. New Orleans! | Can't-Miss Play | NFL Week 17. Online Video. Retrieved from www.youtube.com.

[447] JoeBucsFan.com 2018. Record-breaking Night For America. Online article. Retrieved from www.joebucsfan.com.

[448] Sports Reference, LLC. 2019. 2017 NFL Passing. Online article. Retrieved from www.pro-football-reference.com.

[449] TAMPA BAY BUCCANEERS n.d. Jameis Winston turns 24 with Records in Hand. Online article. Retrieved from www.buccaneers.com.

[450] The Football Database, LLC. 2019. 2017 NFL 300-Yard Passing Games. Online article. Retrieved from www.pro-football-reference.com.

[451] Kacsmar S 2018. 2017 Passing Plus-Minus. Online article. Retrieved from www.footballoutsiders.com.

[452] NFL Enterprises LLC 2019. Next Gen Stats – Passing Leaders – 2017 – Regular Season. Online article. Retrieved from www.nextgenstats.nfl.com.

[453] BrainyMedia Inc 2019. Tom Brady quotes. Online article. Retrieved from www.brainyquote.com.

[454] Solomon J 2013. Jameis Winston: Cocky or competitive? "He doesn't understand failure". Online article. Retrieved from www.al.com.

[455] Sports Reference, LLC. 2019. Player – Kurt Warner – 2000 Game Log. Online article. Retrieved from www.pro-football-reference.com.

[456] Sports Reference, LLC. 2019. Player – Roger Staubach – 1971 Game Log. Online article. Retrieved from www.pro-football-reference.com.

[457] Sports Reference, LLC. 2019. 1972 NFL Passing. Online article. Retrieved from www.pro-football-reference.com.

[458] Sports Reference, LLC. 2019. 2003 NFL Passing. Online article. Retrieved from www.pro-football-reference.com.

[459] Sports Reference, LLC. 2019. 1975 NFL Passing. Online article. Retrieved from www.pro-football-reference.com.

[460] Sports Reference, LLC. 2019. 1988 NFL Passing. Online article. Retrieved from www.pro-football-reference.com.

[461] Sports Reference, LLC. 2019. 2006 NFL Passing. Online article. Retrieved from www.pro-football-reference.com.

[462] Sports Reference, LLC. 2019. 1981 NFL Passing. Online article. Retrieved from www.pro-football-reference.com.

[463] Sports Reference, LLC. 2019. 2007 NFL Passing. Online article. Retrieved from www.pro-football-reference.com.

[464] BrainyMedia Inc 2019. Giordano Bruno quotes. Online article. Retrieved from www.brainyquote.com.

[465] Smartt N 2017. Sexual Harassment In The Workplace In A #MeToo World. Online article. Retrieved from www.forbes.com.

[466] Wikimedia Foundation Inc. 2019. Me Too movement. Online article. Retrieved from www.en.wikipedia.org.

[467] Wong J 2018. #MeToo movement reckons with alleged hypocrisy after Asia Argento accused of sexual abuse. Online article. Retrieved from www.cbc.ca.

[468] Flowers C M 2018. The hypocrisy of #MeToo and female solidarity. Online article. Retrieved from www.philly.com.

[469] De Leon A 2019. #MeToo Hypocrisy – Believe All Women (sometimes). Online article. Retrieved from www.thelibertarianrepublic.com.

[470] Flores L 2019. An Awkward Kiss Changed How I Saw Joe Biden. Online article. Retrieved from www.thecut.com.

[471] Ansari T 2017. The NFL Is Investigating Jameis Winston For Allegedly Groping An Uber Driver In 2016. Online article. Retrieved from www.buzzfeednews.com.

[472] Wikimedia Foundation Inc. 2019. Christie Blatchford. Online article. Retrieved from www.en.wikipedia.org.

[473] Blatchford C 2018. Christie Blatchford: For hypocritical #MeToo movement, it's one strike and you're out. Online article. Retrieved from www.nationalpost.com.

[474] McGovern T 2018. Jameis Winston Dramatically Apologizes To Uber He Allegedly Groped 2 Years Ago & Blames Alcohol. Online article. Retrieved from www.hollywoodlife.com.

[475] Teope H 2018. Jameis Winston expected to be suspended by NFL. Online article. Retrieved from www.nfl.com.

[476] Thomson Reuters 2019. Arizona Revised Statutes Title 13. Criminal Code § 13-1406. Sexual assault; classification; increased punishment. Online article. Retrieved from www.codes.findlaw.com.

[477] USA Today Sports 2017. Ronald Darby on groping accusations against Jameis Winston: 'Just not true'. Online article. Retrieved from www.usatoday.com.

[478] DiBiase L 2018. Friend of Ronald Darby gives conflicting story on Winston. Online article. Retrieved from www.lockedoneagles.com.

[479] Littal R 2018. Jameis Winston's Friend Who is in Jail For Rape Claims Jameis is Lying About 3 People Being in Uber When Jameis Allegedly Grabbed Driver's Private Area (Video). Online article. Retrieved from www.blacksportsonline.com.

[480] Burke T 2018. New Jameis Winston Details Emerge; Convicted Ex-Vanderbilt Football Rapist Says Bucs QB Was Alone With Uber Driver. Online article. Retrieved from www.deadspin.com.

[481] Lavigne P 2018. Friend says Jameis Winston was alone with Uber driver. Online article. Retrieved from www.espn.com.

[482] Rollins K 2018. Friend Says Jameis Winston Was Alone With Uber Driver on Night of Alleged Sexual Abuse. Online article. Retrieved from www.si.com.

[483] Breech J 2018. Jameis Winston suspension: Witness reportedly left out one key detail in Uber story. Online article. Retrieved from www.si.com.

[484] McKenna H 2018. Jameis Winston's Suspension Leaves Us With One Conclusion: He's a Coward. Online article. Retrieved from www.thebiglead.com.

[485] NFL Communications n.d. BUCCANEERS' JAMEIS WINSTON SUSPENDED FOR FIRST THREE REGULAR-SEASON GAMES FOR VIOLATION OF NFL PERSONAL CONDUCT POLICY. Online article. Retrieved from www.nflcommunications.com.

[486] Petchesky B 2018. Jameis Winston Suspended Three Games For Groping Uber Driver. Online article. Retrieved from www.deadspin.com.

[487] Diaz G 2018. Jameis Winston dilemma for Bucs: Cut him or hang onto damaged goods?. Online article. Retrieved from www.orlandosentinel.com.

[488] Florio M 2018. Why weren't Jameis Winston, Ronald Darby punished for not telling the truth? Online article. Retrieved from www.orlandosentinel.com.

[489] NFL.com 2015. NFL releases statement on Patriots' violations. Online article. Retrieved from www.nfl.com.

[490] Gantt D 2015. Goodell cites destroying phone in upholding Tom Brady's suspension. Online article. Retrieved from www.profootballtalk.nbcsports.com.

[491] ESPN.com news services 2016. Tom Brady has 4-game suspension upheld, not ready to accept ruling. Online article. Retrieved from www.espn.com.

[492] Hohler B 2016. Tom Brady drops appeal, accepts four-game Deflategate suspension. Online article. Retrieved from www.bostonglobe.com.

[493] Archer T 2017. Cowboys' Ezekiel Elliott suspended six games for conduct. Online article. Retrieved from www.espn.com.

[494] Hoffman B 2017. Ezekiel Elliott's 6-Game N.F.L. Suspension Reinstated by Court. Online article. Retrieved from www.nytimes.com.

[495] Archer T 2017. Cowboys RB Ezekiel Elliott suspension upheld again after court denies motion. Online article. Retrieved from www.espn.com.

[496] Knoblauch A 2017. Ezekiel Elliott withdraws appeal, will serve suspension. Online article. Retrieved from www.nfl.com.

[497] Hairopoulos K 2017. Decide for yourself: The evidence and arguments surrounding the suspension of Ezekiel Elliott. Online article. Retrieved from www.sportsday.dallasnews.com.

[498] Sessler M 2018. Buccaneers' Jameis Winston suspended three games. Online article. Retrieved from www.nfl.com.

[499] EHM Productions, Inc. 2019. JAMEIS WINSTONAPOLOGIZES FOR UBER INCIDENT ... Blames Alcohol. Online article. Retrieved from www.tmz.com.

[500] Bleacher Report, Inc. 2019. INTERNET REACTS TO JAMEIS SUSPENSION. Online article. Retrieved from www.bleacherreport.com.

[501] Rosvoglou C 2018. Jameis Winston Admits Guilt to Uber Groping Incident in New Statement. Online article. Retrieved from www.12up.com.

[502] Reed J 2018. JAMEIS WINSTON APOLOGY RINGS HOLLOW. Online article. Retrieved from www.sportsnaut.com.

[503] Armour N 2018. With Jameis Winston suspension, NFL saying deflating footballs worse than sexual assault. Online article. Retrieved from www.usatoday.com.

[504] Breech J 2018. Suspended Jameis Winston doesn't admit guilt in Uber case and here's reportedly why. Online article. Retrieved from www.cbssports.com.

[505] NFL Enterprises, LLC. 2019. PERSONAL CONDUCT POLICY League Policies for Players 2016. Online article. Retrieved from www.static.nfl.com.

[506] Williams C 2018. Uber driver sues Jameis Winston. Online article. Retrieved from www.profootballtalk.nbcsports.com.

[507] Laine J 2018. Jameis Winston, Uber driver reach settlement in 2016 groping case. Online article. Retrieved from www.espn.com.

[508] Florio M 2018. Jameis Winston settles with Uber driver. Online article. Retrieved from www.profootballtalk.nbcsports.com.

[509] JoeBucsFan.com 2018. Jameis Reaches Civil Settlement Agreement With Uber Driver. Online article. Retrieved from www.joebucsfan.com.

[510] Dubin J 2018. Buccaneers pick up Jameis Winston's $21 million fifth-year option on rookie contract. Online article. Retrieved from www.cbssports.com.

[511] Laine J 2018. Bucs pick up QB Jameis Winston's fifth-year, $20.9M option for 2019. Online article. Retrieved from www.espn.com.

[512] Jones L 2013. Broncos linebacker Von Miller arrested. Online article. Retrieved from www.usatoday.com.

[513] Klis M and Parker R 2016. Broncos LB Von Miller's legal troubles continue to mount. Online article. Retrieved from www.denverpost.com.

[514] Soignier T 2013. Eagles tackle Jason Peters arrested for drag racing, resisting by flight. Online article. Retrieved from www.usatoday.com.

[515] Associated Press 2012. Bills RB Lynch suspended three games after second run-in with law. Online article. Retrieved from www.nfl.com.

[516] USA TODAY 2019. NFL PLAYER ARRESTS. Online article. Retrieved from www.usatoday.com.

[517] Merron J n.d. Biggest sports gambling scandals. Online article. Retrieved from www.espn.com.

[518] PRO FOOTBALL HALL OF FAME 2019. Players – Paul Hornung. Online article. Retrieved from www.profootballhof.com.

[519] Al Jazeera America, LLC. 2016. The dark side: The secret world of sports doping. Online article. Retrieved from www.america.aljazeera.com.

[520] Brauneck T n.d. NFL BANNED SUBSTANCE LIST. Online article. Retrieved from www.nationalfootballpost.com.

[521] ESPN Enterprises, Inc. n.d. Manning 'disgusted' with Al Jazeera report. Online video. Retrieved from www.espn.com.

[522] Florio M 2018. Al Jazeera claims Peyton Manning's lawyer confirmed HGH use; Manning denies it. Online article. Retrieved from www.profootballtalk.nbcsports.com.

[523] Finn C 2016. NFL media looks other way on Peyton Manning, HGH. Online article. Retrieved from www.bostonglobe.com.

[524] Wilson M and Kaplan P 2017. Peyton Manning accuser Jamie Naughright appears on 'Inside Edition'. Online article. Retrieved from www.knoxnews.com.

[525] Silverman R 2016. Peyton Manning's Forgotten Sex Scandal. Online article. Retrieved from www.thedailybeast.com.

[526] King S 2016. KING: Peyton Manning's squeaky-clean image was built on lies, as detailed in explosive court documents showing ugly smear campaign against his alleged sex assault victim. Online article. Retrieved from www.nydailynews.com.

[527] Inside Edition Inc. 2019 Former Athletic Trainer Speaks Out About Alleged Sexual Assault by Peyton Manning: 'I Was Scared. I Was Intimidated'. Online article. Retrieved from www.insideedition.com.

[528] Breech J 2015. Peyton Manning tops NFL in off-field income; Eli ahead of Tom Brady. Online article. Retrieved from www.cbssports.com.

[529] Badenhausen K 2016. Peyton Manning Retires With Record $400 Million In Career Earnings. Online article. Retrieved from www.forbes.com.

[530] Heath J 2016. Peyton Manning is making just as much from endorsements as he did on the field. Online article. Retrieved from www.broncoswire.usatoday.com.

[531] Barnett Z 2018. Networks are reportedly lining up to make Peyton Manning an even richer man. Online article. Retrieved from www.footballscoop.com.

[532] EHM Productions, Inc. 2019. NFL Superstar Accused of Baby Mama Beatdown. online article. Retrieved from www.tmz.com.

[533] J C 2008. Protection order filed against Larry Fitzgerald Jr. Online article. Retrieved from www.startribune.com.

[534] Montini EJ 2014. Did media give Fitz a bye on '08 domestic disturbance? Online article. Retrieved from www.azcentral.com.

[535] Stern R 2009. Larry Fitzgerald's Alleged Domestic Abuse Buried Deep in Pages of *Arizona Republic*. Online article. Retrieved from www.phoenixnewtimes.com.

[536] Lapointe J 2009. One Step From Super Bowl, Fitzgerald Is Suddenly an Open Book. Online article. Retrieved from www.nytimes.com.

[537] National Football League 2013. Finalists named for Walter Payton NFL Man of the Year Award. Online article. Retrieved from www.nfl.com.

[538] Lease L 2017. Larry Fitzgerald co-winner of Walter Payton Man of the Year award. Online article. Retrieved from www.foxsports.com.

[539] Sports Reference, LLC. 2019. Super Bowl LII – Philadelphia Eagles vs. New England Patriots – February 4th, 2018. Online article. Retrieved from www.pro-football-reference.com.

[540] Frank M 2018. Eagles' Nigel Bradham suspended one game for personal conduct policy violation. Online article. Retrieved from www.usatoday.com.

[541] Reyes L 2016. Eagles' Nigel Bradham arrested after alleged battery of hotel worker. Online article.

[542] McManus T 2017. Eagles LB Nigel Bradham gets deferred prosecution deal. Online article. Retrieved from www.espn.com.

[543] ESPN.com news services 2018. Dante Fowler Jr. suspended 1 game for violating league's conduct policy. Online article. Retrieved from www.abcnews.go.com.

[544] Smith M D 2018. NFL shows once again that its six-game suspension policy is meaningless. Online article. Retrieved from www.profootballtalk.nbcsports.com.

[545] Modisette K 2018. Jameis Winston's suspension inconsistent with Ezekiel Elliott's ban. Online article. Retrieved from www.cowboyswire.usatoday.com.

[546] Reimer A 2018. Absurdity of Brady's Deflategate ban once again exposed by Jameis Winston's 3-game suspension for alleged sexual assault. Online article. Retrieved from www.weei.radio.com.

[547] Thornton J 2018. All of Roger Goodell's 'Transparency' Talk Doesn't Keep Him from Covering Up What Jameis Winston Did. Online article. Retrieved from www.barstoolsports.com.

[548] Mays R 2018. The Shameful Enabling of Jameis Winston. Online article. Retrieved from www.theringer.com.

[549] Steigerwald J 2018. Winston got off easy with three-game suspension. Online article. Retrieved from www.indianagazette.com.

[550] Stites A 2018. How the hell did Jameis Winston not get a 6-game suspension? Online article. Retrieved from www.sbnation.com.

[551] Mattimore R 2018. Presidential Feuds With the Media Are Nothing New. Online article. Retrieved from www.history.com.

[552] Erenow 2019. August 1955 to September 1956 *The Potsdam Papers – "Intellectual Prostitutes" – Margaret Is Married – A Trip to Europe*. Online article. Retrieved from www.erenow.net.

[553] Flood B 2018. ESPN shakes up struggling morning show 'Get Up!', reassigns Michelle Beadle. Online article. Retrieved from www.foxnews.com.

[554] Travis C 2018. ESPN Cuts Ties with Jemele Hill, Demotes Michelle Beadle. Online article. Retrieved from www.outkickthecoverage.com.

[555] Candler M 2017. ESPN PUNDIT WANTS WHITE MEN TO SHUT UP. Online article. Retrieved from www.foxnews.com.

[556] ESPN 2018. Michelle Beadle is done with Jameis Winston getting chances | Get Up! | ESPN. Online video. Retrieved from www.youtube.com.

[557] FSU Seminoles 2018. Fire or Suspend Michelle Beadle. Online article. Retrieved from www.change.org.

[558] Daulerio A J 2018. Did Michelle Beadle Tell Aaron Rodgers, "I Just Wanna Get Fucked" After The ESPYs? ESPN Wants To Know. Online article. Retrieved from www.deadspin.com.

[559] Martin C 2011. ESPN's Beadle Questioned by Bosses About Alleged Unseemly Behavior at ESPY's. Online article. Retrieved from www.adweek.com.

[560] Wikimedia Foundation Inc. 2019. Max Kellerman. Online article. Retrieved from www.en.wikipedia.org.

[561] patghnx 2014. Max and Sam - Young Man Rumble. Online video. Retrieved from www.youtube.com.

[562] ESPN 2018. Jameis Winston is a bust, Bucs should move on at QB –Max Kellerman | First Take. Online video. Retrieved from www.youtube.com.

[563] The Deadline Team 2014. ESPN Slaps Max Kellerman With Suspension After He Admits On-Air To Striking Woman. Online article. Retrieved from www.deadline.com.

[564] Wikimedia Foundation Inc. 2019. Keyshawn Johnson. Online article. Retrieved from www.en.wikipedia.org.

[565] Bender B 2018. 40 most hated NFL players of all time: loudmouths, cheaters, criminals. Online article. Retrieved from www.sportingnews.com.

[566] Braziller Z 2016. ESPN kicks Keyshawn Johnson off NFL pregame show. Online article. Retrieved from www.nypost.com.

[567] Florio M 2016. Keyshawn Johnson returns to ESPN. Online article. Retrieved from www.profootballtalk.nbcsports.com.

[568] Florio M 2018. Keyshawn Johnson says 'there's something wrong mentally' with Jameis Winston. Online article. Retrieved from www.profootballtalk.nbcsports.com.

[569] Rose B 2014. Keyshawn Johnson arrested in Calif. for domestic violence, per report. Online article. Retrieved from www.si.com.

[570] Allen B 2018. Poynter announces new senior media writer. Online article. Retrieved from www.poynter.org.

[571] Concha J 2019. Poynter pulls blacklist of 'unreliable' news websites after backlash. Online article. Retrieved from www.thehill.com.

[572] JoeBucsFan.com 2018. Barber On Tom Jones: Unfair To Jameis Winston. Online article. Retrieved from www.joebucsfan.com.

[573] Tarcho J 2017. Many Coming To Jameis Winston's Defense – Including His Mother. Online article. Retrieved from www.thepewterplank.com.

[574] Jones T 2018. Next move is simple for the Bucs: Get rid of Jameis Winston. Online article. Retrieved from www.tampabay.com.

[575] Jones T 2018. Hey, Bucs, there's no more benefit of the doubt with Jameis Winston. Online article. Retrieved from www.tampabay.com.

[576] Jones T 2018. Jameis Winston's Uber ride will never be forgotten, and shouldn't. Online article. Retrieved from www.tampabay.com.

[577] Short A 2015. 6 Famous People With Shocking Criminal Backgrounds. Online article. Retrieved from www.cracked.com.

[578] BrainyMedia Inc 2019. Vince Lombardi quotes. Online article. Retrieved from www.brainyquote.com.

[579] Laine J 2018. Bucs GM says Jameis Winston may not start Week 4 after suspension. Online article. Retrieved from www.espn.com.

[580] Ledbetter D O 2018. What Dirk Koetter had to say about the Falcons. Online article. Retrieved from www.ajc.com.

[581] Young S M 2018. Dirk Koetter announces Jameis Winston will start Buccaneers' next game. Online article. Retrieved from www.sports.yahoo.com.

[582] JoeBucsFan.com 2018. Vintage Jameis Dedication. Online article. Retrieved from www.joebucsfan.com.

[583] Garafolo M 2018. Jameis Winston organized practices with NFL vets during ban. Online article. Retrieved from www.nfl.com.

[584] Sports Reference, LLC. 2019. Tampa Bay Buccaneers at Chicago Bears – September 30th, 2018. Online article. Retrieved from www.pro-football-reference.com.

[585] Tampa Bay Buccaneers 2018. Dirk Koetter Recaps the Game Against the Bears | Bucs Press Conference. Online video. Retrieved from www.youtube.com.

[586] Sports Reference, LLC. 2019. Tampa Bay Buccaneers at Atlanta Falcons – October 14th, 2018. Online article. Retrieved from www.pro-football-reference.com.

[587] Sports Reference, LLC. 2019. 2018 Cleveland Browns Statistics & Players. Online article. Retrieved from www.pro-football-reference.com.

[588] Sports Reference, LLC. 2019. Pittsburgh Steelers at Cleveland Browns – September 9th, 2018. Online article. Retrieved from www.pro-football-reference.com.

[589] Sports Reference, LLC. 2019. Cleveland Browns at Tampa Bay Buccaneers at Atlanta Falcons – October 21st, 2018. Online article. Retrieved from www.pro-football-reference.com.

[590] ESPN Internet Ventures 2019. NFL Schedule – 2018 – Week 7. Online article. Retrieved from www.espn.com.

[591] Sports Reference, LLC. 2019. Tampa Bay Buccaneers at Cincinnati Bengals – October 28th, 2018. Online article. Retrieved from www.pro-football-reference.com.

[592] Basile N 2016. Not So Super: 15 People Who Have Defeated Superman. Online article. Retrieved from www.cbr.com.

[593] Daily T n.d. Tampa Bucs Gerald McCoy Gives Tour Of His Man Cave. Online article. Retrieved from www.995qyk.com.

[594] Hershey N 2017. This NFL Player Wants To Be Punched By A Superhero. Online article. Retrieved from www.entertainmentbuddha.com.

[595] Kostora N 2012. 10 Veteran NFL Quarterbacks Who Found Success with New Teams. Online article. Retrieved from www.bleacherreport.com.

[596] Sports Reference, LLC. 2019. Player – Norm Van Brocklin. Online article. Retrieved from www.pro-football-reference.com.

[597] Sports Reference, LLC. 2019. Player – Y.A. Tittle. Online article. Retrieved from www.pro-football-reference.com.

[598] Carter B n.d. Unitas surprised them all. Online article. Retrieved from www.espn.com.

[599] Sports Reference, LLC. 2019. Player – Fran Tarkenton. Online article. Retrieved from www.pro-football-reference.com.

[600] Wesseling C 2014. Oakland Raiders' Matt Schaub broken beyond repair? Online article. Retrieved from www.nfl.com.

[601] BrainyMedia Inc 2019. Confucius quotes. Online article. Retrieved from www.brainyquote.com.

[602] Teope H 2018. Jameis Winston: Benching is 'humbling,' minor setback. Online article. Retrieved from www.nfl.com.

[603] Radcliffe JR 2018. Remembering the strange moment the Packers traded Brett Favre, 10 years ago today. Online article. Retrieved from www.usatoday.com.

[604] Associated Press 2009. Favre released by Jets but says he has no intention of NFL return. Online article. Retrieved from www.nfl.com.

[605] Sports Reference, LLC. 2019. Tampa Bay Buccaneers at New York Giants – November 18th, 2018. Online article. Retrieved from www.pro-football-reference.com.

[606] Tampa Bay Buccaneers 2018. Jameis Winston on His Four Touchdown Drives Against Giants | Bucs vs. Giants. Online video. Retrieved from www.youtube.com.

[607] RotoWire Staff 2018. Buccaneers' Jameis Winston: Named as Week 12 starter. Online article. Retrieved from www.cbssports.com.

[608] Tampa Bay Buccaneers 2018. Dirk Koetter Recaps the Hard-Fought Game Against the Giants | Bucs vs. Giants. Online video. Retrieved from www.youtube.com.

[609] Madson K 2018. Kyle Shanahan: Jameis Winston 'can be as good as anyone in this league'. Online article. Retrieved from www.ninerswire.usatoday.com.

[610] Sports Reference, LLC. 2019. San Francisco 49ers at Tampa Bay Buccaneers – November 25th, 2018. Online article. Retrieved from www.pro-football-reference.com.

[611] ESPN Enterprises, Inc. 2019. San Francisco 49ers at Tampa Bay Buccaneers, November 25th, 2018 – Box Score. Online article. Retrieved from www.espn.com.

[612] Jameis1of1 2019. Online article. Retrieved from www.twitter.com, posted by @Jameis1of1 on 2018-11-26

[613] Tampa Bay Buccaneers 2018. Jameis Winston: 'Mike Evans Makes Everyone's Jobs Easier' | Bucs vs. 49ers. Online video. Retrieved from www.youtube.com.

[614] Sports Reference, LLC. 2019. Carolina Panthers at Tampa Bay Buccaneers – December 2nd, 2018. Online article. Retrieved from www.pro-football-reference.com.

[615] Wikia, Inc. 2019. Val-Zod (Earth 2). Online article. Retrieved from www.dc.fandom.com.

[616] Sports Reference, LLC. 2019. New Orleans Saints at Tampa Bay Buccaneers – December 9th, 2018. Online article. Retrieved from www.pro-football-reference.com.

[617] Sports Reference, LLC. 2019. Tampa Bay Buccaneers at Baltimore Ravens – December 16th, 2018. Online article. Retrieved from www.pro-football-reference.com.

[618] Sports Reference, LLC. 2019. Tampa Bay Buccaneers at Dallas Cowboys – December 23rd, 2018. Online article. Retrieved from www.pro-football-reference.com.

[619] Sports Reference, LLC. 2019. Atlanta Falcons at Tampa Bay Buccaneers – December 30th, 2018. Online article. Retrieved from www.pro-football-reference.com.

[620] Kenyon D 2019. Devin White Is Perfect LB to Take over NFL in Patrick Willis, Ray Lewis Mold. Online article. Retrieved from www.bleacherreport.com.

[621] Bratton MW 2018. Ed Orgeron compares Devin White to Ray Lewis, Patrick Willis: 'He's right in that group'. Online article. Retrieved from www.saturdaydownsouth.com.

[622] Scarfo N 2019. 2019 NFL Draft: Devin White measures up to an NFL legend. Online article. Retrieved from www.nflmocks.com.

[623] Kubena B 2019. Here's how LSU LB Devin White's speed makes him the 'freak of nature' of the NFL combine. Online article. Retrieved from www.theadvocate.com.

[624] Teope H 2018. Jameis Winston 'fighting' for Koetter's return in 2019. Online article. Retrieved from www.nfl.com.

[625] Jones K 2018. Buccaneers Fire Head Coach Dirk Koetter After 5–11 Season. Online article. Retrieved from www.si.com.

[626] Diaz G 2016. Diaz: Jameis Winston is reason Dirk Koetter is coaching Bucs. Online article. Retrieved from www.orlandosentinel.com.

[627] Fennelly M 2017. Diaz: Jameis Winston is reason Dirk Koetter is coaching Bucs. Online article. Retrieved from www.orlandosentinel.com.

[628] Sports Reference, LLC. 2019. Tampa Bay Buccaneers at Carolina Panthers – November 4th, 2018. Online article. Retrieved from www.pro-football-reference.com.

[629] Sports Reference, LLC. 2019. Washington Redskins at Tampa Bay Buccaneers – November 11th, 2018. Online article. Retrieved from www.pro-football-reference.com.

[630] TAMPA BAY BUCCANEERS 2019. Mike Evans Shares Thoughts on Bruce Arians, DeSean Jackson & Adam Humphries. Online Video. Retrieved from www.buccaneers.com.

[631] JoeBucsFan.com 2019. Jameis Winston Says He Told Himself To Disregard Coaching. Online article. Retrieved from www.joebucsfan.com.

[632] Florio M 2019. Jameis Winston suggests that he tuned out coaching last year. Online article. Retrieved from www.profootballtalk.nbcsports.com.

[633] Sports Reference, LLC. 2019. Player – Jameis Winston – 2018 Game Log. Online article. Retrieved from www.pro-football-reference.com.

[634] Winston J 2019. Online article. Retrieved from www.twitter.com, posted by Jameis Winston aka @jaboowins on 2019-02-04

[635] Stroud R 2019. As Jameis Winston turns 25, here's how he compares to other NFL quarterbacks at that age. Online article. Retrieved from www.tampabay.com.

[636] Jameis1of1 2018. Online article. Retrieved from www.twitter.com, posted by @Jameis1of1 on 2018-12-30

[637] NFL Enterprises LLC 2019. Next Gen Stats – Passing Leaders – 2018 – Regular Season. Online article. Retrieved from www.nextgenstats.nfl.com.

[638] Kinsley J 2019. Online article. Retrieved from www.twitter.com, posted by Johnny Kinsley aka @Brickwallblitz on 2019-01-31

[639] Kinsley J 2019. Online article. Retrieved from www.twitter.com, posted by Johnny Kinsley aka @Brickwallblitz on 2019-01-25

[640] NFL Matchup on ESPN 2019. Online article. Retrieved from www.twitter.com, posted by NFL Matchup on ESPN aka @NFLMatchup on 2019-01-03

[641] NFL Matchup on ESPN 2019. Online article. Retrieved from www.twitter.com, posted by NFL Matchup on ESPN aka @NFLMatchup on 2019-01-03

[642] NFL Matchup on ESPN 2019. Online article. Retrieved from www.twitter.com, posted by NFL Matchup on ESPN aka @NFLMatchup on 2019-01-03

[643] BrainyMedia Inc 2019. Kurt Warner quotes. Online article. Retrieved from www.brainyquote.com.

[644] Sports Reference, LLC. 2019. Player – Troy Aikman – 1991 Game Log. Online article. Retrieved from www.pro-football-reference.com.

[645] Sports Reference, LLC. 2019. Player – Brett Favre – 1994 Game Log. Online article. Retrieved from www.pro-football-reference.com.

[646] Sports Reference, LLC. 2019. Player – Dan Marino – 1986 Game Log. Online article. Retrieved from www.pro-football-reference.com.

[647] Sports Reference, LLC. 2019. Player – Philip Rivers – 2006 Game Log. Online article. Retrieved from www.pro-football-reference.com.

[648] Sports Reference, LLC. 2019. Player – Aaron Rodgers – 2008 Game Log. Online article. Retrieved from www.pro-football-reference.com.

[649] Sports Reference, LLC. 2019. Player – Steve Young – 1986 Game Log. Online article. Retrieved from www.pro-football-reference.com.

[650] Sports Reference, LLC. 2019. 1994 NFL Passing. Online article. Retrieved from www.pro-football-reference.com.

[651] Sports Reference, LLC. 2019. 1976 NFL Passing. Online article. Retrieved from www.pro-football-reference.com.

[652] Sports Reference, LLC. 2019. 1982 NFL Passing. Online article. Retrieved from www.pro-football-reference.com.

[653] Sports Reference, LLC. 2019. 2008 NFL Passing. Online article. Retrieved from www.pro-football-reference.com.

[654] BrainyMedia Inc 2019. Gil Courtemanche quotes. Online article. Retrieved from www.brainyquote.com.

[655] BrainyMedia Inc 2019. George Orwell online quotes. Online article. Retrieved from www.brainyquote.com.

[656] Curtis B 2017. Sportswriting Has Become a Liberal Profession — Here's How It Happened. Online article. Retrieved from www.theringer.com.

[657] Dougherty M B 2017. The arrogant thinking of liberal sports writers. Online article. Retrieved from www.theweek.com.

[658] Brady J 2016. Inside and out, ESPN dealing with changing political dynamics.Online article. Retrieved from www.espn.com.

[659] Brady J 2017. ESPN awash in rising political tide. Online article. Retrieved from www.espn.com.

[660] Duffy T 2017. Big Lead Sports Media Politics Survey: Only 4% of Media Surveyed Voted for Donald Trump. Online article. Retrieved from www.thebiglead.com.

[661] Gallup, Inc. 2019. Party Affiliation. Online article. Retrieved from www.news.gallup.com.

[662] Ballotpedia n.d. Presidential election, 2016. Online article. Retrieved from www.ballotpedia.org.

[663] Ley T 2018. John Skipper Says He Left ESPN After Someone He Bought Cocaine From Tried To Extort Him. Online article. Retrieved from www.deadspin.com.

[664] Bataglio S 2019. ESPN President Jimmy Pitaro is fighting the cord-cutting wave. Online article. Retrieved from www.latimes.com.

[665]The Shakur Estate 2017. Online article. Retrieved from www.twitter.com, posted by @2PAC on 2017-12-20

[665.1] BrainyMedia Inc 2019. Jim Morrison quotes. Online article. Retrieved from www.brainyquote.com.

[666] Brangin A 2019. Tennessee House Speaker's Top Aide Resigns After Accusations of Framing Black Activist and Sending Racist and Sexist Texts. Online article. Retrieved from www.theroot.com.

[667] The History Place 2000. Presidential Impeachment Proceedings – Bill Clinton. Online article. Retrieved from www.historyplace.com.

[668] Lusterberg R 2014. JAMEIS WINSTON IS SCREAMING OUT FOR HELP. Online article. Retrieved from www.psychologyofsports.com.

[669] Myerberg P 2014. AJ McCarron's mom apologizes for tweet deriding Jameis Winston. Online article. Retrieved from www.ftw.usatoday.com.

[670] Wilson D 2014. Winston May be Idiot, but He's Smarter Than You. Online article. Retrieved from www.uatrav.com.

[671] Pasatieri M n,d. Super Bowl Bound – A Prediction of Jameis Winston's Career. Online article. Retrieved from www.nflpam.com.

[672] Genius Media LLC 2019. Wonderlic Score Database. Online article. Retrieved from www.footballiqscore.com.

[673] Wonderlic Test Sample 2019. NFL Wonderlic Scores. Online article. Retrieved from www.wonderlictestsample.com.

[674] Wonderlic Test Sample 2019. Wonderlic Test Scoring – Wonderlic Score by Job Title. Online article. Retrieved from www.wonderlictestsample.com.

[675] Crowe J 2011. Passing the test off the football field Making the grade off the football field. Online article. Retrieved from www.baltimoresun.com.

[676] Wikimedia Foundation Inc. 2019. Pat McInally. Online article. Retrieved from www.en.wikipedia.org.

[677] Jones T 2017. Jones: Jameis Winston's pep talk to kids sends wrong message (w/video). Online article. Retrieved from www.tampabay.com.

[678] Winston J 2019. Online article. Retrieved from www.twitter.com, posted by Jameis Winston aka @Jaboowins on his Twitter biography.

[679] Lancaster J 2016. Jameis Winston Gets Baptized at Spiritual Retreat. Online article. Retrieved from www.charismanews.com.

[680] Laine J 2018. Buccaneers QB Jameis Winston's fiancee delivers baby boy. Online article. Retrieved from www.espn.com.

[681] Rodgers M 2017. Jameis Winston delivers wrong message to kids.Online article. Retrieved from www.usatoday.com.

[682] Yarcho J 2017. Many Coming To Jameis Winston's Defense – Including His Mother. Online article. Retrieved from www.thepewterplank.com.

[683] Clark R P 2017. Tampa Bay's Jameis Winston said the wrong thing for the right reason. Online article. Retrieved from www.theundefeated.com.

[684] Fennelly M 2018. Bucs fans wear Jameis Winston's No. 3, some uneasily. Online article. Retrieved from www.tampabay.com.

[685] Hill A 2018. Online article. Retrieved from www.twitter.com, posted by Antonio Hill aka @buc_king on 2018-07-30

[686] Jameis1of1 2018. Online article. Retrieved from www.twitter.com, posted by @Jameis1of1 on 2018-07-31

[687] Bucs Nationa 2018. Online article. Retrieved from www.twitter.com, posted by Bucs Nation aka @Bucs_Nation on 2018-07-30

[688] Montanez F G 2018. Online article. Retrieved from www.twitter.com, posted by Felix G. Montanez aka @fgmontanez on 2018-07-30

[689] Srinivasan A 2018. Fitzpatrick becomes 1st player with 3 straight games of over 400 passing yards. Online article. Retrieved from www.msn.com.

[690] Laine J 2018. How does Ryan Fitzpatrick's start compare historically? Stats show favorably. Online article. Retrieved from www.espn.com,

[691] Smith M D 2018. Ryan Fitzpatrick has been outplaying Jameis Winston for two years. Online article. Retrieved from www.profootballtalk.nbcsports.com.

[692] Kaczynski T 1995. Industrial Society and Its Future. Online article. Retrieved from www.theanarchistlibrary.org.

[693] Sports Reference, LLC. 2019. Player – Ryan Fitzpatrick – 2018 Game Log. Online article. Retrieved from www.pro-football-reference.com.

[694] Associated Press 2018. Bucs pass baton to Fitzpatrick against Panthers. Online article. Retrieved from www.thescore.com.

[695] Miklasz B 2009. Warner's ending with Rams was abrupt He came out of nowhere in 1999 season to lead team to a Super Bowl title Several things appeared to strain his relationship with coach Mike Martz. Online article. Retrieved from www.stltoday.com.

[696] Sports Reference, LLC 2019. Player – Marc Bulger. Online article. Retrieved from www.sports-reference.com.

[697] Sports Reference, LLC. 2019. 2011 Green Bay Packers Statistics & Players. Online article. Retrieved from www.pro-football-reference.com.

[698] Sports Reference, LLC. 2019. Detroit Lions at Green Bay Packers – January 1st, 2012. Online article. Retrieved from www.pro-football-reference.com,

[699] Sports Reference, LLC 2019. Player – Steve McNair. Online article. Retrieved from www.sports-reference.com.

[700] Sports Reference, LLC. 2019. 2003 Tennessee Titans Statistics & Players. Online article. Retrieved from www.pro-football-reference.com.

[701] Sports Reference, LLC. 2019. Player – Billy Volek – 2004 Game Log. Online article. Retrieved from www.pro-football-reference.com,

[702] Sports Reference, LLC 2019. Player – Billy Volek. Online article. Retrieved from www.sports-reference.com.

[703] Sports Reference, LLC 2019. Player – Ryan Fitzpatrick. Online article. Retrieved from www.sports-reference.com.

[704] Hermsmeyer J 2018. Jameis Winston Is A Better Quarterback Than Ryan Fitzpatrick. Online article. Retrieved from www.fivethirtyeight.com.

[705] Sports Reference, LLC. 2019. 2017 Tampa Bay Buccaneers Statistics & Players. Online article. Retrieved from www.pro-football-reference.com,

[706] Sports Reference, LLC. 2019. 2018 Tampa Bay Buccaneers Statistics & Players. Online article. Retrieved from www.pro-football-reference.com,

[707] Nesbitt A 2019. NFL fans had fun ripping the Miami Dolphins for signing Ryan Fitzpatrick. Online article. Retrieved from www.ftw.usatoday.com.

[708] Teope H 2019. Cardinals trade QB Josh Rosen to Dolphins for picks. Online article. Retrieved from www.nfl.com.

[709] Orr C 2018. QB Stock Watch: Will Jameis Winston Be on the Tampa Bay Buccaneers in 2019? Online article. Retrieved from www.si.com.

[710] Bennett D 2018. Why it's time for Buccaneers to move on from Jameis Winston. Online article. Retrieved from www.sportsnet.ca.

[711] Heifetz D 2018. Jameis Winston Shouldn't Be an NFL Starting Quarterback. So What Should the Bucs Do? Online article. Retrieved from www.theringer.com.

[712] Easterling L 2018. Yes, the Jameis Winston era needs to end in Tampa Bay. Online article. Retrieved from www.bucswire.usatoday.com.

[713] Sports Reference, LLC. 2019. 1973 Pittsburgh Steelers Statistics & Players. Online article. Retrieved from www.pro-football-reference.com.

[714] Sports Reference, LLC. 2019. 2007 New York Giants Statistics & Players. Online article. Retrieved from www.pro-football-reference.com.

[715] McKenna H 2018. Winston, Draft an Elite QB High in 2019. Online article. Retrieved from www.thebiglead.com.

[716] Miller M 2018. 2019 NFL Mock Draft: Matt Miller's Latest Picks Entering Final Month of Season. Online article. Retrieved from www.bleacherreport.com.

[717] Trapasso P 2018. 2019 NFL Mock Draft: Buccaneers replace Jameis Winston with a turnover-averse quarterback. Online article. Retrieved from www.cbssports.com.

[718] Cherepinsky W 2019. 2019 NFL Mock Draft – Round 4. Online article. Retrieved from www.walterfootball.com.

[719] Sports Reference, LLC 2019. Player – Joe Flacco. Online article. Retrieved from www.sports-reference.com.

[720] Wikimedia Foundation Inc. 2019. 2019 NFL Draft. Online article. Retrieved from www.en.wikipedia.org.

[721] Wagner-McGough 2019. Raiders GM Mike Mayock on Derek Carr's proposal to fight ESPN host: 'I like the attitude'. Online article. Retrieved from www.cbssports.com.

[722] Biler D 2018. Baker Mayfield took on Colin Cowherd and 'won the interview' with more than just his shirt. Online article. Retrieved from www.washingtonpost.com.

[723] Olojede Z 2019. Baker Mayfield Says Colin Cowherd 'Needs to be put in His Place,' Defends Odell Beckham Jr. Online article. Retrieved from www.complex.com.

[724] Martinelli M R 2019. Baker Mayfield calls Colin Cowherd a 'donkey' in response to latest Browns take. Online article. Retrieved from www.ftw.usatoday.com.

[725] Kirkpatrick C 1991. The No Fun League. Online article. Retrieved from www.si.com.

[726] Barnwell B 2018. Ranking the best and worst potential NFL head-coaching openings. Online article. Retrieved from www.espn.com.

[727] Battista J 2018. Ranking NFL coaching vacancies: Browns, Packers most alluring. Online article. Retrieved from www.nfl.com.

[728] Salem D 2019. NFL Offseason 2019: Ranking the 8 coaching vacancies worst to first. Online article. Retrieved from www.nflspinzone.com.

[729] Brinson W 2019. Ryan Tannehill traded from Dolphins to Titans, shaking up the QB situation in Tennessee. Online article. Retrieved from www.cbssports.com.

[730] Clayton J 2018. Ranking the open NFL head coaching jobs, from best to worst. Online article. Retrieved from www.washingtonpost.com.

[731] Lauletta T 2019. The vacant NFL head coaching jobs ranked and the candidates rumored to be in the mix for them. Online article. Retrieved from www.businessinsider.com.

[732] Chiari M n.d. Kliff Kingsbury Fired as Texas Tech Head Coach After 6 Seasons. Online article. Retrieved from www.bleacherreport.com.

[733] Foxworth D 2019. All the reasons the Cardinals' decision to hire Kliff Kingsbury is troubling. Online article. Retrieved from www.theundefeated.com.

[734] Dunne T 2019. WHAT HAPPENED IN GREEN BAY. Online article. Retrieved from www.bleacherreport.com.

[735] Radcliffe J R 2019. National writers and pundits react to the Packers hiring Matt LaFleur as head coach. Online article. Retrieved from www.jsonline.com.

[736] Anderson L 2015. Bruce Arians: The NFL's Ultimate Quarterback Whisperer. Online article. Retrieved from www.bleacherreport.com.

[737] Kelly N 2019. The football life and times of Bruce Arians. Online article. Retrieved from www.tampabay.com.

[738] Laine J 2016. Jameis Winston: Bruce Arians 'inspired me to go after a Super Bowl'. Online article. Retrieved from www.espn.com.

[739] Tampa Bay Buccaneers 2019. Bruce Arians 'Extremely Excited' to Work with Jameis Winston & Coaching Staff | Buccaneers Slice. Online Video. Retrieved from www.youtube.com.

[740] Benjamin C 2019. Bruce Arians says Buccaneers will be built around Jameis Winston, thinks QB 'can win it all'. Online article. Retrieved from www.cbssports.com.

[741] Reynolds S 2019. SR's Fab 5: Bucs QB Winston A Perfect Fit For Arians' Offense. Online article. Retrieved from www.pewterreport.com.

[742] BrainyMedia Inc 2019. Michael Jordan quotes. Online article. Retrieved from www.brainyquote.com.

[743] BrainyMedia Inc 2019. Tiger Woods quotes. Online article. Retrieved from www.brainyquote.com.

[744] Sports Reference, LLC. 2019. 2015 Tampa Bay Buccaneers Statistics & Players. Online article. Retrieved from www.pro-football-reference.com.

[745] Sports Reference, LLC. 2019. 1989 Dallas Cowboys Statistics & Players. Online article. Retrieved from www.pro-football-reference.com.

[746] Sports Reference, LLC. 2019. 1990 Dallas Cowboys Statistics & Players. Online article. Retrieved from www.pro-football-reference.com.

[747] Sports Reference, LLC. 2019. 1991 Dallas Cowboys Statistics & Players. Online article. Retrieved from www.pro-football-reference.com.

[748] Sports Reference, LLC. 2019. 1992 Dallas Cowboys Statistics & Players. Online article. Retrieved from www.pro-football-reference.com.

[749] Sports Reference, LLC. 2019. 1970 Pittsburgh Steelers Statistics & Players. Online article. Retrieved from www.pro-football-reference.com.

[750] Sports Reference, LLC. 2019. 1971 Pittsburgh Steelers Statistics & Players. Online article. Retrieved from www.pro-football-reference.com.

[751] Sports Reference, LLC. 2019. 1972 Pittsburgh Steelers Statistics & Players. Online article. Retrieved from www.pro-football-reference.com.

[752] Sports Reference, LLC. 2019. 2001 New England Patriots Statistics & Players. Online article. Retrieved from www.pro-football-reference.com.

[753] Sports Reference, LLC. 2019. 2002 New England Patriots Statistics & Players. Online article. Retrieved from www.pro-football-reference.com.

[754] Sports Reference, LLC. 2019. 2003 New England Patriots Statistics & Players. Online article. Retrieved from www.pro-football-reference.com.

[755] Sports Reference, LLC. 2019. 2004 New England Patriots Statistics & Players. Online article. Retrieved from www.pro-football-reference.com.

[756] Sports Reference, LLC. 2019. 2002 San Diego Chargers Statistics & Players. Online article. Retrieved from www.pro-football-reference.com.

[757] Sports Reference, LLC. 2019. 2003 San Diego Chargers Statistics & Players. Online article. Retrieved from www.pro-football-reference.com.

[758] Sports Reference, LLC. 2019. 2004 San Diego Chargers Statistics & Players. Online article. Retrieved from www.pro-football-reference.com.

[759] Sports Reference, LLC. 2019. 2005 San Diego Chargers Statistics & Players. Online article. Retrieved from www.pro-football-reference.com.

[760] Sports Reference, LLC. 2019. 1983 Denver Broncos Statistics & Players. Online article. Retrieved from www.pro-football-reference.com.

[761] Sports Reference, LLC. 2019. 1984 Denver Broncos Statistics & Players. Online article. Retrieved from www.pro-football-reference.com.

[762] Sports Reference, LLC. 2019. 1985 Denver Broncos Statistics & Players. Online article. Retrieved from www.pro-football-reference.com.

[763] Sports Reference, LLC. 2019. 1986 Denver Broncos Statistics & Players. Online article. Retrieved from www.pro-football-reference.com

[764] Sports Reference, LLC. 2019. 1992 Green Bay Packers Statistics & Players. Online article. Retrieved from www.pro-football-reference.com.

[765] Sports Reference, LLC. 2019. 1993 Green Bay Packers Statistics & Players. Online article. Retrieved from www.pro-football-reference.com.

[766] Sports Reference, LLC. 2019. 1994 Green Bay Packers Statistics & Players. Online article. Retrieved from www.pro-football-reference.com.

[767] Sports Reference, LLC. 2019. 1995 Green Bay Packers Statistics & Players. Online article. Retrieved from www.pro-football-reference.com.

[768] Sports Reference, LLC. 2019. 1973 San Diego Chargers Statistics & Players. Online article. Retrieved from www.pro-football-reference.com.

[769] Sports Reference, LLC. 2019. 1974 San Diego Chargers Statistics & Players. Online article. Retrieved from www.pro-football-reference.com.

[770] Sports Reference, LLC. 2019. 1975 San Diego Chargers Statistics & Players. Online article. Retrieved from www.pro-football-reference.com.

[771] Sports Reference, LLC. 2019. 1976 San Diego Chargers Statistics & Players. Online article. Retrieved from www.pro-football-reference.com.

[772] Sports Reference, LLC. 2019. 1967 Miami Dolphins Statistics & Players. Online article. Retrieved from www.pro-football-reference.com.

[773] Sports Reference, LLC. 2019. 1968 Miami Dolphins Statistics & Players. Online article. Retrieved from www.pro-football-reference.com.

[774] Sports Reference, LLC. 2019. 1969 Miami Dolphins Statistics & Players. Online article. Retrieved from www.pro-football-reference.com.

[775] Sports Reference, LLC. 2019. 1970 Miami Dolphins Statistics & Players. Online article. Retrieved from www.pro-football-reference.com.

[776] Sports Reference, LLC. 2019. 1986 Buffalo Bills Statistics & Players. Online article. Retrieved from www.pro-football-reference.com.

[777] Sports Reference, LLC. 2019. 1987 Buffalo Bills Statistics & Players. Online article. Retrieved from www.pro-football-reference.com.

[778] Sports Reference, LLC. 2019. 1988 Buffalo Bills Statistics & Players. Online article. Retrieved from www.pro-football-reference.com.

[779] Sports Reference, LLC. 2019. 1989 Buffalo Bills Statistics & Players. Online article. Retrieved from www.pro-football-reference.com.

[780] Sports Reference, LLC. 2019. 2004 New York Giants Statistics & Players. Online article. Retrieved from www.pro-football-reference.com.

[781] Sports Reference, LLC. 2019. 2005 New York Giants Statistics & Players. Online article. Retrieved from www.pro-football-reference.com.

[782] Sports Reference, LLC. 2019. 2006 New York Giants Statistics & Players. Online article. Retrieved from www.pro-football-reference.com.

[783] Sports Reference, LLC. 2019. 1998 Indianapolis Colts Statistics & Players. Online article. Retrieved from www.pro-football-reference.com.

[784] Sports Reference, LLC. 2019. 1999 Indianapolis Colts Statistics & Players. Online article. Retrieved from www.pro-football-reference.com.

[785] Sports Reference, LLC. 2019. 2000 Indianapolis Colts Statistics & Players. Online article. Retrieved from www.pro-football-reference.com.

[786] Sports Reference, LLC. 2019. 2001 Indianapolis Colts Statistics & Players. Online article. Retrieved from www.pro-football-reference.com.

[787] Sports Reference, LLC. 2019. 1983 Miami Dolphins Statistics & Players. Online article. Retrieved from www.pro-football-reference.com.

[788] Sports Reference, LLC. 2019. 1984 Miami Dolphins Statistics & Players. Online article. Retrieved from www.pro-football-reference.com.

[789] Sports Reference, LLC. 2019. 1985 Miami Dolphins Statistics & Players. Online article. Retrieved from www.pro-football-reference.com.

[790] Sports Reference, LLC. 2019. 1986 Miami Dolphins Statistics & Players. Online article. Retrieved from www.pro-football-reference.com.

[791] Sports Reference, LLC. 2019. 1979 San Francisco 49ers Statistics & Players. Online article. Retrieved from www.pro-football-reference.com.

[792] Sports Reference, LLC. 2019. 1980 San Francisco 49ers Statistics & Players. Online article. Retrieved from www.pro-football-reference.com.

[793] Sports Reference, LLC. 2019. 1981 San Francisco 49ers Statistics & Players. Online article. Retrieved from www.pro-football-reference.com.

[794] Sports Reference, LLC. 2019. 1982 San Francisco 49ers Statistics & Players. Online article. Retrieved from www.pro-football-reference.com.

[795] Sports Reference, LLC. 2019. 1984 Houston Oilers Statistics & Players. Online article. Retrieved from www.pro-football-reference.com.

[796] Sports Reference, LLC. 2019. 1985 Houston Oilers Statistics & Players. Online article. Retrieved from www.pro-football-reference.com.

[797] Sports Reference, LLC. 2019. 1986 Houston Oilers Statistics & Players. Online article. Retrieved from www.pro-football-reference.com.

[798] Sports Reference, LLC. 2019. 1987 Houston Oilers Statistics & Players. Online article. Retrieved from www.pro-football-reference.com.

[799] Sports Reference, LLC. 2019. 2006 San Diego Chargers Statistics & Players. Online article. Retrieved from www.pro-football-reference.com.

[800] Sports Reference, LLC. 2019. 2007 San Diego Chargers Statistics & Players. Online article. Retrieved from www.pro-football-reference.com.

[801] Sports Reference, LLC. 2019. 2008 San Diego Chargers Statistics & Players. Online article. Retrieved from www.pro-football-reference.com.

[802] Sports Reference, LLC. 2019. 2009 San Diego Chargers Statistics & Players. Online article. Retrieved from www.pro-football-reference.com.

[803] Sports Reference, LLC. 2019. 2008 Green Bay Packers Statistics & Players. Online article. Retrieved from www.pro-football-reference.com.

[804] Sports Reference, LLC. 2019. 2009 Green Bay Packers Statistics & Players. Online article. Retrieved from www.pro-football-reference.com.

[805] Sports Reference, LLC. 2019. 2010 Green Bay Packers Statistics & Players. Online article. Retrieved from www.pro-football-reference.com

[806] Sports Reference, LLC. 2019. 2004 Pittsburgh Steelers Statistics & Players. Online article. Retrieved from www.pro-football-reference.com.

[807] Sports Reference, LLC. 2019. 2005 Pittsburgh Steelers Statistics & Players. Online article. Retrieved from www.pro-football-reference.com.

[808] Sports Reference, LLC. 2019. 2006 Pittsburgh Steelers Statistics & Players. Online article. Retrieved from www.pro-football-reference.com.

[809] Sports Reference, LLC. 2019. 2007 Pittsburgh Steelers Statistics & Players. Online article. Retrieved from www.pro-football-reference.com.

[810] Sports Reference, LLC. 2019. 1971 Oakland Raiders Statistics & Players. Online article. Retrieved from www.pro-football-reference.com.

[811] Sports Reference, LLC. 2019. 1972 Oakland Raiders Statistics & Players. Online article. Retrieved from www.pro-football-reference.com.

[812] Sports Reference, LLC. 2019. 1973 Oakland Raiders Statistics & Players. Online article. Retrieved from www.pro-football-reference.com.

[813] Sports Reference, LLC. 2019. 1974 Oakland Raiders Statistics & Players. Online article. Retrieved from www.pro-football-reference.com.

[814] Sports Reference, LLC. 2019. 1969 Dallas Cowboys Statistics & Players. Online article. Retrieved from www.pro-football-reference.com.

[815] Sports Reference, LLC. 2019. 1970 Dallas Cowboys Statistics & Players. Online article. Retrieved from www.pro-football-reference.com.

[816] Sports Reference, LLC. 2019. 1971 Dallas Cowboys Statistics & Players. Online article. Retrieved from www.pro-football-reference.com.

[817] Sports Reference, LLC. 2019. 1973 Dallas Cowboys Statistics & Players. Online article. Retrieved from www.pro-football-reference.com.

[818] Sports Reference, LLC. 2019. 1999 St. Louis Rams Statistics & Players. Online article. Retrieved from www.pro-football-reference.com.

[819] Sports Reference, LLC. 2019. 2000 St. Louis Rams Statistics & Players. Online article. Retrieved from www.pro-football-reference.com.

[820] Sports Reference, LLC. 2019. 2001 St. Louis Rams Statistics & Players. Online article. Retrieved from www.pro-football-reference.com.

[821] Sports Reference, LLC. 2019. 2002 St. Louis Rams Statistics & Players. Online article. Retrieved from www.pro-football-reference.com.

[822] Sports Reference, LLC. 2019. 1985 Tampa Bay Buccaneers Statistics & Players. Online article. Retrieved from www.pro-football-reference.com.

[823] Sports Reference, LLC. 2019. 1987 San Francisco 49ers Statistics & Players. Online article. Retrieved from www.pro-football-reference.com.

[824] Sports Reference, LLC. 2019. 1988 San Francisco 49ers Statistics & Players. Online article. Retrieved from www.pro-football-reference.com.

[825] NFL Enterprises LLC 2019. A Football Life: Bruce Arians, the quarterback whisperer. Online Video. Retrieved from www.nfl.com.

[826] Inabinett M 2019. Bruce Arians on Jameis Winston: 'No reason he can't be really, really successful'. Online article. Retrieved from www.al.com.

[827] Sports Reference, LLC. 2019. NFL Passes Intercepted Single-Season Leaders. Online article. Retrieved from www.pro-football-reference.com.

[828] Sports Reference, LLC. 2019. NFL Passes Intercepted Career Leaders. Online article. Retrieved from www.pro-football-reference.com.

[829] Wikimedia Foundation Inc. 2019. George C. Parker. Online article. Retrieved from www.en.wikipedia.org.

[830] Sports Reference, LLC. 2019. NFL Fumbles Career Leaders. Online article. Retrieved from www.pro-football-reference.com.

[831] Sports Reference, LLC 2019. Player – Ken O'Brien. Online article. Retrieved from www.sports-reference.com.

[832] Feldmann M 2002. Favre has career-high 6 interceptions. Online article. Retrieved from www.journaltimes.com.

[833] BrainyMedia Inc 2019. Dan Marino quotes. Online article. Retrieved from www.brainyquote.com.

[834] The Sports Xchange 2019. GM Licht says Winston is Bucs' quarterback. Online article. Retrieved from www.upi.com.

[835] Horing A 2009. Did Kurt Warner Deserve to Be Benched So Many Times? Online article. Retrieved from www.bleacherreport.com.

[836] Somers K 2017. Kurt Warner voted into Pro Football Hall of Fame. Online article. Retrieved from www.azcentral.com.

[837] Klein G 2017. Kurt Warner took a one-of-a-kind route to the Hall of Fame. Online article. Retrieved from www.latimes.com.

[838] Deen S 2017. FSU's Jimbo Fisher: Jameis Winston has Pro Football Hall of Fame potential. Online article. Retrieved from www.orlandosentinel.com.

[839] BrainyMedia Inc 2019. Benjamin Haydon quotes. Online article. Retrieved from www.brainyquote.com.

[840] BrainyMedia Inc 2019. Arthur Schopenhauer quotes. Online article. Retrieved from www.brainyquote.com.

[841] BrainyMedia Inc 2019. Tony Dungy quotes. Online article. Retrieved from www.brainyquote.com.

[842] Hooper E 2017. Jameis Winston proud to launch Dream Forever Foundation. Online article. Retrieved from www.tampabay.com.

[843] JAMEIS WINSTON'S DREAM FOREVER FOUNDATION 2019. Page - About. Online article. Retrieved from www.jameiswinston3.org.

[844] JAMEIS WINSTON'S DREAM FOREVER FOUNDATION 2019. Page - Programs. Online article. Retrieved from www.jameiswinston3.org.

[845] Laine J 2018. Jameis Winston, WWE star treat Tampa youth to 'Black Panther' screening. Online article. Retrieved from www.espn.com.

[846] JAMEIS WINSTON'S DREAM FOREVER FOUNDATION 2019. Page - News. Online article. Retrieved from www.jameiswinston3.org.

[847] Victory D 2019. Tampa Bay QB Jameis Winston kicks off Dream Forever Week with shopping spree for area youth. Online article. Retrieved from www.al.com.

[848] Laine J 2019. Special Olympics sees powerful ally in Bucs QB Jameis Winston. Online article. Retrieved from www.espn.com.

[849] Goodreads, Inc. 2019. Sojourner Truth quotes. Online article. Retrieved from www.goodreads.com.

[850] Romano J 2019. NEW PODCAST: Jameis Winston, Tampa Bay Buccaneers QB. Online Audio Retrieved from www.sportsspectrum.com.

[851] BrainyMedia Inc 2019. Tara Westover quotes. Online article. Retrieved from www.brainyquote.com.

BIBLIOGRAPHY

Alabama High School Football Historical Society Online Pages

Alabama High School Football Historical Society 2018. Hueytown Yearly Summary. Online article. Retrieved from www.ahsfhs.org,

Alabama High School Football Historical Society 2018. Spanish Fort Football Team History. Online article. Retrieved from www.ahsfhs.org,

Alabama High School Football Historical Society 2018. Hueytown Football Team History – Year 2011. Online article. Retrieved from www.ahsfhs.org,

Alabama High School Football Historical Society 2018. Alabama High School Football Players – Jameis Winston. Online article. Retrieved from www.ahsfhs.org.

Articles

Abdul-Jabbar K 2019. Kareem Abdul-Jabbar: LeBron James Is Bigger Than the 'GOAT' Debate, He's a Hero for Our Time. Online article. Retrieved from www.newsweek.com.

Al Jazeera America, LLC. 2016. The dark side: The secret world of sports doping. Online article. Retrieved from www.america.aljazeera.com.

Allen B 2018. Poynter announces new senior media writer. Online article. Retrieved from www.poynter.org.

All State Sugar Bowl 2019. 66th Annual Sugar Bowl Classic – January 4, 2000. Online article. Retrieved from www.allstatesugarbowl.org,

Anderson L 2014. Jameis Winston has 'embarrassed' Hueytown, residents say. Online article. Retrieved from www.al.com.

Anderson L 2015. Bruce Arians: The NFL's Ultimate Quarterback Whisperer. Online article. Retrieved from www.bleacherreport.com.

Ansari T 2017. The NFL Is Investigating Jameis Winston For Allegedly Groping An Uber Driver In 2016. Online article. Retrieved from www.buzzfeednews.com.

Archer T 2017. Cowboys' Ezekiel Elliott suspended six games for conduct. Online article. Retrieved from www.espn.com.

Archer T 2017. Cowboys RB Ezekiel Elliott suspension upheld again after court denies motion. Online article. Retrieved from www.espn.com.

Armour N 2018. With Jameis Winston suspension, NFL saying deflating footballs worse than sexual assault. Online article. Retrieved from www.usatoday.com.

Associated Press 2009. Favre released by Jets but says he has no intention of NFL return. Online article. Retrieved from www.nfl.com.

Associated Press 2012. Bills RB Lynch suspended three games after second run-in with law. Online article. Retrieved from www.nfl.com.

Associated Press 2013. Jameis Winston (4 total TDs) helps No. 1 FSU to 2nd straight ACC Title. Online article. Retrieved from www.espn.com.

Associated Press 2013. No. 3 Clemson handed worst Death Valley defeat by No. 5 Florida State, QB Winston. Online article. Retrieved from www.foxnews.com.

Associated Press 2014. Florida State wins national title with touchdown in final seconds. Online article. Retrieved from www.foxnews.com.

Associated Press 2017. Brady throws for 303 yards, Patriots hold off Bucs 19-14. Online article. Retrieved from www.espn.com.

Associated Press 2017. Bucs: Injured QB Jameis Winston will start against Bills. Online article. Retrieved from www.usatoday.com.

Associated Press 2017. Winston throws late TD pass, Buccaneers beat Saints 31-24. Online article. Retrieved from www.usatoday.com.

Associated Press 2018. Bucs pass baton to Fitzpatrick against Panthers. Online article. Retrieved from www.thescore.com.

Axon R 2014. As incidents mount for Jameis Winston, so does concern. Online article. Retrieved from www.usatoday.com.

Axon R 2014. Jameis Winston stopped by police at gunpoint in 2012 incident. Online article. Retrieved from www.usatoday.com.

Axon R 2015. Judge dismisses one of Jameis Winston's counterclaims, upholds defamation claim. Online article. Retrieved from www.usatoday.com.

Badenhausen K 2016. Peyton Manning Retires With Record $400 Million In Career Earnings. Online article. Retrieved from www.forbes.com.

Ballotpedia n.d. Presidential election, 2016. Online article. Retrieved from www.ballotpedia.org.

Barnett Z 2018. Networks are reportedly lining up to make Peyton Manning an even richer man. Online article. Retrieved from www.footballscoop.com.

Barnwell B 2015. The Year the NFL Went Insane and Gave a Kicker the MVP Award. Online article. Retrieved from www.grantland.com.

Barnwell B 2018. Ranking the best and worst potential NFL head-coaching openings. Online article. Retrieved from www.espn.com.

Barrabi T 2019. Super Bowl rings: Fun facts on cost, history and more. Online article. Retrieved from www.foxbusiness.com.

Basile N 2016. Not So Super: 15 People Who Have Defeated Superman. Online article. Retrieved from www.cbr.com.

Bataglio S 2019. ESPN President Jimmy Pitaro is fighting the cord-cutting wave. Online article. Retrieved from www.latimes.com.

Battista J 2016. SOPHOMORE YEAR: THE PROGRESSION OF JAMEIS WINSTON. Online article. Retrieved from www.nfl.com.

Battista J 2018. Ranking NFL coaching vacancies: Browns, Packers most alluring. Online article. Retrieved from www.nfl.com.

Beaudry P 2009. Hueytown Gophers Reloading for 2009. Online article. Retrieved from www.highschoolsports.al.com.

Belden S 2017. Jon Gruden says he may return to coaching, and 2 teams appear to be the most likely destinations. Online article. Retrieved from www.businessinsider.com.

Bender B 2018. 40 most hated NFL players of all time: loudmouths, cheaters, criminals. Online article. Retrieved from www.sportingnews.com.

Benjamin C 2019. Bruce Arians says Buccaneers will be built around Jameis Winston, thinks QB 'can win it all'. Online article. Retrieved from www.cbssports.com.

Bennett D 2018. Why it's time for Buccaneers to move on from Jameis Winston. Online article. Retrieved from www.sportsnet.ca.

Bieler D 2017. Buccaneers' Jameis Winston loses his mind after losing fumble to Panthers. Online article. Retrieved from www.washingtonpost.com.

Biler D 2018. Baker Mayfield took on Colin Cowherd and 'won the interview' with more than just his shirt. Online article. Retrieved from www.washingtonpost.com.

Blatchford C 2018. Christie Blatchford: For hypocritical #MeToo movement, it's one strike and you're out. Online article. Retrieved from www.nationalpost.com.

Bleacher Report Inc. 2019. Deshaun Watson Becomes 4th Rookie Quarterback with 5 TD Passes in a Game. Online article. Retrieved from www.bleacherreport.com.

Bleacher Report, Inc. 2019. INTERNET REACTS TO JAMEIS SUSPENSION. Online article. Retrieved from www.bleacherreport.com.

Bleacher Report Inc. 2019. Winston Becomes First Player Since Favre to Throw Pick-6 on 1st Pass. Online article. Retrieved from www.bleacherreport.com.

Boren C 2017. Jameis Winston's shoulder injury may keep him out 'an extended period,' not just a few weeks. Online article. Retrieved from www.washingtonpost.com.

Boren C 2017. UPDATE: Jameis Winston's shoulder injury may keep him out 'an extended period', not just a few weeks. Online article. Retrieved from www.washingtonpost.com.

Bradley K 2013. Jameis Winston: Take notice, FSU quarterback is the real deal. Online article. Retrieved from www.sportingnews.com.

Brady J 2016. Inside and out, ESPN dealing with changing political dynamics.Online article. Retrieved from www.espn.com.

Brady J 2017. ESPN awash in rising political tide. Online article. Retrieved from www.espn.com.

Brangin A 2019. Tennessee House Speaker's Top Aide Resigns After Accusations of Framing Black Activist and Sending Racist and Sexist Texts. Online article. Retrieved from www.theroot.com.

Bratton MW 2018. Ed Orgeron compares Devin White to Ray Lewis, Patrick Willis: 'He's right in that group'. Online article. Retrieved from www.saturdaydownsouth.com.

Brauneck T n.d. NFL BANNED SUBSTANCE LIST. Online article. Retrieved from www.nationalfootballpost.com.

Braziller Z 2016. ESPN kicks Keyshawn Johnson off NFL pregame show. Online article. Retrieved from www.nypost.com.

Breech J 2018. Jameis Winston suspension: Witness reportedly left out one key detail in Uber story. Online article. Retrieved from www.si.com.

Breech J 2015. Peyton Manning tops NFL in off-field income; Eli ahead of Tom Brady. Online article. Retrieved from www.cbssports.com.

Breech J 2018. Suspended Jameis Winston doesn't admit guilt in Uber case and here's reportedly why. Online article. Retrieved from www.cbssports.com.

BrethalyzerAlcoholTester 2016. Blood Alcohol Chart For Estimation. Online article. Retrieved from www.breathalyzeralcoholtester.com.

Brinson W 2019. Ryan Tannehill traded from Dolphins to Titans, shaking up the QB situation in Tennessee. Online article. Retrieved from www.cbssports.com.

Brisbee G 2015. How to throw a no-hitter and lose by 4 runs. Online article. Retrieved from www.sbnation.com.

Brooke T 2014. Jameis Winston Named MVP of 2014 BCS National Championship Game. Online article. Retrieved from www.bleacherreport.com.

Brown R 2016. How Jameis Winston compares to QBs who have been Rookie of the Year. Online article. Retrieved from www.espn.com.

Burke T 2018. New Jameis Winston Details Emerge; Convicted Ex-Vanderbilt Football Rapist Says Bucs QB Was Alone With Uber Driver. Online article. Retrieved from www.deadspin.com.

California Innocent Project 2019. Freed Clients – Brian Banks. Online Article. Retrieved from www.californiainnocenceproject.org.

Candler M 2017. ESPN PUNDIT WANTS WHITE MEN TO SHUT UP. Online article. Retrieved from www.foxnews.com.

Carter B n.d. Unitas surprised them all. Online article. Retrieved from www.espn.com.

CBS Interactive Inc. 2019. All-Time Football Players-Quarterback. Online article. Retrieved from www.247sports.com.

CBS Interactive Inc. 2019. Player – Jameis Winston. Online article. Retrieved from www.247sports.com.

CBS Interactive Inc. 2019. 2012 Top Football Recruits. Online article. Retrieved from www.247sports.com.

Chavez C 2017. Watch: Jameis Winston Flips Out On Sideline After Panthers Comeback. Online article. Retrieved from www.si.com.

Cherepinsky W 2019. 2015 NFL Draft Scouting Report: Jameis Winston. Online article. Retrieved from www.walterfootball.com.

Cherepinsky W 2019. 2019 NFL Mock Draft – Round 4. Online article. Retrieved from www.walterfootball.com.

Chiari M n.d. Kliff Kingsbury Fired as Texas Tech Head Coach After 6 Seasons. Online article. Retrieved from www.bleacherreport.com.

Chiari M 2017. Jameis Winston to Start vs. Bills Despite Shoulder Injury. Online article. Retrieved from www.bleacherreport.com.

Clark C 2013. Jameis Winston dazzles as No. 12 Florida State routs Pitt. Online article. Retrieved from www.usatoday.com.

Clark R P 2017. Tampa Bay's Jameis Winston said the wrong thing for the right reason. Online article. Retrieved from www.theundefeated.com.

Clayton J 2018. Ranking the open NFL head coaching jobs, from best to worst. Online article. Retrieved from www.washingtonpost.com.

Concha J 2019. Poynter pulls blacklist of 'unreliable' news websites after backlash. Online article. Retrieved from www.thehill.com.

Crowe J 2011. Passing the test off the football field Making the grade off the football field. Online article. Retrieved from www.baltimoresun.com.

Curtis B 2017. Sportswriting Has Become a Liberal Profession — Here's How It Happened. Online article. Retrieved from www.theringer.com.

Daily T n.d. Tampa Bucs Gerald McCoy Gives Tour Of His Man Cave. Online article. Retrieved from www.995qyk.com.

DaSilva C 2016. Jameis Winston had a remarkable 55-game streak snapped Sunday. Online article. Retrieved from www.foxsports.com.

Daulerio A J 2018. Did Michelle Beadle Tell Aaron Rodgers, "I Just Wanna Get Fucked" After The ESPYs? ESPN Wants To Know. Online article. Retrieved from www.deadspin.com.

Deen S 2017. FSU's Jimbo Fisher: Jameis Winston has Pro Football Hall of Fame potential. Online article. Retrieved from www.orlandosentinel.com.

De Leon A 2019. #MeToo Hypocrisy – Believe All Women (sometimes). Online article. Retrieved from www.thelibertarianrepublic.com.

Diaz G 2016. Diaz: Jameis Winston is reason Dirk Koetter is coaching Bucs. Online article. Retrieved from www.orlandosentinel.com.

Diaz G 2018. Jameis Winston dilemma for Bucs: Cut him or hang onto damaged goods?. Online article. Retrieved from www.orlandosentinel.com.

DiBiase L 2018. Friend of Ronald Darby gives conflicting story on Winston. Online article. Retrieved from www.lockedoneagles.com.

Dougherty M B 2017. The arrogant thinking of liberal sports writers. Online article. Retrieved from www.theweek.com.

Dubin J 2018. Buccaneers pick up Jameis Winston's $21 million fifth-year option on rookie contract. Online article. Retrieved from www.cbssports.com.

Duffy T 2017. Big Lead Sports Media Politics Survey: Only 4% of Media Surveyed Voted for Donald Trump. Online article. Retrieved from www.thebiglead.com.

Dufresne C 2014. A Seminole moment: Florida State wins thrilling BCS finale, 34-31. Online article. Retrieved from www.articles.latimes.com.

Dunne T 2019. WHAT HAPPENED IN GREEN BAY. Online article. Retrieved from www.bleacherreport.com.

Easterling L 2018. Yes, the Jameis Winston era needs to end in Tampa Bay. Online article. Retrieved from www.bucswire.usatoday.com.

EHM Productions, Inc. 2019. JAMEIS WINSTONAPOLOGIZES FOR UBER INCIDENT ... Blames Alcohol. Online article. Retrieved from www.tmz.com.

EHM Productions, Inc. 2019. NFL Superstar Accused of Baby Mama Beatdown. online article. Retrieved from www.tmz.com.

Elliott B 2014. Jameis Winston, squirrel hunter: The important stuff and some Florida State laughs. Online article. Retrieved from www.tomahawknation.com.

Elliott B 2012. The Jameis Winston Experience: Seminoles Sign Top Quarterback. Online article. Retrieved from www.tomahawknation.com.

Erenow 2019. August 1955 to September 1956 *The Potsdam Papers – "Intellectual Prostitutes" – Margaret Is Married – A Trip to Europe*. Online article. Retrieved from www.erenow.net.

ESPN.com news services 2018. Dante Fowler Jr. suspended 1 game for violating league's conduct policy. Online article. Retrieved from www.abcnews.go.com.

ESPN.com news services 2013. Jameis Winston in 2 minor incidents. Online article. Retrieved from www.espn.com.

ESPN.com news services 2013. Jameis Winston: Store employee "hooked us up" with crab legs. Online article. Retrieved from www.espn.com.

ESPN.com news services 2013. Jameis Winston wins Heisman. Online article. Retrieved from www.espn.com.

ESPN.com news services 2016. Tom Brady has 4-game suspension upheld, not ready to accept ruling. Online article. Retrieved from www.espn.com.

ESPN Enterprises, Inc. 2017. Bucs GM: Jameis Winston is 'best leader I think I've ever been around'. Online article. Retrieved from www.espn.com.

Farrar D 2019. The biggest draft bust in the history of every NFL team. Online article. Retrieved from www.touchdownwire.usatoday.com.

Feldmann M 2002. Favre has career-high 6 interceptions. Online article. Retrieved from www.journaltimes.com.

Fennelly M 2017. Diaz: Jameis Winston is reason Dirk Koetter is coaching Bucs. Online article. Retrieved from www.orlandosentinel.com.

Fennelly M 2018. Bucs fans wear Jameis Winston's No. 3, some uneasily. Online article. Retrieved from www.tampabay.com.

Finn C 2016. NFL media looks other way on Peyton Manning, HGH. Online article. Retrieved from www.bostonglobe.com.

Fischer B 2015. Bucs GM: We spoke with over 75 people vetting Jameis Winston. Online article. Retrieved from www.nfl.com.

Flood B 2018. ESPN shakes up struggling morning show 'Get Up!', reassigns Michelle Beadle. Online article. Retrieved from www.foxnews.com.

Flores L 2019. An Awkward Kiss Changed How I Saw Joe Biden. Online article. Retrieved from www.thecut.com.

Florio M 2016. Keyshawn Johnson returns to ESPN. Online article. Retrieved from www.profootballtalk.nbcsports.com.

Florio M 2018. Al Jazeera claims Peyton Manning's lawyer confirmed HGH use; Manning denies it. Online article. Retrieved from www.profootballtalk.nbcsports.com.

Florio M 2018. Jameis Winston settles with Uber driver. Online article. Retrieved from www.profootballtalk.nbcsports.com.

Florio M 2018. Keyshawn Johnson says 'there's something wrong mentally' with Jameis Winston. Online article. Retrieved from www.profootballtalk.nbcsports.com.

Florio M 2018. Why weren't Jameis Winston, Ronald Darby punished for not telling the truth? Online article. Retrieved from www.orlandosentinel.com.

Florio M 2019. Jameis Winston suggests that he tuned out coaching last year. Online article. Retrieved from www.profootballtalk.nbcsports.com.

Flowers C M 2018. The hypocrisy of #MeToo and female solidarity. Online article. Retrieved from www.philly.com.

Fornelli T 2014. VIDEO: Jameis Winston leaving Publix with crab legs. Online article. Retrieved from www.cbssports.com.

Fox Media LLC and Fox Sports Interactive Media, LLC. 2017. Jameis Winston Named NFC Offensive Player Of The Week. Online article. Retrieved from www.foxsports.com.

Fox Sports Interactive Media, LLC. 2019. Full copy of Jameis Winston hearing decision. Online article. Retrieved from www.foxsports.com.

Foxworth D 2019. All the reasons the Cardinals' decision to hire Kliff Kingsbury is troubling. Online article. Retrieved from www.theundefeated.com.

Frank M 2018. Eagles' Nigel Bradham suspended one game for personal conduct policy violation. Online article. Retrieved from www.usatoday.com.

Frank R 2015. Big Eagles fan Jameis Winston 'so excited' for trip to Linc. Online article. Retrieved from www.nbcsports.com.

FSU Seminoles 2018. Fire or Suspend Michelle Beadle. Online article. Retrieved from www.change.org.

Gaines C 2015. NFL Draft expert says Jameis Winston is the 2nd-best quarterback prospect of the past 10 years. Online article. Retrieved from www.businessinsider.com.

Gallup, Inc. 2019. Party Affiliation. Online article. Retrieved from www.news.gallup.com.

Gantt D 2015. Goodell cites destroying phone in upholding Tom Brady's suspension. Online article. Retrieved from www.profootballtalk.nbcsports.com.

Garafolo M 2018. Jameis Winston organized practices with NFL vets during ban. Online article. Retrieved from www.nfl.com.

Genius Media LLC 2019. Wonderlic Score Database. Online article. Retrieved from www.footballiqscore.com.

Goodbread C 2015. Ex-GM blasts Jameis Winston – JaMarcus Russell comparison. Online article. Retrieved from www.nfl.com.

Graham T 2011. Tom Brady first unanimous MVP. Online article. Retrieved from www.espn.com.

Gretz B 2016. Jameis Winston plays letter-perfect game in Tampa Bay Buccaneers' win. Online article. Retrieved from www.bucswire.upi.com.

Hairopoulos K 2017. Decide for yourself: The evidence and arguments surrounding the suspension of Ezekiel Elliott. Online article. Retrieved from www.sportsday.dallasnews.com.

Hale D 2013. The legend of Jameis Winston. Online article. Retrieved from www.espn.com.

Hale D 2014. Winston the same despite opinion. Online article. Retrieved from www.espn.com.

Harrison E 2015. NFL Power Rankings, Week 14: Seahawks climb; Patriots drop. Online article. Retrieved from www.nfl.com.

Hanzus D 2016. Buccaneers promote OC Dirk Koetter to head coach. Online article. Retrieved from www.nfl.com.

Heath J 2016. Peyton Manning is making just as much from endorsements as he did on the field. Online article. Retrieved from www.broncoswire.usatoday.com.

Heifetz D 2018. Jameis Winston Shouldn't Be an NFL Starting Quarterback. So What Should the Bucs Do? Online article. Retrieved from www.theringer.com.

Hendershott A 2017. Hollywood's dishonest campus rape panic. Online article. Retrieved from www.washingtontimes.com.

Hermsmeyer J 2018. Jameis Winston Is A Better Quarterback Than Ryan Fitzpatrick. Online article. Retrieved from www.fivethirtyeight.com.

Hershey N 2017. This NFL Player Wants To Be Punched By A Superhero. Online article. Retrieved from www.entertainmentbuddha.com.

The History Place 2000. Presidential Impeachment Proceedings – Bill Clinton. Online article. Retrieved from www.historyplace.com.

Hohler B 2016. Tom Brady drops appeal, accepts four-game Deflategate suspension. Online article. Retrieved from www.bostonglobe.com.

Hoffman B 2017. Ezekiel Elliott's 6-Game N.F.L. Suspension Reinstated by Court. Online article. Retrieved from www.nytimes.com.

Hooper E 2017. Jameis Winston proud to launch Dream Forever Foundation. Online article. Retrieved from www.tampabay.com.

Horing A 2009. Did Kurt Warner Deserve to Be Benched So Many Times? Online article. Retrieved from www.bleacherreport.com.

Howard Chelsea 2017. Buccaneers QB Jameis Winston re-injured shoulder in Buffalo. Online article. Retrieved from www.sportingnews.com.

Huguenin M 2015. Mayock on Florida State's Jameis Winston: 'He scares me'. Online article. Retrieved from www.nfl.com.

Huguenin M 2015. Steve Mariucci: Jameis Winston 'most astute X's and O's guy'. Online article. Retrieved from www.nfl.com.

Hunt K 2017. Jameis Winston: 'I want to be the greatest of all time one day'. Online article. Retrieved from www.chopchat.com.

Inabinett M 2019. Bruce Arians on Jameis Winston: 'No reason he can't be really, really successful'. Online article. Retrieved from www.al.com.

Inside Edition Inc. 2019 Former Athletic Trainer Speaks Out About Alleged Sexual Assault by Peyton Manning: 'I Was Scared. I Was Intimidated'. Online article. Retrieved from www.insideedition.com.

Jameis Winston 2017. Online article. Retrieved from www.instagram.com, posted by Jameis Winston on 2019-02-04

Jasner A 2015. Bucs QB Jameis Winston ties NFL rookie record with 5 TD passes. Online article. Retrieved from www.espn.com.

J C 2008. Protection order filed against Larry Fitzgerald Jr. Online article. Retrieved from www.startribune.com.

JoeBucsFan.com 2018. Barber On Tom Jones: Unfair To Jameis Winston. Online article. Retrieved from www.joebucsfan.com.

JoeBucsFan.com 2018. Jameis Reaches Civil Settlement Agreement With Uber Driver. Online article. Retrieved from www.joebucsfan.com.

JoeBucsFan.com 2018. Record-breaking Night For America. Online article. Retrieved from www.joebucsfan.com.

JoeBucsFan.com 2018. Vintage Jameis Dedication. Online article. Retrieved from www.joebucsfan.com.

JoeBucsFan.com 2019. Jameis Winston Says He Told Himself To Disregard Coaching. Online article. Retrieved from www.joebucsfan.com.

Johnston J 2017. Jameis Winston guides Tampa Bay Bucs to improbable win over New Orleans Saints. Online article. Retrieved from www.upi.com.

Jones K 2018. Buccaneers Fire Head Coach Dirk Koetter After 5–11 Season. Online article. Retrieved from www.si.com.

Jones L 2013. Broncos linebacker Von Miller arrested. Online article. Retrieved from www.usatoday.com.

Jones T 2017. Jones: Jameis Winston's pep talk to kids sends wrong message (w/video). Online article. Retrieved from www.tampabay.com.

Jones T 2018. Hey, Bucs, there's no more benefit of the doubt with Jameis Winston. Online article. Retrieved from www.tampabay.com.

Jones T 2018. Jameis Winston's Uber ride will never be forgotten, and shouldn't. Online article. Retrieved from www.tampabay.com.

Jones T 2018. Next move is simple for the Bucs: Get rid of Jameis Winston. Online article. Retrieved from www.tampabay.com.

Kalaf S 2015. Marcus Mariota Looked Fantastic. Online article. Retrieved from www.nfl.com.

Kelly N 2019. The football life and times of Bruce Arians. Online article. Retrieved from www.tampabay.com.

Kennedy W 2017. Jameis Winston injury: status uncertain for Buffalo Bills game. Online article. Retrieved from www.buffalorumblings.com.

Kenyon D 2019. Devin White Is Perfect LB to Take over NFL in Patrick Willis, Ray Lewis Mold. Online article. Retrieved from www.bleacherreport.com.

King P 2015. How Winston Became the Buccaneers' No. 1 Hope. Online article. Retrieved from www.si.com.

King P 2016. Jameis Winston: What I Learned. Online article. Retrieved from www.si.com.

King P 2015. The Bucs Start Here. Online article. Retrieved from www.si.com.

King S 2016. KING: Peyton Manning's squeaky-clean image was built on lies, as detailed in explosive court documents showing ugly smear campaign against his alleged sex assault victim. Online article. Retrieved from www.nydailynews.com.

Kinsman v. Winston, Case 6:15-cv-00696-ACC-GJK, Document 7, Filed 2015-05-15

Kirkpatrick C 1991. The No Fun League. Online article. Retrieved from www.si.com.

Kirpalani S 2015. The Jameis Winston You Don't Know – According to Childhood Mentor Otis Leverette. Online article. Retrieved from www.bleacherreport.com.

Klein G 2017. Kurt Warner took a one-of-a-kind route to the Hall of Fame. Online article. Retrieved from www.latimes.com.

Klemko R 2015. T-Minus 7 Days: The Draft's QB's, Now and Then. Online article. Retrieved from www.si.com.

Klis M and Parker R 2016. Broncos LB Von Miller's legal troubles continue to mount. Online article. Retrieved from www.denverpost.com.

Knoblauch A 2017. Ezekiel Elliott withdraws appeal, will serve suspension. Online article. Retrieved from www.nfl.com.

Kostora N 2012. 10 Veteran NFL Quarterbacks Who Found Success with New Teams. Online article. Retrieved from www.bleacherreport.com.

Kubena B 2019. Here's how LSU LB Devin White's speed makes him the 'freak of nature' of the NFL combine. Online article. Retrieved from www.theadvocate.com.

Laine J 2018. Bucs GM says Jameis Winston may not start Week 4 after suspension. Online article. Retrieved from www.espn.com.

Laine J 2018. Bucs pick up QB Jameis Winston's fifth-year, $20.9M option for 2019. Online article. Retrieved from www.espn.com.

Laine J 2017. Bucs QB Jameis Winston exits game with shoulder injury. Online article. Retrieved from www.abcnews.go.com.

Laine J 2017. Jameis Winston 1st in NFL history with consecutive 4,000-yard passing seasons to start career. Online article. Retrieved from www.espn.com.

Laine J 2016. Jameis Winston: Bruce Arians 'inspired me to go after a Super Bowl'. Online article. Retrieved from www.espn.com.

Laine J 2018. Buccaneers QB Jameis Winston's fiancee delivers baby boy. Online article. Retrieved from www.espn.com.

Laine J 2018. How does Ryan Fitzpatrick's start compare historically? Stats show favorably. Online article. Retrieved from www.espn.com,

Laine J 2018. Jameis Winston, Uber driver reach settlement in 2016 groping case. Online article. Retrieved from www.espn.com.

Laine J 2018. Jameis Winston, WWE star treat Tampa youth to 'Black Panther' screening. Online article. Retrieved from www.espn.com.

Laine J 2019. Special Olympics sees powerful ally in Bucs QB Jameis Winston. Online article. Retrieved from www.espn.com.

Lam Q M 2016. Jameis Winston wins Pepsi Rookie of the Year award. Online article. Retrieved from www.nfl.com.

Lancaster J 2016. Jameis Winston Gets Baptized at Spiritual Retreat. Online article. Retrieved from www.charismanews.com.

Lapointe J 2009. One Step From Super Bowl, Fitzgerald Is Suddenly an Open Book. Online article. Retrieved from www.nytimes.com.

Lauletta T 2019. The vacant NFL head coaching jobs ranked and the candidates rumored to be in the mix for them. Online article. Retrieved from www.businessinsider.com.

Lavigne P 2018. Friend says Jameis Winston was alone with Uber driver. Online article. Retrieved from www.espn.com.

Lease L 2017. Larry Fitzgerald co-winner of Walter Payton Man of the Year award. Online article. Retrieved from www.foxsports.com.

Ledbetter D O 2017. Is Jameis Winston the next Josh Freeman? Online article. Retrieved from www.ajc.com.

Ledbetter D O 2018. What Dirk Koetter had to say about the Falcons. Online article. Retrieved from www.ajc.com.

Ley T 2018. John Skipper Says He Left ESPN After Someone He Bought Cocaine From Tried To Extort Him. Online article. Retrieved from www.deadspin.com.

Littal R 2018. Jameis Winston's Friend Who is in Jail For Rape Claims Jameis is Lying About 3 People Being in Uber When Jameis Allegedly Grabbed Driver's Private Area (Video). Online article. Retrieved from www.blacksportsonline.com.

Lusterberg R 2014. JAMEIS WINSTON IS SCREAMING OUT FOR HELP. Online article. Retrieved from www.psychologyofsports.com.

Madson K 2018. Kyle Shanahan: Jameis Winston 'can be as good as anyone in this league'. Online article. Retrieved from www.ninerswire.usatoday.com.

Martin C 2011. ESPN's Beadle Questioned by Bosses About Alleged Unseemly Behavior at ESPY's. Online article. Retrieved from www.adweek.com, 2018-11-27

Martinelli M R 2019. Baker Mayfield calls Colin Cowherd a 'donkey' in response to latest Browns take. Online article. Retrieved from www.ftw.usatoday.com.

Mather V 2017. Jameis Winston Is Having a Great Season; the Bucs Are Not. Online article. Retrieved from www.nytimes.com.

Mattimore R 2018. Presidential Feuds With the Media Are Nothing New. Online article. Retrieved from www.history.com.

Mays R 2018. The Shameful Enabling of Jameis Winston. Online article. Retrieved from www.theringer.com.

McElroy W 2015. Is 'the Hunting Ground' documentary or propaganda? Online article. Retrieved from www.thehill.com.

McGarry T 2013. Jameis Winston is chasing the Heisman trophy. Online article. Retrieved from www.ftw.usatoday.com.

McGovern T 2018. Jameis Winston Dramatically Apologizes To Uber He Allegedly Groped 2 Years Ago & Blames Alcohol. Online article. Retrieved from www.hollywoodlife.com.

McIntyre J and Lisk J 2014. The List of Successful Starting NFL QBs at Age 21 is Very Short, and Johnny Manziel is 21. Online article. Retrieved from www.al.com.

McKenna H 2018. Jameis Winston's Suspension Leaves Us With One Conclusion: He's a Coward. Online article. Retrieved from www.thebiglead.com.

McKenna H 2018. Winston, Draft an Elite QB High in 2019. Online article. Retrieved from www.thebiglead.com.

McManus T 2017. Eagles LB Nigel Bradham gets deferred prosecution deal. Online article. Retrieved from www.espn.com.

McQuade D 2017. Jameis Winston Melts Down After Panthers Comeback. Online article. Retrieved from www.deadspin.com.

Merron J n.d. Biggest sports gambling scandals. Online article. Retrieved from www.espn.com.

Miklasz B 2009. Warner's ending with Rams was abrupt He came out of nowhere in 1999 season to lead team to a Super Bowl title Several things appeared to strain his relationship with coach Mike Martz. Online article. Retrieved from www.stltoday.com.

Miller D n.d. Report: Newton Faced Possible Expulsion Upon Leaving Florida. Online article. Retrieved from www.nationalfootballpost.com.

Miller M 2015. NFL Draft Big Boards 2015: Matt Miller's Final Rankings. Online article. Retrieved from www.bleacherreport.com.

Miller M 2018. 2019 NFL Mock Draft: Matt Miller's Latest Picks Entering Final Month of Season. Online article. Retrieved from www.bleacherreport.com.

MLB Advanced Media, LP 2018. No-hit games in losing effort. Online article. Retrieved from www.mlb.mlb.com.

Modisette K 2018. Jameis Winston's suspension inconsistent with Ezekiel Elliott's ban. Online article. Retrieved from www.cowboyswire.usatoday.com.

Montini EJ 2014. Did media give Fitz a bye on '08 domestic disturbance? Online article. Retrieved from www.azcentral.com.

Mott B 2016. Jameis Winston's inspiring letter to teammates guides Bucs to big win. Online article. Retrieved from www.bucswire.usatoday.com.

Muldowney C 2013. Jameis Winston's Pop Warner Highlights Will Make You Drool. Online article. Retrieved from www.rantsports.com.

Myerberg P 2014. AJ McCarron's mom apologizes for tweet deriding Jameis Winston. Online article. Retrieved from www.ftw.usatoday.com.

Nathan A 2016. NFL Rookie of the Year 2015-16: Award Winners, Voting Results, Twitter Reaction. Online article. Retrieved from www.bleacherreport.com.

National Football League 2013. Finalists named for Walter Payton NFL Man of the Year Award. Online article. Retrieved from www.nfl.com.

Nesbitt A 2019. NFL fans had fun ripping the Miami Dolphins for signing Ryan Fitzpatrick. Online article. Retrieved from www.ftw.usatoday.com.

Newberg J 2011. Jameis Winston picks Noles over Tide. Online article. Retrieved from www.espn.com.

NFL.com 2015. NFL releases statement on Patriots' violations. Online article. Retrieved from www.nfl.com.

NFL Communications n.d. BUCCANEERS' JAMEIS WINSTON SUSPENDED FOR FIRST THREE REGULAR-SEASON GAMES FOR VIOLATION OF NFL PERSONAL CONDUCT POLICY. Online article. Retrieved from www.nflcommunications.com.

NFL Enterprises, LLC. 2019. PERSONAL CONDUCT POLICY League Policies for Players 2016. Online article. Retrieved from www.static.nfl.com.

Nohe P 2015. NFL Combine Review: QB Jameis Wiinston. Online article. Retrieved from www.chopchat.com.

Norris M 2016. Jameis Winston Replaces Tom Brady at 2016 NFL Pro Bowl. Online article. Retrieved from www.bleacherreport.com.

O'Connor I 2015. Why No.1 pick Jameis Winston is monumental risk for Buccaneers. Online article. Retrieved from www.espn.com.

Olojede Z 2019. Baker Mayfield Says Colin Cowherd 'Needs to be put in His Place,' Defends Odell Beckham Jr. Online article. Retrieved from www.complex.com.

Orr C 2017. DeSean Jackson agrees to three-year deal with Bucs. Online article. Retrieved from www.nfl.com.

Orr C 2018. QB Stock Watch: Will Jameis Winston Be on the Tampa Bay Buccaneers in 2019? Online article. Retrieved from www.si.com.

Over The Cap 2019. Player – Jameis Winston. Online article. Retrieved from www.overthecap.com.

Pasatieri M n,d. Super Bowl Bound – A Prediction of Jameis Winston's Career. Online article. Retrieved from www.nflpam.com.

Patsko S 2018. How many Pro Football Hall of Famers are like Joe Thomas and never played a playoff game? Online article. Retrieved from www.cleveland.com.

Pelissero T, Axon R and Corbett J 2015. Jameis Winston: The personal insiders' view of his past, present, future. Online article. Retrieved from www.usatoday.com.

Petchesky B 2018. Jameis Winston Suspended Three Games For Groping Uber Driver. Online article. Retrieved from www.deadspin.com.

Philipse S 2017. Jameis Winston sets league and team records in week 17. Online article. Retrieved from www.bucsnation.com.

Philipse S 2016. Jameis Winston snubbed for Offensive Rookie of the Year. Online article. Retrieved from www.bucsnation.com.

Philipse S 2015. Mel Kiper, Todd McShay call Jameis Winston best on-field prospect. Online article. Retrieved from www.bucsnation.com.

Philipse S 2015. Why no one is talking about the Buccaneers tanking for Jameis Winston. Online article. Retrieved from www.nucsnation.com.

Pierre N 2014. Florida State admin has "no further comment" on Jameis Winston's full-game suspension. Online article. Retrieved from www.tallahassee.com.

Pompei D 2016. The Dream Team That Wasn't: A Cautionary Tale for Free Agency. Online article. Retrieved from www.bleacherreport.com.

PROFOOTBALLDOC 2017. UPDATE: Jameis Winston showing signs of rotator cuff injury. Online article. Retrieved from www.sandiegouniontribune.com.

PRO FOOTBALL HALL OF FAME 2019. Measurement Monday Class of 2019. Online article. Retrieved from www.profootballhofl.com.

Pro Football Writers of America 2019. Rams' Gurley PFWA Rookie/Offensive Rookie of the Year, Chiefs' Peters Defensive Rookie of the Year; 2015 All-Rookie Team named. Online article. Retrieved from www.profootballwriters.org.

Radcliffe JR 2018. Remembering the strange moment the Packers traded Brett Favre, 10 years ago today. Online article. Retrieved from www.usatoday.com.

Radcliffe J R 2019. National writers and pundits react to the Packers hiring Matt LaFleur as head coach. Online article. Retrieved from www.jsonline.com.

Rauf B 2017. These Are The 6 NFL Teams That Will Fire Their Coach This Season. Online article. Retrieved from www.chatsports.com.

Reed J 2018. JAMEIS WINSTON APOLOGY RINGS HOLLOW. Online article. Retrieved from www.sportsnaut.com.

Reed S 2017. Bucs QB Jameis Winston joins Dan Marino in elite company. Online article. Retrieved from www.chicagotribune.com.

Reedy J 2016. Jameis Winston, rape accuser settle lawsuit. Online article. Retrieved from www.orlandosentinel.com.

Reimer A 2018. Absurdity of Brady's Deflategate ban once again exposed by Jameis Winston's 3-game suspension for alleged sexual assault. Online article. Retrieved from www.weei.radio.com.

Reimer A 2015. Bucs rookie LB Kwon Alexander suspended 4 games for PED violation. Online article. Retrieved from www.sbnation.com.

Reineking J 2018. Jets rookie QB Sam Darnold throws pick-six on first pass in NFL debut vs. Lions. Online article. Retrieved from www.usatoday.com.

Renner M 2017. Bad luck is plaguing Marcus Mariota. Poor play is ruining Jameis Winston. Online article. Retrieved from www.washingtonpost.com.

Reyes L 2016. Eagles' Nigel Bradham arrested after alleged battery of hotel worker. Online article. Retrieved from www.usatoday.com.

Reyes L 2016. In Jameis Winston, Buccaneers see limitless potential. Online article. Retrieved from www.usatoday.com.

Reynolds S 2019. SR's Fab 5: Bucs QB Winston A Perfect Fit For Arians' Offense. Online article. Retrieved from www.pewterreport.com.

Rodgers M 2017. Jameis Winston delivers wrong message to kids.Online article. Retrieved from www.usatoday.com.

Rohan T 2013. Winston Solidifies Stardom by Overwhelming Clemson. Online article. Retrieved from www.nytimes.com.

Roling C 2016. Jameis Winston escapes defenders, completes bomb to Mike Evans (video). Online article with video. Retrieved from www.thesportsdaily.com.

Rollins K 2018. Friend Says Jameis Winston Was Alone With Uber Driver on Night of Alleged Sexual Abuse. Online article. Retrieved from www.si.com.

Rose B 2014. Keyshawn Johnson arrested in Calif. for domestic violence, per report. Online article. Retrieved from www.si.com.

Rosvoglou C 2018. Jameis Winston Admits Guilt to Uber Groping Incident in New Statement. Online article. Retrieved from www.12up.com.

RotoWire Staff 2018. Buccaneers' Jameis Winston: Named as Week 12 starter. Online article. Retrieved from www.cbssports.com.

Ruiz S 2017. Jameis Winston throws furious tantrum at ref after losing fumble late in loss. Online article. Retrieved from www.ftw.usatoday.com.

Salem D 2019. NFL Offseason 2019: Ranking the 8 coaching vacancies worst to first. Online article. Retrieved from www.nflspinzone.com.

Scarfo N 2019. 2019 NFL Draft: Devin White measures up to an NFL legend. Online article. Retrieved from www.nflmocks.com.

Schlabach M 2013. FSU's Jameis Winston not charged. Online article. Retrieved from www.espn.com.

Schlabach M 2014. Winston hearing pushed to Dec. 1. Online article. Retrieved from www.espn.com.

Schofield M 2015. Getting To Know Jameis Winston. Online article. Retrieved from www.insidethepylon.com.

Schow A 2016. Ten years after Duke Lacrosse rape hoax, media has learned nothing. Online article. Retrieved from www.washingtonexaminer.com.

Schow A 2015. 'The Hunting Ground' crew caught editing Wikipedia to make facts conform to film. Online article. Retrieved from www.washingtonexaminer.com.

Sessler M 2018. Buccaneers' Jameis Winston suspended three games. Online article. Retrieved from www.nfl.com.

Shammas M 2015. Harvard Law Professors Defend Law Student Brandon Winston, Denouncing His Portrayal in "The Hunting Ground". Online article. Retrieved from variety.com.

Short A 2015. 6 Famous People With Shocking Criminal Backgrounds. Online article. Retrieved from www.cracked.com.

Silagyi K 2017. Jameis Winston is injured, but Bills know Bucs' QB presents huge challenge. Online article. Retrieved from www.billswire.usatoday.com.

Silverman R 2016. Peyton Manning's Forgotten Sex Scandal. Online article. Retrieved from www.thedailybeast.com.

The SI Staff 2017. NFL Predictions: Playoff Picks, Super Bowl LII Winner, Awards and More. Online article. Retrieved from www.si.com.

SI Wire 2015. Florida State quarterback Jameis Winston to enter NFL draft. Online article. Retrieved from www.si.com.

Skybox 360 Media, LLC. 2019. Montana drives 49ers past Bengals in Super Bowl XXIII. Online article. Retrieved from www.49erswebzone.com.

Smartt N 2017. Sexual Harassment In The Workplace In A #MeToo World. Online article. Retrieved from www.forbes.com.

Smith M D 2015. Jimbo doesn't understand why there is a question about Jameis. Online article. Retrieved from www.profootballtalk.nbcsports.com.

Smith M D 2018. NFL shows once again that its six-game suspension policy is meaningless. Online article. Retrieved from www.profootballtalk.nbcsports.com.

Smith M D 2018. Ryan Fitzpatrick has been outplaying Jameis Winston for two years. Online article. Retrieved from www.profootballtalk.nbcsports.com.

Soave R 2015. How the Hunting Ground Spreads Myths About Campus Rape. Online article. Retrieved from www.reason.com.

Soignier T 2013. Eagles tackle Jason Peters arrested for drag racing, resisting by flight. Online article. Retrieved from www.usatoday.com.

Solomon J 2013. Jameis Winston: Cocky or competitive? "He doesn't understand failure". Online article. Retrieved from www.al.com.

Somers K 2016. Buccaneers' Jameis Winston Loves Bruce Arians – and Vice Versa. Online article. Retrieved from www.azcentral.com.

Somers K 2017. Kurt Warner voted into Pro Football Hall of Fame. Online article. Retrieved from www.azcentral.com.

Sports 1 Marketing, n.d. Top NFL Sports Agents Create a Legacy. Online article. Retrieved from www.sports1marketing.com.

Sports Reference, LLC. 2019. 2017 NFL Top 100. Online article. Retrieved from www.pro-football-reference.com.

The Sports Xchange 2019. GM Licht says Winston is Bucs' quarterback. Online article. Retrieved from www.upi.com.

Srinivasan A 2018. Fitzpatrick becomes 1st player with 3 straight games of over 400 passing yards. Online article. Retrieved from www.msn.com.

Steigerwald J 2018. Winston got off easy with three-game suspension. Online article. Retrieved from www.indianagazette.com.

Stern R 2009. Larry Fitzgerald's Alleged Domestic Abuse Buried Deep in Pages of *Arizona Republic*. Online article. Retrieved from www.phoenixnewtimes.com.

Stites A 2017. Jameis Winston had a meltdown on the sideline after a game-clinching fumble. Online article. Retrieved from www.sbnation.com.

Stites A 2018. How the hell did Jameis Winston not get a 6-game suspension? Online article. Retrieved from www.sbnation.com.

Streeter K 2015. JAMEIS WINSTON IS ON THE CLOCK. Online article. Retrieved from www.espn.com.

Stroud R 2015. Bucs' Jameis Winston off the field: So far, so very good. Online article. Retrieved from www.tampabay.com.

Stroud R 2017. Jameis Winston restores the Bucs faith, then lobbies for the return of head coach Dirk Koetter. Online article. Retrieved from www.tampabay.com.

Stroud R 2019. As Jameis Winston turns 25, here's how he compares to other NFL quarterbacks at that age. Online article. Retrieved from www.tampabay.com.

Student Sports LLC 2019. Elite 11 History. Online article. Retrieved from www.elite11.com.

TAMPA BAY BUCCANEERS n.d. Jameis Winston turns 24 with Records in Hand. Online article. Retrieved from www.buccaneers.com.

Tarcho J 2017. Many Coming To Jameis Winston's Defense – Including His Mother. Online article. Retrieved from www.thepewterplank.com.

Taylor Jr. S 2015. A Smoking-Gun E-mail Exposes the Bias of The Hunting Ground. Online article. Retrieved from www.nationalreview.com.

Taylor Jr. S 2015. The Cinematic Railroading of Jameis Winston. Online article. Retrieved from www.nationalreview.com.

Teope H 2018. Jameis Winston: Benching is 'humbling,' minor setback. Online article. Retrieved from www.nfl.com.

Teope H 2018. Jameis Winston expected to be suspended by NFL. Online article. Retrieved from www.nfl.com.

Teope H 2018. Jameis Winston 'fighting' for Koetter's return in 2019. Online article. Retrieved from www.nfl.com.

Teope H 2019. Cardinals trade QB Josh Rosen to Dolphins for picks. Online article. Retrieved from www.nfl.com.

The Deadline Team 2014. ESPN Slaps Max Kellerman With Suspension After He Admits On-Air To Striking Woman. Online article. Retrieved from www.deadline.com.

The Football Database, LLC. 2019. 2017 NFL 300-Yard Passing Games. Online article. Retrieved from www.pro-football-reference.com.

Thomson Reuters 2019. Arizona Revised Statutes Title 13. Criminal Code § 13-1406. Sexual assault; classification; increased punishment. Online article. Retrieved from www.codes.findlaw.com.

Thornton J 2018. All of Roger Goodell's 'Transparency' Talk Doesn't Keep Him from Covering Up What Jameis Winston Did. Online article. Retrieved from www.barstoolsports.com.

T.I. Gotham Inc. 2019. Best Rookie Quarterback Seasons in NFL History. Online article. Retrieved from www.si.com.

Tracy M 2014. Jameis Winston Suspended for First Half of Florida State-Clemson Game. Online article. Retrieved from www.nytimes.com.

Trapasso P 2018. 2019 NFL Mock Draft: Buccaneers replace Jameis Winston with a turnover-averse quarterback. Online article. Retrieved from www.cbssports.com.

Travis C 2018. ESPN Cuts Ties with Jemele Hill, Demotes Michelle Beadle. Online article. Retrieved from www.outkickthecoverage.com.

USA TODAY 2019. NFL PLAYER ARRESTS. Online article. Retrieved from www.usatoday.com.

USA Today Sports 2017. Ronald Darby on groping accusations against Jameis Winston: 'Just not true'. Online article. Retrieved from www.usatoday.com.

USA Today Sports Digital Properties 2019. Aaron Rodgers' 2011 season ranked among best ever from NFL QB. Online article. Retrieved from www.packerswire.usatoday.com.

Van Denburg H 2010. Brett Favre 'We Want Somme Pussy' video surfaces. Online article. Retrieved from www.citypages.com.

Variety Media, LLC 2015. Variety Critics Pick Their Least Favorite Films of 2015 – Ella Taylor. Online article. Retrieved from www.variety.com.

Victory D 2019. Tampa Bay QB Jameis Winston kicks off Dream Forever Week with shopping spree for area youth. Online article. Retrieved from www.al.com.

Wagner-McGough S 2017. Jameis Winston loses his mind after fumble that sealed the Buccaneers' loss. Online article. Retrieved from www.cbssports.com.

Wagner-McGough 2019. Raiders GM Mike Mayock on Derek Carr's proposal to fight ESPN host: 'I like the attitude'. Online article. Retrieved from www.cbssports.com.

Ward R 2014. Lakers News: Kobe Bryant Reveals Origin of 'Black Mamba' Nickname. Online article. Retrieved from www.lakersnation.com

Wesseling C 2014. Oakland Raiders' Matt Schaub broken beyond repair? Online article. Retrieved from www.nfl.com.

Wikia, Inc. 2019. Val-Zod (Earth 2). Online article. Retrieved from www.dc.fandom.com.

Williams C 2018. Uber driver sues Jameis Winston. Online article. Retrieved from www.profootballtalk.nbcsports.com.

Williams N 2015. 2015 NFL Draft: Jameis Winston's rots helped shape him for the storms. Online article. Retrieved from www.al.com.

Wilson D 2014. Winston May be Idiot, but He's Smarter Than You. Online article. Retrieved from www.uatrav.com.

Wilson M and Kaplan P 2017. Peyton Manning accuser Jamie Naughright appears on 'Inside Edition'. Online article. Retrieved from www.knoxnews.com.

Wilson R 2015. Jimbo Fisher: Jameis Winston 'is as smart as anybody I've been around'. Online article. Retrieved from www.cbssports.com.

Wilson R 2015. Report: Jimbo Fisher said EJ Manuel didn't have tools to be NFL starter. Online article. Retrieved from www.cbssports.com.

Wiltfong S 2011. Elite 11: Winston got in early. Online article. Retrieved from www.247sorts.com.

Wong J 2018. #MeToo movement reckons with alleged hypocrisy after Asia Argento accused of sexual abuse. Online article. Retrieved from www.cbc.ca.

Wonderlic Test Sample 2019. NFL Wonderlic Scores. Online article. Retrieved from www.wonderlictestsample.com.

Wonderlic Test Sample 2019. Wonderlic Test Scoring – Wonderlic Score by Job Title. Online article. Retrieved from www.wonderlictestsample.com.

Yarcho J 2017. Many Coming To Jameis Winston's Defense – Including His Mother. Online article. Retrieved from www.thepewterplank.com.

Yoffe E 2015. The Hunting Ground: The failures of a new documentary about rape on college campuses. Online article. Retrieved from www.slate.com.

Young S M 2018. Dirk Koetter announces Jameis Winston will start Buccaneers' next game. Online article. Retrieved from www.sports.yahoo.com.

Zierlein L 2015. Prospects – Jameis Winston. Online article. Retrieved from www.nfl.com.

Books

The Holy Bible, King James Version 1769. Online Publishing, Inc. The power Biblecd Program

Kaczynski T 1995. Industrial Society and Its Future. Online article. Retrieved from www.theanarchistlibrary.org.

Lewis CS 1954. Mere Christianity: A Revised and Amplified Edition, with a New Introduction, of the Three Books, Broadcast Talks, Christian Behaviour, and Beyond Personality. London, UK: The Macmillan Company

Lombardi M 2004. Gridiron Genius: A Master Class in Winning Championships and Building Dynasties in the NFL. New York, NY, USA: Crown Archetype

Travis C 2018. Republicans Buy Sneakers Too: How the Left Is Ruining Sports with Politics. New York, NY, USA: Broadside Books

Dictionary

Dictionary.com, LLC 2019. Entry for 'Phenom'. *Dictionary.com*. Online article. Retrieved from www.dictionary.com.

Florida State Seminoles Individual Game Online Pages – Sorted by Game Date

Sports Reference, LLC. 2019. Florida State at Pitt Box Score, September 2, 2013. Online article. Retrieved from www.sports-reference.com.

Sports Reference, LLC. 2019. Nevada at Florida State Box Score, September 14, 2013. Online article. Retrieved from www.sports-reference.com.

Sports Reference, LLC. 2019. Bethune-Cookman at Florida State Box Score, September 21, 2013. Online article. Retrieved from www.sports-reference.com.

Sports Reference, LLC. 2019. Florida State at Boston College Box Score, September 28, 2013. Online article. Retrieved from www.sports-reference.com.

Sports Reference, LLC. 2019. Maryland at Florida State Box Score, October 5, 2013. Online article. Retrieved from www.sports-reference.com.

Sports Reference, LLC. 2019. Florida State at Clemson Box Score, October 19, 2013. Online article. Retrieved from www.sports-reference.com.

Sports Reference, LLC. 2019. North Carolina State at Florida State Box Score, October 26, 2013. Online article. Retrieved from www.sports-reference.com.

Sports Reference, LLC. 2019. Miami (FL) at Florida State Box Score, November 2, 2013. Online article. Retrieved from www.sports-reference.com.

Sports Reference, LLC. 2019. Florida State at Wake Forest Box Score, November 9, 2013. Online article. Retrieved from www.sports-reference.com.

Sports Reference, LLC. 2019. Syracuse at Florida State Box Score, November 16, 2013. Online article. Retrieved from www.sports-reference.com.

Sports Reference, LLC. 2019. Idaho at Florida State Box Score, November 23, 2013. Online article. Retrieved from www.sports-reference.com.

Sports Reference, LLC. 2019. Florida State at Florida Box Score, November 30, 2013. Online article. Retrieved from www.sports-reference.com.

Sports Reference, LLC. 2019. Duke vs Florida State Box Score, December 7, 2013. Online article. Retrieved from www.sports-reference.com.

ESPN Enterprises, Inc. 2019. VIZIO BCS NATIONAL CHAMPIONSHIP - Gamecast. Online article. Retrieved from www.espn.com.

ESPN Enterprises, Inc. 2019. VIZIO BCS NATIONAL CHAMPIONSHIP – Play-by-Play. Online article. Retrieved from www.espn.com.

Heisman Trophy Voting – Sorted by Year

Sports Reference, LLC 2019. 1992 Heisman Trophy Voting. Online article. Retrieved from www.sports-reference.com.

Sports Reference, LLC 2019. 1993 Heisman Trophy Voting. Online article. Retrieved from www.sports-reference.com.

Sports Reference, LLC 2019. 1995 Heisman Trophy Voting. Online article. Retrieved from www.sports-reference.com.

Sports Reference, LLC 2019. 1996 Heisman Trophy Voting. Online article. Retrieved from www.sports-reference.com.

Sports Reference, LLC 2019. 2003 Heisman Trophy Voting. Online article. Retrieved from www.sports-reference.com.

Sports Reference, LLC 2019. 2004 Heisman Trophy Voting. Online article. Retrieved from www.sports-reference.com.

Sports Reference, LLC 2019. 2005 Heisman Trophy Voting. Online article. Retrieved from www.sports-reference.com.

Sports Reference, LLC 2019. 2007 Heisman Trophy Voting. Online article. Retrieved from www.sports-reference.com.

Sports Reference, LLC 2019. 2008 Heisman Trophy Voting. Online article. Retrieved from www.sports-reference.com.

Sports Reference, LLC 2019. 2009 Heisman Trophy Voting. Online article. Retrieved from www.sports-reference.com.

Sports Reference, LLC 2019. 2013 Heisman Trophy Voting. Online article. Retrieved from www.sports-reference.com.

Sports Reference, LLC 2019. 2014 Heisman Trophy Voting. Online article. Retrieved from www.sports-reference.com.

Jameis Winston's Dream Forever Foundation Website Pages

JAMEIS WINSTON'S DREAM FOREVER FOUNDATION 2019. Page - About. Online article. Retrieved from www.jameiswinston3.org.

JAMEIS WINSTON'S DREAM FOREVER FOUNDATION 2019. Page - Programs. Online article. Retrieved from www.jameiswinston3.org.

JAMEIS WINSTON'S DREAM FOREVER FOUNDATION 2019. Page - News. Online article. Retrieved from www.jameiswinston3.org.

Miscellaneous NCAA Team Online Pages – Sorted by Year

Sports Reference, LLC 2019. 2005 USC Trojans Stats. Online article. Retrieved from www.sports-reference.com.

Sports Reference, LLC 2019. 2006 Florida Gators Stats. Online article. Retrieved from www.sports-reference.com.

Sports Reference, LLC 2019. 2007 Florida Gators Stats. Online article. Retrieved from www.sports-reference.com.

Sports Reference, LLC. 2019. 2013 Florida State Seminoles Schedule and Results. Online article. Retrieved from www.sports-reference.com.

Miscellaneous NFL Individual Game Online Pages – Sorted by Date

Sports Reference, LLC. 2019. Chicago Bears at Minnesota Vikings – September 17th, 1961. Online article. Retrieved from www.pro-football-reference.com.

Sports Reference, LLC. 2019. Seattle Seahawks at New England Patriots – September 19th, 1993. Online article. Retrieved from www.pro-football-reference.com.

Sports Reference, LLC. 2019. Super Bowl XL - Seattle Seahawks vs. Pittsburgh Steelers - February 5th, 2006. Online article. Retrieved from www.pro-football-reference.com.

ESPN Enterprises, Inc. 2019. Cleveland Browns at Detroit Lions, November 22nd, 2009 – Box Score. Online article. Retrieved from www.espn.com.

Sports Reference, LLC. 2019. Detroit Lions at Green Bay Packers – January 1st, 2012. Online article. Retrieved from www.pro-football-reference.com,

Sports Reference, LLC. 2019. Wild Card – Detroit Lions at Seattle Seahawks – January 7th, 2017. Online article. Retrieved from www.pro-football-reference.com.

ESPN Enterprises, Inc. 2019. Kansas City Chiefs at Houston Texans, October 8th, 2017 – Box Score. Online article. Retrieved from www.espn.com.

Sports Reference, LLC. 2019. Kansas City Chiefs at Houston Texans – October 8th, 2017. Online article. Retrieved from www.pro-football-reference.com.

Sports Reference, LLC. 2019. Super Bowl LII – Philadelphia Eagles vs. New England Patriots – February 4th, 2018. Online article. Retrieved from www.pro-football-reference.com.

Sports Reference, LLC. 2019. Pittsburgh Steelers at Cleveland Browns – September 9th, 2018. Online article. Retrieved from www.pro-football-reference.com.

Miscellaneous Statistics Online Pages

6th Ring. NFL QB playoff records, stats. Online article. Retrieved from www.6thring.com.

ESPN Internet Ventures 2019. NFL Schedule – 2018 – Week 7. Online article. Retrieved from www.espn.com.

ESPN Internet Ventures 2019. NFL History – Passing Yardage Leaders. Online article. Retrieved from www.espn.com.

Kacsmar S 2018. 2017 Passing Plus-Minus. Online article. Retrieved from www.footballoutsiders.com.

NFL Enterprises LLC 2019. Next Gen Stats – Glossary. Online article. Retrieved from www.nextgenstats.nfl.com.

NFL Enterprises LLC 2019. Next Gen Stats – Passing Leaders – 2016 – Regular Season. Online article. Retrieved from www.nextgenstats.nfl.com.

NFL Enterprises LLC 2019. Next Gen Stats – Passing Leaders – 2017 – Regular Season. Online article. Retrieved from www.nextgenstats.nfl.com.

NFL Enterprises LLC 2019. Next Gen Stats – Passing Leaders – 2018 – Regular Season. Online article. Retrieved from www.nextgenstats.nfl.com.

Sports Reference, LLC. 2019. 2010 NFL Standings & Team Stats. Online article. Retrieved from www.pro-football-reference.com.

Sports Reference, LLC. 2019. 2012 NFL Rushing. Online article. Retrieved from www.pro-football-reference.com.

Sports Reference, LLC. 2019. 2016 NFL Standings & Team Stats – Rushing Offense. Online article. Retrieved from www.pro-football-reference.com.

Sports Reference, LLC. 2019. NFL Fumbles Career Leaders. Online article. Retrieved from www.pro-football-reference.com.

Sports Reference, LLC 2019. Passing Efficiency Rating Single Season Leaders and Records. Online article. Retrieved from www.sports-reference.com.

Sports Reference, LLC. 2019. NFL Passes Intercepted Career Leaders. Online article. Retrieved from www.pro-football-reference.com.

Sports Reference, LLC. 2019. NFL Passes Intercepted Single Game Leaders. Online article. Retrieved from www.pro-football-reference.com.

Sports Reference, LLC. 2019. NFL Passes Intercepted Single-Season Leaders. Online article. Retrieved from www.pro-football-reference.com.

The Football Database, LLC. 2019. NFL Regular Season Quarterback Win/Loss Records. Online article. Retrieved from www.pro-football-reference.com.

NCAA Award Winner Lists

Sports Reference, LLC 2019. ACC Offensive Player of the Year Winners. Online article. Retrieved from www.sports-reference.com.

Sports Reference, LLC 2019. ACC Player of the Year Winners. Online article. Retrieved from www.sports-reference.com.

Sports Reference, LLC 2019. AP Player of the Year Award Winners. Online article. Retrieved from www.sports-reference.com.

Sports Reference, LLC 2019. Consensus All-America Teams (2010-2018). Online article. Retrieved from www.sports-reference.com.

Sports Reference, LLC 2019. Davey O'Brien Award Winners. Online article. Retrieved from www.sports-reference.com.

Sports Reference, LLC 2019. Manning Award Winners. Online article. Retrieved from www.sports-reference.com.

Sports Reference, LLC 2019. Walter Camp Player of the Year Award Winners. Online article. Retrieved from www.sports-reference.com.

NCAA Individual Player Online Pages

Sports Reference, LLC 2019. Player – Marcus Mariota. Online article. Retrieved from www.sports-reference.com.

Sports Reference, LLC 2019. Player – Charlie Ward. Online article. Retrieved from www.sports-reference.com.

Sports Reference, LLC 2019. Player – Jameis Winston. Online article. Retrieved from www.sports-reference.com.

Sports Reference, LLC 2019. Player – Danny Wuerffel. Online article. Retrieved from www.sports-reference.com.

NFL / AFL Seasonal Passing Statistics – Sorted by Year

Sports Reference, LLC. 2019. 1961 NFL Passing. Online article. Retrieved from www.pro-football-reference.com.

Sports Reference, LLC. 2019. 1967 NFL Passing. Online article. Retrieved from www.pro-football-reference.com.

Sports Reference, LLC. 2019. 1968 AFL Passing. Online article. Retrieved from www.pro-football-reference.com.

Sports Reference, LLC. 2019. 1968 NFL Passing. Online article. Retrieved from www.pro-football-reference.com.

Sports Reference, LLC. 2019. 1969 NFL Passing. Online article. Retrieved from www.pro-football-reference.com.

Sports Reference, LLC. 2019. 1970 NFL Passing. Online article. Retrieved from www.pro-football-reference.com.

Sports Reference, LLC. 2019. 1971 NFL Passing. Online article. Retrieved from www.pro-football-reference.com.

Sports Reference, LLC. 2019. 1972 NFL Passing. Online article. Retrieved from www.pro-football-reference.com.

Sports Reference, LLC. 2019. 1973 NFL Passing. Online article. Retrieved from www.pro-football-reference.com.

Sports Reference, LLC. 2019. 1974 NFL Passing. Online article. Retrieved from www.pro-football-reference.com.

Sports Reference, LLC. 2019. 1975 NFL Passing. Online article. Retrieved from www.pro-football-reference.com.

Sports Reference, LLC. 2019. 1976 NFL Passing. Online article. Retrieved from www.pro-football-reference.com.

Sports Reference, LLC. 2019. 1979 NFL Passing. Online article. Retrieved from www.pro-football-reference.com.

Sports Reference, LLC. 2019. 1980 NFL Passing. Online article. Retrieved from www.pro-football-reference.com.

Sports Reference, LLC. 2019. 1981 NFL Passing. Online article. Retrieved from www.pro-football-reference.com.

Sports Reference, LLC. 2019. 1982 NFL Passing. Online article. Retrieved from www.pro-football-reference.com.

Sports Reference, LLC. 2019. 1983 NFL Passing. Online article. Retrieved from www.pro-football-reference.com.

Sports Reference, LLC. 2019. 1984 NFL Passing. Online article. Retrieved from www.pro-football-reference.com.

Sports Reference, LLC. 2019. 1985 NFL Passing. Online article. Retrieved from www.pro-football-reference.com.

Sports Reference, LLC. 2019. 1986 NFL Passing. Online article. Retrieved from www.pro-football-reference.com.

Sports Reference, LLC. 2019. 1987 NFL Passing. Online article. Retrieved from www.pro-football-reference.com.

Sports Reference, LLC. 2019. 1988 NFL Passing. Online article. Retrieved from www.pro-football-reference.com.

Sports Reference, LLC. 2019. 1989 NFL Passing. Online article. Retrieved from www.pro-football-reference.com.

Sports Reference, LLC. 2019. 1990 NFL Passing. Online article. Retrieved from www.pro-football-reference.com.

Sports Reference, LLC. 2019. 1991 NFL Passing. Online article. Retrieved from www.pro-football-reference.com.

Sports Reference, LLC. 2019. 1992 NFL Passing. Online article. Retrieved from www.pro-football-reference.com.

Sports Reference, LLC. 2019. 1993 NFL Passing. Online article. Retrieved from www.pro-football-reference.com.

Sports Reference, LLC. 2019. 1994 NFL Passing. Online article. Retrieved from www.pro-football-reference.com.

Sports Reference, LLC. 2019. 1998 NFL Passing. Online article. Retrieved from www.pro-football-reference.com.

Sports Reference, LLC. 2019. 1999 NFL Passing. Online article. Retrieved from www.pro-football-reference.com.

Sports Reference, LLC. 2019. 2000 NFL Passing. Online article. Retrieved from www.pro-football-reference.com.

Sports Reference, LLC. 2019. 2001 NFL Passing. Online article. Retrieved from www.pro-football-reference.com.

Sports Reference, LLC. 2019. 2002 NFL Passing. Online article. Retrieved from www.pro-football-reference.com.

Sports Reference, LLC. 2019. 2003 NFL Passing. Online article. Retrieved from www.pro-football-reference.com.

Sports Reference, LLC. 2019. 2004 NFL Passing. Online article. Retrieved from www.pro-football-reference.com.

Sports Reference, LLC. 2019. 2005 NFL Passing. Online article. Retrieved from www.pro-football-reference.com.

Sports Reference, LLC. 2019. 2006 NFL Passing. Online article. Retrieved from www.pro-football-reference.com.

Sports Reference, LLC. 2019. 2007 NFL Passing. Online article. Retrieved from www.pro-football-reference.com.

Sports Reference, LLC. 2019. 2008 NFL Passing. Online article. Retrieved from www.pro-football-reference.com.

Sports Reference, LLC. 2019. 2009 NFL Passing. Online article. Retrieved from www.pro-football-reference.com.

Sports Reference, LLC. 2019. 2012 NFL Passing. Online article. Retrieved from www.pro-football-reference.com.

Sports Reference, LLC. 2019. 2015 NFL Passing. Online article. Retrieved from www.pro-football-reference.com.

Sports Reference, LLC. 2019. 2016 NFL Passing. Online article. Retrieved from www.pro-football-reference.com.

Sports Reference, LLC. 2019. 2017 NFL Passing. Online article. Retrieved from www.pro-football-reference.com.

Sports Reference, LLC. 2019. 2018 NFL Passing. Online article. Retrieved from www.pro-football-reference.com.

NFL Individual Player Online Pages

ESPN Enterprises, Inc. 2019. NFL – Player – Cam Newton. Online article. Retrieved from www.espn.com.

ESPN Enterprises, Inc. 2019. NFL – Player – Russell Wilson. Online article. Retrieved from www.espn.com.

PRO FOOTBALL HALL OF FAME 2019. Players – Paul Hornung. Online article. Retrieved from www.profootballhof.com.

Sports Reference, LLC. 2019. Player – Troy Aikman. Online article. Retrieved from www.pro-football-reference.com.

Sports Reference, LLC. 2019. Player – Steve Bartkowski. Online article. Retrieved from www.pro-football-reference.com.

Sports Reference, LLC. 2019. Player – Drew Bledsoe. Online article. Retrieved from www.pro-football-reference.com.

Sports Reference, LLC. 2019. Player – Sam Bradford. Online article. Retrieved from www.pro-football-reference.com.

Sports Reference, LLC. 2019. Player – Terry Bradshaw. Online article. Retrieved from www.pro-football-reference.com.

Sports Reference, LLC. 2019. Player – Tom Brady. Online article. Retrieved from www.pro-football-reference.com.

Sports Reference, LLC 2019. Player – Marc Bulger. Online article. Retrieved from www.pro-football-reference.com.

Sports Reference, LLC. 2019. Player – Drew Brees. Online article. Retrieved from www.pro-football-reference.com.

Sports Reference, LLC. 2019. Player – David Carr. Online article. Retrieved from www.pro-football-reference.com.

Sports Reference, LLC. 2019. Player – Tim Couch. Online article. Retrieved from www.pro-football-reference.com.

Sports Reference, LLC. 2019. Player – John Elway. Online article. Retrieved from www.pro-football-reference.com.

Sports Reference, LLC. 2019. Player – Mike Evans. Online article. Retrieved from www.pro-football-reference.com.

Sports Reference, LLC. 2019. Player – Brett Favre. Online article. Retrieved from www.pro-football-reference.com.

Sports Reference, LLC 2019. Player – Ryan Fitzpatrick. Online article. Retrieved from www.pro-football-reference.com.

Sports Reference, LLC 2019. Player – Joe Flacco. Online article. Retrieved from www.pro-football-reference.com.

Sports Reference, LLC. 2019. Player – Dan Fouts. Online article. Retrieved from www.pro-football-reference.com.

Sports Reference, LLC. 2019. Player – Bob Griese. Online article. Retrieved from www.pro-football-reference.com.

Sports Reference, LLC. 2019. Player – Brent Grimes. Online article. Retrieved from www.pro-football-reference.com.

Sports Reference, LLC. 2019. Player – Rex Grossman. Online article. Retrieved from www.pro-football-reference.com.

Sports Reference, LLC. 2019. Player – Stan Humphries. Online article. Retrieved from www.pro-football-reference.com.

Sports Reference, LLC. 2019. Player – Jim Kelly. Online article. Retrieved from www.pro-football-reference.com.

Sports Reference, LLC. 2019. Player – Andrew Luck. Online article. Retrieved from www.pro-football-reference.com.

Sports Reference, LLC. 2019. Player – Eli Manning. Online article. Retrieved from www.pro-football-reference.com.

Sports Reference, LLC. 2019. Player – Peyton Manning. Online article. Retrieved from www.pro-football-reference.com.

Sports Reference, LLC. 2019. Player – Dan Marino. Online article. Retrieved from www.pro-football-reference.com.

Sports Reference, LLC. 2019. Player – Baker Mayfield. Online article. Retrieved from www.pro-football-reference.com.

Sports Reference, LLC 2019. Player – Steve McNair. Online article. Retrieved from www.pro-football-reference.com.

Sports Reference, LLC. 2019. Player – Joe Montana. Online article. Retrieved from www.pro-football-reference.com.

Sports Reference, LLC. 2019. Player – Warren Moon. Online article. Retrieved from www.pro-football-reference.com.

Sports Reference, LLC. 2019. Player – Cam Newton. Online article. Retrieved from www.pro-football-reference.com.

Sports Reference, LLC 2019. Player – Ken O'Brien. Online article. Retrieved from www.pro-football-reference.com.

Sports Reference, LLC. 2019. Player – Carson Palmer. Online article. Retrieved from www.pro-football-reference.com.

Sports Reference, LLC. 2019. Player – Jim Plunkett. Online article. Retrieved from www.pro-football-reference.com.

Sports Reference, LLC. 2019. Player – Philip Rivers. Online article. Retrieved from www.pro-football-reference.com.

Sports Reference, LLC. 2019. Player – Aaron Rodgers. Online article. Retrieved from www.pro-football-reference.com.

Sports Reference, LLC. 2019. Player – Ben Roethlisberger. Online article. Retrieved from www.pro-football-reference.com.

Sports Reference, LLC. 2019. Player – JaMarcus Russell. Online article. Retrieved from www.pro-football-reference.com.

Sports Reference, LLC. 2019. Player – Alex Smith. Online article. Retrieved from www.pro-football-reference.com.

Sports Reference, LLC. 2019. Player – Ken Stabler. Online article. Retrieved from www.pro-football-reference.com.

Sports Reference, LLC. 2019. Player – Matthew Stafford. Online article. Retrieved from www.pro-football-reference.com.

Sports Reference, LLC. 2019. Player – Roger Staubach. Online article. Retrieved from www.pro-football-reference.com.

Sports Reference, LLC. 2019. Player – Fran Tarkenton. Online article. Retrieved from www.pro-football-reference.com.

Sports Reference, LLC. 2019. Player – Vinny Testaverde. Online article. Retrieved from www.pro-football-reference.com.

Sports Reference, LLC. 2019. Player – Y.A. Tittle. Online article. Retrieved from www.pro-football-reference.com.

Sports Reference, LLC. 2019. Player – Norm Van Brocklin. Online article. Retrieved from www.pro-football-reference.com.

Sports Reference, LLC 2019. Player – Billy Volek. Online article. Retrieved from www.pro-football-reference.com.

Sports Reference, LLC. 2019. Player – Kurt Warner. Online article. Retrieved from www.pro-football-reference.com.

Sports Reference, LLC. 2019. Player – Russell Wilson. Online article. Retrieved from www.pro-football-reference.com.

Sports Reference, LLC. 2019. Player – David Woodley. Online article. Retrieved from www.pro-football-reference.com.

Sports Reference, LLC. 2019. Player – Steve Young. Online article. Retrieved from www.pro-football-reference.com.

NFL Individual Player Season Game Logs

Sports Reference, LLC. 2019. Player – Troy Aikman – 1989 Game Log. Online article. Retrieved from www.pro-football-reference.com.

Sports Reference, LLC. 2019. Player – Troy Aikman – 1990 Game Log. Online article. Retrieved from www.pro-football-reference.com.

Sports Reference, LLC. 2019. Player – Troy Aikman – 1991 Game Log. Online article. Retrieved from www.pro-football-reference.com.

Sports Reference, LLC. 2019. Player – Terry Bradshaw – 1970 Game Log. Online article. Retrieved from www.pro-football-reference.com.

Sports Reference, LLC. 2019. Player – Tom Brady – 2001 Game Log. Online article. Retrieved from www.pro-football-reference.com.

Sports Reference, LLC. 2019. Player – Drew Brees – 2001 Game Log. Online article. Retrieved from www.pro-football-reference.com.

Sports Reference, LLC. 2019. Player – Drew Brees – 2002 Game Log. Online article. Retrieved from www.pro-football-reference.com.

Sports Reference, LLC. 2019. Player – John Elway – 1983 Game Log. Online article. Retrieved from www.pro-football-reference.com.

Sports Reference, LLC. 2019. Player – Mike Evans – 2017 Game Log. Online article. Retrieved from www.pro-football-reference.com.

Sports Reference, LLC. 2019. Player – Brett Favre – 1991 Game Log. Online article. Retrieved from www.pro-football-reference.com.

Sports Reference, LLC. 2019. Player – Brett Favre – 1992 Game Log. Online article. Retrieved from www.pro-football-reference.com.

Sports Reference, LLC. 2019. Player – Brett Favre – 1993 Game Log. Online article. Retrieved from www.pro-football-reference.com.

Sports Reference, LLC. 2019. Player – Brett Favre – 1994 Game Log. Online article. Retrieved from www.pro-football-reference.com.

Sports Reference, LLC. 2019. Player – Ryan Fitzpatrick – 2018 Game Log. Online article. Retrieved from www.pro-football-reference.com.

Sports Reference, LLC. 2019. Player – Dan Fouts – 1973 Game Log. Online article. Retrieved from www.pro-football-reference.com.

Sports Reference, LLC. 2019. Player – Josh Freeman – 2011 Game Log. Online article. Retrieved from www.pro-football-reference.com.

Sports Reference, LLC. 2019. Player – Bob Griese – 1967 Game Log. Online article. Retrieved from www.pro-football-reference.com.

Sports Reference, LLC. 2019. Player – Matt Hasselbeck – 2015 Game Log. Online article. Retrieved from www.pro-football-reference.com.

Sports Reference, LLC. 2019. Player – Jim Kelly – 1986 Game Log. Online article. Retrieved from www.pro-football-reference.com.

Sports Reference, LLC. 2019. Player – Jacky Lee – 1960 Game Log. Online article. Retrieved from www.pro-football-reference.com.

Sports Reference, LLC. 2019. Player – Eli Manning – 2004 Game Log. Online article. Retrieved from www.pro-football-reference.com.

Sports Reference, LLC. 2019. Player – Peyton Manning – 1998 Game Log. Online article. Retrieved from www.pro-football-reference.com.

Sports Reference, LLC. 2019. Player – Dan Marino – 1983 Game Log. Online article. Retrieved from www.pro-football-reference.com.

Sports Reference, LLC. 2019. Player – Dan Marino – 1984 Game Log. Online article. Retrieved from www.pro-football-reference.com.

Sports Reference, LLC. 2019. Player – Dan Marino – 1985 Game Log. Online article. Retrieved from www.pro-football-reference.com.

Sports Reference, LLC. 2019. Player – Dan Marino – 1986 Game Log. Online article. Retrieved from www.pro-football-reference.com.

Sports Reference, LLC. 2019. Player – Marcus Mariota – 2017 Game Log. Online article. Retrieved from www.pro-football-reference.com.

Sports Reference, LLC. 2019. Player – Joe Montana – 1979 Game Log. Online article. Retrieved from www.pro-football-reference.com.

Sports Reference, LLC. 2019. Player – Warren Moon – 1984 Game Log. Online article. Retrieved from www.pro-football-reference.com.

Sports Reference, LLC. 2019. Player – Philip Rivers – 2004 Game Log. Online article. Retrieved from www.pro-football-reference.com.

Sports Reference, LLC. 2019. Player – Philip Rivers – 2006 Game Log. Online article. Retrieved from www.pro-football-reference.com.

Sports Reference, LLC. 2019. Player – Aaron Rodgers – 2005 Game Log. Online article. Retrieved from www.pro-football-reference.com.

Sports Reference, LLC. 2019. Player – Aaron Rodgers – 2008 Game Log. Online article. Retrieved from www.pro-football-reference.com.

Sports Reference, LLC. 2019. Player – Ben Roethlisberger – 2004 Game Log. Online article. Retrieved from www.pro-football-reference.com.

Sports Reference, LLC. 2019. Player – Ken Stabler– 1970 Game Log. Online article. Retrieved from www.pro-football-reference.com.

Sports Reference, LLC. 2019. Player – Roger Staubach – 1969 Game Log. Online article. Retrieved from www.pro-football-reference.com.

Sports Reference, LLC. 2019. Player – Roger Staubach – 1971 Game Log. Online article. Retrieved from www.pro-football-reference.com.

Sports Reference, LLC. 2019. Player – Billy Volek – 2004 Game Log. Online article. Retrieved from www.pro-football-reference.com.

Sports Reference, LLC. 2019. Player – Kurt Warner – 1998 Game Log. Online article. Retrieved from www.pro-football-reference.com.

Sports Reference, LLC. 2019. Player – Kurt Warner – 1999 Game Log. Online article. Retrieved from www.pro-football-reference.com.

Sports Reference, LLC. 2019. Player – Kurt Warner – 2000 Game Log. Online article. Retrieved from www.pro-football-reference.com.

Sports Reference, LLC. 2019. Player – Jameis Winston – 2015 Game Log. Online article. Retrieved from www.pro-football-reference.com.

Sports Reference, LLC. 2019. Player – Jameis Winston – 2016 Game Log. Online article. Retrieved from www.pro-football-reference.com.

Sports Reference, LLC. 2019. Player – Jameis Winston – 2017 Game Log. Online article. Retrieved from www.pro-football-reference.com.

Sports Reference, LLC. 2019. Player – Jameis Winston – 2018 Game Log. Online article. Retrieved from www.pro-football-reference.com.

Sports Reference, LLC. 2019. Player – Steve Young – 1985 Game Log. Online article. Retrieved from www.pro-football-reference.com.

Sports Reference, LLC. 2019. Player – Steve Young – 1986 Game Log. Online article. Retrieved from www.pro-football-reference.com.

NFL Team Season Statistics & Players Online Pages – Sorted by Year

Sports Reference, LLC. 2019. 1967 Miami Dolphins Statistics & Players. Online article. Retrieved from www.pro-football-reference.com.

Sports Reference, LLC. 2019. 1968 Miami Dolphins Statistics & Players. Online article. Retrieved from www.pro-football-reference.com.

Sports Reference, LLC. 2019. 1969 Dallas Cowboys Statistics & Players. Online article. Retrieved from www.pro-football-reference.com.

Sports Reference, LLC. 2019. 1969 Miami Dolphins Statistics & Players. Online article. Retrieved from www.pro-football-reference.com.

Sports Reference, LLC. 2019. 1969 Pittsburgh Steelers Statistics & Players. Online article. Retrieved from www.pro-football-reference.com.

Sports Reference, LLC. 2019. 1970 Dallas Cowboys Statistics & Players. Online article. Retrieved from www.pro-football-reference.com.

Sports Reference, LLC. 2019. 1970 Miami Dolphins Statistics & Players. Online article. Retrieved from www.pro-football-reference.com.

Sports Reference, LLC. 2019. 1970 New England Patriots Statistics & Players. Online article. Retrieved from www.pro-football-reference.com.

Sports Reference, LLC. 2019. 1970 Pittsburgh Steelers Statistics & Players. Online article. Retrieved from www.pro-football-reference.com.

Sports Reference, LLC. 2019. 1971 Dallas Cowboys Statistics & Players. Online article. Retrieved from www.pro-football-reference.com.

Sports Reference, LLC. 2019. 1971 Oakland Raiders Statistics & Players. Online article. Retrieved from www.pro-football-reference.com.

Sports Reference, LLC. 2019. 1971 Pittsburgh Steelers Statistics & Players. Online article. Retrieved from www.pro-football-reference.com.

Sports Reference, LLC. 2019. 1972 Oakland Raiders Statistics & Players. Online article. Retrieved from www.pro-football-reference.com.

Sports Reference, LLC. 2019. 1972 Pittsburgh Steelers Statistics & Players. Online article. Retrieved from www.pro-football-reference.com.

Sports Reference, LLC. 2019. 1973 Dallas Cowboys Statistics & Players. Online article. Retrieved from www.pro-football-reference.com.

Sports Reference, LLC. 2019. 1973 Oakland Raiders Statistics & Players. Online article. Retrieved from www.pro-football-reference.com.

Sports Reference, LLC. 2019. 1973 Pittsburgh Steelers Statistics & Players. Online article. Retrieved from www.pro-football-reference.com.

Sports Reference, LLC. 2019. 1973 San Diego Chargers Statistics & Players. Online article. Retrieved from www.pro-football-reference.com.

Sports Reference, LLC. 2019. 1974 Atlanta Falcons Statistics & Players. Online article. Retrieved from www.pro-football-reference.com.

Sports Reference, LLC. 2019. 1974 Oakland Raiders Statistics & Players. Online article. Retrieved from www.pro-football-reference.com.

Sports Reference, LLC. 2019. 1974 San Diego Chargers Statistics & Players. Online article. Retrieved from www.pro-football-reference.com.

Sports Reference, LLC. 2019. 1975 San Diego Chargers Statistics & Players. Online article. Retrieved from www.pro-football-reference.com.

Sports Reference, LLC. 2019. 1976 San Diego Chargers Statistics & Players. Online article. Retrieved from www.pro-football-reference.com.

Sports Reference, LLC. 2019. 1979 San Francisco 49ers Statistics & Players. Online article. Retrieved from www.pro-football-reference.com.

Sports Reference, LLC. 2019. 1980 San Francisco 49ers Statistics & Players. Online article. Retrieved from www.pro-football-reference.com.

Sports Reference, LLC. 2019. 1981 San Francisco 49ers Statistics & Players. Online article. Retrieved from www.pro-football-reference.com.

Sports Reference, LLC. 2019. 1982 San Francisco 49ers Statistics & Players. Online article. Retrieved from www.pro-football-reference.com.

Sports Reference, LLC. 2019. 1983 Denver Broncos Statistics & Players. Online article. Retrieved from www.pro-football-reference.com.

Sports Reference, LLC. 2019. 1983 Miami Dolphins Statistics & Players. Online article. Retrieved from www.pro-football-reference.com.

Sports Reference, LLC. 2019. 1984 Denver Broncos Statistics & Players. Online article. Retrieved from www.pro-football-reference.com.

Sports Reference, LLC. 2019. 1984 Houston Oilers Statistics & Players. Online article. Retrieved from www.pro-football-reference.com.

Sports Reference, LLC. 2019. 1984 Miami Dolphins Statistics & Players. Online article. Retrieved from www.pro-football-reference.com.

Sports Reference, LLC. 2019. 1985 Denver Broncos Statistics & Players. Online article. Retrieved from www.pro-football-reference.com.

Sports Reference, LLC. 2019. 1985 Houston Oilers Statistics & Players. Online article. Retrieved from www.pro-football-reference.com.

Sports Reference, LLC. 2019. 1985 Miami Dolphins Statistics & Players. Online article. Retrieved from www.pro-football-reference.com.

Sports Reference, LLC. 2019. 1985 Tampa Bay Buccaneers Statistics & Players. Online article. Retrieved from www.pro-football-reference.com.

Sports Reference, LLC. 2019. 1986 Buffalo Bills Statistics & Players. Online article. Retrieved from www.pro-football-reference.com.

Sports Reference, LLC. 2019. 1986 Denver Broncos Statistics & Players. Online article. Retrieved from www.pro-football-reference.com

Sports Reference, LLC. 2019. 1986 Houston Oilers Statistics & Players. Online article. Retrieved from www.pro-football-reference.com.

Sports Reference, LLC. 2019. 1986 Miami Dolphins Statistics & Players. Online article. Retrieved from www.pro-football-reference.com.

Sports Reference, LLC. 2019. 1986 Tampa Bay Buccaneers Statistics & Players. Online article. Retrieved from www.pro-football-reference.com.

Sports Reference, LLC. 2019. 1987 Buffalo Bills Statistics & Players. Online article. Retrieved from www.pro-football-reference.com.

Sports Reference, LLC. 2019. 1987 San Francisco 49ers Statistics & Players. Online article. Retrieved from www.pro-football-reference.com.

Sports Reference, LLC. 2019. 1987 Houston Oilers Statistics & Players. Online article. Retrieved from www.pro-football-reference.com.

Sports Reference, LLC. 2019. 1988 Buffalo Bills Statistics & Players. Online article. Retrieved from www.pro-football-reference.com.

Sports Reference, LLC. 2019. 1988 Dallas Cowboys Statistics & Players. Online article. Retrieved from www.pro-football-reference.com.

Sports Reference, LLC. 2019. 1988 San Francisco 49ers Statistics & Players. Online article. Retrieved from www.pro-football-reference.com.

Sports Reference, LLC. 2019. 1989 Buffalo Bills Statistics & Players. Online article. Retrieved from www.pro-football-reference.com.

Sports Reference, LLC. 2019. 1989 Dallas Cowboys Statistics & Players. Online article. Retrieved from www.pro-football-reference.com.

Sports Reference, LLC. 2019. 1990 Dallas Cowboys Statistics & Players. Online article. Retrieved from www.pro-football-reference.com.

Sports Reference, LLC. 2019. 1991 Dallas Cowboys Statistics & Players. Online article. Retrieved from www.pro-football-reference.com.

Sports Reference, LLC. 2019. 1992 Dallas Cowboys Statistics & Players. Online article. Retrieved from www.pro-football-reference.com.

Sports Reference, LLC. 2019. 1992 Green Bay Packers Statistics & Players. Online article. Retrieved from www.pro-football-reference.com.

Sports Reference, LLC. 2019. 1992 New England Patriots Statistics & Players. Online article. Retrieved from www.pro-football-reference.com.

Sports Reference, LLC. 2019. 1993 Green Bay Packers Statistics & Players. Online article. Retrieved from www.pro-football-reference.com.

Sports Reference, LLC. 2019. 1994 Green Bay Packers Statistics & Players. Online article. Retrieved from www.pro-football-reference.com.

Sports Reference, LLC. 2019. 1995 Green Bay Packers Statistics & Players. Online article. Retrieved from www.pro-football-reference.com.

Sports Reference, LLC. 2019. 1997 Indianapolis Colts Statistics & Players. Online article. Retrieved from www.pro-football-reference.com.

Sports Reference, LLC. 2019. 1998 Indianapolis Colts Statistics & Players. Online article. Retrieved from www.pro-football-reference.com.

Sports Reference, LLC. 2019. 1999 Indianapolis Colts Statistics & Players. Online article. Retrieved from www.pro-football-reference.com.

Sports Reference, LLC. 2019. 1999 St. Louis Rams Statistics & Players. Online article. Retrieved from www.pro-football-reference.com.

Sports Reference, LLC. 2019. 2000 Indianapolis Colts Statistics & Players. Online article. Retrieved from www.pro-football-reference.com.

Sports Reference, LLC. 2019. 2000 St. Louis Rams Statistics & Players. Online article. Retrieved from www.pro-football-reference.com.

Sports Reference, LLC. 2019. 2001 Indianapolis Colts Statistics & Players. Online article. Retrieved from www.pro-football-reference.com.

Sports Reference, LLC. 2019. 2001 New England Patriots Statistics & Players. Online article. Retrieved from www.pro-football-reference.com.

Sports Reference, LLC. 2019. 2001 St. Louis Rams Statistics & Players. Online article. Retrieved from www.pro-football-reference.com.

Sports Reference, LLC. 2019. 2002 New England Patriots Statistics & Players. Online article. Retrieved from www.pro-football-reference.com.

Sports Reference, LLC. 2019. 2002 San Diego Chargers Statistics & Players. Online article. Retrieved from www.pro-football-reference.com.

Sports Reference, LLC. 2019. 2002 St. Louis Rams Statistics & Players. Online article. Retrieved from www.pro-football-reference.com.

Sports Reference, LLC. 2019. 2003 Cincinnati Bengals Statistics & Players. Online article. Retrieved from www.pro-football-reference.com.

Sports Reference, LLC. 2019. 2003 New England Patriots Statistics & Players. Online article. Retrieved from www.pro-football-reference.com.

Sports Reference, LLC. 2019. 2003 San Diego Chargers Statistics & Players. Online article. Retrieved from www.pro-football-reference.com.

Sports Reference, LLC. 2019. 2003 Tennessee Titans Statistics & Players. Online article. Retrieved from www.pro-football-reference.com.

Sports Reference, LLC. 2019. 2004 New England Patriots Statistics & Players. Online article. Retrieved from www.pro-football-reference.com.

Sports Reference, LLC. 2019. 2004 New York Giants Statistics & Players. Online article. Retrieved from www.pro-football-reference.com.

Sports Reference, LLC. 2019. 2004 Pittsburgh Steelers Statistics & Players. Online article. Retrieved from www.pro-football-reference.com.

Sports Reference, LLC. 2019. 2004 San Diego Chargers Statistics & Players. Online article. Retrieved from www.pro-football-reference.com.

Sports Reference, LLC. 2019. 2004 San Francisco 49ers Statistics & Players. Online article. Retrieved from www.pro-football-reference.com.

Sports Reference, LLC. 2019. 2005 New York Giants Statistics & Players. Online article. Retrieved from www.pro-football-reference.com.

Sports Reference, LLC. 2019. 2005 Pittsburgh Steelers Statistics & Players. Online article. Retrieved from www.pro-football-reference.com.

Sports Reference, LLC. 2019. 2005 San Diego Chargers Statistics & Players. Online article. Retrieved from www.pro-football-reference.com.

Sports Reference, LLC. 2019. 2006 New York Giants Statistics & Players. Online article. Retrieved from www.pro-football-reference.com.

Sports Reference, LLC. 2019. 2006 Oakland Raiders Statistics & Players. Online article. Retrieved from www.pro-football-reference.com.

Sports Reference, LLC. 2019. 2006 Pittsburgh Steelers Statistics & Players. Online article. Retrieved from www.pro-football-reference.com.

Sports Reference, LLC. 2019. 2006 San Diego Chargers Statistics & Players. Online article. Retrieved from www.pro-football-reference.com.

Sports Reference, LLC. 2019. 2007 Green Bay Packers Statistics & Players. Online article. Retrieved from www.pro-football-reference.com.

Sports Reference, LLC. 2019. 2007 New York Giants Statistics & Players. Online article. Retrieved from www.pro-football-reference.com.

Sports Reference, LLC. 2019. 2007 Pittsburgh Steelers Statistics & Players. Online article. Retrieved from www.pro-football-reference.com.

Sports Reference, LLC. 2019. 2007 San Diego Chargers Statistics & Players. Online article. Retrieved from www.pro-football-reference.com.

Sports Reference, LLC. 2019. 2008 Detroit Lions Statistics & Players. Online article. Retrieved from www.pro-football-reference.com.

Sports Reference, LLC. 2019. 2008 Green Bay Packers Statistics & Players. Online article. Retrieved from www.pro-football-reference.com.

Sports Reference, LLC. 2019. 2008 San Diego Chargers Statistics & Players. Online article. Retrieved from www.pro-football-reference.com.

Sports Reference, LLC. 2019. 2009 Green Bay Packers Statistics & Players. Online article. Retrieved from www.pro-football-reference.com.

Sports Reference, LLC. 2019. 2009 San Diego Chargers Statistics & Players. Online article. Retrieved from www.pro-football-reference.com.

Sports Reference, LLC. 2019. 2009 St. Louis Rams Statistics & Players. Online article. Retrieved from www.pro-football-reference.com.

Sports Reference, LLC. 2019. 2010 Carolina Panthers Statistics & Players. Online article. Retrieved from www.pro-football-reference.com.

Sports Reference, LLC. 2019. 2010 Green Bay Packers Statistics & Players. Online article. Retrieved from www.pro-football-reference.com

Sports Reference, LLC. 2019. 2011 Green Bay Packers Statistics & Players. Online article. Retrieved from www.pro-football-reference.com.

Sports Reference, LLC. 2019. 2011 Indianapolis Colts Statistics & Players. Online article. Retrieved from www.pro-football-reference.com.

Sports Reference, LLC. 2019. 2011 New England Patriots Statistics & Players. Online article. Retrieved from www.pro-football-reference.com.

Sports Reference, LLC. 2019. 2014 Tampa Bay Buccaneers Statistics & Players. Online article. Retrieved from www.pro-football-reference.com.

Sports Reference, LLC. 2019. 2015 Tampa Bay Bucccaneers Statistics & Players. Online article. Retrieved from www.pro-football-reference.com.

Sports Reference, LLC. 2019. 2016 Detroit Lions Statistics & Players. Online article. Retrieved from www.pro-football-reference.com,

Sports Reference, LLC. 2019. 2016 Seattle Seahawks Statistics & Players. Online article. Retrieved from www.pro-football-reference.com.

Sports Reference, LLC. 2019. 2016 Tampa Bay Buccaneers Statistics & Players. Online article. Retrieved from www.pro-football-reference.com.

Sports Reference, LLC. 2019. 2017 Tampa Bay Buccaneers Statistics & Players. Online article. Retrieved from www.pro-football-reference.com,

Sports Reference, LLC. 2019. 2018 Cleveland Browns Statistics & Players. Online article. Retrieved from www.pro-football-reference.com.

Sports Reference, LLC. 2019. 2018 Tampa Bay Buccaneers Statistics & Players. Online article. Retrieved from www.pro-football-reference.com,

Online Audio Clips

Romano J 2019. NEW PODCAST: Jameis Winston, Tampa Bay Buccaneers QB. Online Audio Retrieved from www.sportsspectrum.com.

Sports Talk Florida 2015. Tampa Bay Buccaneers 2015 NFL Draft: GM Jason Licht Press Conference. Online Video. Retrieved from www.youtube.com.

Winston J 2013. Jameis Winston Heisman Trophy Acceptance Address. Online Audio with Transcript. Retrieved from www.americanrhetoric.com.

Winston J 2019. Tiki and Tierney 2-1-19 Hour 2. Online interview. Retrieved from www.omny.fm.

Online Videos

Alex Friedman 2013. Jameis Winston Heisman Trophy Speech. Online Video. Retrieved from www.youtube.com.

Denver Broncos 2016. Miller sacks Newton forcing a fumble for the second time | Plays of the Week | SuperBowl 50. Online Video. Retrieved from www.youtube.com.

dmstr25 2017. CNN host stunned when Clay Travis says he believes in the First Amendment and boobs. Online Video. Retrieved from www.youtube.com.

ESPN 2018. Michelle Beadle is done with Jameis Winston getting chances | Get Up! | ESPN. Online video. Retrieved from www.youtube.com.

ESPN 2018. Jameis Winston is a bust, Bucs should move on at QB –Max Kellerman | First Take. Online video. Retrieved from www.youtube.com.

ESPN Enterprises, Inc. n.d. Manning 'disgusted' with Al Jazeera report. Online video. Retrieved from www.espn.com.

NBC Universal 2019. PROFOOTBALLTALK Bucs' Koetter has seven-week audition to save job. Online Video. Retrieved from www.nbcsports.com.

NFL 2017. Jameis Winston Tosses Game-Winning TD Pass vs. New Orleans! | Can't-Miss Play | NFL Week 17. Online Video. Retrieved from www.youtube.com.

NFL Enterprises LLC 2019. A Football Life: Bruce Arians, the quarterback whisperer. Online Video. Retrieved from www.nfl.com.

NFL Enterprises LLC 2019. Jameis Winston almost comes to tears after beating Eagles. Online Video. Retrieved from www.nfl.com.

NFL Enterprises LLC 2019. Jameis Winston gets philosophical in postgame press conference. Online Video. Retrieved from www.nfl.com.

patghnx 2014. Max and Sam - Young Man Rumble. Online video. Retrieved from www.youtube.com.

raidergirlsdotcom 2011. Amazing Bo Jackson Tecmo Bowl Run – 1 quarter long! Online Video. Retrieved from www.youtube.com.

Tampa Bay Buccaneers 2018. Dirk Koetter Recaps the Hard-Fought Game Against the Giants | Bucs vs. Giants. Online video. Retrieved from www.youtube.com.

Tampa Bay Buccaneers 2018. Jameis Winston on His Four Touchdown Drives Against Giants | Bucs vs. Giants. Online video. Retrieved from www.youtube.com.

Tampa Bay Buccaneers 2019. Bruce Arians 'Extremely Excited' to Work with Jameis Winston & Coaching Staff | Buccaneers Slice. Online Video. Retrieved from www.youtube.com.

TAMPA BAY BUCCANEERS 2019. Mike Evans Shares Thoughts on Bruce Arians, DeSean Jackson & Adam Humphries. Online Video. Retrieved from www.buccaneers.com.

Tampa Bay Buccaneers 2018. Dirk Koetter Recaps the Game Against the Bears | Bucs Press Conference. Online video. Retrieved from www.youtube.com.

TAMPA BAY BUCCANEERS 2019. Mike Evans Shares Thoughts on Bruce Arians, DeSean Jackson & Adam Humphries. Online Video. Retrieved from www.buccaneers.com.

Todd's TV 2014. Jameis Winston Post-Game Interview BCS Championship Game. Online Video. Retrieved from www.youtube.com.

Wantitall MG 2017. Jameis Winston Goes Off On Official!! Online Video. Retrieved from www.youtube.com.

Quotes

BrainyMedia Inc 2019. Tom Brady quotes. Online article. Retrieved from www.brainyquote.com.

BrainyMedia Inc 2019. Giordano Bruno quotes. Online article. Retrieved from www.brainyquote.com.

BrainyMedia Inc 2019. Confuscius quotes. Online article. Retrieved from www.brainyquote.com.

BrainyMedia Inc 2019. Gil Courtemanche quotes. Online article. Retrieved from www.brainyquote.com.

BrainyMedia Inc 2019. Miguel de Cervantes quotes. Online article. Retrieved from www.brainyquote.com.

BrainyMedia Inc 2019. Frederick Douglass quotes. Online article. Retrieved from www.brainyquote.com.

BrainyMedia Inc 2019. Tony Dungy quotes. Online article. Retrieved from www.brainyquote.com.

BrainyMedia Inc 2019. Albert Einstein quotes. Online article. Retrieved from www.brainyquote.com.

BrainyMedia Inc 2019. Brett Favre quotes. Online article. Retrieved from www.brainyquote.com.

BrainyMedia Inc 2019. Gandhi quotes. Online article. Retrieved from www.brainyquote.com.

BrainyMedia Inc 2019. Jon Gruden quotes. Online article. Retrieved from www.brainyquote.com.

BrainyMedia Inc 2019. Benjamin Haydon quotes. Online article. Retrieved from www.brainyquote.com.

BrainyMedia Inc 2019. Edmund Hillary quotes. Online article. Retrieved from www.brainyquote.com.

BrainyMedia Inc 2019. Vladimir Lenin quotes. Online article. Retrieved from www.brainyquote.com.

BrainyMedia Inc 2019. William Mather Lewis quotes. Online article. Retrieved from www.brainyquote.com.

BrainyMedia Inc 2019. Vince Lombardi quotes. Online article. Retrieved from www.brainyquote.com.

BrainyMedia Inc 2019. Michael Jordan quotes. Online article. Retrieved from www.brainyquote.com.

BrainyMedia Inc 2019. Peyton Manning quotes. Online article. Retrieved from www.brainyquote.com.

BrainyMedia Inc 2019. Dan Marino quotes. Online article. Retrieved from www.brainyquote.com.

BrainyMedia Inc 2019. Joe Montana quotes. Online article. Retrieved from www.brainyquote.com.

BrainyMedia Inc 2019. Warren Moon quotes. Online article. Retrieved from www.brainyquote.com.

BrainyMedia Inc 2019. Jim Morrison quotes. Online article. Retrieved from www.brainyquote.com.

BrainyMedia Inc 2019. George Orwell online quotes. Online article. Retrieved from www.brainyquote.com.

BrainyMedia Inc 2019. Karl Pearson quotes. Online article. Retrieved from www.brainyquote.com.

BrainyMedia Inc 2019. Arthur Schopenhauer quotes. Online article. Retrieved from www.brainyquote.com.

BrainyMedia Inc 2019. William Shakespeare quotes. Online article. Retrieved from www.brainyquote.com.

BrainyMedia Inc 2019. George Bernard Shaw quotes. Online article. Retrieved from www.brainyquote.com.

BrainyMedia Inc 2019. Thomas Sowell quotes. Online article. Retrieved from www.brainyquote.com.

BrainyMedia Inc 2019. Charles Spurgeon quotes. Online article. Retrieved from www.brainyquote.com.

BrainyMedia Inc 2019. W. Clement Stone quotes. Online article. Retrieved from www.brainyquote.com.

BrainyMedia Inc 2019. Kurt Warner quotes. Online article. Retrieved from www.brainyquote.com.

BrainyMedia Inc 2019. George Washington quotes. Online article. Retrieved from www.brainyquote.com.

BrainyMedia Inc 2019. Tara Westover quotes. Online article. Retrieved from www.brainyquote.com.

BrainyMedia Inc 2019. E.B. White quotes. Online article. Retrieved from www.brainyquote.com.

BrainyMedia Inc 2019. Marianne Williamson quotes. Online article. Retrieved from www.brainyquote.com.

BrainyMedia Inc 2019. Tiger Woods quotes. Online article. Retrieved from www.brainyquote.com.

BrainyMedia Inc 2019. Malcolm X quotes. Online article. Retrieved from www.brainyquote.com.

Goodreads, Inc. 2019. Vince Lombardi Jr. quotes. Online article. Retrieved from www.goodreads.com.

Goodreads, Inc. 2019. Sojourner Truth quotes. Online article. Retrieved from www.goodreads.com.

Tampa Bay Buccaneers Individual Game Online Pages – Sorted by Game Date

Sports Reference, LLC. 2019. Tennessee Titans at Tampa Bay Buccaneers – September 13th, 2015. Online article. Retrieved from www.pro-football-reference.com.

Sports Reference, LLC. 2019. Chicago Bears at Tampa Bay Buccaneers – December 27th, 2015. Online article. Retrieved from www.pro-football-reference.com.

Sports Reference, LLC. 2019. Tampa Bay Buccaneers at Carolina Panthers – January 3rd, 2015. Online article. Retrieved from www.pro-football-reference.com.

Sports Reference, LLC. 2019. Tampa Bay Buccaneers at New Orleans Saints – September 20th, 2015. Online article. Retrieved from www.pro-football-reference.com.

Sports Reference, LLC. 2019. Tampa Bay Buccaneers at Houston Texans – September 27th, 2015. Online article. Retrieved from www.pro-football-reference.com.

Sports Reference, LLC. 2019. Carolina Panthers at Tampa Bay Buccaneers – October 4th, 2015. Online article. Retrieved from www.pro-football-reference.com.

Sports Reference, LLC. 2019. Jacksonville Jaguars at Tampa Bay Buccaneers – October 11th, 2015. Online article. Retrieved from www.pro-football-reference.com.

Sports Reference, LLC. 2019. Tampa Bay Buccaneers at Washington Redskins – October 25th, 2015. Online article. Retrieved from www.pro-football-reference.com.

Sports Reference, LLC. 2019. Tampa Bay Buccaneers at Atlanta Falcons – November 1st, 2015. Online article. Retrieved from www.pro-football-reference.com.

Sports Reference, LLC. 2019. New York Giants at Tampa Bay Buccaneers – November 8th, 2015. Online article. Retrieved from www.pro-football-reference.com.

Sports Reference, LLC. 2019. Dallas Cowboys at Tampa Bay Buccaneers – November 15th, 2015. Online article. Retrieved from www.pro-football-reference.com.

Sports Reference, LLC. 2019. Tampa Bay Buccaneers at Philadelphia Eagles – November 22nd, 2015. Online article. Retrieved from www.pro-football-reference.com.

Sports Reference, LLC. 2019. Tampa Bay Buccaneers at Indianapolis Colts – November 29th, 2015. Online article. Retrieved from www.pro-football-reference.com.

Sports Reference, LLC. 2019. Atlanta Falcons at Tampa Bay Buccaneers – December 6th, 2015. Online article. Retrieved from www.pro-football-reference.com.

Sports Reference, LLC. 2019. New Orleans Saints at Tampa Bay Buccaneers – December 13th, 2015. Online article. Retrieved from www.pro-football-reference.com.

Sports Reference, LLC. 2019. Tampa Bay Buccaneers at St. Louis Rams – December 17th, 2015. Online article. Retrieved from www.pro-football-reference.com.

Sports Reference, LLC. 2019. Tampa Bay Buccaneers at Atlanta Falcons – September 11th, 2016. Online article. Retrieved from www.pro-football-reference.com.

Sports Reference, LLC. 2019. Tampa Bay Buccaneers at Arizona Cardinals – September 18th, 2016. Online article. Retrieved from www.pro-football-reference.com.

Sports Reference, LLC. 2019. Los Angeles Rams at Tampa Bay Buccaneers – September 25th, 2016. Online article. Retrieved from www.pro-football-reference.com.

Sports Reference, LLC. 2019. Denver Broncos at Tampa Bay Buccaneers – October 2nd, 2016. Online article. Retrieved from www.pro-football-reference.com.

Sports Reference, LLC. 2019. Tampa Bay Buccaneers at Carolina Panthers – October 10th, 2016. Online article. Retrieved from www.pro-football-reference.com.

Sports Reference, LLC. 2019. Tampa Bay Buccaneers at San Francisco 49ers – October 23rd, 2016. Online article. Retrieved from www.pro-football-reference.com.

Sports Reference, LLC. 2019. Oakland Raiders at Tampa Bay Buccaneers – October 30th, 2016. Online article. Retrieved from www.pro-football-reference.com.

Sports Reference, LLC. 2019. Atlanta Falcons at Tampa Bay Buccaneers – November 3rd, 2016. Online article. Retrieved from www.pro-football-reference.com.

Sports Reference, LLC. 2019. Chicago Bears at Tampa Bay Buccaneers – November 13th, 2016. Online article. Retrieved from www.pro-football-reference.com.

Sports Reference, LLC. 2019. Tampa Bay Buccaneers at Kansas City Chiefs – November 20th, 2016. Online article. Retrieved from www.pro-football-reference.com.

Sports Reference, LLC. 2019. Seattle Seahawks at Tampa Bay Buccaneers – November 27th, 2016. Online article. Retrieved from www.pro-football-reference.com.

Sports Reference, LLC. 2019. Tampa Bay Buccaneers at San Diego Chargers – December 4th, 2016. Online article. Retrieved from www.pro-football-reference.com.

Sports Reference, LLC. 2019. New Orleans Saints at Tampa Bay Buccaneers – December 11th, 2016. Online article. Retrieved from www.pro-football-reference.com.

Sports Reference, LLC. 2019. Tampa Bay Buccaneers at Dallas Cowboys – December 18th, 2016. Online article. Retrieved from www.pro-football-reference.com.

Sports Reference, LLC. 2019. Tampa Bay Buccaneers at New Orleans Saints – December 24th, 2016. Online article. Retrieved from www.pro-football-reference.com.

Sports Reference, LLC. 2019. Carolina Panthers at Tampa Bay Buccaneers – January 1st, 2017. Online article. Retrieved from www.pro-football-reference.com.

Sports Reference, LLC. 2019. Chicago Bears at Tampa Bay Buccaneers – September 17th, 2017. Online article. Retrieved from www.pro-football-reference.com.

Sports Reference, LLC. 2019. Tampa Bay Buccaneers at Minnesota Vikings – September 24th, 2017. Online article. Retrieved from www.pro-football-reference.com.

Sports Reference, LLC. 2019. New York Giants at Tampa Bay Buccaneers – October 1st, 2017. Online article. Retrieved from www.pro-football-reference.com.

Sports Reference, LLC. 2019. New England Patriots at Tampa Bay Buccaneers – October 5th, 2017. Online article. Retrieved from www.pro-football-reference.com.

Sports Reference, LLC. 2019. Tampa Bay Buccaneers at Arizona Cardinals – October 15th, 2017. Online article. Retrieved from www.pro-football-reference.com.

Sports Reference, LLC. 2019. Tampa Bay Buccaneers at Buffalo Bills – October 22nd, 2017. Online article. Retrieved from www.pro-football-reference.com.

Sports Reference, LLC. 2019. Carolina Panthers at Tampa Bay Buccaneers – October 29th, 2017. Online article. Retrieved from www.pro-football-reference.com.

Sports Reference, LLC. 2019. Tampa Bay Buccaneers at New Orleans Saints – November 5th, 2017. Online article. Retrieved from www.pro-football-reference.com.

Sports Reference, LLC. 2019. Tampa Bay Buccaneers at Green Bay Packers – December 3rd, 2017. Online article. Retrieved from www.pro-football-reference.com.

Sports Reference, LLC. 2019. Detroit Lions at Tampa Bay Buccaneers – December 10th, 2017. Online article. Retrieved from www.pro-football-reference.com.

Sports Reference, LLC. 2019. Atlanta Falcons at Tampa Bay Buccaneers – December 18th, 2017. Online article. Retrieved from www.pro-football-reference.com.

Sports Reference, LLC. 2019. Tampa Bay Buccaneers at Carolina Panthers – December 24th, 2017. Online article. Retrieved from www.pro-football-reference.com.

Sports Reference, LLC. 2019. New Orleans Saints at Tampa Bay Buccaneers – December 31st, 2017. Online article. Retrieved from www.pro-football-reference.com.

Sports Reference, LLC. 2019. Tampa Bay Buccaneers at Chicago Bears – September 30th, 2018. Online article. Retrieved from www.pro-football-reference.com.

Sports Reference, LLC. 2019. Tampa Bay Buccaneers at Atlanta Falcons – October 14th, 2018. Online article. Retrieved from www.pro-football-reference.com.

Sports Reference, LLC. 2019. Cleveland Browns at Tampa Bay Buccaneers at Atlanta Falcons – October 21st, 2018. Online article. Retrieved from www.pro-football-reference.com.

Sports Reference, LLC. 2019. Tampa Bay Buccaneers at Cincinnati Bengals – October 28th, 2018. Online article. Retrieved from www.pro-football-reference.com.

Sports Reference, LLC. 2019. Tampa Bay Buccaneers at Carolina Panthers – November 4th, 2018. Online article. Retrieved from www.pro-football-reference.com.

Sports Reference, LLC. 2019. Washington Redskins at Tampa Bay Buccaneers – November 11th, 2018. Online article. Retrieved from www.pro-football-reference.com.

Sports Reference, LLC. 2019. Tampa Bay Buccaneers at New York Giants – November 18th, 2018. Online article. Retrieved from www.pro-football-reference.com.

Sports Reference, LLC. 2019. San Francisco 49ers at Tampa Bay Buccaneers – November 25th, 2018. Online article. Retrieved from www.pro-football-reference.com.

ESPN Enterprises, Inc. 2019. San Francisco 49ers at Tampa Bay Buccaneers, November 25th, 2018 – Box Score. Online article. Retrieved from www.espn.com.

Sports Reference, LLC. 2019. Carolina Panthers at Tampa Bay Buccaneers – December 2nd, 2018. Online article. Retrieved from www.pro-football-reference.com.

Sports Reference, LLC. 2019. New Orleans Saints at Tampa Bay Buccaneers – December 9th, 2018. Online article. Retrieved from www.pro-football-reference.com.

Sports Reference, LLC. 2019. Tampa Bay Buccaneers at Baltimore Ravens – December 16th, 2018. Online article. Retrieved from www.pro-football-reference.com.

Sports Reference, LLC. 2019. Tampa Bay Buccaneers at Dallas Cowboys – December 23rd, 2018. Online article. Retrieved from www.pro-football-reference.com.

Sports Reference, LLC. 2019. Atlanta Falcons at Tampa Bay Buccaneers – December 30th, 2018. Online article. Retrieved from www.pro-football-reference.com.

Tweets

Bucs Nationa 2018. Online article. Retrieved from www.twitter.com, posted by Bucs Nation aka @Bucs_Nation on 2018-07-30

Hill A 2018. Online article. Retrieved from www.twitter.com, posted by Antonio Hill aka @buc_king on 2018-07-30

Jameis1of1 2018. Online article. Retrieved from www.twitter.com, posted by @Jameis1of1 on 2018-07-31

Jameis1of1 2019. Online article. Retrieved from www.twitter.com, posted by @Jameis1of1 on 2018-11-26

Jameis1of1 2018. Online article. Retrieved from www.twitter.com, posted by @Jameis1of1 on 2018-11-28

Jameis1of1 2018. Online article. Retrieved from www.twitter.com, posted by @Jameis1of1 on 2018-12-30

Kinsley J 2019. Online article. Retrieved from www.twitter.com, posted by Johnny Kinsley aka @Brickwallblitz on 2019-01-25

Kinsley J 2019. Online article. Retrieved from www.twitter.com, posted by Johnny Kinsley aka @Brickwallblitz on 2019-01-31

Montanez F G 2018. Online article. Retrieved from www.twitter.com, posted by Felix G. Montanez aka @fgmontanez on 2018-07-30

NFL Matchup on ESPN 2019. Online article. Retrieved from www.twitter.com, posted by NFL Matchup on ESPN aka @NFLMatchup on 2019-01-03

NFL Matchup on ESPN 2019. Online article. Retrieved from www.twitter.com, posted by NFL Matchup on ESPN aka @NFLMatchup on 2019-01-03

NFL Matchup on ESPN 2019. Online article. Retrieved from www.twitter.com, posted by NFL Matchup on ESPN aka @NFLMatchup on 2019-01-03

Schrager P 2015. Online article. Retrieved from www.twitter.com, posted by Peter Schrager aka @PSchrags on 2015-04-22

The Shakur Estate 2017. Online article. Retrieved from www.twitter.com, posted by @2PAC on 2017-12-20

Winston J 2019. Online article. Retrieved from www.twitter.com, posted by Jameis Winston aka @Jaboowins on his Twitter biography.

Winston J 2019. Online article. Retrieved from www.twitter.com, posted by Jameis Winston aka @Jaboowins on 2019-02-04

Winston J 2019. Online article. Retrieved from www.twitter.com, posted by Jameis Winston aka @jaboowins on 2019-02-04

Winston J 2019. Online article. Retrieved from www.twitter.com, posted by Jameis Winston aka @Jaboowins on 2017-02-20

Wikipedia Articles

Wikimedia Foundation Inc. 2019. Pat McInally. Online article. Retrieved from www.en.wikipedia.org.

Wikimedia Foundation Inc. 2019. 1990 NFL Draft. Online article. Retrieved from www.en.wikipedia.org.

Wikimedia Foundation Inc. 2019. 2019 NFL Draft. Online article. Retrieved from www.en.wikipedia.org.

Wikimedia Foundation Inc. 2019. 1994 Orange Bowl. Online article. Retrieved from www.en.wikipedia.org.

Wikimedia Foundation Inc. 2019. George C. Parker. Online article. Retrieved from www.en.wikipedia.org.

Wikimedia Foundation Inc. 2019. 1997 Sugar Bowl. Online article. Retrieved from www.en.wikipedia.org.

Wikimedia Foundation Inc. 2019. 2004 NFL Draft. Online article. Retrieved from www.en.wikipedia.org.

Wikimedia Foundation Inc. 2019. 2014 BCA National Championship Game. Online article. Retrieved from www.en.wikipedia.org.

Wikimedia Foundation Inc. 2019. Christie Blatchford. Online article. Retrieved from www.en.wikipedia.org.

Wikimedia Foundation Inc. 2019. Tommie Frazier. Online article. Retrieved from www.en.wikipedia.org.

Wikimedia Foundation Inc. 2019. Major B. Harding. Online article. Retrieved from www.en.wikipedia.org.

Wikimedia Foundation Inc. 2019. Keyshawn Johnson. Online article. Retrieved from www.en.wikipedia.org.

Wikimedia Foundation Inc. 2019. Max Kellerman. Online article. Retrieved from www.en.wikipedia.org.

Wikimedia Foundation Inc. 2019. Matt Leinart. Online article. Retrieved from www.en.wikipedia.org.

Wikimedia Foundation Inc. 2019. Jason Licht. Online article. Retrieved from www.en.wikipedia.org.

Wkipedia 2019. List of NCAA major college football yearly passing leaders. Online article. Retrieved from www.en.wikipedia.org.

Wikimedia Foundation Inc. 2019. List of Pro Football Hall of Fame inductees. Online article. Retrieved from www.en.wikipedia.org.

Wikimedia Foundation Inc. 2019. List of Tampa Bay Buccaneers seasons. Online article. Retrieved from www.en.wikipedia.org.

Wikimedia Foundation Inc. 2019. A.J. McCarron. Online article. Retrieved from www.en.wikipedia.org.

Wikimedia Foundation Inc. 2019. Me Too movement. Online article. Retrieved from www.en.wikipedia.org.

Wikimedia Foundation Inc. 2019. 2011 Philadelphia Eagles season. Online article. Retrieved from www.en.wikipedia.org.

Wikimedia Foundation Inc. 2019. Tim Tebow. Online article. Retrieved from www.en.wikipedia.org.

INDEX

**Other than Jameis Winston and the 21 Legendary Quarterbacks
Who Appear on Nearly Every Statistical Chart**

A

Abdul-Jabbar, Kareem, 30, 78
Aguayo, Roberto, 129
Alexander, Kwon, 102-03
Allen, Breion, 201, 333
Allen, Kyle, 41
Alva, Edward Patrick, 59
Apostle Paul, 332
Argento, Asia, 182
Arredonodo, Jose, 158
Arians, Bruce, 36, 129, 295-96, 305
Axon, Rachel, 90

B

Babin, Chad, 70
Bajakian, Mike, 128
Baker, Chris, 161
Banks, Brandon, 187-88
Banks, Brian, 61, 190
Banks, James, 41
Barber, Peyton, 159
Barber, Ronde, 215
Barber, Steve, 158
Barkley, Matt, 41
Barnett, Blake, 39, 41
Barnwell, Bill, 293
Bartkowski, Steve, 125
Battista, Judy, 293-94
Bayless, Skip, 255
Beadle, Michelle, 207-11, 213-14, 259
Bellichick, Bill, 128
Benjamin, Kelvin, 74
Bennett, Donnovan, 285-86
Berlin, Brock, 39, 41
Biden, Joe, 182
Blatchford, Christie, 183
Bledsoe, Drew, 98, 104-05, 112, 125, 230

Bomar, Rhett, 39, 41
Bonds, Barry, 333
Boseman, Chadwick, 60
Boyd, Tajh, 41, 64, 67
Bradford, Sam, 89, 126
Bradham, Nigel, 198, 201-04
Brady, Jim, 259
Breech, John, 194
Bridgewater, Teddy, 94
Brown, Jim, 79, 315
Browne, Max, 41
Brantley, John, 39, 41
Brate, Cameron, 106, 157, 159, 165, 223
Brunell, Mark, 123
Bruno, Giordano, 180
Bryant, Kobe, 28, 30, 33, 69, 332
Bryant, Matt, 225
Bundchen, Gisele, 276
Burcham, Neal, 39
Bush, Reggie, 81
Butkus, Dick, 113

C

Campbell, Jason, 41
Carr, David, 126
Carr, Derek, 291
Carroll, Patricia, 52
Casada, Glen, 261
Catanzaro, Chandler, 225
Cervantes, Miguel de, 33
Cherepinsky, Walter, 89
Christ, Jesus, ix, xv, xviii, xxiii, 62, 181, 188, 269, 332, 337-39
Claiborne, Morris, 266
Clark, Corey, 65
Clark, Roy Peter, 270
Clausen, Casey, 41
Clausen, Jimmy, 41

Clayton, John, 294
Clinton, Bill, 261
Coe, Tom, 52
Concannon, Jack, 112
Confucius, 230, 336
Conway, Anne C., 55
Cothren, Cade, 261-62
Cousins, Kirk, 137-38
Corbett, Jim, 90
Corp, Aaron, 41
Couch, Tim, 110, 126
Courtemanche, Gil, 255
Cowherd, Colin, 255, 291-92
Craig, Dameyune, xii, 71
Crist, Dayne, 41
Croyle, Brodie, 39, 41
Curtis, Bryan, 258
Cutler, Jay, 255

D

Dalton, Andy, 124, 290
Darby, Ronald, 186-88
Darnold, Sam, 98, 104-05, 163, 255, 285
Darragh, Dan, 104-05
Davis, Chris, 74
Davis, Troy, 84
Dick, Kirby, 58-59
Dickey, Lynn, 112
Dilfer, Trent, 39, 121
DiMaggio, Joe, 134
Dougherty, Michael B., 258
Douglass, Frederick, 64, 273
Driskel, Jeff, 39, 41
Dykstra, Lenny, xxi
Dungy, Tony, 330, 333
Dylan, Bob, 266

E

Eason, Jacob, 41
Ebron, Eric, 158
Edwards, Trent, 41
Einstein, Albert, 27
Eisen, Rich, 90, 296
Elliott, Ezekiel, 191-92, 194, 198, 212, 217-18, 221, 275
Evans, Mike, 51-52, 131, 164-65, 236-37, 277

F

Felder, Kenny, 276
Fennelly, Martin, 276-78
Fields, Justin, 39
Finley, Ryan, 290
Fisher, Jimbo, xii, 70, 75, 92-93, 326-27
Fitzgerald, F. Scott, 153
Fitzgerald, Larry, 198, 200-01, 203-04
Fitzpatrick, Ryan, 222, 224, 227-28, 232, 237, 278-84, 290
Flacco, Joe, 123, 289
Flores, Lucy, 182
Flynn, Matt, 281
Folk, Nick, 153
Fowler, Dante, 198, 202-04
Frazier, Tommie, 80
Freeman, Devonta, 72-73
Freeman, Josh, 104-05, 160
Freeman, Mark, xii, 34-35
French, My-lihn, 200

G

Gabbert, Blaine, 39
Gandhi, xv, 32, 181
Garafolo, Mike, 223-24
George, Eddie, 80
George, Jeff, 125, 266
Genske, Greg, 276
Gilbert, Garrett, 41
Gioannetti, Anthony, 46
Glazer (family), xii
Glennon, Mike, 96
Godwin, Chris, 165, 236
Lenin, Vladimir, 61

Goff, Jared, 110
Goldberg, Whoopi, 182
Gostkowski, Stephen, 153
Graham, Otto, 108, 198
Green, Fred, xii, 34
Greene, Rashad, 73
Grier, Will, 289
Griffin, Archie, 79, 199
Griffin III, Robert, 104
Grimes, Brent, 51-52
Grogan, Steve, 124
Grossman, Rex, 121
Gruden, Jon, 88, 326
Gurley, Todd, 103

H

Hackenberg, Christian, 41
Hale, David, 43
Hanratty, Terry, 112
Harbaugh, Jim, 47-48
Hardy, Greg, 61
Harding, Major Best, 53-54
Haskins, Dwayne, 40, 163
Hasselbeck, Matt, 84, 102
Hawkins, Andy, 158
Haydon, Benjamin, 328
Heaps, Jake, 39
Hendershott, Anne, 56
Henne, Chad, 41
Henson, Drew, 95
Herdy, Amy, 60
Hill, Antonio, 277
Hill, Jemele, 273
Hillary, Edmund, 127
Hornung, Paul, 198
Hostetler, Jeff, 121
Howard, Cecil, 41
Howard, O.J., 159
Hundley, Brett, 157
Humphries, Adam, 106, 155, 165
Humphries, Stan, 121

J

Jackson, Bo, 131
Jackson, DeSean, 151, 159, 227, 232
Jackson, Lamar, 104-05, 235, 266

James, LeBron, 28, 30, 38, 78, 263
Jansen, Tim, 53
Jefferson, Thomas, 86, 206
John the Baptist, xvi, xviii
Johnson, Brad, 121, 124
Johnson, Ken, 158
Johnson, Keyshawn, 207, 213-14
Jones, Tom, 207, 215-20, 267-70
Jordan, Michael, 30, 243, 297
Joseph (in the Bible), 331
Joyner, Lamarcus, 64, 72

K

Kaczynski, Ted, 278
Kaepernick, Colin, 89
Kalaf, Samer, 98
Keenum, Case, 129
Kellerman, Max, 207, 211-14, 255, 259, 291
Kent, Clark, 234
Kiel, Gunner, 41
King David, 331
King, Peter, 87, 94, 97, 106
Kinsley, Jonathan, 243
Kinsman, Erica, 51-57, 59-60, 68
Kiper, Mel, 88
Klemko, Robert, 89
Koetter, Dirk, 106, 127, 132, 136, 156, 159, 165, 221-22, 224, 232-33, 236-39
Kosar, Bernie, 112

L

LaFleur, Matt, 295
Lagercrantz, David, xxi
Laine, Jenna, 275, 278
Landry, Greg, 112
Lane, Robert, 41
Lauletta, Tyler, 294
Leak, Chris, 41, 82
Lee, Jacky, 112
Lee, Xavier, 41
Leinart, Matt, 81-83, 85, 324

Leverette, Otis, xvi-xix, 34, 36-37, 61-62, 223, 326, 340

Lewis, C.S., 43

Lewis, William Mather, 58, 255

Lewis, Ray, 236, 326

Licht, Jason, xii, 87-88, 93-94, 107, 128, 156, 222, 263, 290, 314-15

Little, Floyd, 113

Lock, Drew, 289

Lomax, Neil, 117, 147, 176, 251

Lombardi, Michael, 35

Lombardi, Vince, 130, 221, 230

Luck, Andrew, 88-89, 110, 126

Lujak, Johnny, 79

Lustberg, Richard, 262-63

Luther, Martin, 332

Lynch, Marshawn, 197

M

Maddox, Tommy, 112

Magnum, Tanner, 39

Mahomes, Patrick, 233-34, 241, 244, 265, 286-87

Mallett, Ryan, 41

Manuel, E.J., 41,93, 95, 326

Manziel, Johnny, 94

Mariota, Marcus, 87, 91, 95, 98, 160

Mariucci, Steve, 90

Marshall, Nick, 72

Martin, Mike, 70

Martino, Freddie, 131

Mather, Victor, 159

Mauer, Joe, 41

Mayfield, Baker, 115, 126, 226, 265, 267, 291

Mayock, Mike, 88, 291

McCarron, A.J., 80, 84, 263, 265

McCarron, Dee Dee, 263

McCoy, Gerald, 228, 234, 334

McCoy, LeSean, 155

McElroy, Wendy, 57

McInally, Pat, 266

McKenna, Henry, 289

McMahon, Jim, 121

McNabb, Donovan, 123, 230, 266

McNair, Steve, 281

McShay, Todd, 88

Meggs, Willie, 52

Milano, Alyssa, 182

Miller, Braxton, 41

Miller, Matt, 89, 289

Miller, Reggie, 243

Miller, Stu, 158

Miller, Von, 197

Mirer, Rick, 98

Mock, Chance, 41

Montanez, Felix G., 277-78

Morelli, Anthony, 41

Morrison, Jim, 261

Morton, Craig, 123

Moseley, Mark, 84

Moss, Randy, 326

Muldowney, Connor, 35

Murphy, Louis, 223

Murray, Aaron, 39

Murray, Kyler, 41

Murray, Patrick, 159

Mustain, Mitch, 41

N

Naughtright, Jamie, 199

Nazario, Angela, 200-01

Newton, Cam, 41-42, 51, 81-82, 85, 89, 126, 136, 139, 161-162, 164, 234, 265, 267

O

O'Brien, Ken, 311

O'Connor, Ian, 91

Olson, Ben, 39, 41

O'Neil, Titus, 334

Orwell, George, 257

Orr, Conor, 285

P

P., Kate, 182-87, 189-92, 194-96, 199

Pagel, Mike, 112

Palmer, Carson, 126, 154

Parcels, Bill, 35

Parker, George, 307

Pasatieri, Michael, 264

Patchett, Ann, 22

Patterson, Shea, 39, 41

Pearson, Karl, 30

Pellew, Herley, 335

Pelissero, Tom, 90, 188, 194

Pelosi, Nancy, 182

Perrilloux, Ryan, 41

Peters, Jason, 197

Peterson, Adrian, 154

Philips, Casey, 295

Plunkett, Jim, 123, 125

Ponder, Christian, 64

Prater, Matt, 158

Prescott, Dak, 235, 262

Pryor, Terrelle, 41

R

Reed, Joe, 177

Reid, Bobby, 41

Reynolds, Scott, 296

Rice, Jerry, 302

Rice, Ray, 49

Romano, Jason, 337

Romo, Tony, 124

Roosevelt, Theodore, 86, 206

Rosen, Josh, 41, 104-05, 284, 293-94

Russell, JaMarcus, 95, 110, 126

Ryan, Matt, 99, 102, 110, 128, 158, 225, 313

S

Saban, Nick, 44, 80

Salem, Dan, 293-94

Salem, Todd, 293-94

Sanchez, Mark, 39, 41, 113

Sanders, Barry, 79, 315

Sanders, Randy, xii

Santos, Cairos, 235

Sapp, Warren, 326

Sayers, Gale, 113

Schofield, Mark, 89

Schopenhauer, Arthur, 328-30
Schrager, Peter, 88
Scott, Matt, xii, 37, 264
Scruggs, Mark, 187
Shakespeare, William, 77
Shakur, Tupac, xv, 181, 261
Shanahan, Kyle, 233
Shaw, George Bernard, 31
Shaw, Kenny, 73
Shepard, Russell, 41
Shockley, D.J., 41
Short, Kawaan, 162
Shorts, Cecil, 132
Sims, Phillip, 41
Simpson, O.J., xxi, 333
Skipper, John, 258, 260
Smith, Alex, 104-05, 124, 126, 132, 311
Smith, Jeff, 36
Smith, Stephen A., 166, 255
Smoker, Jeff, 41
Soave, Robby, 57
Sowell, Thomas, 15, 26, 29, 181
Spurgeon, Charles, 49
Stafford, Matthew, 39-42, 89, 101-02, 104-05, 110, 126, 158
Starr, Bart, 264
Steinbeck, John, xx
Steinberg, Leigh, 91
Stone, W. Clement, 32
Streeter, Kurt, 91
Stroud, Rick, 97

T

Tagovailoa, Tua, 39-40
Tarkenton, Fran, 104-05, 112-13, 121, 123, 169, 229
Taylor, Ella, 58
Taylor, Lawrence, xxi
Taylor Jr., Stuart, 57
Taylor, Tyrod, 41
Tebow, Tim, 41, 81-83, 85, 324
Testaverde, Vinny, 125
Theismann, Joe, 77, 123
Thompson, Ms., 192

Tittle, Y.A., 229
Tollner, Bruce, 91
Tollner, Ryan, 91
Torretta, Gino, 79
Tracy, Marc, 49
Trapasso, Chris, 290
Travis, Clay, 91, 208, 258-60, 272-73
Trubisky, Mitchell, 225
Truman, Harry, 206, 215
Trump, Donald, 206, 260
Truth, Sojourner, 336
Tuiasosopo, Matt, 39, 41
Tyson, Mike, xxi

U

Unitas, Johnny, 229

V

Van Brocklin, Norm, 228
Vick, Marcus, 41
Vick, Michael, 72, 108
Volek, Billy, 281

W

Wahlberg, Mark, 219-20
Walker, Ms., 54
Ward, Charlie, 65, 81, 83-85
Washington, George, 26, 86
Watson, Deshaun, 101-02, 262, 265
Weaver, Jered, 158
Weinke, Chris, 81-82, 85
Weinstein, Harvey, 56,182
Wentz, Carson, 255
Westover, Tara, 340
White, Danny, 123
White, Devin, 236
White, E.B., 29
White, LenDale, 81
White, Sean, 39
Whitfield, George, 223
Whitfield, Levonte, 73
Williams, Doug, 121
Williams, Katt, 52
Williams, P.J., 72

Williams, Terry Tempest, xxii
Williamson, Marianne, 151
Wilson, Larry, 113
Wilson, Russell, 51, 129, 132-34, 139, 234, 244, 262, 267, 287
Wilson, Woodrow, 206
Winston, Antonor, xii, xvii, 34, 199
Winston, Antonor Malachi, 269, 276
Winston, Loretta, xii, 34, 270
Woodley, David, 112, 121
Woods, Tiger, 297
Woulard, Asiantii, 39
Wright, Kyle, 39, 41
Wuerffel, Danny, 81, 83-85

X

X, Malcolm, xxvi, 32, 206

Y

Young, Matt, 158
Young, Vince, 41-42, 266

Z

Zwick, Justin, 41

ABOUT THE AUTHOR

Jameis1of1 is a Biblical Christian, husband and father first and foremost. He is also a theologian, businessman, freelance writer, published author of numerous works in various genres under both his real name as well as a number of pennames, and is an investor in various high-end items ranging from rare sports cards to real estate and from comics to commodities.

You may personally correspond with Jameis1of1 on Twitter: @Jameis1of1

Made in the USA
Middletown, DE
08 December 2019